LA ROCHELLE AND THE ATLANTIC ECONOMY

DURING THE EIGHTEENTH CENTURY

LA ROCHELLE

and the Atlantic Economy

during the Eighteenth

Century ⁓ JOHN G. CLARK

THE JOHNS HOPKINS UNIVERSITY PRESS

Baltimore and London

330.944
C 67n

This book has been brought to publication with the generous assistance
of the Andrew W. Mellon Foundation.

The Johns Hopkins University Press, Baltimore, Maryland 21218
The Johns Hopkins Press Ltd., London

Library of Congress Cataloging in Publication Data
Clark, John Garretson, 1932–
   La Rochelle and the Atlantic economy during the eighteenth century.
   Includes index.
   1. La Rochelle—Economic conditions. 2. La Rochelle—Commerce—History.
3. La Rochelle—Social conditions. 4. Merchants—France—La Rochelle—History.
5. La Rochelle—Harbor—History. I. Title.
HC278.R5C55   330.944'64   80—29275
ISBN 0–8018–2529–6

To all of the Rochelais
who extended such gracious hospitality
to all of the Clarks

Contents

List of Tables

List of Figures

Preface and Acknowledgments

 Vessels from La Rochelle sailed into my historical consciousness while I was engaged in studying aspects of eighteenth-century New Orleans. New Orleans was an eighteenth-century backwater until France ceded Louisiana to Spain and until the American colonists, in separating themselves from Great Britain, displayed an intense interest in who controlled the delta of the Mississippi River. Given the normal paucity of trade goods available at New Orleans and the difficulty of conducting business there, the persistence of Rochelais entries and the commitment of one Rochelais family, the Rasteau, aroused my curiousity. Who was this Jacques Rasteau, this venturer to New Orleans, Pensacola, Mobile, Havana, and Vera Cruz who sent his ships out under the command of his sons and who exiled one high-strung son to New Orleans as the family agent? I thought that a biography of this Huguenot merchant family would be a rewarding project and that La Rochelle might be an intriguing place to live.

Once in La Rochelle, it became apparent that Rasteau was but one of a group of 90 to 100 powerful *négociant-armateurs* who dominated the commerce and society of the city. From that point on, as I delved into the incredibly rich documentary and manuscript materials available in Rochelais archives, the project expanded by its own momentum to encompass the political economy of La Rochelle. I have attempted at all times to place La Rochelle within a holistic economic context, so that family structure, kinship relations, marriage patterns, relations with the central government, local industry, and so on are analyzed along with trade patterns, specific commodity trades, the slave trade, and business organization. Data comparing La Rochelle with competing French ports was used when available.

My research in La Rochelle went smoothly, without a hitch, because of the efficiency, cooperation, and goodwill of the staffs of La Rochelle Municipal Library, the Archives of the Department of Charente-Maritime, and the La Rochelle Chamber of Commerce.

Numerous other people and groups eased the path to this end result. The University of Kansas provided summer research support through the General Research Fund and, most critically, granted me a sabbatical leave. The American Philosophical Society and the Council on Economic History awarded me financial grants-in-aid to supplement the sabbatical salary.

Librarians at the University of Kansas, the New York Public Library, and the Library of Congress were also of great help.

My deepest thanks are offered to Theodore Wilson and Betsy Kuznesof, of the Department of History at the University of Kansas, and to Robert Forster, Department of History, The Johns Hopkins University, who read and critiqued the entire manuscript. Lynn Nelson, David Katzman and Richard Sheridan, all from the University of Kansas, offered useful criticism of particular chapters. To my wife, Lois, who typed and edited at least two full drafts, I offer a finished product, the threat of new projects, and my love.

All of the above contributed to the good in the book; I am responsible for the bad.

LA ROCHELLE AND THE ATLANTIC ECONOMY
DURING THE EIGHTEENTH CENTURY

ONE

La Rochelle: Its
Economy and the System
of Privilege

 The port cities of France that achieved high prosperity
during the eighteenth century generally enjoyed some
outstanding advantage or set of advantages that provided
the competitive edge necessary to attract a continuous flow of goods to their
wharves and warehouses. A commodious and deep harbor, superior transportation to interior trade centers, a hinterland specializing in the large-scale
production of some valuable commodity, tariff or tax rates more favorable than
those levied at competitive ports—the presence of any one of these factors
might prove sufficiently attractive to merchants to compensate for the absence
of other advantages. Although lacking specific advantages over competing
ports, La Rochelle flourished during most of the tumultuous eighteenth
century, an accomplishment inexplicable in economic terms alone.

THE CHARACTER OF THE CITY AND ITS PORT

Situated on the Bay of Biscay, equidistant from Nantes to the north and
Bordeaux to the south, La Rochelle strained to meet the competition of those
dynamic maritime centers. During the eighteenth century, La Rochelle's busi-
nessmen frequently complained that the condition of the port caused great
inconvenience to shipping, prompting shippers to bypass the port and greatly
increasing operating costs for residents. The old port, entered via a narrow
channel that passed between the massive stone Towers of St. Nicolas and of
the Chain, was scarcely three-hundred yards long and half as wide and subject
to severe tides. It was slowly silting up. At low tide, seagoing vessels could
neither enter nor exit, and only vessels of under 150 tons could navigate the
channel. So small was the old port that vessels were required to moor side by
side, at right angles to the quay, thus increasing the hazard of fire and hindering
the transfer of goods.

Figure 1.1
View of the Inner Port of La Rochelle

This view exaggerates the size of the inner port, which could accommodate but few ocean-going vessels. At left-center are the two towers guarding the entrance from *l'avant port,* where most vessels first moored. At right-center is the Grosse Horloge, through which one still enters the main part of the city.

Vessels approaching the city normally anchored first in the outport, formed between the foundation of the Dike of Richelieu and the two towers, where they awaited favorable tides and a berth inside the harbor. Many vessels availed themselves of lighter service to speed up unloading and loading. Others with cargoes for La Rochelle put in to the south at the mouth of the Charente River, near Rochefort, and contracted with coasting vessels to transfer the goods to La Rochelle. Still others sailed north to Marans, a small port at the mouth of the Seudre River.

Colbert, the visionary French minister of finance from the 1660s into the 1680s, had pressured the great commercial companies of the North, of Senegal, and of Guinea to locate their headquarters at La Rochelle. To upgrade facilities for those state-sponsored firms, Colbert authorized public expenditures to deepen the channel, improve the docks and wharves, and modernize the dry docks. To eliminate some of the hazards of the approach to the port, a lighthouse was constructed on Île de Ré, the closest of three offshore islands that buffered the roadstead from the worst effects of Atlantic storms. A relatively safe roadstead determined that La Rochelle would be selected during the War of the Austrian Succession and the Seven Years' War as a staging point for convoys destined for the French colonies. But from the 1690s to the French Revolution, in spite of persistent clamor from the Rochelais, port work proceeded only fitfully. By the late 1780s, the roadstead was in such poor condition that merchants set up observation posts along the ramparts between the Tower of Four Sergeants and the Tower of the Chain to search out their vessels with spyglasses and dispatch lighters to them.[1]

Although La Rochelle's harbor caused merchants and sailors some inconvience and additional expense, approaches to the port presented fewer dangers to navigation than the trip up the Loire to Nantes, the Gironde to Bordeaux, the Charente to Rochefort, or the Adour to Bayonne. To reach Bordeaux, vessels had to navigate sixty miles of the Gironde Estuary to the confluence of the Garonne and Dordogne and then sail another twenty miles up the Garonne to the city. The port of Dunkirk was so choked with silt by the 1780s that only the smallest of vessels dared enter.[2] Physically disadvantaged ports, however, generally appeared to possess some other locational advantage.

As a result of the riverine location of Nantes and Bordeaux, La Rochelle enjoyed certain cost advantages over those larger competitors. But other, more serious disabilities weakened the city's economic position. The absence of a wealthy and productive interior, tributary to La Rochelle, counted as a weighty locational disadvantage. Merchants and manufacturers in Nantes and Bordeaux exploited extensive and productive hinterlands by means of their river system. Nantes served as an outport of Paris (as did Le Havre), and while river transport on the Loire was sorely burdened by feudal tolls, it was far cheaper and swifter than the overland traffic that connected La Rochelle to the interior. Bordeaux dominated a fertile, wine-producing hinterland, whose rivers carried to the port wheat from the Middle Garonne and Acquitaine and lumber, wool, cheese, and coal from Languedoc, Provence, and Rouissillon. Le Havre, too, benefited from its location on the Seine and its relative proximity to northern Europe.[3]

La Rochelle, like Saint-Malo, Brest, and Rochefort, lacked the interior connections of Le Havre, Nantes, and Bordeaux. But Brest and Saint-Malo trafficked in the manufactures of Brittany, whereas Rochefort was a bastion of the royal navy. La Rochelle was a sealocked port, separated from her immediate hinterland on three sides by miles of salt marshes stretching from the Seudre to the Charente rivers. The soils of Aunis, the small province of which La Rochelle was the center, were too poor to support cereals. The region's products—salt, wines (of poor quality), and *eaux-de-vie*—provided an important component of the city's trade with France's colonies and with northern Europe. However, during the eighteenth century, production of those goods fluctuated wildly, taxes imposed a heavy burden on producers and shippers, and the markets for salt and brandies were penetrated by competitors. Manufacturing, except for sugar refining, formed an insignificant part of the local economy.[4] Locational disadvantages, weak agricultural linkages, and

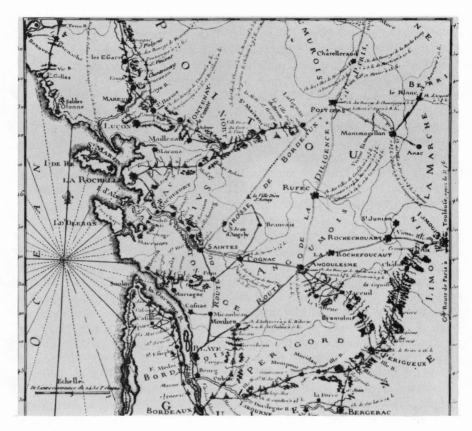

Figure 1.2
La Rochelle's Economic Hinterland

The Rochelais hinterland extended to Fontenay to the northeast, through Niort and Poitiers to the east, and southeast into the brandy country around Saint-Jean-d'Angely, Saintes, and Cognac.

the absence of a manufacturing sector or convenient access to manufacturing centers, limited the growth potential of the city during the Old Regime.

Between 1675 and 1700, about 25,000 people lived in La Rochelle. War and religious persecution reduced that number to 20,000 by 1728, and by 1787, only 17,250 remained. In fact, forty-one other cities in France were larger than La Rochelle in 1787, Nantes by two and one-half times and Bordeaux by five times. Brest, Dunkirk, and Le Havre each boasted populations of more than 20,000. However, La Rochelle's population exceeded those of its other competitors such as Saint-Malo, Lorient, Rochefort, Bayonne, and Morlaix. In 1700, residents of these cities were among the 16 percent of the

French population who lived in towns over 3,000, a proportion rising to about 23 percent by the 1790s. In Aunis and Saintonge (the province bordering Aunis on the east), the population was largely rural, but less so than in many interior provinces because of employment in fishing and other maritime occupations.[5]

In one crucial respect, the composition of the Rochelais population changed dramatically during the seventeenth and eighteenth centuries, the proportion of Protestants to Roman Catholics having been reversed. In 1610, three of four Rochelais were Protestant. The Protestant population was decimated, however, during the period of insurgency of the 1620s and the seige and capture of the city by the forces of Cardinal Richelieu in 1628. In the 1630s Protestants comprised no more than 45 percent of the total. The Protestant population held fairly steady between 1660 and 1685, but the revocation of the Edict of Nantes in 1685 caused several thousand Protestants to flee the city, and Protestant immigration was prohibited. By 1730, only one of four residents adhered to *la religion reputée reformée*.[6] Members of this small group, however, provided most of the city's entrepreneurial leadership and dominated the maritime sector.

While its concentration of Huguenots distinguished La Rochelle from most French cities, in other respects its urban character resembled that of other ports. The city's walls enclosed an area of about four kilometers, with faubourgs encroaching upon the countryside along three sides. Within the walls, the place was incredibly crowded and noisy. Hundreds of transients— seamen and ordinary men and women seeking employment—jostled peasants and fishermen and fishmongers hawking their wares. Local merchants and shopkeepers, artisans and laborers scurried about on their daily rounds. Human- and horse-drawn vehicles jammed the narrow streets leading to the port. Only the numerous arcaded sidewalks somewhat protected pedestrians. At low tide, the stench of organic decay mingled with the odors of tar or fish and with the smell of daily deposits of garbage and excreta that covered the streets and sidewalks with a slimy and slippery film.

Contemporary descriptions of the city penned after 1750 indicate that the spatial arrangement of the city's housing was basically undifferentiated by economic function or status. Quarters of the town formerly inhabited by particular kinds of skilled worker and shipkeeper housed people of diverse occupations. A port location was still required by some economic functions (such as shipbuilding and repair) but most were diffused throughout the city. Similarly, the residences of rich and poor were intermingled. An analysis, written in about 1780, of the rental value of property in the five parishes of the city confirmed the diffusion of wealth and poverty. Dwellings with an annual rental of under 300 *livres tournois* (lt.) comprised no less than 50 percent of all residences in each parish. A common laborer—earning one and one-half lt. daily—could not aspire to a dwelling costing more than 200 lt. annually. Lux-

Figure 1.3
Plan of La Rochelle in 1820

The city plan of 1820 indicates that little had changed since 1750. Beyond the walls were marshes and scattered farms and estates. Today, center city exists much as depicted in this map. The main harbor is now the anchorage of fishing boats and pleasure craft.

urious homes, then, inhabited mostly by the great merchants, stood side by side with respectable residences of shopowners and artisans and the squalid quarters of the poor.

With a shrinking population base, the city did not expand notably during the eighteenth century. It was not until the end of the Old Regime that a few public buildings such as *l'hôtel de la Bourse* (now the Chamber of Commerce) were constructed, and a few wealthy citizens built luxurious homes. Such construction did not reflect any great increment to the city's wealth generated by rising per capita income, but only the expenditure by merchants of accrued capital gains. Commenting on the city's physical embellishment in 1787, Pierre Jean

Van Hoogwerf, an established merchant, wrote that the city was no wealthier, and probably poorer, than in earlier times.[7] Van Hoogwerf's assessment was correct. La Rochelle's economy, severely damaged during both the Seven Years' War and the War of the American Revolution, failed to recover fully during the 1780s. Entering the revolutionary period in a precarious economic condition, the city's commercial and maritime strength disintegrated, never to be reconstituted.

THE STATE AS THE SOURCE OF PRIVILEGE

As the Rochelais perceived their commercial situation, inferior location and port facilities composed but a part of their economic problem. The other, and perhaps the dominant, source of difficulty was the national government. By the eighteenth century, unchallenged supremacy resided in the state. The notion of the state as a force for national unity and economic integration had been born and launched upon its checkered career.

In France, the Bourbon monarchy, through violence and compromise, had achieved ascendency by the second half of the seventeenth century. Dissidence had been crushed, as at La Rochelle in 1628, and as in the case of the *Fronde* some two decades later. Though the power of the crown was great, it was not sufficiently strong to completely undermine traditional designations of status. France during the Old Regime was, above all else, a corporate state. Virtually everyone belonged to some corporate or institutional body through which rights, duties, and economic opportunities were filtered and from which status was derived. Above the crown was privilege. Privilege reposed in individuals, occupations, social classes, provinces, and municipalities. Privilege permeated the fabric of French society—its liberties, customs, and traditions, its attitudes and institutions.[8]

In the ongoing competition among French ports, privilege was no less a determinant of success than were so-called natural economic advantages. Privilege shuffled economic advantages about randomly and subjectively, without regard to supply and demand factors, production or technological considerations, or economies and diseconomies of scale. As a combination of social and political imperatives upon which was superimposed the doctrine of state intervention in all phases of the economy, privilege obstructed the economic development of eighteenth-century France.

Privilege acted as a double-edged sword, prohibiting as well as allowing, exacting from as well as bestowing upon. Used by the central government to reward the powerful and to achieve fiscal ends, it frequently protected inefficiency and stifled initiative. Each municipality in France bore the burden—or reaped the fruits—of privilege. Penetrating all phases of the economic life of communities, it seemed to be an effective instrument of centralized control, for it fostered divisiveness by rewarding some with favors that were denied to others.[9] La Rochelle experienced the power of the state when Louis XIII stripped the privilege of self-government from the city after its capitulation to Richelieu.

The economic vitality of the ports depended in large part upon the system of privilege. Some cities were exempted from certain taxes and subjected to others. Certain tariffs were levied in some cities and not in others. Of essential importance, ports were prohibited from plying or were permitted to ply certain branches of trade. Port cities had no alternative but to attempt to gain additional privileges, to disencumber themselves from onerous obligations, and to oppose cities engaged in the same exercises.

In La Rochelle, as in all other seaports, local officials and merchants were sensitive to any shift in advantage that threatened to disturb the status quo. The economic and political elites within each municipality derived their formal status and power essentially from the system of privilege; thus, their self-interest moderated any inclination to attack the system in a fundamental way. The Huguenot bourgeoisie of La Rochelle, for instance, discriminated against because of their religion and their class, abstained from frontal assaults against religious intolerance and confined their efforts to occasional petitions objecting to anti-Protestant legislation. Nor did they attack economic privilege with demands for free trade. Instead, they launched vigorous attacks only against extensions of privilege to competing ports, zealously resisted any diminution of their own privilege, and energetically sought new privileges. Municipal chauvinism, community paranoia, and entrenched economic elites characterized La Rochelle even before the consolidation of state power against the city. However, state success in eliminating overt separatist tendencies also nurtured new forms of local attachment and new strategies to achieve local ends.

The doctrine of *exclusivisme,* that mercantilistic relationship between the mother country and her colonies that justified the monopolistic control of colonial trade by the metropole, affirmed the system of privilege as national economic policy. Any effort on the part of colonial or royal interests to disturb that relationship or any evidence of laxity in enforcing it evoked immediate protest from and cooperation among ports empowered to participate in the colonial trade. Prior to 1700, this privilege was possessed by La Rochelle, Bordeaux, Nantes, Rouen, and Marseilles. Dunkirk, Bayonne, and the ports of Languedoc gained entry between 1704 and 1716. The letters patent of 1717 codified these and other regulations. Between 1717 and 1784, when the *arrêt du conseil* of October 1784 opened the colonial trade to all ports of the realm that could handle vessels of 150 tons, other ports sought the privilege and the privileged ports opposed them. La Rochelle and her allies used their combined influence against Rochefort (1726 and 1763), Saint-Malo (1733, 1737, 1758), Granville (1737), Saint-Valéry-sur-Somme (1714 and 1749), and Caen and Cherbourg (1756).[10]

The letters patent of 1717 and 1727 expressly prohibited foreigners from trading with the colonies. During wartime, however, English naval strength frequently prevented French shippers from adequately supplying the colonies, sorely tempting the French government to open the trade to neutral shipping. In 1757, commercial bodies in La Rochelle, Nantes, Bordeaux, Lille, and Saint-Malo simultaneously sent protests to the minister of the Marine, arguing that French merchants alone could supply the colonies. This debate erupted again during the War of the American Revolution and, shortly after the war, the *arrêt* of August 1784 revoked those sections of the letters patent of 1727 prohibiting foreign trade with the colonies. *Mémoires* opposing the new policy poured into the Ministry of the Marine. Bayonne, Dunkirk, and Marseilles expressed astonishment and consternation at the sudden sacrifice of long-standing French interests to the interests of a few rich colonists and English, Dutch, and French merchants. La Rochelle's Chamber of Commerce predicted disaster.[11]

Cooperative attitudes, however, often fractured under the pressure of other issues. In 1756, La Rochelle stood alone in protesting the suspension of article two of the letters patent of 1717, which required that vessels return from the colonies directly to the port of departure. As in 1726, when they had blocked an attempt by Breton ports to waive this regulation, the Chamber of Commerce at La Rochelle and individual merchants foresaw local ruin. Regulation, they liked to argue, maintained an equality among the ports of the realm. The ports of lower Brittany enjoyed an excellent route to the interior in the Loire, while northern Brittany obtained many articles for the colonial trade from northern Europe more cheaply than La Rochelle. Bretons made their *armements* (outfitted their vessels) with less expense than La Rochelle. If they were to unload at La Rochelle, the Rochelais asserted, the Bretons could sell for 10 percent less and ruin local vendors and the economy of the city as a whole.[12] Thus the Rochelais invoked privilege against locational advantage. During the course of the eighteenth century, commercial interests in La Rochelle also found time to join with their peers in Rouen in opposing the establishment of a chamber of commerce at Amiens, to attack the abuse of free port status by Marseilles, Bayonne, and Dunkirk, and, in 1778, to launch a campaign to obtain free port status in the trade with England's rebellious thirteen colonies.[13]

Logic did not prevent the Rochelais from criticizing the principle of the free port while seeking the privilege for themselves. In 1664, La Rochelle and several other ports had gained the designation *port franc,* allowing them to import foreign merchandise without payment of duties. They lost the privilege in 1688, at which point only Marseilles, Dunkirk, and Bayonne remained so designated. Lorient received free port status in 1784. According to the Rochelais, the free ports had contributed to the ruination of domestic manufacturing, engaged in extensive smuggling with England and Ireland, and held an unfair advantage in trading with the colonies. Legitimate commerce suffered, or so went the reasoning, while the entire realm was penalized by the loss of tax revenues.

In 1778, the Franco-American commercial treaty promised at least one free port in France, and Rochelais mustered their energies and influence to obtain that status. Many of them had American friends, such as Benjamin Franklin, and relatives, including such former Rochelais as John Jay and the prominent Faneuil family of Boston. Jacques Torterue Bonneau, La Rochelle's permanent representative in Paris was joined by Daniel Garesché, the most prominent Rochelais merchant during the 1780s, to aid the campaign for free port status. Bonneau was a cousin of Jay's, and Garesché had numerous relatives in New Rochelle and New York City. Between 1778 and 1783, Bonneau and Garesché conferred frequently with Jay, Franklin, and Thomas Jefferson. The military commander of Aunis, the count of Puysegeur, used his influence, as did some French nobility who had invested in Rochelais commerce. But in 1786, the Farmers General announced their opposition to granting free port status to La Rochelle. In 1787 the Rochelais effort was put to one side to await the outcome of the Assembly of Notables, and the city's campaign was soon lost in the confusion of revolution.[14]

Through most of the eighteenth century, Rochelais were at least as successful as their peers in other ports in defending their own privileges. They enjoyed special privileges in the fur trade with New France and in trading with Louisiana, managing to get them restored after that colony had been ceded to Spain in 1765. In their efforts to expand the privileges of La Rochelle and minimize those of their competitors, Rochelais leaders functioned within the system, making effective use of local and extralocal institutions to express their views and gain outside support.

ROCHELAIS DEFENSES AGAINST THE STATE

If privilege was whimsy, it was also politics. The Rochelais protected themselves against the encroachment of the state by developing efficient local institutions. Given the frailty of La Rochelle's economic position, the city's economic notables were ever prepared to respond to challenges, for a moment's hesitation would allow competitors to seize the initiative. Thus, matters of apparently little moment were attended to as carefully as issues of obvious consequence.

Ironically, the dominant institutional ramparts manned by the Rochelais—the Chamber of Commerce, the *juridiction consulaire,* and the municipal government—were creatures of the state. The chamber was actively involved in the total economic life of the city but possessed less formal authority than the other institutions. Yet in spite of the absence of extensive formal power, the chamber, mouthpiece of elite merchants, carried the most prestige. The city government was endowed with fiscal and substantive powers, particularly over municipal services, while the juridiction consulaire handled admiralty functions.[15] During the eighteenth century, these three bodies promoted the welfare of La Rochelle with vigor. While their leaders never dared to criticize the crown, they displayed no such timidity in opposing government policies that might adversely affect the interests of La Rochelle.

Chambers of commerce were not formally organized in France until 1702, though unofficial assemblies of notable merchants had existed much earlier. Merchants at Marseilles had organized as early as 1599, taking the name Chamber of Commerce in 1650. It remained the only chamber in France until 1700, when Dunkirk received authorization to form a similar body. A law of 1701 then sanctioned the creation of chambers in the principal cities of the realm. Between 1702 and 1726, a series of arrêts du conseil authorized chambers in Lyons, Rouen, Toulouse, Montpellier, Bordeaux, Lille, and La Rochelle. Shortly thereafter similar bodies were formed in Bayonne, Nantes, and Saint-Malo. Amiens received one in 1761. La Rochelle's chamber was organized in 1719.[16]

From the beginning of discussions between Rochelais merchants and royal authorities over the establishment of a chamber, the officials of the juridiction consulaire had voiced opposition. They feared a diminution of their authority over commerce and a consequent reduction in status. Too, they expressed apprehension that the new body would be dominated by Protestants. When the consulaire authority realized that the crown insisted upon the chamber's organization, its leaders proposed that Protestants be declared ineligible to vote for both the director of the new body and for the Rochelais deputy to the royal Council of Commerce.

Members of the juridiction consulaire, while all Catholics, did not represent Catholic opinion in La Rochelle. Catholic unity against Huguenot membership in the new body, anticipated by consulaire officials, failed to materialize. Most significantly for the future economic health of the city, Catholic merchants, who frequently participated in maritime ventures with Protestants, did not voice any opposition to a full role for Protestants in the chamber. Moreover, the royal government recognized the real power of Protestant merchants in La Rochelle. Royal selection of three Protestants, including David Oüalle as the first director and two Catholics as the first chamber members, demonstrated this fact. Of the thirty-eight directors who served between 1719 and 1790, nineteen were Protestants. To avoid antagonizing the juridiction consulaire as well as any other Catholics who harbored anti-Protestant feelings, the royal government appointed only Catholics as deputies to the Council of Commerce until 1777, when a Huguenot, Pierre Isaac Rasteau, was selected.

During the lifetime of the Chamber of Commerce, its Protestant and Catholic members presented a common front against the crown and its agents, against the ambitions of rival cities, and against their local adversaries in the juridiction consulaire. The first chamber chose to exclude the judges of the consulaire, unlike the chambers of other cities which provided seats for the judges, because not all of the judges were merchants. All efforts by other classes to participate were resisted. The Rochelais Chamber of Commerce represented a mercantile constituency, but that constituency consisted only of the city's elite merchants. While members of the body portrayed themselves as representatives of general Rochelais economic interests, in fact they represented only the most powerful merchants—*les négociants* or *les armateurs*—and not artisans, shopkeepers, petty wholesalers, nor others not engaged in overseas commerce. The chamber was an exclusive body functioning in an exclusive system to maintain those privileges essential to *le commerce du grande cours.*[17]

The essential responsibility of all French chambers was to nominate three persons for the position of deputy to the Council of Commerce, from which list the crown selected the deputy. Otherwise, the role of the chambers remained ill-defined. Always anxious to seize any chance, the Chamber of Commerce of La Rochelle intruded into every issue that remotely affected trade. At one time or another, the chamber administered port activities (a major function of Marseilles's chamber) and financial exchange, mediated business disputes, supported petitions forwarded by merchants to the central government, participated in bankruptcy proceedings, joined the city government in promoting public works, organized relief during local crises, fielded militia units, and served as collector of economic data.

La Rochelle and other cities each supported in Paris a deputy to the Council of Commerce (renamed Bureau of Commerce in 1722). Acting solely in a consultative capacity, the deputies could address issues only when their advice was sought. Theoretically, each deputy represented the total economic interests of the realm. In fact, most spent their time lobbying for hometown interests. Since the crown paid an inadequate salary, local chambers provided stipends to cover living costs in Paris. Chambers demanded loyalty in return and frequently launched recall efforts when deputies did not attend to business. With the exception of their first deputy, Antoine Héron (1700–12), the Rochelais were quite satisfied with the performance of their representatives, all of whom were distinguished local merchants and well known nationally.[18]

Each of La Rochelle's deputies maintained an extensive, almost daily, correspondence with the La Rochelle Chamber of Commerce.[19] All described their activities, asked for aid or information, and sought advice on particular issues. Rochelais deputies were not afraid to reprimand the chamber for committing strategic errors, writing impolitic letters, or failing to provide necessary information. Most of their time was devoted to finding their way through the bureaucratic maze to the proper person with whom to conduct business and then waiting in his anteroom for an interview. As semiprofessional lobbyists, they sought support from other deputies over issues of common concern, particularly colonial trade, and then coordinated the strategy of the deputies and the separate chambers of commerce. Of necessity, given the competitive framework within which the cities existed, coalitions shifted rapidly.

La Rochelle's deputies kept abreast of all rumors and actual developments. Rumor stimulated as much activity as fact, and the Rochelais were not above pulling out of an alliance with other ports when a rumor or fact was judged to have no bearing on La Rochelle. Thus, little collegiality evolved within the Council of Commerce, and while not consciously discouraged by the crown, the system of interurban competition over privilege militated against the evolution of unity.

For elite merchants, the La Rochelle Chamber of Commerce functioned as the major institutional buffer against the power of the state and as an officially recognized forum in which to articulate their opinions. The chamber represented those merchants who controlled the greater share of local investment capital and shipping upon which the prosperity of the city rested. To an extent, then, particularistic interests converged with the public interest. Yet the chamber also took positions beneficial to its constituents but harmful to others in the city. In disputes with the Farmers General, for example, the chamber was prepared to grant concessions that would worsen the tax burdens of lesser merchants in exchange for reductions in taxes exacted from elite merchants. Linking prosperity with the maintenance of privilege, the chamber vigorously defended the prerogatives of its members.

La Rochelle's elite merchants found in the municipal government still another institution responsive to their needs. Though the city government possessed little autonomy, within the limits of municipal jurisdiction the city and the chamber acted virtually in tandem. With Richelieu's establishment of the intendants and their increasing authority, the autonomy of municipalities, hitherto governed by local and customary law, was doomed. The replacement of local by national laws occurred much more swiftly in La Rochelle, however, than in other French communities.

In arms against the crown in the late 1620s, La Rochelle suffered siege, defeat, and occupation. In 1628, its municipal government was suppressed. The city was administered by the *conseil de direction,* a group of royal appointees, until 1694, at which time Louis XIV established a new form of municipal government. This comprised a *corps du presidial,* composed of royal placemen, and a *corps de ville,* consisting of a mayor, four *échevins* (aldermen), and 12 *assesseurs* chosen from the city's principal citizens. The *corps de ville,* in effect a city council, operated under the control of the *corps du presidial.* Then, in 1717, all city governments formed since 1690 were abrogated, and cities returned to the forms existing in 1690. Since La Rochelle had had no organization at that time, a special royal declaration established a city government of a mayor, aldermen, councilors, and an attorney.

The crown selected a mayor and two aldermen every December from a list of three nominees for each position. The city council consisted of two aldermen, two councilors representing "bourgeois sans professions des avocats ou médecins," two councilors from the *commerçans en gros,* and two councilors-at-large. On paper, the city government appeared more representative of the city's population than did the Chamber of Commerce. In reality, the great merchants gained rapid ascendancy. One of them normally filled the mayor's chair, and they held both the aldermanic and at-large positions on the council, in addition to the seats reserved for wholesale merchants. The typical council seated as many as six or seven elite merchants.

The intendant, not the city government, held real power over municipal affairs. With the establishment of the intendancy system, the crown gained control over municipal finances. In effect, cities became an integral part of the regime's fiscal system, and the intendant guaranteed a continuous flow of local funds to the royal treasury. Hardly a *sol* could be spent by the city government without the approval of the intendant. In 1733, the city government decided to purchase a building for the meeting of the council. The intendant, Bignon, ordered postponement of the purchase until his return to the city and then vetoed the proposal, arguing that the city debt to the royal government was too great to allow for additional expenses.

City officials served more or less at the pleasure of the intendant. His opinions, in fact, ruled in the selection of those officials. Aggressive intendants such as Bignon and Antoine Claude de Pleuve informed La Rochelle's municipal officers of their preferred choices for mayor and alderman. In 1748, de Pleuve reminded the mayor and aldermen of the impending election, commenting that he was sorry to see the incumbent mayor's term end. It did not. Municipal officers understood the message, included the incumbent's name as their first choice, and Joseph Pascaud was duly reelected.

Municipal responsibilities for the provision of services and the advancement of the commercial fortunes of the city clashed with the ever more pressing financial needs of the crown, which viewed municipalities as predictable and convenient sources of tax revenues. This contest between the local units and the central government matched antagonists of unequal power. The combined influence of the chamber and the municipal government succeeded in an occasional skirmish, but when the stakes were great, local welfare as interpreted by the merchant elite gave way to the centralizing momentum of royal officials and to that group's immediate needs. The infrequent cooperation of the juridiction consulaire, adamantly anti-Protestant and obsessed with protecting its small area of competence, added nothing to the strength of the local alliance. Although defeated on issue after issue, the Rochelais persisted in defending local welfare against the incursions of royal government.[20] The question of monopolistic commercial companies exemplifies an issue in which defeat and unflagging opposition followed in sequence throughout the eighteenth century.

Monopoly extended privilege to economic affairs. From the monopoly of the metropole in colonial trade to the sole right of Rochelais *painetiers* to vend bread, it pervaded the whole of the French economy. Monopoly served the state by enhancing its power. At the local level the system shielded occupational groups against competition. During the eighteenth century, merchant attitudes toward monopoly often fluctuated, mostly in response to perceived advantages and disadvantages. While the great merchants operated world wide and managed a trade far larger than that of merchants or craftsmen dependent on the local market, the former held as narrow a concept of the marketplace as the latter. Both sought a controlled market situation that would protect them from outside competition. Artisans remained united in their opposition to uncontrolled entry into their specialties. In La Rochelle, wheelwrights in 1704, cloth merchants in 1708, potteryware dealers in 1710, and drygoods vendors in 1757 and 1759, protested the illegal competition of outsiders. The city's artisans protested just as vigorously in 1757 when the intendant established an *adjudicataire du bois de chauffage*, who had the sole privilege of selling firewood. The motives of the artisans differed little from those of the large merchants who fought the participation of other ports in colonial trade.[21]

Local self-interest motivated wholesale merchants to both favor and oppose monopoly. During the eighteenth century, the national monopoly of colonial trade received consistent support, while the monopolies of the commercial companies were the target of unyielding hostility—unyielding, that is, if the company headquarters were situated in some other city. During Colbert's time, much of La Rochelle's prosperity derived from the operations of the Company of the North, the Company of Acadia, the Royal Company of Guinea, and the Company of Senegal, all headquartered in La Rochelle. The dominant monopolistic company of the eighteenth century, established by John Law as the Company of the West in 1717 (Company of the Indies, 1719), was initially supported by most merchants from the Atlantic ports as a pump-priming effort to revive the French economy. But support rapidly turned to opposition when Law's behemoth collapsed in 1719.[22]

When reorganization was accomplished in 1723, the merchants of the major ports united against the company, a hostility maintained until its privileges were suspended in 1769. At Nantes, which enjoyed a monopoly of sales of the company's goods between 1723 and 1733, the organization was viewed favorably until 1723, when it refused to grant permission to individuals to ply the slave trade.[23] Chambers of commerce at Nantes, La Rochelle, and Bordeaux had approved of the original company of John Law, as had the chambers at Lyons, Tours, Orleans, and Amiens, because a branch of the Banque générale, formed in 1716 (Banque royale, 1717) was established in each city with a royal mint. Rouen's Chamber of Commerce opposed this policy since that city did not have a mint. During the 1720s, the Company of the Indies maintained two stores in La Rochelle, under the management of an important Rochelais merchant, Paul Depont des Granges. Depont purchased goods, especially brandy, for the company's ventures and generated some support through his operations, but favor dissipated when the decision about the slave trade became known.

In 1724, Nicolas Claëssen, the deputy of commerce from La Rochelle, reported to the chamber his efforts to push for freedom of commerce in West Africa. Thereafter, deputies focused much of their attention on subverting the company. In 1733, merchants in Nantes, La Rochelle, and other ports strongly protested when Lorient received the privilege of selling all company goods. Lorient became a favorite target of Rochelais abuse. Even when, in 1769, the Company of the Indies lost all its privileges, opponents of large-scale monopoly could not relax their vigilance since others were eager to pursue the quest for domination.

In 1777, the Company of French Guiana received the slave trade monopoly. Pierre Isaac Rasteau and deputies from other cities joined in petitioning the Ministry of the Marine against the suspension of free trade in slaves. Then, in 1785, a new Company of the Indies received a charter. Special deputies streamed into Paris as aides to the regulars in escalating a campaign against the new company. The intrusion of the revolution aggravated the situation since the National Assembly in 1790 forced Lorient to share its privileges with Toulon. Lorient's Chamber of Commerce appealed to other cities to oppose Toulon's partial monopoly. Rochelais and others evinced little sympathy for Lorient and increased their pressure on the assembly to rescind the company's charter or at least to open up all ports to its trade. The second Company of the Indies collapsed during the first revolutionary war.[24]

Rochelais merchants accepted the system of privilege. To do otherwise would have been revolutionary. Privilege bestowed upon them a rank in society superior to most. It defended their entrenchment in the Chamber of Commerce. Some Rochelais, Protestants and Catholics alike, sought and obtained positions in the administrative hierarchy, offices carrying titles but few functions. Privilege, then, had claims upon La Rochelle's elite merchants. They responded with unswerving loyalty to the regime.

But the system also placed economic burdens upon the merchants. True, *exclusivisme* created what was essentially a closed economy, one that subordinated colonial interests to those of the mother country and in which the French armateur-négociant reigned supreme in commercial matters. However, total exclusivism was never attained. La Rochelle's merchants complained to the state about inefficient and sporadic enforcement of the monopoly. Compromises weakened the hold of merchants on colonial markets. Rochelais commercial interests disputed such policies. Chartered monopolies denied merchants access to lucrative trades. Merchants attacked these concrete manifestations of privilege, using available institutions and working through the political system. Taxes, above all else, aroused their ire. Arbitrary assessment, inefficient collection, and wasteful use of taxes returned to the Rochelais few benefits commensurate with their sums exacted. The tax structure diverted capital to the state away from investment in economic enterprise.

THE STATE AS A COMPETITOR FOR CAPITAL

Three economies, each with its own special focus and at a different stage of development, coexisted in eighteenth-century France. A subsistence rural economy consisted largely of peasants, most of whom were so marginally integrated with regional markets that the nation was only imperfectly fed. France lacked a national grain market, and the suffering caused by harvest failures in Aunis or Saintonge was not assuaged by the existence of surplus crops in the Mediterranean plains or even in Brittany. The second economy was based on the coastal and major river cities, connected by major waterways, which serviced each other's needs and the markets of the colonies and foreign nations. The primary economic hinterlands of the coastal cities lay overseas rather than inland. The peasantry consumed only small quantities of the goods distributed by the coastal entrepots, and the luxury market within France was finite and of marginal significance. Relative to the agriculture sector, the coastal-river sector was dynamic. The third economy—the state—fulfilled its own needs by milking the other parts of the triad.

The state invested little in the creation of social overhead capital and returned little to society in the form of growth-promoting services. The royal government spent enormous sums in protecting privilege and in maintaining the court of Versailles. Venality skimmed vast amounts of money from the rural and coastal-riverine economies, creating a superstructure of functionaries with varying degrees of status but few duties beyond the collection of fees.

Descriptions of the economy of the Old Regime as divided into rural and commercial-industrial-urban sectors, with little interconnection between them, largely overlook the distinct and competitive interests of the state.[25] Nor was the economy of France in the process of integration, in which the various sectors would become increasingly complementary and supportive.[26] Rather, the economy contained a dormant sector, a dynamic sector, and an exploitive and unproductive sector. More than simply an obstruction to the economic growth of an independent and self-contained Atlantic economy of port cities, the state was a distinct economic system, ordering priorities according to its own economic imperatives and displaying only scant regard for the welfare of the weaker economic sectors.[27]

Although the capital supply of France expanded during the eighteenth century, so did the needs of government. Each war, from the War of the League of Augsburg (1688–97) to the War of the American Revolution (1778–83), was an unmitigated disaster for the coastal-river sector, largely because the French navy failed to protect the merchant marine or the colonies.[28] While the wars used resources unproductively, however, the daily operation of the state economic system was both the primary cause of capital depletion and of counterproductive resource use. Taxes and the sale of offices competed directly for funds that in England went into private enterprise. The system of privilege induced investment in landed wealth, in spite of small returns, rather than in commerce or industry.[29]

State fiscal considerations prompted a commitment to monopoly that narrowed the commercial options of merchants. The state dispensed privileges to the cities, which then sought to perpetuate them. Port was pitted against port, each seeking only to aggrandize or save itself. The state did not serve as the arbiter or mediator of disputes between aggressive urban commercial interests; indeed, the state, as the source of privilege, instigated the disputes. To catalog the failures of the Old Regime serves only to emphasize that the failures were those of a regime separate and apart from the body politic, yet possessing overwhelming economic power. The state's intervention in the economy served narrow purposes: its own fiscal needs.

At La Rochelle, the priorities established by the royal government for the expenditure of municipal funds did not meet the needs of the city. Moreover, the crown responded lackadaisically to the persistent Rochelais pleas for funds to improve the port. Money, appropriated in 1728 for port work, was not released until 1732 and then accomplished little since the funds were insufficient. The maintenance of troops used for port work was charged to La Rochelle. Petitions and special envoys to Paris produced no results through the 1740s and the 1750s. In 1768, the royal government appropriated 150,000 lt. for port work but compelled the city to match that sum by public subscription. Some improvements resulted, but not enough, and not before the project fell victim to the War of the American Revolution. The enormous royal debt of the 1780s and hard times in La Rochelle precluded further work. In 1790, the traveler François Marlin observed that La Rochelle had almost lost its harbor.[30]

In 1765, La Rochelle's debt exceeded 200,000 lt., all traceable to wartime expenses forced on the city by the royal government at a time when revenues from local taxes were so low that borrowing was required. In that same year, the government ordered the city to construct a new arsenal, costing 60,000 lt., or have its revenues seized. Municipal revenues were only two times greater than the projected cost of the arsenal. Out of these limited funds the city attempted to repair the port, extend the water system to unserved parts of the city, meet other municipal needs, and reduce its debt. At the same time La Rochelle's assessed property valuation resulted in annual taxes of 10,000 lt., and the city was encumbered by other royal charges amounting to 134,000 lt.[31] La Rochelle paid greater annual sums to the government than went into its yearly budget. In addition to municipal taxes, a multitude of other taxes and fees were assessed against individuals and various groups. Still larger sums were exacted by tariffs and other charges against commerce.

All through the eighteenth century, the municipal government, the Chamber of Commerce, and the juridiction consulaire engaged in a running controversy with various agencies of the royal government, notably the Farmers General, over the levying of taxes. Most of these taxes were assessed directly against commerce or paid out of commercial profits. Taxes did not reenter the local economy in the form of services or social overhead, as royal indifference to port repair demonstrated. Moreover, most taxes were farmed or attached to offices. Holders of those privileges required sufficiently large returns to meet their contractual obligations to the crown and to amortize their original investment while reaping a suitable annual profit. No evidence has been uncovered of a single local tax concessionaire investing in Rochelais commerce during the eighteenth century.[32]

Temporary impositions, demanded by some national crisis such as war or so-called free gifts to the crown, tended to become permanent and institutionalized. In 1701, a tax called "la grande et petite traitte" was levied temporarily on the tonnage of goods imported or exported by Rochelais merchants. In 1728, estimates placed the cost of the duty between 120 lt. and 200 lt. per departing vessel, or about 4,480 lt. annually for those vessels alone that were headed for the colonies. The tax was still collected in 1730. Surtaxes were also levied from time to time against the city's tax base, and lifting the surtax did not result in a proportionate lowering of the tax base.[33]

Rochelais obduracy with regard to the payment of taxes chargeable against the city frequently centered on the imposition of the *taille,* a tax falling on real estate and houses and one of the heaviest burdens carried by the peasantry. In 1634, the taille was replaced at La Rochelle by an *abonnement* (lump sum payment) of 4,000 lt. But sometime prior to 1720, the tax obligation of the Rochelais changed from a lump sum to a share of the tax charged to each generality. Rochelais fought this rule for forty-five years before abonnement was reestablished. During that period, the Rochelais paid some 50 to 100 percent more than under abonnement. As was the case with most French taxes, the burden on the bourgeois and other lesser classes was disproportionately heavy because large numbers of officeholders and *gentilshommes* were exempted from the taille.

In 1765, with abonnement in effect again, the issue took a new turn. Holders of the tax farm of two nearby rural parishes attempted to collect the taille on the rural properties of Rochelais residents. The city, with support from the intendant, successfully argued the illegality of this application of the tax since the obligation of residents of the city was fully discharged through the abonnement. But this urban victory unleashed a dispute between rural interests largely manufacturers of brandy, and Rochelais owners of rural property. The country group opposed the pretensions of the urbanites to exemptions, claiming that the latter owned 75 percent of the taillable land in some parishes, which left the remaining 25 percent to sustain the full burden of the tax. The owners of rural property in La Rochelle, including a number of armateurs, replied that their lands were worked profitably only because of the exemption and that the livelihood of the peasant cultivators would be destroyed should the lands become taxable. In 1782, an arrêt du conseil subjected those lands to the taille, but by 1786 most Rochelais landowners had obtained individual exemptions.[34]

In the short run, privilege produced generally favorable results for the urban owners of rural property. In the long run, however, the gains were debatable, since the end product of the lands in question was brandy, a major component of La Rochelle's trade.[35] Charges against these lands, in addition to stiff taxes on the brandy itself, simply lowered brandy's margin of profit (or increased the quantity necessary to purchase some other commodity), enhanced the competitiveness of Spanish and Portuguese brandies, and thus reduced the "liquid" capital available to Rochelais merchants for reinvestment.

Many tariffs, taxes, and fees diverted capital from the maritime economy. Three issues in particular, all involving charges, engaged the attention of the Rochelais: the tariff called *domaine d'occident,* perceived inequities of commercial regulations, and the exactions of venal officeholders.

In 1674, when the islands of the Antilles (West Indies) came under direct royal control, they formed the crown's domaine d'occident. Taxes at various rates had been levied on both imports to and exports from the Antilles during the seventeenth century. In 1674, *le droit du domaine d'occident* was established as a tax of 3 percent of the value of the goods coming from the American colonies. The tax was put to farm in 1681, and in 1699, *la ferme du domaine d'occident* was separated from other farms and leased for twelve-year periods. Beginning in 1727, and presumably for three years only, the crown added an additional one-half percent to cover expenses encountered in preventing interloping in the islands. But renewal occurred at the end of every three years—without any appreciable reduction in smuggling. From time to time adjustments were made in order to stimulate a particular part of the colonial trade, as in the reduction of the tax by 50 percent on goods from the colonies that had been purchased through the barter or sale of slaves. Until 1714, the duty was collected at the colonial port; thereafter, collection in specie occurred in the French port.[36]

During the first years of the eighteenth century a system developed whereby each port negotiated separately with the Farmers General the value of the colonial product upon which the tax was charged.[37] The percentage was fixed, but the value of the product varied with market and with other conditions. The market price, then, became the critical point at issue. The deputy of commerce from each port managed these negotiations armed with detailed instructions supplied by the local chamber of commerce.

Except during the 1720s, when the Company of the Indies managed the negotiations with ports, the initial offers of the ports were invariably much lower than the initial demand of the farm and the final compromise much closer to the farm's figure than to the port's offer. La Rochelle's first offer always fell considerably lower than the farm's initial figure. Indeed, the Rochelais offer, if traced from year to year, rarely reflected accurately the actual trends of export prices. Export prices for sugar and indigo increased steadily from 1770 to 1776, but the trend line of the Rochelais offer sloped downward. The farm, of course, did not accept the Rochelais proposals. In general, established rates reflected fluctuations in prices better than did the Rochelais offers. Since appeals to the controller-general about the rates set by the farm had little effect, the Rochelais started from the lowest possible level before yielding to the upward pull of the farm. In at least one instance La Rochelle's deputy, Pierre Isaac Rasteau, admonished the chamber for submitting patently unrealistic offers, which served only to make the farm less willing to compromise.

During the 1780s the Farmers General attempted to bring assessments closer to real value. This stimulated greater cooperation among the several ports most affected. In 1783 and 1784, the controller-general sided with the ports and ordered a general reduction of 15 percent in all rates. But the normal procedure left individual ports in isolated negotiation with the farm. At frequent intervals, the controller-general received strenuous protests from each port charging that its rates were higher than those of its competitors. Merchants in Nantes and Bordeaux were particularly sensitive to inequities since they lived in the tariff zone designated *Provinces Réputées Étrangères.* Not only did local tariff barriers exist, but the ports paid tariffs when their goods entered all other zones. La Rochelle was located in the *Provinces des Cinq Grosses Fermes,* a free trade zone consisting of the most populous and wealthiest areas of France. Inferior transportation to the interior and La Rochelle's focus on colonial and foreign trade minimized the advantages of location in that tariff zone.[38]

Between 1767 and 1776, domaine d'occident duties for raw sugar, coffee, cotton, and indigo alone cost La Rochelle's merchants about 655,000 lt. annually, or 19 percent of the value of all Rochelais imports from the colonies and 7 percent of all imports. In more concrete terms, the average annual value of outbound cargoes in Rochelais vessels between 1780 and 1784, the closest years for which this data was calculable, ran at 152,800 lt. In any given year, then, the domaine d'occident absorbed capital sufficient for the outfit of four additional vessels.[39]

Commercial regulations varied widely from port to port. The free ports operated under regulations similar to those operative within the third tariff zone, the *Province à l'Instar de l'Etranger.* They traded freely with foreign lands but were treated as foreigners in their relations with the rest of France. La Rochelle operated in a different system, Nantes and Bordeaux in still another. But the "systems" were not really systems, for within each system tariffs were applied unequally. Exceptions to one duty or another were frequently granted and as frequently retracted, and the duties applied at each port differed. Nantes complained that local duties on sugars put it at a disadvantage in competing with La Rochelle. La Rochelle claimed that furs from Louisiana and other colonies entered Bordeaux more cheaply. Bordeaux asserted that the free ports engaged in a vast conspiracy to substitute northern European and Italian wines for Bordelais wines in the colonial trade. Every port demanded the consistent application of *droits de frêt* (tonnage duties) against foreign shipping entering French ports. It was a costly procedure, made the more complicated and expensive by the connection between the sale of offices and the imposition of charges.[40]

Wartime exigencies, debilitating privileges, a ponderous bureaucracy, and the erosion of local autonomy combined to produce venal officeholders and venality in office. The wars of Louis XIV, particularly the War of the Spanish Succession, prompted the creation and sale of numerous offices in La Rochelle and elsewhere. In 1691, the crown created the *offices de courtiers commissionaires,* sold them for 100,000 lt. each, and authorized the holders to institute a tax of 20 *sols* per cask of wine. The *offices de controlleurs des exploits,* purchased by a Parisian for 100,000 lt. in 1703, established a new fee for legal services. An *office des droits de courtiers jaugeur et inspecteur aux boissons,* created in 1706, charged fees for inspecting wine casks. In the 1720s, the *office de juré-mesurer de charbon de terre,* purchased for 150,000 lt., was established at La Rochelle, Rochefort, and Île de Ré. This last farmer aroused the animosity of coal dealers, brandy manufacturers, and sugar refiners by levying duties on the loaded tonnage of coal freighters rather than on the tonnage of coal carried. And in 1753, an arrêt du conseil authorized the appointment of four *agréeurs à l'embarquement,* three *agréeurs à l'acceptation,* and a number of *courtiers en jurande,* to verify the weight, quality, and packaging of brandy.[41]

Such offices represented but a few of those existing in La Rochelle and but a fraction of those suffocating France. According to one estimate, these positions tied up close to one billion lt. in capital value. Venal offices were negotiable, long-term investments, as much an investment in status as in an income-producing position.[42] But in La Rochelle, it was not the status-carrying offices such as *tresorier de France* that burdened commerce but the swarm of small officeholders levying fees, each seeking to enlarge his income by a liberal interpretation of the rights inherent in the position. Hardly a commodity moved but a fee was levied against it. How much these exactions diminished available capital cannot be calculated, but it must have been substantial.

CONCLUSION

All communities, save the most isolated, are integrated into some larger society through a complex network of political and socioeconomic linkages. That integration may be either functional or dysfunctional. If the functional exists, a two-way flow of resources occurs. Reciprocity in exchange will operate, based upon economic advantages and specialization. Economic reciprocity between a governmental unit and its subordinate communities will involve the outward flow of taxes and human resources and an inward flow of services that the community cannot provide for itself. The government will attempt to mediate conflicting demands for services by evaluating community needs according to some objective measure of community resources or capabilities. The goals of government will include the achievement of a balance between tax output and service input and the equalization of the basic services available to all communities. Such a model, of course, has never existed in the real world. But its opposite, a dysfunctional model, approximates the web of relationships binding La Rochelle to the royal government.

La Rochelle was functionally integrated with the Atlantic world of seaborne commerce, a system encompassing the coastal-riverine cities of France, the commercial centers of western Europe (including the Mediterranean), the West African coast, and the colonies of the Western Hemisphere. With the exception of a few interior centers, the Rochelais commercial network connected but loosely with the atomized markets of France. A mutual purpose permeated the relationships between merchants in La Rochelle, Nantes, Bordeaux, London, Amsterdam, Hamburg, and other places. Investment capital, goods, information, and people flowed between these centers.[43]

State power impinged upon this system at all points, superimposing its own priorities and neglecting those of the Rochelais. That the elite Rochelais and their peers elsewhere embraced certain of the state's priorities—exclusivisme, for example—should not obscure the Rochelais' demand for a level of enforcement beyond the capabilities of the state. When local and state priorities dovetailed, the Rochelais remained vigilant, sensitive to the demonstrated readiness of the state to compromise or abrogate local advantages. During the eighteenth century, the long struggle of port interests against monopolistic companies and in favor of a total exclusion of foreign trade with the colonies demonstrated that vigilance. For the most part, however, state priorities did not converge with the long-term interests of the Rochelais economy. Indeed, the state and La Rochelle engaged in an unequal competition for finite economic resources.

An arsenal instead of port construction; a municipal government heavily indebted as a result of royal exactions and unable to contribute to the creation of social overhead; the proliferation of venal officeholders and accompanying fees; heavy, inequitable and arbitrarily levied direct and indirect taxes on commerce—all these factors worked to lower the efficiency of the port and to reduce the capital employed in commerce. Severely disadvantaged by a small harbor with inferior access to the interior, and inhibited by a relatively poor agricultural hinterland, La Rochelle's possibilities for economic growth were further circumscribed by the capital-depleting exactions of the state.

Within the walls of La Rochelle, an economic elite strove to increase its wealth through commerce and to ward off the power of the state. The economic strength of the city rested on the relationships developed among members of the elite and between them and their contacts overseas. Effective local institutions depended upon such relationships.[44] Within the elite families, social and economic functions were inseparable and mutually sustaining. Kinship systems, cemented by bonds of religion but rarely producing serious strife between Huguenot and Roman Catholic, united the primary holders of investment capital. Kinship and local loyalties became interwoven with the Rochelais economic system, a system operating within a larger society, including some of France, but more importantly, embracing the Atlantic world and worlds beyond.

TWO

The Seaborne Commerce
of La Rochelle

 The sea ruled the lives of the residents of La Rochelle. It sustained the city's economy more fully than at Nantes or Bordeaux where the people lived some distance from the ocean and could gain livelihoods in trades only secondarily associated with the maritime sector. Whereas great arterial waterways connected Bordeaux and Nantes with the interior, of necessity the Rochelais were attuned to the sea. Rumors of war, promises of peace, results of new tariff negotiations, and other information arrived from London or Amsterdam earlier via ship than via coach from Paris.

Up and down the coast in the immediate vicinity of La Rochelle, smaller ports functioned in part as the provincial capital's appendages—coasting goods to and from that city, sending their young men to serve on Rochelais vessels, and in general, contributing to the role of La Rochelle as a regional center. In eighteenth-century La Rochelle, ships and cargoes were the measure of the city.

THE SIZE OF THE ROCHELAIS FLEET

The number and tonnage of ships in the prerevolutionary French merchant marine has not been established with any precision. Estimates vary widely. In 1730, Court de Maurepas, minister of the Marine, estimated the fleet at 3,000 vessels of all sizes. Most other counts for the 1730s ran from 5,500 to 6,500, reflecting, if correct, an addition to the fleet of over 2,000 vessels since 1715. Tonnage for the 1730s and 1740s probably approached 270,000 tons. By the end of the Old Regime, the total fleet probably did not contain many more vessels than the high estimate for the 1730s. The tonnage employed during the 1780s, however, certainly exceeded 700,000 tons, an increase resulting from the greater size of ships constructed but a portion of which may be accounted for by the purposeful overestimation of tonnage by shipowners.[1]

Vessels were divided into three separate but overlapping categories. Those engaged in trips to the Western Hemisphere and African or Pacific waters were classified as *vaisseaux de long cours* and composed the high seas merchant fleet. Vessels plying the waters to England and Ireland, Holland, the Scandinavian states, and to Baltic and Mediterranean ports of call conducted *le grand cabotage*. Those ships running between French Atlantic ports participated in *le petit cabotage*. By and large, the high seas vessels were of greater tonnage than the others. *Terreneuviers* (fishing ships) were generally included in counts of the high seas fleet, although they were normally smaller than vessels engaged in le grand cabotage. Many French vessels engaged in *le long cours* in one year were destined for le grand cabotage to Spain, Portugal, Italy, or the Levant in another year.

French maritime strength lay in its high seas fleet and domestic coasters. Le grand cabotage was dominated by foreigners.[2] The high seas fleet composed about one-half of the total tonnage and local coasters probably another one-third. Of the two major forms of shipping, the information for each port concerning vaisseaux de long cours is much more complete and reliable than data on local coasting. But the latter was essential for La Rochelle and other ports that depended upon outside sources of supply for trade goods produced in France. No less essential was le grand cabotage, which moved to French ports the trade goods unobtainable in France or purchased more cheaply abroad and which carried away the vast quantities of colonial products that financed the trade cycle. In this traffic, foreign, rather than local, merchants profited from freight charges.

In any year between the 1660s and the 1780s, La Rochelle's high seas fleet ranked among the most important in France. Its position relative to the size of the fleets in other ports shifted downward between the 1680s and 1715, recovered and stabilized through 1763, and then gradually declined. Table 2.1 offers a comparison of the vessels over 100 tons registered at various French ports for the years 1664, 1686, and 1704, and for the following years shows departures le long cours.[3]

La Rochelle's maritime strength peaked between 1682 and 1686. The impressive size of the Rochelais fleet owed much to the patronage of Colbert, who influenced the Companies of the North, of Senegal, and of Guinea to locate their headquarters in the city. Those companies owned about 1,500 tons of the port's estimated 11,000 tons of shipping. But growth in the trade with the French West Indies provided the impetus for tripling of tonnage between 1664 and 1682. Trade with the Antilles supplied La Rochelle with those commodities—among which sugar was preeminent—which could be profitably reexported to northern Europe. Unfortunately disaster struck in 1685 with the revocation of the Edict of Nantes. Many prominent Huguenot merchants hurriedly liquidated their businesses and fled to England or to Holland. By 1687, La Rochelle's fleet numbered only sixty-five vessels. The next year France went to war. Such serious losses followed that in 1690 the Rochelais fleet numbered but thirty-six vessels. The fleet did not again approach the size attained in 1682 until the late 1730s and early 1740s.

Table 2.1. Number of Vessels Registered at or Departing from French Ports, 1664–1787

Year	La Rochelle	Nantes	Bordeaux	Le Havre	Saint-Malo	Lorient	Marseilles	Bayonne
1664	18	12	11	75	48		21	19
1686	93	84		114	117		47	61
1704	45	151	29	60	90		72	18
1722	16	80	120	25				
1727	23	108				13		
1729	38		123			20		
1730	34			45		18		
1740	42		99	50				
1741	43	113						
1750	48	100	127	45			12	12
1754	37	113	188	49			38	17
1755	31	68	192	47			35	17
1770	34	98		57				
1786	47	127	281	110	11	96	126	
1787	34	116	245	119	18	85	146	16

Source: See note 3.

As table 2.1 indicates, many ports entered the eighteenth century with diminished maritime strength as a result of the War of the League of Augsburg and found little opportunity to reconstruct their fleets because of the outbreak in 1701 of the War of the Spanish Succession. After 1715, the Rochelais fleet reflected this pattern, gaining strength between wars and losing ground during wars. While its size relative to the Nantais fleet remained more or less stable and improved relative to the ships of Saint-Malo and Bayonne, it fell far behind those of Le Havre, Bordeaux, and Marseilles. Table 2.2 records the fluctuating pattern of departures experienced by La Rochelle, much of it reflecting wartime losses and the steady abandonment of colonies in North America. Only during the periods 1750–54 and 1780–89 did average annual tonnage approach the 11,000 tons attributed to the port during the 1680s. While it is likely that the tonnage for the 1780s was inflated, the figures in table 2.2 do accentuate the impact of recurrent military crises upon Rochelais efforts to expand their fleet and their trade zones.[4]

By shifting the focus of discussion from general size to shipping commitments to specific markets, the impingement of war and diplomacy and the economic policies of the royal government become clear. The primary destinations of the Rochelais high seas fleet and the number of vessels plying those routes are displayed in table 2.3.

La Rochelle's négociants responded to the coming of peace in 1715 by outfitting seventy-two vessels in that year and the next. They then adopted a more cautious policy of outfitting no more than twenty-eight vessels annually between 1718 and 1728 (see table 2.2). Great economic uncertainty prevailed in France during those years. Brutal deflationary policies were pursued by the

Table 2.2. *Number and Tonnage of Vessels Outfitted for* le long cours *at La Rochelle, 1715–89 (by five-year periods)*

Five-year period	Number of vessels outfitted	Average tonnage per vessel	Total average tonnage
1715–19	116	146	3,387
1720–24	113	138	3,119
1725–29	115	158	3,634
1730–34	172	175	6,020
1735–39	181	195	7,059
1740–44	183	188	6,881
1745–49	244	196	9,565
1750–54	237	232	10,997
1755–59	130	189	4,914
1760–64	126	193	4,864
1765–69	203	198	8,039
1770–74	156	211	6,583
1775–79	140	235	6,580
1780–84	179	283	10,131
1785–89	166	425	14,110

Source: See table 2.1.

state between 1713 and 1715 with the objective of scaling down the enormous government debt. Monetary devaluations of about 30 percent precipitated a rash of failures and a general depression throughout France. This was followed by the inflationary schemes of John Law, which generated a wildly speculative atmosphere. After the collapse of Law's company in 1720, the government renewed its harsh deflationary tactics, manipulating the currency to serve its own purposes. Further deflation, coupled with poor harvests in 1725 necessitating the use of specie to purchase grain from abroad, aggravated specie shortages and set off fluctuations in foreign exchange in which French money of account lost value relative to foreign money.

The Rochelais, playing it close to the vest through 1725, accepted with relief the government's decision in 1726 to stabilize the currency. But in 1727, France went to war against Spain for the second time within a decade, resulting in the closing of important Spanish markets and higher risks along the routes to the West Indies. Thus, Rochelais shipowners postponed until 1729 all decisions regarding the expansion of their operations.[5]

Once a modicum of economic stability within a relatively peaceful international setting had been achieved (the War of the Polish Succession, 1733–38, did not disturb the colonial trade), the Rochelais fleet expanded rather rapidly until the beginning of the Seven Years' War (see tables 2.2 and 2.3). Even during the years of French participation in the War of the Austrian Succession, 1743–48, Rochelais armements remained at a high level. In 1744 and 1745, armements numbered twenty-one and twenty-six respectively while departures during the war averaged forty-three annually. During the brief interim between that war and the next, the Rochelais fleet reached its

Table 2.3. Destination of Vessels Outfitted at La Rochelle, 1710–92 (by decade)

Destination	1710–19	1720–29	1730–39	1740–49	1750–59	1760–69	1770–79	1780–92
French West Indies	64	42	3	11	6	4	7	8
Santo Domingo	17	110	202	167	81	110	94	116
Guadeloupe	4	3	0	2	0	20	7	4
Martinique	5	3	5	42	21	41	24	15
Cayenne	2	3	11	11	5	50	16	6
Louisiana	2	4	22	49	54	33	0	0
Canada and offshore islands	20	30	39	52	133	14	9	11
Africa–West Indies	8	11	65	84	35	23	73	118
Îles de France and de Bourbon	0	0	0	0	0	0	13	28
United States	0	0	0	0	0	0	0	7
Local waters (fishing)	5	16	1	2	27	24	44	47
Western Europe (coasting)	6	0	1	5	1	2	3	15
Other	8	6	4	2	4	8	6	3
Total	141	228	353	427	367	329	296	378

Source: See table 2.1.

29

numerical peak with as many as sixty-one departures in 1747 and an annual average of forty-eight departures for the period 1745–54.

The West Indian trade engaged the bulk of eighteenth century shipping in La Rochelle, as it did in Nantes and Bordeaux. Le Havre and Marseilles both became more heavily involved in the colonial trade during the century, but for neither port did the islands constitute the key sector. As a primary destination, the West Indies received less than 50 percent of La Rochelle's vessels in only two decades, 1750–59 and 1780–89 (see table 2.3). If the vessels outfitted for the slave trade are included in the West Indian count, the proportion of West Indian voyages fell below 65 percent only between 1750 and 1759. In that decade, La Rochelle expanded its trade with both Louisiana and Canada.

Trading patterns at Nantes and Bordeaux replicated La Rochelle's concentration of the West Indies. Of the Antillian possessions, Santo Domingo was the principal destination for La Rochelle's vessels as well as for those of Nantes, Le Havre, and Marseilles. Bordeaux's orientation remained toward Martinique and Guadeloupe until after the War of the American Revolution, when Santo Domingo became the focus. Indeed, so great was Bordeaux's expansion during the 1780s that its ventures composed 40 percent of all French departures for Santo Domingo, over 50 percent for Guadeloupe, and about one-third for Martinique. For the Rochelais, Guadeloupe and Martinique served as alternative ports of call when poor market conditions prevailed at the Santo Domingan ports of Cap française, Port-au-Prince, or Les Cayes.

Shipping figures for the Canadian trade fail to distinguish between terreneuviers and trading vessels. Most Rochelais ventures to New France consisted of the latter. Between 1749 and 1756, the height of the Canadian trade, Le Havre outfitted 333 vessels for Canada, Bordeaux 179, Marseilles 167, and La Rochelle 121. Except for La Rochelle, terreneuviers composed a large but unknown number of those vessels. La Rochelle's interest in the general Canadian trade probably exceeded that of the other ports. With Louisiana, the Rochelais established an absolute preponderance. After an initial period between 1731 and 1738 when the Rochelais and Bordelais shared the trade, Rochelais ships accounted for about 45 percent of all vessels calling at New Orleans. Another 14 percent were military ships or ships leased to the crown, some of the latter owned by Rochelais. During the two decades 1740–69, Canada and Louisiana together attracted 34 percent of all Rochelais ventures (see table 2.3). The cession of those colonies caused severe stress in La Rochelle, a condition never fully compensated for by the development of new markets in the Indian Ocean or by increased attention to the slave trade.[6]

Slaving ventures to West Africa and thence to the Antilles were by the far most difficult voyages. Taking advantage of prevailing seasonal winds that propelled slavers toward West Africa, from there to the West Indies, and then east toward Europe, eased navigational problems. Colonial demands for slaves to open up new agricultural lands and to replace the dead and disabled hardly abated at any time during the eighteenth century. Monopolistic companies, vigorous foreign competition, the everpresent threat of disease and black resistance, and large capital requirements all made slaving the most risky of the trades, but if successful, the most lucrative.

Between 1717 and 1720, Law's Company of the Indies, by absorbing the Company of Senegal and the Company of Africa, controlled all rights to the slave trade on the coast of Africa between the Sierra Leone River and the Cape of Good Hope. During its short life, the company followed earlier practices by issuing a limited number of permissions to private individuals to engage in the slave trade in return for a fee paid for each slave transported from Africa. The Company of the Indies lost all of its privileges in 1721 but reemerged in 1723, reorganized and restored to its fiscal and commercial privileges.[7]

In 1723, the company discontinued slave trade permissions, intending to conduct the entire trade itself. Nantes, in particular, suffered from this decision, and La Rochelle and Bordeaux joined Nantes in protesting the new policy. Within three years, the permission-fee system was reinstated. The company focused its attention on the East Indies and commanded insufficient resources to monopolize the slave trade or the trades with Santo Domingo and Louisiana. The company ceded Louisiana to the crown in 1731, having already renounced most of its other privileges in America. In 1730, the tobacco monopoly was leased to the Farmer's General, leaving in company hands only the trade in beaver and slaves, the latter open to private enterprise for a fee. In the middle 1730s, the company suggested that it abandon the slave trade entirely, but the government rejected the notion of totally free trade since it received a percentage of the fees collected by the company. Until the end of the decade, the company sent one or two vessels annually to West Africa. Nonetheless, individuals could participate in the trade.

French naval strength in West African waters provided private slavers little protection against the aggressive competition of the English. While none of the Engish, Dutch, Portuguese, or French establishments in Africa were colonies—the Europeans paid tribute to local rulers—all but the French maintained at least token military forces at coastal factories. French ships generally operated in Senegal even though the great reservoir of slaves was in Guinea. Frequently, English warships chased the French from the Senegalese coast, and Senegal itself was occupied by the English between 1763 and 1783. While the Dutch, too, were firmly established along the Guinea coast, their more strictly commercial purposes enabled French traders to deal with them. Stiff competition caused French traders to shift their efforts further south near the Congo River.[8]

During the eighteenth century, Nantes retained its position as the leading slave trading port in France. Prior to 1725, perhaps 80 percent of all French slavers outfitted on the Loire. This virtual monopoly declined between 1725 and 1749 as La Rochelle and Bordeaux claimed some of the trade. Nantes, however, still accounted for close to 60 percent of all French deliveries to the islands. During this period La Rochelle sent out six or seven slavers per year while Bordeaux averaged about five slavers annually, and Nantes close to fifteen. Between 1763 and 1778, Bordeaux's average rose to ten and La Rochelle and a new participant, Le Havre, each sent out eight or nine annually; Nantes averaged about twenty. During the 1780s, Nantes dispatched about forty slavers per year, or 40 percent of the French total, Bordeaux and Le Havre sent fourteen to fifteen per year, or 20 percent for each, and La Rochelle contributed an average of thirteen annually, or 15 percent. Most of the remaining five percent originated at Dunkirk, Saint-Malo, Honfleur, and Bayonne. Rochelais slaving tonnage surpassed that of Bordeaux and Le Havre, so the deliveries from the three ports were probably equal. By the 1780s almost one in three Rochelais departures headed for Africa.[9]

Nantes's early supremacy in the slave trade stemmed from its position as the sole market for the sale of goods of the Company of the Indies. Necessary contacts were established during this period with Dutch and Flemish suppliers of appropriate trade goods and with Dutch contacts in West Africa.[10] These advantages, soon shared by other ports, prompted a shift to slave trading at Nantes when the company opened it to individuals. By the 1780s, slaving's apparent advantages made it a central endeavor of the great Atlantic ports. Rochelais efforts to develop commerce with the United States faltered, according to a Rochelais firm, because its armateurs abandoned North America in order to concentrate on the slave trade.[11]

At the same time that the vessels of France's Atlantic ports turned increasingly toward the coast of West Africa for cargoes of blacks, other vessels also turned their prows southwestward. But instead of stopping at Senegal, they continued around the Cape of Good Hope and into the Indian Ocean. Until the demise of the Company of the Indies in 1769, the trade with the East Indies, India, and China was the exclusive privilege of that company, operating out of Lorient. Between 1769 and the formation of a second Company of the Indies in 1785, La Rochelle and other ports energetically pursued the East Indian trade.[12]

Once in the Indian Ocean, French vessels made for Île de France (Île Maurtius under Dutch occupancy, which ended in 1712), located 350 miles east of Madagascar. Île de Bourbon (also known as Île de Réunion), its neighbor to the southeast, lacked a suitable port so it was bypassed for Île de France. Coffee harvested on Île de Bourbon, slaves from the coast of East Africa via Madagascar, Indian cloths and Bengal silks from Pondicherry (at the southern end of the coast of Coromandel), Chinese porcelains, and spices from the Dutch East Indies—all could be obtained in abundance at Port Louis, the major city of Île de France. Vessels continuing on to Pondicherry or Canton revictualed at Port Louis. With the opening of Île de France to private trade, the slave trade shifted somewhat from the west to the east coast of Africa and vessels followed a circuitous trade route from France to Île de France and East Africa, then to the Antilles, and then home.

During the period 1769–85, La Rochelle, unobstructed by monopoly, sent 26 vessels to the Indian Ocean while Nantes, Bordeaux, and Marseilles each contributed over 40. Saint-Malo outfitted 32 vessels. Lorient, the headquarters of the defunct Company of the Indies, profiting from the requirement (opposed by the other ports) that all East Indian cargoes be discharged there, outfitted 120 vessels. It is unlikely that more than 25 or 30 of these ships were controlled by Lorient's merchants; most were financed by individuals from other communities. Then, in 1785, a new Company of the Indies received its charter.

Capitalized at 20 million lt. (raised to 40 million in 1786), the company immediately aroused the antagonism of merchants in La Rochelle and elsewhere. Licensing by the company regulated private participation in the East Indian trade. Too, the failure of the company to allow the merchants of the major ports to obtain shares of either the first or second stock issues exacerbated the opposition. Charles Lanesse, merchant of Bordeaux, warned the La Rochelle Chamber of Commerce that "le privilege exclusif" threatened all ports, pointing out that the administration of the company did not include any merchants from the ports engaged in the trade.[13]

While the various ports, through their representatives in Paris, coordinated their attacks on the company, permissions were obtained and vessels continued to travel to Île de France. The company, outfitting fewer than ten vessels annually, lacked the strength to completely control the trade. One estimate for the six years 1785–90 credits armateurs at Lorient with outfitting twenty-two vessels for the East Indies, Bordeaux with twenty-one, Marseilles twenty, Nantes fourteen, Saint-Malo thirteen, and La Rochelle ten.[14] The vitality of this trade despite the length of the voyage, the greater tonnage of vessels, and the high costs of financing suggests that at the very end of the Old Regime the ports were slowly turning their attention away from the Antilles.[15]

La Rochelle committed relatively few vessels to the codfishing fleet which cast its nets along Newfoundland's Grand Banks, but it served as an important port of discharge for the catch of non-Rochelais fishermen. Saint-Malo, Dunkirk, Dieppe, Granville, and other ports sent as many as 175 fishing vessels to Newfoundland's waters during each year of the two decades prior to the French Revolution, of which some 20 to 25 ships annually sold their cod at La Rochelle. Many others stopped at La Rochelle to obtain salt. Nantes and Marseilles both claimed preeminence as fish markets. Each of those two ports probably attracted twice as many fishing vessels as either La Rochelle, Bordeaux, Dieppe, or Honfleur. All of the French ports suffered severe competition from New England fishermen. With each war, the French foothold slipped: first with the loss of Newfoundland and the islands of Saint-Pierre and Miquelon in 1713, then with the loss of Louisbourg and Acadia in 1745, and finally in 1763 with the loss of all of Canada. Saint Pierre and Miquelon were returned to France in 1763, and the French retained fishing rights on the Grand Banks. New England fishermen, however, marketed a good part of their catch in the West Indies and over the years effectively penetrated the French islands. In so doing, they not only denied markets to French fishermen guaranteed in the letters patent of 1717 but also diverted colonial staples from French ports to English and New England ports. Government subsidies to fishing vessels, offered after 1767, were insufficient to restore the French fishing fleet to its mid-eighteenth century strength.[16]

While the fishing fleet declined during the last half of the century, the French share of le grand cabotage remained at the same low level throughout the century. The merchants of the Atlantic ports ignored the traffic, preferring to concentrate their capital in maintaining a high seas fleet. Consequently, the Dutch, English, Danes, and Germans managed and owned the shipping that carried colonial goods to northern Europe.

A Rochelais analysis of le grand cabotage in 1783 contended that Dutch superiority in the northern trade resulted from lower costs per voyage than the French could achieve. Because of regulations fixing the size of a vessel's crew, French crews were frequently twice as large of those on Dutch vessels of equivalent size. Moreover, Dutch vessels were more efficient, and the Dutch were more experienced in navigating the dangerous Baltic Sea. Such disadvantages, the study concluded, readily explained the virtual absence of French bottoms passing into and out of the Baltic. In 1767 and 1768, a total of 12,988 vessels entered or left the Baltic, of which 16 were French, 4,601 Dutch, and 3,066 English. Swedes, Danes, and Germans shared the remainder.[17] During the years of peace in the 1750s and 1760s, arrivals at La Rochelle from northern Europe probably surpassed the number of vessels outfitted for le long cours. Bordeaux alone absorbed some one-third of all vessels passing out of the Baltic for French ports and quite possibly an equal share of the Dutch traffic.[18]

By far the larger number of vessels arriving at La Rochelle consisted of coasters. In 1764 and 1765, 2,688 ships of all types anchored at La Rochelle. Of those, 916 had come from Normandy, Brittany, and ports to the south. Ports within fifty miles—Les Sables d'Olonne, Île de Ré, Tremblade, Marrennes, Marans, and ports along the Charente River—accounted for 57 percent of all arrivals and 34 percent of total tonnage. Rochelais merchants probably owned less than 15 percent of those vessels.[19]

The precise number of vessels le long cours owned fully or in part by Rochelais can only be estimated. The individual who registered a vessel at the Admiralty—the armateur—need not have been the owner either in full or in part. Armateurs frequently acted as agents for owners, non-Rochelais as well as Rochelais. Available evidence about the numbers of non-Rochelais-owned vessels departing from the port suggests at least part Rochelais ownership of most vessels outfitted there. In any given year, La Rochelle residents owned in whole or in part about twice the number of vessels that departed.[20]

The Rochelais obtained their vessels by purchase and by construction in La Rochelle and other ports. Typically, a flurry of purchases occurred at the conclusion of a war as buyers sought to replace vessels seized or destroyed by the enemy. Some replacements were captured English ships. Still others bought French vessels captured by the English. The Rasteaus purchased *la Marthe* (170 tons), formerly a Nantes vessel, at Bristol. At least five other Rochelais concluded similar purchases in England at the same time.[21]

Rochelais vessels changed hands quite frequently at public auction. In July 1749, after the public crier had announced the sale for several days, the merchants of the city gathered to bid on *le Saint Charles* (220t). Jacques Rasteau père opened the bidding at 12,000 lt. Other bids forced Rasteau to 17,600 lt. when Robert Deverigny closed the sale with an offer of 18,000 lt. Deverigny soon sold the vessel to Elie Giraudeau and other investors for 21,000 lt. Vessels were sold as partnerships ended, as estates were settled, during bankruptcy proceedings, and at other times.[22]

Merchants contracted for the construction of new vessels in other cities and at home. Notices of proprietorship for vessels constructed elsewhere most frequently identified shipyards at Nantes and Rochefort, but Saint-Malo, Bayonne, and even Archangel received some Rochelais business. During the 1780s, the firm of Lepage Brothers constructed most of the vessels at La Rochelle. In 1784 and 1785, this firm constructed at least seventeen ships, six over 100 tons, for Rochelais customers. A few of their vessels were speculative ventures but most were built on contract. In 1787, Lepage Brothers constructed several ships in excess of 500 tons for use in the East Indian trade.[23]

Estimates of cost per ton of vessels constructed for or purchased by Rochelais during the eighteenth century, calculated on the basis of known tonnage and known sale or construction prices, suggest that costs per ton rose steadily until the 1780s. Averaging 81 lt. per ton during the period 1710–29, 111 lt. for 1748–67, and 158 lt. for 1780–84, costs then declined to an average of 110 lt. per ton for 1785–90, reflecting the economies realized by the construction or purchase of larger vessels. The rising commitment of Rochelais merchants to the East Indian and slave trade resulted in the acquisition of ships of larger tonnage.[24]

The purchase and construction of vessels accelerated at the conclusion of each of the last three wars fought against England. Since Chapter 7 will discuss in detail the effects of war on Rochelais shipping, only the magnitude of the losses will be treated here. Relatively good data is available for the War of the Austrian Succession and the Seven Years' War. Between 1743, when France entered the conflict, and November 1745, La Rochelle lost 30 vessels and cargoes worth 8.6 million lt. The Rasteaus, again hit hard, suffered the capture of three vessels worth over 900,000 lt. In 1757 and 1758, 70 more Rochelais ships worth at least 10 million lt. fell prey to the English, leaving the port a fleet of fewer than ten ships. Nantes's fleet was reduced by 110 vessels, many of which were slavers, valued at 17 million lt. Relatively fewer losses were sustained during the American Revolution because of improved convoy systems, unusual French naval parity with England in Atlantic waters, and the absence of North American privateers operating along West Indian sea lanes. In both La Rochelle and Bordeaux, the construction and purchase of new vessels between 1778 and 1783 more than compensated for wartime losses.

The exigencies of war and the losses incurred tended to concentrate the colonial trade in fewer hands. Small operators (outfitting fewer than ten ventures during a given decade) were less likely to resume operations after the American war than after the Seven Years' War. Between 1763 and 1770, small armateurs readied 20 percent of the vessels departing La Rochelle but only 12 percent from 1781 to 1785. As the needs of trade demanded larger ships and longer voyages, fewer individuals or firms possessed the necessary capital to undertake such ventures.[25]

Despite serious wartime losses, particularly during the Seven Years' War, fleet tonnage at the major ports rapidly regained and then frequently surpassed prewar levels. La Rochelle outfitted over 10,000 tons annually in 1763, 1764, and 1765, compared with an annual tonnage of 7,205 for the five years 1750–54. Rochelais annual tonnage during the 1770s fluctuated between 5,000 and 8,000 tons but jumped to over 10,000 in 1781, 12,000 in 1784, and then to an average of 17,567 for the three years 1785–87. Such dramatic increments to the port's tonnage garnered La Rochelle little or no ground on her competitors.

THE VALUE AND COMPOSITION OF LA ROCHELLE'S EXTERIOR TRADE

La Rochelle's merchant community failed to match the rapid pace of economic growth achieved by its major competitors. Although La Rochelle's commerce did expand in absolute terms, its share of national commerce declined during the century. The following discussion of the composition and value of the city's trade with its primary markets provides a basis for comparison between ports and delineates the market setting within which the Rochelais strove to advance.

The total value of external commerce at La Rochelle increased between 1718 and 1780. But as table 2.4 demonstrates, the three major wars fought during those years either slowed down or drastically reversed prior trends.[26] Although data for the 1780s are incomplete, figures on shipping presented earlier in this chapter support the conclusion that La Rochelle's commerce during the period at least equaled the magnitude achieved between 1774 and 1778. The total value of imports and exports at La Rochelle rose by 65 percent from 1718 to 1778, an annual growth rate of just over one percent, but the port's trade grew much less rapidly than the total external trade of the nation or of its major competitors.

France's external commerce rose by at least 3 percent per annum between 1717 and 1787, rising from a total of 114 million lt. (current value) to 1.1 billion lt. During the same period, Bordeaux's commerce increased at an

Table 2.4. *Average Value of Imports and Exports at La Rochelle, 1718–80 (lt. in thousands)*

Year	Import	Export	Year	Import	Export
1718–22	5,786	7,114	1754	10,600	9,787
1723–27	6,329	6,321	War		
1728–32	5,788	7,149	1755–63	3,765	4,986
1733–37	5,896	7,403	1764–68	6,311	6,808[c]
1738–42[a]	8,216	8,852	1769–73	6,468	9,411
War			1774–78	10,178	11,157
1743–48	8,583	8,636[b]	War		
1749–53	10,297	10,942	1779–80	3,906	4,018

[a] Figures unavailable for: 1742, 1743, 1745, 1755, 1763, 1777.
[b] 1744 and 1746 only.
[c] 1764 missing.
Source: See note 26.

annual rate above 4 percent. Between 1730 and 1778, the annual rate of growth at Marseilles exceeded 6 percent. Nantes's external trade doubled in value while that of Le Havre–Rouen tripled. The slower pace of La Rochelle's growth reduced its share of the nation's external commerce from some six percent during the period 1728–1732 to under four percent in the 1740s and to between two and three percent following the American Revolution. La Rochelle's trade about equaled that of Marseilles from 1728 to 1732, whereas it was one-half that of Nantes's and Le Havre–Rouen's and 60 percent of Bordeaux's. Fifty years later, Marseilles's trade exceeded that of La Rochelle by almost eight times. Bordeaux's trade was seven times greater and Le Havre–Rouen's four times larger. La Rochelle kept pace only with Nantes.[27]

Differentials between La Rochelle and the four dominant ports in the volume of trade were wider in the trade with Europe than in that with the colonies. While La Rochelle retained a share of 2 to 3 percent of the total trade with Europe during the eighteenth century, the European trade of Marseilles and Bordeaux was fourteen and ten times greater respectively than La Rochelle's by 1778. During the 1730s the differential had been about two times larger. In the colonial trade, however, the Rochelais maintained a greater, but similarly declining, significance. La Rochelle's share of the colonial trade had surpassed 20 percent during the 1730s but had declined to 7 percent by the 1770s. By 1778, the colonial trade at Marseilles, Nantes, and Le Havre-Rouen was twice La Rochelle's, while Bordeaux's trade, averaging 68 million lt. for the years 1773–78, exceeded La Rochelle's by four times. Values are not available for the 1780s, but the number and tonnage of armements suggest that La Rochelle's relative position remained stable with all the ports but Bordeaux. In 1786 and 1787, when La Rochelle outfitted 81 ships le long cours, Bordelais armements totaled 526. Although the average tonnage per Rochelais ship may have been somewhat larger, it is likely that Bordeaux's colonial trade was at least five times that of La Rochelle's. In 1770 and 1771,

Bordeaux claimed 59 percent of the Antilles trade. While this share declined thereafter, the port still controlled 40 percent at the end of the 1780s. Marseilles and Le Havre-Rouen each claimed about 20 percent. By the time of the French Revolution, Bordeaux and Marseilles each controlled about 25 percent of the total exterior trade of France.[28]

The origin of La Rochelle's imports, the destination of exports, and the percentage of total value of imports and exports by place are summarized in table 2.5. This table makes clear the dominance of the colonies, which normally provided La Rochelle with well above one-half of its imports and received an increasing share of exports. The proportion of colonial trade to total trade was greater at La Rochelle than at Marseilles. The latter's imports from and exports to the colonies fluctuated between 10 and 20 percent of total trade after 1750. At La Rochelle, the colonial trade accounted for over 60 percent of exterior commerce from 1749 to 1753, and above 50 percent from 1774 to 1778. At Bordeaux colonial commerce contributed 46 percent of total trade in 1776, and 49 percent at Nantes from 1775 to 1778.

Virtually the entire import of colonial commodities at La Rochelle—accounting for about one-half of all imports between 1764 and 1778—were reexported to northern and other European markets. This reexport trade, as Ernest Labrousse in 1944 and Thomas M. Doerflinger more recently have pointed out, probably contributed about one-third of total French exports during the 1770s and 1780s. Reexports were relatively more important at La Rochelle, Nantes, and Bordeaux than at Le Havre–Rouen or Marseilles. After mid-century, Nantais and Bordelais reexports contributed between 20 and 30 percent of their total trade. At La Rochelle, reexports contributed 35 to 40 percent of total trade, underscoring the more intense dependence of that port upon the Antilles trade. In addition, the disposition of salt and brandy receipts at La Rochelle was almost totally accounted for by exports to European ports, and the disposition of French and European goods imported at La Rochelle was accounted for by exports to the colonies or West Africa. La Rochelle, to a relatively greater extent than her larger competitors, served as a point of long distance transshipment of goods. But in a general way, all of the ports functioned within the same system. Most of the goods received at Bordeaux, whether products of her hinterland or of France or Europe, went into the foreign or colonial trade. Rochelais brandies or Bordelais wines, as an example, shipped to Breton or Norman ports composed a large part of the latter's reexport trade to foreign or colonial markets. The major current of goods flowed between ports and from ports to overseas markets, a pattern perhaps even more descriptive of La Rochelle than other ports because of inferior connections with the interior.[29]

Foreign suppliers provided the greatest portion of goods used in the slave and colonial trades. In the 1776 voyage to Guinea of the slaver *le Meulan* only one-third of its typical cargo originated in France.[30] Unlike Nantes, which provided some of its own manufactured goods, particularly apparel and hardware, or Bordeaux, which exported wines and cereals obtained from its hinter-

Table 2.5. Rochelais Imports (I) and Exports (E) by Percentage of Total Value, 1718–80

Year	Market	Colonies	England	Holland	The North[a]	Spain and Portugal	Italy and Switzerland
1718–27	I	74	12	8	5	1	
	E	28	11	38	16	2	6
1728–37	I	71	10	10	8	1	
	E	37	8	28	19	2	4
1738–42	I	70	9	12	8	1	
	E	40	8	21	23	1	6
1743–48	I	86	3	5	5	1	
	E	31	1	18	37	1	10
1749–54	I	77	8	7	8	1	
	E	44	9	13	26	2	5
1755–63	I	59	3	23	11	4	
	E	28	1	27	30	2	10
1764–78	I	55	7	25	5	7	
	E	53	7	8	23	1	5
1779–80	I	57	1	13	19	1	
	E	22	0	3	38	1	5

[a] Including the Hanseatic cities, Germany, Denmark, Sweden, and Russia.
Sources: Récapitulation entrées, and Récapitulation sorties.

land, La Rochelle contributed only salt and brandy as an export of local production. The value of salt exports declined quickly after 1740 and, by the 1770s, was of little significance. Until the 1770s, brandy normally furnished less than 20 percent of Rochelais exports to the colonies. The bulk of that commodity was exported to northern Europe. After 1770, the slave trade took most of the port's brandy exports (see table 8.2). The abrupt decline in brandy shipments to northern Europe reflected the weakening competitive position of local vis-à-vis Spanish and Portuguese brandies.

Holland and the Hanseatic cities of Hamburg, Lübeck, and Bremen furnished the greatest quantity and variety of goods used in La Rochelle's colonial trade and were the primary European markets for both La Rochelle's exports and reexports. The leading categories of goods imported from those places consisted of manufactured and unfinished metals, finished cloths, wood products, and foods. The Dutch supplied large quantities of cheese (some 10 percent of imports from Holland in most years) and cauris (cowry, a type of strung seashell) for the slave trade, while the Baltic ports forwarded planks, staves, barrels, and other products of the forest.

Holland and the North received large quantities of goods from La Rochelle, especially salt, brandy, sugar, and indigo. During wartime the share of domestic goods, largely salt and brandy, rose relative to the share of colonial products. During the Seven Years' War, 69 percent of the total value of Rochelais exports to the North consisted of brandy and 18 percent sugar and indigo. Before the war, between 1749 and 1754, 59 percent of those exports consisted of sugar and indigo and 18 percent brandy. Prior to 1742, domestic commodities formed one-half of all shipments; after 1749, colonial goods normally made up the bulk of the cargoes. Sugar and indigo formed 60 percent of the value of Rochelais exports to the North between 1774 and 1778. Between 1720 and 1778, exports to Holland and the North of salt, brandy, all sugars, indigo, and coffee (beginning in the 1740s) usually contributed between 25 and 45 percent of total Rochelais exports. Holland and the North received virtually all of their salt and, until the 1770s, above one-third of their brandy from La Rochelle.[31]

Just as the Rochelais share of total French foreign trade declined during the eighteenth century, so too did La Rochelle ship a diminishing share of colonial products to northern Europe. Holland and the North received 11,156,000 lt. in sugars, indigo, and coffee from French sources in 1750, of which 9 percent came from La Rochelle. In 1776, less than 2 percent originated at La Rochelle. After 1742, the North, especially the Hanse towns, surpassed Holland as the primary European destination of Rochelais exports (see table 2.5). Bordeaux, Marseilles, and Le Havre–Rouen dominated this trade, while Nantes and La Rochelle slipped into a secondary position. The value of Bordelais exports to the North exceeded La Rochelle's by about twenty times during the 1760s and 1770s while Rochelais exports to Holland—including Bordelais wines— equaled no more than one-quarter of the value of Bordeaux's shipments.

Other markets also figured in the foreign trade of La Rochelle. But as table 2.5 indicates, such places as England, Spain, Portugal, and Italy were of marginal significance compared with Dutch or Hanse ports. England, Spain, and Portugal supplied a fairly constant share of La Rochelle's imports during the eighteenth century. Rochelais exports to England declined and exports to Spain and Portugal were small. In contrast, Le Havre's commerce with Spain and Portugal consistently accounted for more than 25 percent of its exterior trade, while traffic with the North generated less than 15 percent. Rochelais exports to England consisted mostly of indigo and brandy, in exchange for butter, Irish salt beef, and coal from British markets. Imports from Spain were of considerable importance to La Rochelle after 1768. But of the goods making up that trade—wool, furs, indigo, and piasters—only wool was of Spanish origin. The other commodities were from Louisiana and had formed part of the receipts from the colonies prior to the cession of Louisiana to Spain in 1763.[32]

Rochelais exports to the Italian peninsula and to Swiss cities fluctuated between 4 and 10 percent of total Rochelais exports (see table 2.5). Indigo shipments to Italian and Swiss markets greatly exceeded the value of all other goods. Italian ports occasionally received large cargoes of sugar and smaller quantities of coffee and furs and skins. During the period 1747–61, furs, skins and hides composed 75 percent of La Rochelle's shipments to the Swiss. In most other years, indigo was the principal commodity. Even though Rochelais armateurs, such as Nicolas Schaaf and Pierre Jean Van Hoogwerf, outfitted an occasional vessel for the Mediterranean, Dutch and German shipowners controlled le grand cabotage. The Mediterranean trade, dominated by Marseilles, was of greater relative importance to La Rochelle than to Norman and Breton ports or to Bordeaux.

CONCLUSION

During the last three decades of the Old Regime, La Rochelle's economy became increasingly dependent upon the colonial trade, particularly upon the slave trade. The proportion of slavers to other vessels le long cours outfitted by Rochelais reflected this dependence. Too, the value of goods exported to Africa as a percentage of all exports to the colonies rose from 33 percent in 1769 and 1770 to 75 percent in 1775 and 69 percent in 1776. As the relative importance of the colonial trade intensified at La Rochelle, it remained stable at Nantes, Marseilles, and Bordeaux. At Le Havre–Rouen, colonial imports rose rapidly but exports to the colonies declined. The primary trade focus of Le Havre–Rouen remained Europe and Paris. Marseilles retained a Mediterranean orientation, and the Antilles trade was of less significance than at Le Havre–Rouen. Bordeaux, which came to dominate colonial imports during the 1770s and 1780s, developed its European export sector more successfully than La Rochelle or Nantes.

While the colonies received well under 50 percent of La Rochelle's exports between 1718 and 1768, that proportion soared to 69 percent prior to the American Revolution and remained around that level through 1789. At Le Havre–Rouen, the colonial trade accounted for about 33 percent of total trade between 1773 and 1778. At Marseilles, the proportion remained between 15 and 20 percent from 1730 through the 1770s. At Bordeaux, the share of total trade attributable to colonial commerce rose from 34 percent between 1717 and 1721 to over 40 percent after 1770. During the same period, the percentage of total Bordelais exports directed to the colonies declined from 22 percent to under 15 percent.[33]

For La Rochelle, Bordeaux, and Nantes, the colonial connection provided the initial stimulus to growth and remained the decisive factor during the eighteenth century. While other trade orientations remained paramount at Le Havre–Rouen and Marseilles, the colonial trade provided a new growth sector supplemental to the dominant sectors. Earlier in the century, when Marseilles began venturing more heavily in the Antilles trade than previously, reexports of colonial staples to northern Europe represented the addition of new commodities rather than new markets. To a degree unmatched at other ports, La Rochelle's economy rested almost solely on the colonial connection. The Rochelais, disadvantaged by severe locational constraints, never evolved those supplementary trades which afforded some balance to the commerce of their rivals and which allowed some economic flexibility when political or economic events disrupted the colonial exchange. La Rochelle was ill-prepared, then, to respond to politically or economically induced changes in the prevailing commercial system.

THREE

The Négociant *Families* *of La Rochelle*

Fewer than one hundred families controlled the commerce of the port of La Rochelle during the eighteenth century. The dominant firms in the city were family enterprises, most of which attained prominence after the War of the Spanish Succession and continued to function into the 1780s. Family and business were inseparable. Indeed, so intertwined were social attitudes and goals with economic attitudes and goals that a study of family in La Rochelle inevitably becomes an investigation of the city's primary socioeconomic unit.

Elsewhere in France, family units of a structure and function similar to the Rochelais rose during the eighteenth century, forming part of an expanding middle stratum of society. There were, however, identifiable substrata within the middle class, and efforts to construct models of the bourgeoisie and its family structure have often failed to distinguish these strata from one another. Much as history in general has told the tale of notables, so have historians of the bourgeoisie molded archetypes largely from the *haute bourgeoisie* of Paris and other large cities. The great financiers of Paris and other large cities, the *rentiers* (investor bourgeoisie), and the administrative bourgeoisie, however, pursued goals, developed life styles, and evolved world views that differed markedly from the round of life in which La Rochelle's elite merchants moved.[1]

Both speculators and port merchants lived in a world of risk far more precarious than the rentiers. Port merchants, however, could not assume the degree of risk acceptable to *agioteurs* (speculators). Rochelais merchants such as Claude Etienne Belin, Jacques Rasteau, or Paul Depont des Granges preferred moderate returns on their investments to the gambles of instant winning and losing of fortunes, which typified the life of speculators. Rochelais négociant families were, in effect, economic units organized into *comptoirs* (business or counting houses), responsible for maintaining and expanding the family capital and devoted to the economic security of the next generation. With so much at stake, the négociant families would not venture all on one throw of the die. In their everyday business routine, these Rochelais fell somewhere between the agioteur and the rentier.[2]

The primary purpose of this and the following two chapters is to analyze La Rochelle's négociant families and their kinship networks as an economic system of capital accumulation and circulation. The system performed essential functions. It assured that capital would remain in circulation for mercantile purposes rather than being hoarded or channeled into lands and rents. It preserved family wealth for succeeding generations so that the family comptoir was perpetuated and strengthened. Insofar as the system worked, the dominant families performed social, if not public, purposes. Their collective efforts sustained the essential viability of La Rochelle as a central entrepôt in the colonial trade in the face of counterpressures that would otherwise have hastened its decline. The central devices to preserve wealth within the kinship networks—the dowry, inheritance, and career programs for the male line—will form the substance of this chapter.

La Rochelle's elite merchants confronted different problems than did their peers in Amsterdam or Nantes.[3] City size and location were crucial; the Rochelais had to try harder just to remain competitive. Too, most of La Rochelle's elite merchants were Huguenots, existing as a tiny minority in a sea of Roman Catholicism and subjected to various legal constraints. These and other disadvantages demanded a cohesiveness within and between the Rochelais family networks that other port cities with greater resources found less necessary.

During the eighteenth century, some ninety families provided economic and municipal leadership in La Rochelle. From this group came the men and women who owned and managed the merchant fleet, who mobilized capital for investment purposes, and who directed the major economic institutions of the city—the Chamber of Commerce, the jurisdiction consulaire, the sugar refineries, the comptoirs, and the insurance companies. These ninety families encompassed virtually the entire economic elite of La Rochelle.

While the socioeconomic characteristics of Rochelais families resembled those evolved by families in other times and places, the Rochelais experience reflected a highly refined response to discrete historical conditions that, beginning in the early seventeenth century, reduced the economic, social, and political options available to Protestants in the city and which eliminated municipal autonomy until the eighteenth century. Although not wholly fettered by historical circumstances, the Rochelais socioeconomic structure did evolve from particular historical experiences. In La Rochelle, religion formed the strongest bond between elite families, three quarters of which were Huguenot. Kinship ties never, and socializing but rarely, crossed religious lines, even though Protestants and Catholics mingled freely and informally and cooperated closely and effectively in political activities that bore on the port's economic life. Protestants competed with Catholics for business with no more sharpness or animosity than in the competition with other Protestants. Joint ventures between Protestants and Catholics, though not unusual, were less the norm than cooperation between religious confreres. In the public sphere, then, Protestants and Catholics alike functioned not as members of antagonistic religions but as members of the same social class. In contrast, Protestant négociants in Nantes, Bordeaux, and Marseilles seemed much less cohesive. In Marseilles, Huguenots exerted less influence on business and municipal affairs than in La Rochelle. For example, no Protestants served in the Marseilles Chamber of Commerce until the 1780s. Unlike the case of La Rochelle, a narrow group of families did not control most of the seats in Marseille's chamber.

Size and its magnetic qualities accounted for part of the difference between La Rochelle and its larger rivals. By the end of the Old Regime, 46 percent of the négociants at Marseilles were either foreign or non-Marseillais French, compared with under 5 percent at La Rochelle. Protestants, some of whom were non-Marseillais, composed only 20 percent of the négociants at the Mediterranean port. Finally, fewer than 100 négociants of all types operated at La Rochelle while some 750 conducted affairs at Marseilles and at least 400 at Nantes. In a port so small and so economically dependent upon a relatively small group of merchant families as La Rochelle, each family's success contributed not only to its own prosperity but to the strength of all. Conversely, economic instability within one family comptoir threatened the stability of all. Successful competition with larger and wealthier coastal rivals depended upon efficient business organization and the wise utilization of a narrower range of resources. The elite Rochelais shared perceptions about the needs of the port and about threats to its vitality.[4] Such consensus on policy issues affecting their oceanic commerce was both cause and effect of the similar ways in which they organized their family life, passed wealth from one generation to the next, and strove to strengthen the kinship unit.

FAMILY ORIGINS

The religious wars of the early seventeenth century and the persecution that followed had decimated the Protestant population of La Rochelle. In 1685, the revocation of the Edict of Nantes precipitated another round of persecution and Protestant migration. However, the remaining small group of *religionnaires* (Huguenots) provided the greater portion of the economic leadership that sustained the city's position during the troubled and war-torn eighteenth century. Catholics were not unimportant; of the twenty-six leading families included in table 3.1, eight were Catholics.[5]

The steady erosion of Protestant strength between 1628 and 1700, affecting merchants as well as other occupational groups, determined that few of the Protestants in La Rochelle in 1700 would be descendants of the Rochelais of 1600. Richelieu's victory in 1628 caused thousands of Huguenots to emigrate. In 1661, some 1,800 Protestants, all residents of the city since

Table 3.1. Rank Score, and Religion of the Leading Rochelais Families, by Maritime and General Economic Significance

Maritime Significance

Rank	Family	Score	Religion
1	Rasteau	297	P[a]
2	Garesché	221	P
3	Belin	180	P
4	Vivier	154	P
5	Giraudeau	147	P
6	Delacroix	111	P
7	Carayon	111	P
8	Bonneau	106	P
9	Bonfils	103	P
10	Seignette	96	P
11	Perdriau	78	P
12	Depont	77	P
13	Suidre	75	P
14	Goguet	68	RC
15	Pascaud	66	RC
16	Guibert	65	P

General Economic Significance

Rank	Family	Score	Religion
1	Belin	475	P
2	Rasteau	447	P
3	Seignette	361	P
4	Vivier	359	P
5	Pascaud	301	RC[b]
6	Garesché	281	P
7	Goguet	273	RC
8	Giraudeau	257	P
9	Bonneau	256	P
10	Carayon	236	P
11	Delacroix	236	P
12	Depont	222	P
13	Gastumeau	185	RC
14	Bridault	175	RC
15	Bonfils	173	P
16	Papineau	170	RC
17	Admyrauld	151	P
18	de Butler	147	RC
19	Legrix	145	RC
20	Van Hoogwerf	144	P
21	Lefebvre	143	RC
22	Suidre	140	P
23	Bernon	138	P
24	Dubeignon	125	P
25	Labbé	120	P
26	Perdriau	113	P

[a] P = Protestant
[b] RC = Roman Catholic

1628, were expelled and an additional 3,000 Protestants fled following the revocation. In the single year 1688, an estimated 500 Rochelais arrived in Holland. According to the intendant of La Rochelle, writing in 1698, his *généralité* (district) had lost within a decade one-third of its population through war, internal emigration, and the emigration of religionnaires, including a large number of armateurs and seamen from La Rochelle and Île de Ré.[6]

Still, a central core of Protestant merchants persisted. Prior to the 1680s, the richest and most active merchants of the port had been Protestants, and the revocation had not totally displaced the merchant class of La Rochelle. While whole families and lines of other families fled, others remained who had been longtime residents of the city. Few could trace their line back to the fourteenth century as did the Depont or Vivier families, or even to the sixteenth century as did the Belin, but several families who chose not to emigrate had been active merchants in the city during the period immediately following the city's capitulation to Cardinal Richelieu. The latter included the Auboyneau, Bonneau, Lepage, and Seignette families. Others—the Delacroix, de Butler, Denis, and Robert families—had engaged vigorously in maritime trade since the 1660s.

Belins had been merchants in La Rochelle during the late sixteenth century, but it was Allard Belin fils (1650–1746) who founded the powerful merchant dynasty that operated during the eighteenth century. His older brother, Ozée (b. 1642), had received the office *ouvrier de pleine part de la monnaye royalle* upon the death of his father in 1684, just as the father had succeeded his father in that office in 1646. Allard fils, as had his father and grandfather, succeeded in 1684 to the office *prévôt de la monnaye*. Allard and Ozée then passed these offices to their sons. In other respects, the careers of Allard and Ozée and their children diverged. Ozée's line held offices in the juridiction consulaire, purchased estates in Saintonge and Aunis and in the West Indies, and eschewed direct participation in the management of maritime commerce. Allard and, ultimately, his sons, Elie Allard (d. 1780) and Claude Etienne (1697–1779), managed the family business and held prestigious offices in the Chamber of Commerce (see Belin genealogy, table 3.3).[7]

The Deponts, among the oldest ennobled families in the French provinces, had filled municipal offices in La Rochelle during the late fourteenth century. In the early seventeenth century, they had outfitted vessels for Canada, as had the Bonneau, Delacroix, and Denis families, and by the late seventeenth century, Paul Depont, Seigneur des Granges, was a leading Rochelais armateur, a position retained until his death in 1744. Only one son of three followed Paul's vocation, and that son engaged in brokerage and wholesaling instead of shipowning. The other sons managed the extensive landed properties of the family while holding a variety of offices in the généralité of La Rochelle. Paul's grandson, Jean Samuel, obtained the post of intendant of Moulins in 1765, advancing to the intendancy of Metz in 1778.[8]

Less ancient than the Belin and less distinguished than the Depont, the Bonneau, Delacroix, and Seignette families had been firmly established in the port at the time of the siege. Nicolas Bonneau had outfitted one or two vessels annually for Morocco between 1630 and 1660, some under his command, while also venturing to the Antilles, Canada, Spain, and the Baltic Sea. His sons and grandsons were leading Rochelais armateurs, bankers, sugar refiners, and officeholders during the entire eighteenth century. Originally from Holland, the Delacroixs had been merchants of Calais and La Rochelle prior to the 1660s. Jehain Delacroix (d. 1669), his sons, Adrian and Abraham, Abraham's son, Théodore (d. 1735), and Théodore fils aîné (d. 1770) followed a career line similar to the Bonneaus.[9]

Diverging slightly from the pattern of the Bonneaus and the Delacroixs, Jean Seignette père had moved to La Rochelle in 1592 as an apothecary, one of the last three Rochelais Protestants in the profession. Protestants were no longer admitted into that occupation after 1628, and in 1678 a statute prohibited all religionnaires from working as apothecaries. However, Jean's son, Elie

(b. 1657), had continued to practice his specialty until 1691, when renewed persecution resulted in a brief banishment to Besançon. Permitted to return, Elie and his sons (particularly Elie fils) and their descendants built up one of the most powerful merchant houses in the city and held a variety of offices, some of which were ordinarily inaccessible to Huguenots.[10]

Compared with the above families, the Rasteaus, Giraudeaus, and Viviers were newcomers to La Rochelle. Jacques Rasteau père (1680–1756) first appeared in local records in 1696 as captain of the vessel *le Saint Mathieu,* returned from Martinique. Although the origins of the Rasteau family are unknown, Jacques's lineage must have been acceptable, for he married Suzanne Sara Seignette prior to 1714, at which time he relinquished his maritime command and became a fulltime armateur. During the next eight decades, Jacques's numerous sons moved one by one into the family comptoir, several after stints as ships' captains, or joined the mercantile houses of uncles in Santo Domingo. The youngest son, Paul, judged by his father to be the most irresponsible of the boys, was sent to New Orleans in 1736 to handle the firm's affairs. The Rasteaus quickly accrued commercial distinctions, but unlike the Belins or Seignettes, royal office either eluded them or formed no part of their ambitions. Elie Giraudeau (d. 1749) assumed his place in the chronicles of La Rochelle at about the same time as Jacques Rasteau, and the Giraudeau family experienced an occupational and social history similar to the Rasteaus. Jean Vivier (1672–1732) and his family gained wealth and honors that may have surpassed those of his contemporaries, the Rasteaus and Giraudeaus. Much more ancient in lineage than the Belins, the Vivier clan had provided councillors to the parlement of Paris in the fourteenth century and had played a heroic role in the siege of La Rochelle in 1628. They remained obscure for the remainder of the seventeenth century. Jean rebuilt the family's fortunes toward the end of the century, capitalizing on the same opportunities that had brought success to Jacques Rasteau and Elie Giraudeau. The Viviers were a renewed old family.[11]

These families and others, including such prominent Catholics as the Pascauds, de Butlers, and Goguets, provided continuity between the early seventeenth and the eighteenth century.[12] Almost without exception the mercantile activities of these families persisted over three to four generations, reaching to the French Revolution and beyond. A close perusal of table 3.2, listing the number of vessels outfitted by the leading twenty-six families, discloses that only the Rasteaus, Viviers, and Giraudeaus served as armateurs during each of the seven decades. But all of the other families, excepting the de Butlers and Delacroixs, continued to make capital investments in shipping, to underwrite insurance, or to pursue a brokerage and commission business. The outfitting of vessels was but one phase—if the most important—of the complex activities of these families.

Continuity between the generations was assured by a variety of devices, including marriage and dowry, estate inheritance, and career training for the young. All eased the entry of sons as full partners into the family comptoir, a

Table 3.2. Number and Percentage of Rochelais Vessels Outfitted by Leading Families, by Economic Significance, 1720–89

Rank	Family	1720–29	1730–39	1740–49	1750–59	1760–69	1770–79	1780–89
1	Belin	24	26	17	6	6	0	0
2	Rasteau	24	36	27	26	27	9	13
3	Seignette	0	11	15	7	2	8	10
4	Vivier	3	0	5	1	11	2	2
5	Pascaud	4	11	14	5	0	0	0
6	Garesché	4	0	7	9	10	34	40
7	Goguet	0	0	0	12	8	16	13
8	Giraudeau	3	18	14	9	1	0	0
9	Bonneau	16	16	16	11	10	6	5
10	Carayon	0	0	0	3	0	5	9
11	Delacroix	11	53	0	2	5	0	0
12	Depont	17	11	3	0	0	0	0
12	Gastumeau[a]	0	0	0	0	0	0	0
14	Bridault[a]	0	0	0	0	0	0	0
15	Bonfils	1	0	14	14	14	0	0
16	Papineau[a]	0	0	0	0	0	0	0
17	Admyrauld	0	0	2	9	6	13	8
18	de Butler	7	9	1	0	0	0	0
19	Legrix[a]	0	0	0	0	0	0	0
20	Van Hoogwerf	0	0	0	0	0	7	12
21	Lefebvre	0	0	3	2	5	0	0
22	Suidre	0	0	0	1	12	32	7
23	Bernon	4	0	0	3	10	13	7
24	Dubeignon	0	9	15	5	0	0	0
25	Labbé	0	10	24	2	0	0	0
26	Perdriau	4	1	9	21	3	0	0
	% of Rochelais vessels out-fitted by above	53.5	59.7	43.5	40.3	39.5	48.9	36.5

[a] no connection with shipping

prelude to their ultimate succession as heads of firms. During the 1740s, a number of sons of established négociants began to operate with their fathers and on their own. Pierre Jacques and Pierre Isaac Rasteau assumed increasing responsibilities during the 1740s and succeeded their father in 1748. Concurrently, Jean Elie Giraudeau l'aîné and Antoine Giraudeau, Pierre Hardy fils, Jacques Carayon fils aîné, and Trésahar Bonfils inherited control of the economic networks created by their parents. Passing the management of economic interests from one generation to the next represented the achievement of basic family goals, which were achieved in part through strategic marriage alliances with other Protestant houses. Proscriptive laws against members of the Protestant sect intensified the quest for intergenerational continuity.

RELIGIOUS DISABILITIES AND CAREER CHOICES

Family papers and public documents offer only tantalizing hints of the intensity of family commitment to Protestantism. During a time of great personal travail, Pierre Isaac Rasteau recalled in a letter to a friend the feeling of warmth and oneness experienced while worshipping at home with his parents and siblings.[13] It is not possible to determine the degree to which even nominal adherence worked to the disadvantage of a particular family. The Seignettes were forced out of one profession into another and made a fortune. Nor is it possible to identify all of those Protestant families whose faith remained intact and distinguished them from those, less persevering, who renounced their faith publicly yet practiced it in private, or from those who fully recanted. The sect persisted in La Rochelle. Numerous Huguenot merchants made no effort to hide their allegiance to the faith. Many practiced its tenets in the privacy of their homes. Religion affected their lives. Protestant teaching, along with money and property, passed from parent to children. This much is known. Still, most of the practical and daily meaning of their faith and the consequences of loyalty to it remain essentially unknown.

During the long period between 1628 and the end of the Old Regime, informal and statutory persecution imposed onerous burdens and severe restraints upon La Rochelle's Huguenots. Although the intensity of persecution moderated during the 1760s, in law Protestants remained a marginal group until shortly before the Revolution. Denied rights enjoyed by Catholic members of their class, Rochelais Protestants adapted their familial and business structures to conditions of nonfreedom imposed by royal authority.

Proscriptive laws prohibited La Rochelle's religionnaires from holding municipal office while other laws, passed prior to the revocation, denied Protestants entry into certain occupations or professions. At the same time, laws forbade Protestant immigration to the city. Persecution and discrimination intensified during the years preceding the revocation. Government orders were withdrawn from Protestant stores. Only Catholics could serve as harbor pilots. Reductions occurred in the allowable number of Protestant masters in various trades. In 1684, the Protestant temple was forcibly closed. In late September 1685, only days before the revocation, a company of soldiers appeared in the city with orders to convert Protestants to Catholicism, by force if necessary.

The revocation destroyed freedom of conscience for French Huguenots and stripped essential civil liberties from those who did not convert. Enforcement waxed and waned through the following years. In the 1680s and 1690s, newly converted Rochelais Catholics whom the clergy declared to have "relapsed" at death were dragged through the streets and thrown into the dump. The daughters of one merchant, Jean Ribant, were carried away to a convent in 1692. In 1724, an edict imposed heavy sentences upon those still attending Protestant services, condemned ministers to death, required Catholic baptism within twenty-four hours of birth, prescribed a Catholic education for all children until age sixteen, declared the illegality of Huguenot marriages, and reconfirmed the occupational prohibitions of earlier years.

Sporadic enforcement of discriminatory laws and informal persecution persisted through the 1750s. Meschinet de Richemond's daughter was forced into a convent in 1733. Others girls were placed in convents in 1735 when authorities uncovered a clandestine Protestant school in which the Admyraulds participated. La Rochelle's prisons frequently confined Protestants discovered at worship. Between 1748 and 1755, some sixty-eight people were arrested and detained in the city's jails. And in 1754, a church court at La Rochelle condemned Protestant minister Louis Gibert in absentia, publicly burned his books, papers, and sermons, and hung him in effigy. Persecution eased off following the conclusion of the Seven Years' War, and in 1787, an edict restored civil status to Protestants.[14]

Religious intolerance and its legal codification failed to eradicate the sect in La Rochelle. Prominent Rochelais merchants held religious services at home and conducted Protestant baptisms and marriages. Notarized baptismal and marriage certificates reflected the lack of civil rights. For example, the baptismal paper of Jean Ezeckiel Couillandeau in 1708 stated that Jean was the son of Jean père and Jeanne Grazellie, "sa prétendue femme, n'étant pas mariés en face de l'Eglise" (his so-called wife, not having been married by the Church). In 1770, a statement attested to the baptism of Etienne Catherine, daughter of Elie Louis Seignette, a merchant and master of the mint, and Claire Doublet, "sa prétendue femme." By the 1770s, at least twenty Protestant households, the Belins, Admyraulds, Rasteaus, and Seignettes among them, held Sunday meetings. Pastors circulated freely from household to household. In 1775, a group of Rochelais Protestants, including the male heads of the Rasteau, Carayon, and Giraudeau families, and the pastor Bétrine petitioned the crown for the restoration of their rights.[15]

Persecution of Protestants, particularly during the first half of the eighteenth century, in part derived from suspicion about the ultimate loyalty of the sectarians to France. Protestant behavior during the wars of the late seventeenth and early eighteenth centuries allayed many of the doubts of Louis XIV's government and of the Regency. Thus, the French government and royal officials in La Rochelle provided a full role for Huguenots in the La Rochelle Chamber of Commerce. Concurrently, however, the government had to demonstrate a responsiveness to Catholic pressures to end Protestantism in the realm. Outbreaks of bigotry at La Rochelle in the mid-eighteenth century coincided with periods of intense nationalistic hatred of England. But the wartime record of the Protestants offered impressive proof of their loyalty to the crown. When a large English fleet menaced the city in 1757, the merchant community organized and commanded its defense. Huguenots commanded four of the five batteries; Pierre Jacques Rasteau's battery defended the entrance to the port. Virtually the entire merchant community, some ninety-six négociants, manned the ramparts. In recognition of this service, Louis XV authorized the removal from the city gate of the plaques celebrating the fall of the city in 1628. Meanwhile, royal officials ignored manifestations of Protestantism in the city.[16]

Despite the long period of discrimination, the merchants of La Rochelle prospered. Family wealth increased. The municipality and the royal government bestowed honors upon Huguenot families. Sons followed fathers in business, while matrimony forged useful alliances between the families. Children were raised in the Protestant way and as adults enjoyed amicable and often close relationships with Catholic merchants. It has been suggested that since French law prohibited Protestants from entering such prestigious professions as law, medicine, and the military, as well as many skilled crafts, they had no choice but to pursue careers in commerce. According to this explanation, Huguenots were driven into commerce and forced to evolve closely-knit family units in order to survive in a world hostile to their religious beliefs.[17]

Explicit evidence is lacking which shows that Protestants were forced into commercial roles against their inclinations. Protestant merchants had been dominant in La Rochelle prior to the revocation of the Edict of Nantes. The sons of merchants had normally adopted the vocation of the fathers as a matter of course, a practice replicated in the eighteenth century. Private letters to family and friends of the Rasteau, Belin, Vivier, Seignette, and other elite families contained no allusions to lack of occupational choice. Nor were regrets expressed about their vocational life. Rochelais data fail to support such notions, allegedly prevalent among the bourgeoisie, as loss of a sense of purpose, low self-esteem, or psychological resentment over the lack of mobility. In La Rochelle, the elite merchants did not appear disjointed nor split. They did not behave as though they longed to leave their class and ascend into the nobility. Nor did they retire as early as possible, giving up the active life of commerce for one of passive security.[18]

Indeed, the three or four generations of Rochelais responsible for the port's vitality believed that their occupation afforded many satisfactions and the opportunity to enjoy a full life. During the difficult days of the American Revolution, Pierre Jean Van Hoogwerf wrote of disruption of trade, loss of vessels, wild fluctuation of prices, and other threats to solvency. But he also expressed total commitment to his occupation and he planned for the future. From 1776 to 1778, Van Hoogwerf lobbied actively and successfully to succeed the retiring resident consul of Denmark and to obtain official status in La Rochelle as the commercial agent of the Dutch government. Justifiably, he expected to benefit from these appointments by expanding his contacts. Increased profits would result, he hoped, and thus allow him to replace his wartime losses.

Similarly, the correspondence between Trésahar Bonfils and his uncle and business associate Théodore Delacroix, as the young Bonfils toured southern Europe on a business trip during the early 1750s, conveyed a young man's wonder at the complexity and variety of the world. While approving business decisions made by his uncle and advising on possibilities for the sale of goods, Trésahar roamed through Italy. As he traveled about selling sugars and making maritime insurance in the name of the firm, he commented on the architectural and artistic marvels encountered, as well as upon the superiority of Rochelais commercial organization compared with that of the Italians. Ending up in Paris, Bonfils spent a delightful day meeting and dining with the minister of the Marine, during which time he arranged to lease company vessels to the crown. In June 1780, the Rochelais armateur, Meschinet de Richemond responded affirmatively to an inquiry from a friend in Abbéville about the possibility of the latter's son training in the de Richemond comptoir. De Richemond believed that an enthusiastic young man had much to learn before striking out on his own. Should young de Machey come to La Rochelle, de Richemond promised to demonstrate by example his own enthusiasm for his work. The Van Hoogwerf, Bonfils, and de Richemond letters were hardly written by men who had personal doubts about the importance of what they were doing.[19] What could be more natural than pursuing a commercial career when born and raised in a port city?

Rochelais négociants frequently sent their sons abroad to obtain an education. The practice has been explained as a reflection of the desire of Protestants to avoid compulsory Catholic education. This view overlooks the practical nature of the education received. Sons were sent generally to Holland to learn business practices and acquire language skills in the countinghouse of some merchant, frequently a relative, and to gain experience in states, including England and Geneva, with which the Rochelais conducted important trades. The explanation of escaping parochial schooling also ignores the ability of those who remained in La Rochelle to circumvent the law. Merchants such as Elie Giraudeau and Jacques Bernon had the wherewithal and the inclination to send their sons to Amsterdam for an education; Jacques Rasteau père, possessing the means, instead placed his boys aboard his ships and taught them in his comptoir. Since more complete treatment of training the young will be presented when the social purposes of kin-centered businesses are discussed in Chapter 4, suffice it to say that both Giraudeau's and Rasteau's choices can be explained without reference to religion.[20]

Circumstantial evidence suggests that the merchants of La Rochelle and their sons willingly entered their occupations and that they might well have made the same career decisions even had other choices been open. The sons of Catholic négociants certainly enjoyed more vocational options than their Protestant contemporaries. Honorific titles came relatively more easily to Rochelais Catholics than to Protestants. As we shall see in later pages, a somewhat smaller proportion of Catholics than Protestants engaged in certain kinds of business. But these activities (insurance, for example) were only supplementary to the main business of outfitting vessels, to which Catholics as well as Protestants devoted most of their energies. Catholic comptoirs, like Protestant, passed from father to son. Psychological interpretations of the impact of Protestantism upon career choices and career satisfaction must be offered with greater care and with more attention to actual life histories.

Elite Protestant families suffered only occasional harassment. By and large, local authorities—secular and religious—left them alone on matters of faith. Presumably their great wealth, commercial influence, and proven loyalty to the crown buffered the Protestant families against the law. Membership in a proscribed group, occasional persecution or the threat of persecution, the necessity of worshipping secretly, and other disabilities must, however, have been psychologically traumatic. But in terms of public behavior, Huguenots and Catholics pursued similar objectives. They husbanded their fortunes and assured continuity between generations by advantageous marriages, rigorous training of the young, and wise estate settlements.

KINSHIP SYSTEMS AMONG THE ROCHELAIS

By the 1740s, considerable wealth had been accumulated by many of La Rochelle's merchants. The Depont estate exceeded one million lt. When Jean Vivier père died in 1737, his children divided an estate worth 876,000 lt. Allard Belin's estate in 1748 yielded about 800,000 lt. Bonneaus, Bonfils, Admyraulds and Rasteaus all fell heir to inheritances surpassing 250,000 lt., and it was likely that at least equivalent amounts circulated within the Seignette, de Butler, and Carayon families. During the 1780s, the Weis family, Daniel Garesché, and Pierre Jean Van Hoogwerf, among others, were noted for their riches.[21] These fortunes had been acquired by risk-taking entrepreneurs responsible for even the smallest details of their business and whose ability to analyze detailed economic information enabled them to remain one step ahead of fluctuating world market conditions. Crises in production, markets, and prices could be handled during times of peace by close attention to alternatives. The vagaries of peacetime government policies were also manageable. Only the cumulative effects of a series of world wars proved beyond the merchants' ability to cope.

The affluence of these Rochelais families compared favorably with what might be considered the upper middle class commercial elite in other cities. According to an estimate from Nantes, one family, the Montaudoin, had amassed a fortune of 600,000 lt. by the mid-eighteenth century, while twenty-four others possessed estates valued at over 200,000 lt. By the end of the Old Regime, however, the wealthiest Nantais were far richer than their predecessors and probably the richest Rochelais. At that time, some twelve to twenty families in Nantes had estates worth over one million lt. The négociant William Grou left an estate in 1774 valued at over four million lt. Still, the Rochelais acquired large fortunes, permitting a lifestyle available to only a small fraction of the French population.[22]

Great wealth served many purposes. Family comforts were not overlooked but neither were they permitted to drain wealth from the business. According to one local merchant, however, increasing ostentation surfaced during the difficult days of the 1780s. Pierre Jean Van Hoogwerf claimed that some families depleted their capital by living beyond their means. The Weis firm, as an example, was considered by Pierre Jean to be losing its reputation and its business, yet Conrad Achille Weis offered expensive concerts each Thursday evening to his social circle. Letters from Van Hoogwerf to his sister in 1789 and 1790 indicated that socializing continued, as families offered sumptuous feasts in honor of the officers of the local bourgeois militia company. Pierre Jean complained that he, too, felt compelled to arrange an entertainment so that his loyalties remain above suspicion.[23]

The Admyrauld, Vivier, Delacroix, Carayon, and other families resided in richly furnished homes scattered about the city.[24] Large town houses of three stories, valued at from 20,000 to 30,000 lt., were typical among the wealthy Rochelais négociants. Many of the families were large and gatherings of relatives and friends frequent. The homes of the merchants were filled with finely turned silverware, handpainted silk screens, heavy, brocaded handwoven draperies, massive mirrors in gilded frames, delicate glasswares, ornately carved yet comfortably contoured and upholstered furniture, all of which must have pleased the eyes of guests who gathered for a social evening. Too, in the seventeenth and eighteenth centuries, affluent families moved out of the kitchen into sitting and dining rooms and separate bedrooms for adults and children. Domestics generally lived in, and in the homes of Trésahar Bonfils, Daniel Garesché, Jacques Carayon, and others, black slaves served as domestics. Mademoiselle Bonfils and other young women were tended by Negresses from an early age.[25]

While contemporary evidence from La Rochelle suggests that families during the period 1764–74 typically consisted of two parents and two to three children, many of the négociant families were considerably larger.[26] Jacques and Susan Sara Seignette Rasteau raised thirteen children to adulthood. Allard and Elizabeth Olivier Belin raised nine, three of whom produced twenty children before their parents died. Daniel and Henriette Delacroix brought up thirteen children. With 1 in 4 infants dying during their first year and with 45 percent of the deaths in La Rochelle claiming children between the ages of one and ten years, it is likely that the number of children noted above does not accurately represent the number of births in those families.[27] Moreover, of 58 Huguenot families in the group of 90 for whom information on the number of adult children was discovered, 26 had 1 or 2, 13 had 3, and 19 had 4 or more. Of 13 Roman Catholic households, none had over 4. While some second and third generation families raised as many or more children than the first generation—the Admyrauld and Giraudeau, for example—most second and third generation families were considerably smaller.

The size of the 58 Protestant families offers interesting possibilities for explaining inferentially the compulsion for stability and the habits of cooperation which evolved among those households. Let us assume that all 58 families were first generation, i.e., with families completed by 1730, and project available data on family size into the second and third generations. How many new family units would result? Using the figure of 1.5 children for 26 families, 3 children for 13 families and 5 children for 19 families, the result would be 173 offspring. Assuming that they were evenly distributed by sex and that they all intermarried, 95 new nuclear families would be created. But, as will be demonstrated in a few pages, 82 percent of the marriages involved local partners. Using that proportion, then, 76 new second-generation families would be formed. If carried into the third generation, 91 new households would result.

Such an increase would pose distinct dangers for négociant families located in a port with limited possibilities for growth, and particularly for those new family units initiating commercial careers during the unsettled years which commenced with the Seven Years' War, continued through the War of the American Revolution, and culminated in the hard times of the 1780s. Had not second and third generation families been smaller, the integrity of the négociant subcommunity would have been vulnerable to the threat of splintering under the pressure of intense internal competition.

In an expanding economy, growth permits the establishment of new economic units without necessarily weakening the profitability of older units. The total value of French trade with her colonies more than doubled from 1720 to 1755, doubled again from 1755 to 1778, and reached 276 million lt. in 1787, an increase of 25 percent over 1778. Bordeaux, in particular, experienced a fantastic rise in the total value of its commerce. Nantes, Rouen, and Marseilles also prospered.[28] La Rochelle enjoyed much less spectacular success. The value of its commerce had more than doubled between 1720 and the 1740s, but its trade during the last decade of the Old Regime did not exceed by more than 30 percent the value reached during the 1740s. The Rochelais fleet had not grown, nor had supportive enterprises. La Rochelle's refineries were in decline and so new industries were developed.[29] Commercial opportunities in the city had remained virtually stagnant during the last half of the eighteenth century.

La Rochelle, then, could not sustain a marked increase in numbers of négociants without diminishing the profits of established comptoirs. Since the years between the outbreak of the Seven Years' War and the French involve-

Table 3.3. The Family of Allard (b. ca. 1650–d. 1746) and Elizabeth Olivier Belin

Children[1]	Spouses	Parents of Spouses[2]	Grandchildren
Claude-Etienne (1697–1779)	Marie Anne Carayon	Jacques Carayon père Sara Depont	Elizabeth
			Marie Marie Ettienne
Elie-Allard (d. 1780)	Marguerite Rasteau	Jacques Rasteau père Suzanne Sara Seignette	Marie Cornelie Jacques Allard
Marie Judith	Jean Seignette fils aîné	Jean Seignette père Marie Anne Guillmaud	Allard Louis Benjamin
			Jeanne Judith Elizabeth Judith
Marie Esther	Jacques Bernon fils aîné	Jacques Bernon père ———Depont	?
Marie Madelaine	Nicolas Guyon	? ?	?
Jeanne Marie	Henri Elie Torterue Bonneau	Louis Torterue Bonneau Marie Besnard	Jacques Jeanne Suzanne
Suzanne	Jean Jenner	?	Etienne Isaac
	Pierre Isaac Rasteau[7]	Jacques Rasteau père Suzanne Sara Seignette	Jacques le jeune

[1] Two children died in infancy.
[2] Wife's maiden name used here.
[3] Sister of Marguerite and Pierre Isaac.
[4] Barthellemy's brother, Jean, married the sister of Jean Isaac Raboteau.

ment in the American Revolution, twenty-two years in all, had been punctuated by crises and hard times, self-interest called for fewer children. Capital diffusion among an excessive number of merchants, either within or without the family comptoirs, would have raised the level of competition and reduced the capital strength of each unit. The Rochelais response was to have fewer children. Even with a decline in fertility rates among second and third generation families, the problem of guaranteeing career opportunities to the youth remained of critical importance.[30] Thus, it may be suggested, patterns of intermarriage and such mechanisms as dowry, early partition, and inheritance gained a larger significance as a means of maintaining the cohesion of the négociant kinship groups and preserving intact the capital of the comptoir.

Data existed on the marital alliances of sixty of the ninety sample families. The Belin family will be examined in detail to illustrate the contractual arrangements that bound the parties and the purposes served by such connections. When appropriate, other families will be referred to.

Tables 3.3 and 3.4 summarize the basic information. Table 3.3 carries the Belin family through four generations. Although gaps exist in the material

Spouses	Parents of Spouses	Great-grandchildren	Spouses
Pierre Jean Van Hoogwerf	Gerard Van Hoogwerf		
	Marie Fleurance Delacroix	Suzanne	Etienne Charuyer
		Elizabeth	
		Ettienne	Elizabeth Richard
Jean Baptiste Nairac	(from Bordeaux)		
Pierre Joachim de Baussay	(from La Rochelle)		
Pierre Nicolas Allet	(from La Rochelle)		
Anne Marie Weis	Conrad Achille Weis		
	Madelaine Bernon		
?			
Henriette Rasteau[3]	Jacques Rasteau père		
	Suzanne Sara Seignette		
Jean Isaac Raboteau[4]	(a Rochelais master draper)		
Barthellemy Ranson[4]	André Ranson		
	?		
?			
Nicolas Paillet[5]	Elisée Paillet	Marie Jeanne	Pierre Thouron[6]
	?		
Henriette Madelaine Paillet[5]	Elisée Paillet		
	?		
——— Giraudeau	Ellie Giraudeau		
	?		

[5] Siblings.
[6] The son of Jean Isaac Thouron and Marie Suzanne Admyrauld Thouron.
[7] Rasteau, brother of Marguerite Rasteau, was Suzanne's second husband.

offered, twenty-five families are identified who were connected matrimonially with the children of Allard and Elizabeth Belin, including nine of the leading twenty-six families listed in table 3.1. Table 3.4 extends the genealogical information by showing the family units with whom the Belins were directly involved economically. Belins invested in the ships of or received investments from at least nine of the twenty-five families related to them by marriage. The Rasteau pattern, also depicted in table 3.4, serves as a basis for comparison. Rasteaus married into four of the families who formed part of the Belin kinship group. Nine of the ten families related to the Rasteaus joined with them in various economic ventures. Jacques Rasteau's sons-in-law included six Rochelais armateurs. Interfamily investments connected the Rasteaus with twelve of the families who were similarly involved with the Belins.

An extension of this analysis of marital ties to include the Vivier, Carayon, Seignette, Depont, Delacroix, Bonneau, and Paillet families plus the Belin and Rasteau reveals connections with forty-nine families—more than one-half of the original ninety. Twenty of those families were each allied with at least two of the forty-nine. The Depont, Paillet, Seignette, Garesché, and seven other

Table 3.4. Belin and Rasteau Connections with Other Rochelais Families through Marriage and Maritime Investments

Family	Belin			Rasteau		
	Connection by marriage	Inv. in ships of	Inv. in Belin ships	Connection by marriage	Inv. in ships of	Inv. in Rasteau ships
Olivier						
Carayon	X	X	X	X	X	X
Depont	X	X	X		X	X
Seignette	X		X	X	X	
Rasteau	X	X	X			
Bernon	X			X		X
Guillmaud	X					
Guyon	X		X			
Bonneau	X	X	X			
Besnard	X					X
Jenner	X		X			
Allet	X					
Weis	X			X	X	
Van Hoogwerf	X	X				
Nairac	X	X				
Giraudeau	X			X		X
de Baussay	X					
Raboteau	X					
Paillet	X			X	X	
Ranson	X					
Broussard	X		X			
Charuyer	X					
Delacroix	X					
Richard	X					
Thouron	X				X	
Vivier		X		X	X	X
Bonfils		X				
Chabot		X				
Dubeignon		X				
Garesché		X				X
Admyrauld				X	X	
Suidre				X		X
Manie				X		
Hardy						X
Augier						X
Boulanger						X
Belin				X	X	X

families among the forty-nine provided spouses for at least three other families. All eighteen Huguenot merchants listed on table 3.1 were intermarried with the above nine families.

Rochelais families sought spouses largely from within local society who would assure the perpetuation of the clans. Pierre Goubert has noted that during the seventeenth and part of the eighteenth century, marriage partners were normally born in the same parish. This relative immobility, however, did not last beyond midcentury, by which time people were moving more often and farther away from home.[31] In La Rochelle, sufficient data was available to identify the partners of 105 marriages. In 88 of those unions, or 82 percent, the partners were both Rochelais; in 17 a Rochelais married a non-Rochelais. Of the 88 marriages with local partners, the couples in 70 belonged to the 90 sample families. Most of the marriages involving a non-Rochelais partner joined a Rochelais female with a non-Rochelais négociant, and in several of them the new husband immediately took up residence as a merchant in La Rochelle.[32] Because 82 percent of the marriages joined members of the leading families, it must be concluded that the young were marrying horizontally. Marriage did serve to advance the careers of the males, and, hopefully, guaranteed security for the daughters, but it was not a vehicle for interclass movement.[33]

The extent to which marriages within the négociant subcommunity were arranged cannot be determined with any certainty. Arranged marriages, often through a marriage broker, were common enough in the eighteenth century to sustain the belief that some, perhaps many, of the Rochelais unions carried out prior agreements of family heads. Given the intimate connections between Jacques Rasteau and Allard Belin, it seems reasonable to assume that they discussed, if not arranged, the marriages of Marguerite Rasteau and Elie Allard Belin and Henriette Rasteau and Louis Benjamin Belin. If not arranged in any formal sense, unions between Rasteaus and Belins were not unexpected.

Catholics, too, married locally. Daughters of Jean de Butler married Pascauds and Lapointes; and Victoire Félicité Pascaud, daughter of Joseph Marie Pascaud and Doréthée de Butler Pascaud, married Joseph Denis Goguet. A child of that union married a son of Louis Benjamin Bridault. Another son of Louis Benjamin married Elizabeth Antoinette Lefebvre. Five of the Catholic families identified in table 3.1 were encompassed by those unions. Local marriages, then, predominated among Protestants and Catholics alike.

DOWRIES AND INHERITANCE

By selecting spouses from within a local pool, dowries and inherited wealth accumulated, and the practice of interfamily investments guaranteed the continuous use of that wealth in the local economy.

Dowries in La Rochelle, as elsewhere, assured suitable spouses for daughters. Criteria of suitability varied from place to place and from time to time. Among the Rochelais, marriage neither furthered political ambitions nor served as a means of upward mobility. Marriages united peer families, all of whom pursued similar economic objectives. Kin consistently provided a large proportion of the capital required to outfit Rochelais vessels. Although kin investments declined during the mid-1780s relative to earlier periods (see figure 4.1), by the later years multifamily partnerships were more common. Thus, some of those funds, which in earlier days would have been invested in the name of a particular relative, were subsumed within the organization.[34] Inter-marriage within the négociant families created investment networks. Wealth from dowries formed a common treasury for individuals in the négociant class. Marriage contracts controlled the uses of dowries, minimizing the possibility that money would be withdrawn from commerce. Through investment in Rochelais ventures, dowries produced increments to the total wealth of the families, adding to the capital resources of the city and passing to the next generation through inheritance.

When Suzanne Belin married Pierre Isaac Rasteau during the 1750s, she carried to the union a dowry of 45,000 lt. in cash and 4,000 lt in household items. These assets represented a portion of her inheritance and were to be held in common. Such an arrangement allowed Rasteau to use the cash in his business ventures only with his wife's approval. Since approval was implicit in the marriage agreement, the dowry became part of his working capital. A decade or so earlier, in 1739, Suzanne's older sister Marie Madelaine had married Nicolas Guyon. Her father provided a dowry of 20,000 lt. and an assortment of household items worth at least 10,000 lt. Guyon's marriage increased his capital worth by 20,000 lt. And still another decade earlier, in 1729, when Jeanne Marie Belin wed Henri Elie Torterue Bonneau, the bride contributed a dowry of 20,000 lt. and silverware valued at 4,000 lt. while the groom provided 20,000 lt., of which 14,000 lt. was used in commerce and 6,000 lt. was to enter the household. Three Belin daughters, then, possessed dowries of 103,000 lt. The dowries of the two remaining daughters, married into the Seignette and Bernon families, were not known but must have been equivalent. Still larger than any of the Belin dowries was that of Françoise Depont. In 1710 she married Pierre Morreau fils aîné, bringing with her cash, household items, and property valued at 55,000 lt.[35]

Males commonly, but not invariably, carried a stipulated sum of money or other wealth into a marriage.[36] In the marriages noted above the bridegrooms provided a portion in only one instance, the Belin-Bonneau union. Bonneau had just begun his business at the time of the wedding while Rasteau, Guyon, and Morreau were well established. A similar pattern held in other marriages. Husbands did not bring portions to the unions of Gerard Van Hoogwerf, brother of Pierre Jean, and Marie Fleurance Delacroix in 1727 or Louis Torterue Bonneau and Marie Besnard in 1688, both bridegrooms being experienced négociants; but Etienne Charuyer did bring a portion to his wedding with Suzanne Van Hoogwerf in 1792. At that time Etienne had launched a new business. The possibility that business maturity in a bridegroom precluded the requirement of a monetary contribution might explain each of the above cases. However customary such a practice might have been, exceptions were not wanting. When the widower Nicolas Paillet, an experienced merchant, wed Jeanne Suzanne Bonneau in 1756, both parties contributed 10,000 lt. in cash and other properties.[37]

When bridegrooms provided a portion, the contract generally stipulated that the cash must be used in commerce. Frequently, a part of the bride's dowry was similarly committed. Some contracts stipulated that a part of the dowry be invested by the husband in his business in his wife's name, with the profits accruing to her account. Other contracts left the form of investment to the judgment of the husband, or even to the judgment of the couple. Presumably, such provisions secured the wife against widowhood and resembled the English practice of jointure (a stipulated settlement on the wife in case of widowhood).[38]

In general, dowries quickly turned into working capital. Few probably converted a dowry as rapidly as J. J. Garnault. Writing to his partner, Meschinet de Richemond in late October 1782, Garnault promised that within the week he would send, in short-term paper or specie, the dowry from his marriage to P.C. Lambert's daughter. Garnault's firm was dangerously overextended, and the partners immediately ploughed the dowry into their business in a futile effort to salvage their affairs.[39] Pierre Isaac Rasteau used a portion of the Belin dowry to add capital to his partnership with his brother Pierre Jacques. Similarly, Nicolas Guyon's marriage enabled him to establish a firm in La Rochelle.

Rochelais dowries compared favorably in value with those offered in Rouen during the 1740s and with dowries of up to 30,000 lt. suggested as typical for the larger merchants of Nantes earlier in the century. They were paltry, however, compared with dowries of 100,000 lt. and more given by a few merchants of Nantes toward the end of the Old Regime. Still, Rochelais dowries attested to the wealth of the elite négociants.[40]

Suzanne Belin's dowry came from her inheritance; Marie Madelaine's dowry, in 1739, was given directly by her father. In that year, Allard Belin called the family together to agree to a division of his personal property and the entire property of his recently deceased wife. This was but a partial division of Allard's estate, excluding from it his business assets, which were only divided upon his death in 1747. Attending the Belin meeting were the daughters and their husbands and the sons but not their wives (see table 3.3). The sons-in-law, as husbands of the heirs, enjoyed legal standing in the division and were, in fact, the managers of businesses into which a portion of the inheritance would flow. The daughters-in-law lacked legal standing.

Allard's initial division amounted to 288,000 lt. It consisted of three town houses valued at 50,200 lt., a number of stores and warehouses valued at 28,000 lt., a country house and grounds at Lagord, a small village six kilometers northeast of the city, worth 12,000 lt., a windmill at Aytre, south of the city on the road to Rochefort, worth 2,000 lt., salt lands worth 15,000 lt., income from other landholdings valued at 43,500 lt., land mortgages worth 59,200 lt., and income from other investments made in the name of particular children.[41] For instance, a sum of 5,500 lt. had been invested in 1717 in *rentes viagère,* a form of life annuity, *sur la tête* of Claude Etienne. Similar sums had been invested in the name of each of the other children. These rentes were transferred from Allard's charge to the children, who could dispose of them as they wished. Early partition by equal shares netted each of the heirs above 41,000 lt. While the inheritance laws of the region specified equal division, disposal of a portion of or the whole of an estate prior to death allowed the family head to divide the estate in a way agreeable to the heirs and the parent.

Allard Belin legally controlled the resources that he chose to divide early. The proper moment to initiate an early division was undoubtedly arrived at after full discussion within the family. All interests had to be treated equitably, and the discrete interests of individuals had somehow to be made compatible with the interests of the family at large. Allard was 89 years old at the time of the first division. Lingering illness, an aged man's premonitions, or other such reasons might have defined the proper moment. In other cases, however, early partition occurred while the head of the family was still in the prime of life, many years before retirement. Sons attaining their majority, daughters marrying young négociants, the birth of grandchildren, any or all of these reasons might have provided the stimulus for partition. In any event, available evidence does not reveal family heads hanging on to their wealth until the last bitter moment so as to keep their sons in a position of dependency and subordination. At the time of Allard's death, Claude Etienne had long been his father's partner, extracting his own share from the profits of the firm. As noted again in later pages, Etienne Van Hoogwerf utilized his portion of the early division of his mother's estate to enter into partnership with his father, Pierre Jean.

In the Belin case, early partition assured that family wealth would remain active in the family business. Claude Etienne soon converted a portion of the rentes and his mother's *succession* into liquid capital for use in the comptoir, now managed by himself and his brother, Elie Allard. The latter contributed equivalent sums from his share of the early division and his mother's estate. For both Elie Allard Belin and Etienne Van Hoogwerf, as well as for other young Rochelais, such division brought to a conclusion their years of dependence and propelled them into the adult world.[42]

Final division of Allard's estate occurred following his death in late 1747. The inventory placed a value of 750,000 lt. on his estate, including 256,000 lt. *dettes actives de l'Amérique.* Partition did not include the one-half of the goods in stock that belonged to Claude Etienne or investments made in the name of the firm one-half of which also belonged to the firm. As in the early division the final estate was apportioned into seven equal shares of about 107,000 lt. each. Thus, each heir ultimately received close to 150,000 lt. from the estates of Allard and Elizabeth Belin. When Elizabeth Belin married Pierre Jean Van Hoogwerf, she brought with her these assets as well as the dowry of 49,000 lt.[43]

Claude Etienne continued the family firm in partnership with his brother, Elie Allard. Claude died on January 5, 1779, at which time his daughters and their husbands jointly initiated proceedings for the division of his estate. Table 3.5 traces each division of the estates of Claude and his wife, Marie Anne

Table 3.5. *Inheritances from the Estates of Claude Etienne and Marie Anne Carayon Belin, 1781–81 (lt.)*

| | Received from estates of | | | | |
| | Marie Anne Carayon Belin 1778 1st division | Claude-Etienne Belin 1779 *succession* | Marie Ann Carayon Belin 1779 2nd division | Marie Ann Carayon Belin 1781 *succession* | Total |
Heirs					
Marie Anne Carayon Belin		271,127[a]			
Elizabeth Belin Van Hoogwerf	99,802	125,262	90,376	83,776	399,206
Suzanne Belin de Baussay	99,802	125,262	90,376	83,766	399,206
Marie Belin Nairac	99,802	125,262	90,376	83,766	399,206
Total		646,913			1,197,603

[a] Divided by veuve Belin in the second division

Carayon Belin, beginning with the partial division of Madame Belin's estate prior to her husband's death and continuing through stages until the entire 1.2 million lt. had passed to the heirs. This did not include Belin's shares in vessels currently en route, which were equivalent to the ownership of two vessels and their entire cargoes, or a sum of approximately 200,000 lt.

The notarized inventory of Claude's estate separated it into country estates worth 155,767 lt., city properties at 104,799 lt., salt lands at 16,950 lt., rentes at 160,080 lt., and business assets at 209,316 lt. Most of the rural property had been acquired between 1764 and 1774, whereas the city property had been purchased gradually since 1735. It appears that the larger portion of Belin's wealth, some 65 percent, had been turned into noncommercial and nonliquid form. Using the above categories, however, exaggerates the extent of such conversion since only the salt lands and the business assets appear directly related to the business. In detailing the estate according to commercial and noncommercial wealth a different picture of capital use emerges.

First of all, some 200,000 lt. in outstanding investments in ships and cargoes must be included on the commercial side. This would raise the value of his estate from 646,912 lt. to 846,912 lt. Even with the exclusion of these investments from this calculation, the commercial properties and debts equaled 51 percent of Belin's estate. Inclusion of the value of the shares elevates the commercial proportion to 63 percent. Moreover, the salt and brandy lands valued at 54,948 lt. produced an annual income in commodities that provided part of the cargoes dispatched by Belin, the stores yielded rents, the sugar refinery manufactured a valuable product, and the shares in vessels would yield, presumably, some profit. Income from the rentes might also be used for commercial purposes. On the other hand, some portion of the debts were probably uncollectable. For Belin to have about two-thirds of his worth actively engaged in productive commercial enterprises reflects an overwhelming commitment to capital accumulation.[44]

The saga of Belin wealth can be continued, at least in part, through one more generation. All branches were not equally successful. Jacques Allard, a planter on Santo Domingo and son of Elie Allard Belin, in 1781 renounced his rights to inheritance as "plus onereuse que profitable." Although additional details on this inheritance were not found, in other cases where heirs waived their inheritance rights it meant that the liabilities of the deceased exceeded his assets.[45] Such waivers were not unusual during the years of the American Revolution when numerous bankruptcies plagued the négociants of La Rochelle. But the wealth that passed to Elizabeth Belin Van Hoogwerf (see 3.5) and from her to her spouse, Pierre Jean, survived those trying times.

Elizabeth died in 1786. Pierre Jean divided her estate of 537,913 lt., taking one-half for himself as the law allowed and apportioning the remainder equally among their three children. Included in the division was the original dowry of 45,000 lt. and the whole of Elizabeth's inheritance from her mother and father. Part of Elizabeth's estate had already been divided, one portion forming the dowry of Suzanne in her marriage to Etienne Charuyer, and another portion used by their son Etienne to buy into his father's firm. Thus, Elizabeth's wealth formed part of Van Hoogwerf's actual commercial capital even before her death while the undivided portions, invested to her account by her husband, contributed to the overall strength of the family firm. Now one-half of her total estate was added to Pierre Jean's actual capital worth, while the remainder passed intact to a fourth generation. In time, Pierre Jean's children could expect the remainder, and perhaps more, to come into their possession. It is possible, however, that the French Revolution caused them bitter disappointment.[46]

Other Rochelais families followed similar inheritance practices. Paul Depont des Granges divided part of his estate in 1712 and through codicils kept his will up to date with his expanding wealth. In the original will and the codicils, part of the Depont estate was guaranteed to his unborn grandchildren and great grandchildren. When the daughters married (Marianne Sara to a nobleman, Françoise to Pierre Morreau, a Rochelais merchant, and a third to Louis Charuyer), codicils were added and included in the marriage contracts stipulating that the income from parts of the dowry was inheritable only by the children of the Depont des Granges daughters.

Paul Depont died in 1744, leaving 1.2 million lt., 50 percent in cash, goods, shares of vessels, and two vessels owned in whole. While a large part of the wealth found its way into land rather than into maritime commerce, that land contributed grain, salt, and brandy to La Rochelle's exports.[47] In 1726, Paul had purchased the seigneurie d'Argrefeuille for 65,000 lt. In 1763, brandies from that estate sold in the city for 18,000 lt., hinting strongly at the rapid amortization of that investment. Thus, even an obvious propensity to purchase landed estates—Depont owned six at the time of his death—and to disengage from maritime activities must not produce quick assumptions about the withdrawal of capital from the dynamic sectors of the economy.[48]

CONCLUSION

While the splendor of the Rochelais households pales when compared with that of the court nobility or the haute bourgeoisie of Paris, within their own sphere La Rochelle's elite were the haute bourgeoisie. Protestant, but not ascetic, they took pride in the accomplishments of their families and spent a portion of their ample incomes to provide costly amenities. If their lifestyles were emulative of the aristocratic mode, an assumption unsupported by the evidence from La Rochelle, other and stronger imperatives moderated any propensity to masquerade. La Rochelle's merchants labored hard for their comforts. Responsibility to the family and the risks and competitiveness of their operations counseled the reinvestment of the larger portion of their capital in their businesses.

La Rochelle's négociant class clearly exercised control over the use of accumulated capital. Dowries and the division of estates by early partition and final settlement assured the reinvestment of funds in those maritime and commercial activities upon which the survival of the families depended. Such mechanisms also provided sons and sons-in-law with the capital to establish themselves or to expand their operations. In the process each family member gained economic security, even though some young males, as Chapter 4 will explain, had to make their way in locations other than La Rochelle. Too, the vitality of La Rochelle's economy rested upon the cumulative results of these family practices.

Evidence indicates that treating wealth gained by an individual head of family as the collective possession of the family prevailed among the lesser bourgeois of the city. The estate of Pierre Jean Chauvet, *maître cloutier* (master nailmaker) as had been his father and grandfather, passed, along with the craft, through five generations. Successive generations of the Denis family of druggists and several families of clothiers received wealth and vocational specialities from their forebears.[49] For the Belins and the Chauvets, though distant from one another in wealth and social status, the family served as an efficient medium for distributing accumulated wealth and vocational and social standing among second and third generations.

FOUR

Business Organization
and Family in
La Rochelle

Family-centered firms predominated in La Rochelle and other French ports. The family served not only as the conservator of wealth, maintaining the patrimony in commercial use over a long period of time, but as the decision-making body in the conduct of maritime affairs. In La Rochelle, as in Marseilles, all of the most solid and durable comptoirs were family firms.[1] Rochelais insurance companies, discussed in detail in Chapter 9, proved the only exceptions to the general pattern.

In accounting for the evolution of modern capitalism, some investigators have posited as among the prerequisites the physical separation of business from the household and the separation of the management of the business from that of the home.[2] Implicit here is the identification of family-based firms with traditional (vis-à-vis modern) methods of capital accumulation. As applied to the Rochelais, such an analysis would assume that the linkage of business with the preservation of wealth and the perpetuation of the family, a connection which did indeed exist, prejudiced family businesses against risk-taking and hastened the transfer of capital from use in commerce to more secure and status-enhancing land and rentes. But this does not describe the pattern of capital use adopted by the families dealt with in Chapter 3. Capital allocation among those families produced instead a blend of investments in commerce and related industries, income-producing properties, and lower risk rentes. Neither inflexible in structure nor conservative in decision-making, family firms in La Rochelle were dynamic institutions during the eighteenth century.

BUSINESS STRUCTURES IN LA ROCHELLE

Formal business associations encompassed fathers and sons, widows and sons, and brothers. Partnerships commonly united relatives and, somewhat less commonly, unrelated individuals. Toward the end of the eighteenth century corporate organizations appeared, uniting individuals and families in a larger business structure independent of the family unit. Informal associations also flourished in which individuals—kin or not—joined temporarily to achieve some specific purpose but otherwise operated independently. Great fluidity existed as individuals and families shifted among these varieties of associational forms, frequently participating in two or three simultaneously. From within these types of organizations, merchants managed a complex assortment of business activities including commission and brokerage, insurance, banking and investments, buying and selling on their own account or for others, and owning or supervising merchant vessels.[3]

The types of business organization prevalent in eighteenth-century France have been adequately explained in a number of studies. The Ordinance of Commerce of 1673 recognized three basic forms: the *société générale,* the *société en commandite,* and the *société anonyme.* Joint stock corporations were not mentioned. The société générale (known also as *société ordinaire* or *société nom collectif*) attained the most general use in eighteenth-century La Rochelle and elsewhere. Basically a simple partnership, all associates were jointly and severally responsible for the debts of the société. In practice, partners could write this obligation out of the charters and, in effect, participate with limited liability.

Sociétés en commandite provided for two kinds of investors, the *commandites* (or *complimentaires*) and the *commanditaires.* The former served as the publicly designated managers of the firms who could also invest in the firm and who were liable for the full debt of the société. The latter possessed no authority over the firm, were liable only for the actual amount of their investment and were frequently anonymous, thus providing a safe mechanism for noble investment. Secrecy, though, was not mandatory, and it was possible for commanditaires to participate fully in the operation of the business. Sociétés anonymes maintained the anonymity of participants, and unlike the other organizational types, were not required to register at the juridiction consulaire. They were unimportant in La Rochelle.[4]

Two other types of business organization appeared in La Rochelle, the *sociétés de capitaux* (or *sociétés par action*) and the independent entrepreneur. La Rochelle had experienced the former during the seventeenth century when the headquarters of several commercial companies located there. During the Law era, a branch of the Banque royale had operated in the city, and Paul Depont des Granges had managed the local business of the Company of the Indies. But the most important of the joint stock companies in La Rochelle were the insurance firms established during the 1750s and after. Sociétés par actions, chartered by royal authority, differed from the other organizations in that stock issues sold publicly and were negotiable. Prior to the 1780s, the unlimited liability of stockholders prevailed. Thereafter, corporate charters normally included limited liability clauses.[5]

During the earlier decades of the eighteenth century, independent entrepreneurs had dominated the commercial sector of La Rochelle. As sons came of age or sons-in-law entered the family, heads of households established partnerships with members of their own and other families. The partnership form became more frequent during the 1740s, but the great flexibility inherent in both independent entrepreneurship and kin partnership blurred the difference between them. Both depended upon outside capital, local and nonlocal. The independent entrepreneur drew from family capital as did the family partnership and partnerships between kin. But partnerships did facilitate the entrance of sons or relatives into the family business and, in so doing, guaranteed that capital would remain vested in the firm.

In La Rochelle, shipping enterprises provided the largest outlet for investment capital and accounted for most of the fixed capital. Determining the proportionate share of investment in Rochelais shipping from various categories of investors elucidates the centrality of family and kinship groups to the maritime economy while also calling attention to the significant contribution of nonfamily capital. Individuals or firms normally owned in toto most of the vessels for which they served as armateurs. Rochelais armateurs infrequently subscribed the entire capital required for a venture, however. Both the vessel and the cargo were divided into fractional shares that were then purchased by other investors (the intéressés). Intéressés in Rochelais vessels consisted of four types of investors: an individual armateur or an *armateur en société*, whose investment would include the capital subscribed by members of the nuclear families involved; relatives of the family or families; other Rochelais; and non-Rochelais.[6]

Figure 4.1 displays the shares held by each category of investor (plus unknowns). The availability of data determined the selection of the three time periods. The first two periods, 1719–21/1723–24 and 1748–49, include only those vessels outfitted by individuals listed in table 3.1, while the third period, 1784–87, includes all armateurs.[7]

Armateurs maintained a stable proportion of investment in each of the three periods. With the exception of the firm of Delacroix and Bonfils (an uncle and nephew), the armateurs represented in the two early periods were independent operators. In the later period, however, eight of the nineteen armateurs belonged to partnerships. Five of the eight were associations between fathers and sons that had originated after 1749. Other sociétés générales functioned in La Rochelle prior to the 1740s but few involved the dominant families and fewer still survived the War of the Austrian Succession.

Allard Belin (in the earlier period) and his two sons Claude Etienne and Allard fils (in the middle period) exemplified the pattern of kinship investment. During the five years of the first period, Allard père outfitted six vessels. He held 58 percent of the shares, while members of families joined or to be joined with the Belin by marriage, including Paul Depont des Granges, Elie Giraudeau, Jacques Rasteau père, Jean Seignette, Jacques Carayon, and the widow of his brother Ozée contributed the remaining 42 percent. In 1748–49,

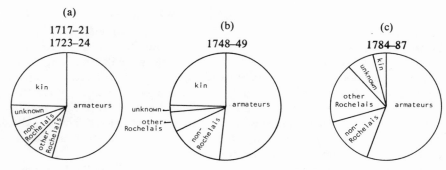

Figure 4.1
Distribution of Shares among Four Groups Investing in Rochelais Vessels, 1719–87
Source: Amirauté de La Rochelle, ACM, Ms. B5726, 5589 (1719–21), 5720–25 (1723–24), 5738–40 (1748–50), 5789–96 (1784–87), and numerous other collections.

Claude and Allard fils each outfitted three vessels. Claude held 17 percent in Allard's armements while Allard held 22 percent in his brother's. Claude was intéressé for 51 percent in his own ventures while Jacques Rasteau, Jacques Carayon, and Paul Belin subscribed the remaining 27 percent. Allard held 33 percent in his own vessels; the Bonneaus and Henri Belin, both kin, held 33 percent, and non-Rochelais owned the remaining 17 percent.

According to figure 4.1c, the investment role of relatives had shrunk radically by the 1780s. In all probability, however, less shrinkage actually occurred. The data base for figure 4.1 c employs all armateurs, and it is likely that some individuals identified as intéressés were also kin, as were perhaps some of the unidentified. For example, Swiss and German relatives of Weis & Sons were commanditaires in the Weis comptoir. These relatives took shares in the six armements prepared by the Weises between 1784 and 1787. But they were not identified as intéressés. In 1786, the Weises outfitted le Reparateur (780t) for Guinea and the Antilles at a total cost of 200,000 lt. While the records indicated that the armateurs held 94 percent of the shares, in fact their kin contributed a portion of the investment ascribed to the armateurs. It is probable that Daniel Garesché, the largest armateur during the period, also received investments from commanditaires. Whatever the actual proportion of shares held by commanditaires who were kin, the value represented therein should be added to the kin sector of figure 4.1c and deducted from the armateurs' portion. Another factor that further qualifies the statistical findings was the greater prevalence during the 1780s of multifamily partnerships (or sociétés générales). Some of the funds, which in earlier days would have been invested in the name of a particular relative, became subsumed within the shares held by the partnership.

Even with these qualifications, which all tend to reduce the degree of kin-investor shrinkage, the role of kin-investors clearly had declined. Table 4.1 reflects a progressive decline in kinship investment for three of the four families

Table 4.1. *Kin Investments in Vessels of Four Families (%)*

Family	1719–21, 1723–24		1748–49		1784–87	
	Armateur	Kin	Armateur	Kin	Armateur	Kin
Carayon	?	?	27	2	61	6
Giraudeau	32	13	31	15	69	?
Vivier	50	50	?	?	23	10
Rasteau	33	29	48	18	48	5

Source: See figure 4.1.

and little change for the Carayon family. During the first period, 1719–24, the Carayons took shares of vessels outfitted by the Rasteau and Belin families (see tables 3.2 and 3.4). While kinship solidarity seems to have been as strong in the 1780s as in earlier years, the size of the clans had diminished as a result of falling fertility rates. Fewer new families were started, fewer new family alliances were forged, and the pool of potential kin-investors contracted. Table 3.2 traces a gradual decline in the shipping role of the leading elite families. By the 1780s, many had ceased outfitting vessels and the share of armements controlled by the entire group had reached a historic low. The leading armateurs of the 1780s—Garesché, Van Hoogwerf, and Goguet—had fewer kin in La Rochelle than the Rasteaus or Viviers, whereas their connections throughout the rest of France seemed superior. Van Hoogwerf purposely sought investors from outside La Rochelle. J. B. Nairac, Samuel de Missy, and Nicolas Suidre, other leading armateurs of this decade, also sought intéressés from among nonkin and non-Rochelais. These and other reasons to be offered in subsequent pages of this chapter may explain in part the decline of kin as investors.

Family organizations, whether formalized in a société générale or not, provided adequate flexibility for Rochelais armateurs. Few options were lost in a partnership even if the partners bound themselves together for a stipulated period of time. George V. Taylor emphasized the great flexibility enjoyed by major partnerships in Lyons, which allowed the firms to expand while conducting vast and complex operations on many fronts—but he also noted the transitory nature of the collaborations. Henri Levy-Bruhl also characterized partnerships as short-lived. In La Rochelle, however, as in Nantes, many firms experienced a long life or were established with longterm goals in mind. They expired because of economic failure, induced perhaps by a war or general hard times, rather than because of a decision of the partners to end the relationship.[8]

In La Rochelle, single entrepreneurs evolved into father and son firms or, if the sons had been too young at the time of the father's death, into firms carried on by the widow, who then brought sons into the firm as they came of age, ultimately turning over to them the entire business. A variety of patterns were, of course, possible. Jacques Carayon, Pierre Gabriel Admyrauld, Elie Giraudeau, Jean Labbé, Marc Antoine Lefebvre, Antoine Pascaud, Jean Chabot, Jacques Bernon, Denis Goguet, Jacques Rasteau, Jean Vivier,

Gerard Van Hoogwerf, Pierre Van Hoogwerf, Emanuel Weis, and others each established sociétés with their sons. The presence of adult sons enabled the Rasteau, Bernon, Chaudruc, and Van Hoogwerf businesses to associate brothers upon the retirement or death of the father. The Belin brothers formed a partnership soon after the initial division of Allard's estate and prior to his death. Allard, in semiretirement, continued to operate on his own, though on a smaller scale than previously. These were not temporary associations.

Other firms reflected different combinations of kin. Louis Auboyneau formed a partnership with his son-in-law Joachim Dussault; the uncle Théodore Delacroix and the nephew Trésahar Bonfils were en société; and the firms of Pierre Samuel de Missy & Meschinet de Richemond and Paillet & Meynardie joined brothers-in-law.

Widowhood thrust additional responsibilities upon the women of merchant families. Upon the deaths of their husbands, the widows Bonfils, Admyrauld, Charuyer, Delacroix, Massieu, Ranson, Pascaud, Carayon, and Lefebvre all assumed control of the family comptoir. The widows Delacroix, Massieu, and Ranson managed their affairs without outside assistance. Others formulated new arrangements with kin. When Elie Bonfils died in 1768, his widow, née Suzanne Garesché, assumed control of the business with the aid of her three sons-in-law, including Elie Giraudeau, and her son Trésahar. An agreement among the heirs left the firm's capital intact and in Suzanne's hands. At the death of Pierre Gabriel Admyrauld, the firm of Admyrauld & Son became Veuve Admyrauld & Son until a younger son, Jean Louis, came of age; it then became Admyrauld Brothers. The Pascaud, Carayon, and Lefebvre establishments replicated the Admyrauld sequence.[9] These widows trained their sons to manage the comptoir, outfitted and dispatched vessels, underwrote insurance, invested funds, and performed other necessary duties. While one cannot penetrate the family sitting room or more intimate corners to learn what husbands and wives talked about, it seems most likely that conversation turned frequently to business affairs. These women were thoroughly knowledgeable about the family enterprise and at all times participated in economic decision-making.

Kinship arrangements kept these firms intact. In the case of the Charuyers, such support meant the difference between disbanding a successful enterprise and continuing it until minor children had matured sufficiently to take control.[10] In 1755, Louis Charuyer and his brother-in-law Pierre Paul François Depont, son of Paul Depont des Granges, formed a société to conduct brokerage and wholesale and retail trade. Each partner contributed 50,000 lt. Louis died in 1759, leaving his widow, née Sara Depont, and seven minor children. Louis left an equity of 83,000 lt. in Charuyer & Depont and an estate valued at 88,000 lt. Depont agreed to continue en société with his sister. In 1771, Sara bought out Pierre and initiated an inventory preparatory to turning the business over to her eldest sons, Jean and Etienne. After settling with Depont and paying all other debts, the firm was worth 127,000 lt. Veuve

Charuyer then made an early division of her estate, providing the two sons each with 33,000 lt., with which they formed a partnership to continue the firm. Sara divided the remainder of her estate in 1776, ceding the totality to Etienne and Jean for use in the business. The brothers agreed to make payments totaling 172,000 lt. to their mother and the remaining children and waived their rights to those payments at Sara's death. Early division, then, transformed Sara's entire estate into a capital loan at a time when Charuyer Brothers sought to expand. By 1782, shortly after Sara's death, the brothers had repaid the loan with interest. The five remaining children received their share of Sara's estate, increased by interest payments, and proceeded with the division of the money plus interest repaid by Charuyer Brothers to their mother.

By 1786 Charuyer Brothers boasted a net worth of 390,000 lt. Jean died in 1788 and Etienne formed a new société with his brother François, in which Etienne invested 75 percent of the capital and François 25 percent. Three years later, Etienne married Suzanne Van Hoogwerf and a dowry of 35,000 lt. in cash (household goods worth 15,000 lt. completed this dowry) entered the firm as a capital loan from Etienne's spouse. François benefited from the injection of this sum into the partnership but would have no claim on the principal should Etienne die.[11] Only a few years earlier, Pierre Jean Van Hoogwerf and his son Etienne had formed a partnership. Etienne's one-third share of 35,000 lt. derived from an early division of Elizabeth Belin Van Hoogwerf's estate. So, too, did the dowry brought by Suzanne to her union with Etienne Charuyer (see table 3.5). Thus, the wealth of the Belin family permeated successive generations, nurturing the commerce of La Rochelle.

Other sociétés générales accomplished similar purposes to the Charuyer partnership. Théodore Delacroix & Company, changed to Delacroix & [Trésahar] Bonfils in 1744, brought into the firm Delacroix's nephew, the son of his sister and Elie Bonfils. Young Bonfils, served, in effect, an apprenticeship—but also received a share of the profits—under his uncle's tutelage. When, in 1757, Trésahar was prepared to operate on his own, the firm was dissolved. To expand his trade, Jean Chaudruc formed a partnership with his son Jacques in 1751, and that firm immediately took on a partner in Canada who held a 25 percent interest. The charter of the Chaudruc firm stipulated that if the partner in Canada returned to La Rochelle he would forfeit for six years his right to either return to Canada or trade there, or pay an indemnity of 10,000 lt. to the firm.[12]

Not all partnerships were registered and not all agreements specified the capitalization. But those that did seemed to be more heavily capitalized than partnerships in Nantes. Of twenty-eight charters at Nantes for which the capital was known, seventeen were capitalized at under 50,000 lt. and only five surpassed 100,000 lt. Most of the Rochelais partnerships exceeded 100,000 lt. in initial capitalization and few fell below 70,000 lt. The société générale established between Pierre Garesché and Charles Billotteau, in which each invested 85,000 lt., can be considered typical for La Rochelle.[13]

For purposes of maritime commerce and related enterprises in La Rochelle, joint stock companies offered no advantages unavailable to partnerships or individual operations. If joint stock companies could expand through the issue of new stock, so, too, could partnerships through the infusion of new funds from a variety of sources including dowries, inheritances, and non-Rochelais investors. Partners invested sums in their business which were differentiated from the working capital and which drew interest much like stock earned dividends. Etienne Charuyer utilized his wife's dowry in that manner. Kin also availed themselves of such options. Odilé Van Hoogwerf regularly invested in her brother's comptoir. Pierre also managed undesignated funds from Rochelais and non-Rochelais, investing them in his own and others' enterprises. The investment of undesignated funds in armements earned interest of 4 to 6 percent, while the investor also received shares in a maritime venture and its profits. Many Rochelais armateurs functioned as investment bankers, managing the money of others and earning a commission for services. In La Rochelle, as in Nantes, merchants did not confine their activities solely to armements.[14]

H. Levy-Bruhl has rightly asserted that, during the eighteenth century, the outright sale of a partner's interest in a firm to a third party occurred rarely.[15] Charters of sociétés générales protected participants against alienation (negotiability of interest in a partnership) through dissolution clauses and clauses awarding prohibitively high indemnities to the remaining partners in the event of an unagreed upon alienation. Since the free choice of one's associates constituted a major advantage of the partnership, such defensive clauses were essential.

Each vessel outfitted at La Rochelle (in which several individuals normally invested) represented a kind of floating corporation. For the periods specified in figure 4.1 armateurs contributed something over one-half of the total value of vessel and cargo. A few armateurs—Elie Bonfils and Jean Vivier during the 1720s and Daniel Garesché in the 1780s—registered full ownership of their ventures at the admiralty office. But even if no hidden investors were involved, full ownership by an individual was the exception to the rule. The pattern in the figures holds for other years as well.

Rochelais armateurs, their relatives, and other Rochelais contributed the bulk of the necessary capital, although the role of non-Rochelais expanded as a comparison of figure 4.1a and 4.1b with 4.1c indicates. Taylor correctly called attention to the lack of fixed assets and investments in maritime commerce since each voyage, although perhaps a joint venture, terminated with the division among the intéressés of the profits or losses.[16] But in focusing on the transitory quality of these operations, Taylor neglected elements of permanence, which permitted armateurs to send their vessels out year after year.

Many armateurs in La Rochelle developed a stable group that purchased shares in their vessels. These shares were negotiable and were frequently sold to third parties. Jean Vivier sold in 1748 a portion of his one-sixth interest in the ship *le Jean Elie* for a profit of 1,500 lt. To pay a debt to Jacques Rasteau père, Vivier ceded to him his share in *la Grande Amazonne*. Robert Deverigny similarly ceded his share in *l'Infante Victoire* to Elie Vivier, who in turn sold it to Elie Weis.[17] None of these transactions accorded the new share owners any management role in the venture nor did it add to or diminish the capital committed to the voyage. Within the parameters set by the single voyage, the shares were as potentially mobile as those offered by a joint stock company.

A reliable group of investors who invested with reasonable consistency in the armements of a Rochelais négociant created, in effect, fixed assets. Whether or not an armateur operated with a stipulated capital, the predictability of investments allowed the better planning of future operations and, by increasing his own investment or widening the pool of intéressés, the expansion of firm's operations. The de Magon firm at Saint-Malo drew capital from Marseilles, Dijon, Vannes, and elsewhere, neglected few areas of commerce, and lasted from 1714 to 1792. In this company, doubly interesting because it united numerous holders of *noblesse de la robe*—a status attained by the purchase of an office that conferred nobility—the investors associated in specific ventures wherein the legal connections ended with a division of the returns. The association continued venture after venture, however, achieving—in fact if not in law—the permanence attributed to joint stock companies.[18]

Table 3.3 suggests the congruence of interfamily investment patterns in ventures launched by the Belin and Rasteau families. The Vivier, Carayon, Depont, Seignette, Dubeignon, and Garesché families all invested in Rasteau and Belin vessels. The Belin family served as armateurs from at least 1714 through 1768 and invested in the ships of others until 1777. Incomplete though the records on intéressé are, the earliest known Rasteau investment in a Belin armement dates to 1721 and the last to 1765. Belins, for their part, invested in at least ten Rasteau vessels between 1746 and 1776. And as will be recounted later in this chapter, Belin financial succor saved Pierre Isaac Rasteau from bankruptcy following the Seven Years' War.

Between 1719 and 1737, Belin and Depont des Granges consistently took shares in one another's vessels. Jean Baptiste Nairac received investments from the Belins in each year from 1765 to 1777. The Gareschés habitually invested in Delacroix & Bonfils voyages and in Bonneau ventures from 1719 through the 1750s, while Bonneau took shares in Belin's ships during the 1740s and the 1750s. During each year of the 1770s, Etienne Belin was an intéressé in the armements of Jacques Carayon fils aîné. Jacques, in his turn, regularly placed funds during the 1780s in the ships of Pierre Jean Van Hoogwerf and Fleuriau Brothers & Thouron. Van Hoogwerf's regular pool of investors also included Wilkens Brothers & Company and J.B. Nairac as well as numerous non-Rochelais. Jean Vivier and Jacques Rasteau were intéressé in each other's vessels. From the late 1740s until at least 1784, the Rasteau Brothers purchased shares in Vivier ships. Admyraulds supported Elie Giraudeau during the 1730s and the 1740s, and during the 1780s Benjamin Giraudeau took shares in most of the voyages launched by the Admyrauld Brothers.

During the years prior to the American Revolution, such formal sociétés tended to include a limited number of individuals, most of them relatives and the remainder Rochelais. Between 1740 and 1749, Jacques Rasteau père organized twenty-seven voyages, of which investors are known for nine. Table 4.2 identifies the investors and their shares for each of the nine Rasteau ships. Table 4.4 list the intéressés in three Van Hoogwerf armements made between 1784 and 1787.

The Rasteau pattern can be considered both typical for the period and transitional; typical because a rather small number of Rochelais, all of whom were kin save Depont des Granges and Gignoux, provided the bulk of the investment above that of Rasteau, and transitional because non-Rochelais investors initially appeared in 1748 and 1749. Non-Rochelais intéressés were not uncommon in prior years (see figure 4.1), but they became increasingly important during and after the 1740s (table 4.4). Before 1740, Rasteau did not seek outside investors and the pool of local investors was quite small. The intéressés in three voyages of the slaver *le Saint Louis* between 1738 and 1743, identified in table 4.3, reflected the consistency of investment of a restricted number of individuals. The very same group also invested during the 1740s in the slaving voyages of Rasteau's *la Victoire*. In effect, the intéressés of *le Saint Louis* and *la Victoire* formed a société. Note the absence of non-Rochelais investors.

By the 1760s and thereafter, the armateurs of La Rochelle had developed regular outside clients for investment in their maritime ventures. In seven voyages of *la Suzanne Marqueritte* from 1765 to 1777, J.B. Nairac armateur, the same group of six Rochelais who had invested in Rasteau's ships, combined with two people from Bordeaux and one from Rouen as intéressés.[19] By the 1780s, Pierre Jean Van Hoogwerf had developed an even broader network of local and nonlocal investors.

Table 4.2. Investors in Nine Rasteau armements, *1740–49*

Investor	No. of vessels invested in	% of shares in each vessel								
Jacques Rasteau	9	48	38	35	50	50	67	33	13	67
Capt. Gignoux	1	4								
Paul Depont	3	13		13	15			13		
Elie Vivier	4	4		6	8	10		10		
Jean Vivier	4	15	31	15			33			
Paul Vivier	2							2	23	9
Veuve Carayon	4	17	25	18	25					
Jacques Carayon fils	2								23	8
Capt. Elie Seignette	1			13						
Allard Belin	1					44				
Allard Belin fils	1					6				
Pierre Jacques Rasteau	2								25	8
Non-Rochelais	3							42	16	8

Table 4.3. *Investors and Their Percentage Shares in Three Voyages of Rasteau's* le Saint Louis

Investor	1st voyage, 1738	2nd voyage, 1740	3rd voyage, 1743
Jacques Rasteau	48	48	35
Paul Depont	13	13	13
Veuve Carayon	17	17	17
Elie Vivier	8	4	8
Jean Vivier	15	15	15
Capt. Gignoux		4	
Capt. Seignette			13

Source: Compte des retours pour compte des intéressés au navire le St. Louis, 6 Novembre 1738, Depont des Granges Papers, ACM, Ms. E486; Compte générale du navire le St. Louis 2ᵉ voyage 1740–41, and Compte générale de navire le St. Louis 3ᵉ voyage 16 février 1743, ACM, Ms. E486.

When Van Hoogwerf solicited investments, he pursued certain objectives. First, he wished to limit his own investment to under 50 percent. This could have been achieved by interesting other Rochelais in his ventures. But he also wished to avoid that if possible so as to incur no obligations to invest in their enterprises. Van Hoogwerf, then, sought subscriptions from outside the city.[20] While he achieved his first goal, as table 4.4 demonstrates, less success accompanied his efforts to limit local investments and expand nonlocal ones. By dividing the shares into very small parts and spreading them among a sizable group, he reduced his obligation to any single individual. Moreover, ten of the twenty Rochelais intéressés did not make armements and none were kin.

One historian of La Rochelle has concluded that during the 1780s armateurs utilized a larger pool of intéressés—each with a smaller share—and sought nonlocal investors more diligently.[21] For two armements managed by Meschinet de Richemond and J.J. Garnault & Co. in 1780, one subscribed three investors and the second, four; in each case two intéressés were non-Rochelais. De Richemond & Garnault retained a 50 percent interest in one venture and a 66 percent interest in the other. Of the nineteen armateurs whose ventures were aggregated in figure 4.1c, only Louis Vivier signed as many investors as Van Hoogwerf for any single voyage. Fourteen of the nineteen armements subscribed no more than six intéressés, forming a pool comparable to that depicted for the Rasteaus in tables 4.2 and 4.3. While the role of relatives diminished and the role of other Rochelais as well as the non-Rochelais assumed greater significance, evidence supporting the typicality of the Van Hoogwerf pattern is inconclusive.

The investment role of non-Rochelais did expand between the 1720s and the 1740s, but it remained stable for the remainder of the Old Regime (figure 4.1). Available capital at La Rochelle may have been inadequate to support fully the city's shipping. Rochelais were net importers of capital, the significance of which will be analyzed in Chapter 10.

Table 4.4. Investors and Their Percentage Shares in Three armements of Pierre Jean Van Hoogwerf, 1784–87

Investor	No. of vessels	% of shares in each vessel		
Pierre Jean Van Hoogwerf	3	46	58	34
Etienne Van Hoogwerf fils	2	2	2	
Capt. André Begeaud	2	5		7
Gustave Gabriel Benoist fils	3	2	2	2
Jacques Carayon fils aîné	3	3	3	3
Casson et femme	1	5		
Louis Fort	2	2	2	
J. B. Nairac	2	3	3	
Noordingh & White	1	3		
Jean David Pinnesseau	2	3	2	
Poupet Frères	2	6	6	
Stockard & d'Ebert et Cie.	1	3		
Charles Vallette	3	3	3	3
Herman Wilkens	3	3	3	3
Capt. Jean de Bosq	1		6	
Dumoustier de Fredilly	1		3	
Joseph Le Carre	2		2	2
Billotteau	1			2
d'Eseuve	1			4
Jenner fils	1			1
Investors from:				
Abbéville	3	5	6	9
Rouen	2	1	4	
Marseilles	1	6		
Santo Domingo	1		8	
Chollet	2		2	2
Amiens	1			1

Source: Van Hoogwerf Papers, ACM, Ms. 4J487; ACM, Ms. 5789–96 (1784–87).

The armateurs' purpose was to obtain sufficient capital to outfit a given number of vessels. Few armateurs wished to assume the entire risk of a trading voyage. Family obligations demanded that the chance to participate in a profitable venture be open to kin. Close Rochelais business associates would also be offered the opportunity to subscribe. The reputation of La Rochelle's armateurs would also make investment in their armements attractive to non-Rochelais. During a period of commercial expansion such as the ten years 1745–54, when the number of Rochelais armements achieved a century high (see table 4.2), the investment needed in order to take advantage of the market exceeded the amount available from traditional sources. The Rasteaus and others tapped nonlocal capital. Again, during the 1780s, when the focus of the port's commerce had swung to slaving and the East Indian trade, both involving large capital inputs for extended time periods, the city's armateurs sought nonlocal subscribers. Their ability to attract outside capital attested to the confidence of outsiders in Rochelais endeavors.

The methods adopted by armateurs to finance their ventures, rarely studied in detail, have sustained broad generalizations about the structure and efficiency of eighteenth-century French maritime commerce. Dividing vessels into shares so as to minimize risk, common enough among most merchants operating in the Atlantic world, has also been viewed as a means by which large businesses could operate on little capital.[22] In La Rochelle, however, as figure 4.1 and the subsequent tables should make clear, direct investment by armateurs accounted for at least half of the capital committed to most armements. Credits sustained a portion of this, but heavy risks remained with armateur. Moreover, armement and *désarmement* (charges incurred upon the vessel's return such as tariffs, taxes, and other fees) required large sums of cash in hand.[23] Access to credit by no means guaranteed that a voyage could be undertaken.

Maritime and commercial business organizations in La Rochelle were characterized by the centrality of family and flexibility of structure.[24] While perhaps ill-suited for purposes of large capital accumulation, they facilitated the accomplishment of goals established by négociant owner-managers. Some sociétés were of limited duration and formed for specific purposes; others undertook a wide variety of operations and enjoyed long lives. Habit, kinship and friendship, and mutual benefit lent structure and permanence to relationships that superficially appeared to be unstructured and highly fluid.

THE SOCIAL PURPOSE OF KIN-CENTERED BUSINESS

The comptoir was the fulcrum of the family unit. Only success in business permitted the elite négociants to maintain their places in society and to achieve the social and economic security that they sought for themselves and their families. Concurrently, the willingness of family members to subordinate personal ambitions to the welfare of the family business and to accept the roles designed for them increased the likelihood of the firm's profitability and longevity. In this way, comptoir and household became integrated parts of a single institution in which social purposes merged smoothly with economic goals. Of numerous account books investigated, only the ledgers of Pierre Jean Van Hoogwerf separated household expenses from the accounts of the business.[25]

Physical distance separated the homes of elite merchants from their comptoirs. Allard Belin, Jean Vivier, and Jacques Rasteau, and their sons after them, walked each morning from their homes to their places of business. During the course of a day, they traversed the city on foot, visiting their warehouses or stores, looking in at the refinery, supervising the loading or unloading of their vessels, registering documents at the admiralty office, and attending auctions. At the comptoir, the négociant scrutinized his accounts, read and wrote innumerable letters, conferred with business associates, and sent subordinates scurrying after this or that piece of information or carrying messages to other comptoirs.

At dusk, the merchant returned to his home, perhaps to an entertainment, but more likely to a quiet meal with his family, followed by an hour's relaxation with his wife before the hearth. One can imagine that during those moments the husband shared the important occurrences of the day with his wife, not as gossip or casual conversation, but as one would impart information to a colleague who might, at any moment, have to act upon it. Discussing the marriage of a daughter or son or the education of a son, acts of grave consequence for the comptoir, must have merited the particular attention of the couple.

Just as dowries and inheritance practices served family and group ends, so too did the education of the young. Male children received an education that trained them to assume those responsibilities necessary to protect and further the interests of the family. Collectively, the effects of such training produced personnel equipped to perform leadership roles in the city.[26]

Given the size of some Rochelais families, the limited careers open to Protestants, and the modest growth of La Rochelle's commercial sector, careful provision had to be made for occupational succession or its equivalent within the male line. Too many sons proved a difficult responsibility. None of the elite families involved more than two sons in the family business at the same time, but numerous families had many more than two sons to place. While declining birth rates after midcentury may have eased the problem somewhat, of necessity other opportunities for employment were sought. Occupational discrimination impinged most severely on Huguenot efforts to place "excess" sons by denying them choices available to the Catholic majority. Commerce alone seemed the most accessible occupation for the scions of such wealthy families. But positions within the city, either as partners in family operations or as independent entrepreneurs, were limited. Migration had to be considered a possibility, and the children prepared for it. Training the young received assiduous attention.

Children of the elite Rochelais families received no formal education in La Rochelle, even though the law prescribed a compulsory Catholic education. Local authorities did not enforce this requirement and allowed Huguenots to educate their children as they wished. The children, then, were taught in the home to read, write, and cipher. When the sons reached adolescence (no information was discovered relating to the education of daughters), their training became more formal and preeminently vocational. As noted in Chapter 3, some young Rochelais acquired their training in the counting houses of foreign merchants while others, remaining in La Rochelle, studied under the supervision of fathers, older brothers, widowed mothers, and relatives. Daniel Garesché fils learned about commerce in the comptoir of Jacques Carayon fils (1709–1802), married his employer's daughter, Marie Anne Sara, in 1767, and went on to become the most prominent armateur in the city during the 1780s.[27]

Many families used their ships as a school and testing ground for their sons. At least seventeen of the ninety elite families—thirteen known to be Protestant and one Catholic—trained shipmasters. The Giraudeaus and Rasteaus each produced four captains and the Bonneaus and Bernons, two each. Other families providing a captain included the Belin, Depont, Seignette, Bonfils, Garesché, Hardy, Lamarque, Auboyneau, Dujardin, Goguet, and Couillandeau. Elie Nicolas Rasteau and two brothers followed in their father's footsteps. After several voyages to the Antilles as a ship's boy, Elie launched his formal nautical training when seventeen years old as an ensign on *la Perle,* commanded by Elie Seignette. After five and one-half years of training, Rasteau faced Louis Herault, Louis Auboyneau, and Jean Elie Giraudeau, sitting as a board of marine examiners with the authority to certify master's status. Upon passing the examination, Elie accepted his first command in 1737 at twenty-three years of age.

Jacques Rasteau had thirteen children to provide for. Each daughter married a Rochelais merchant but all the sons could not share the family business at La Rochelle. Two sons, Pierre Jacques fils aîné and Pierre Isaac, succeeded to Jacques's business. By the late 1740s, the three Rasteau commanders, Elie Nicolas, Jean Benjamin, and Gabriel, had established comptoirs at Port-au-Prince and Cul-de-sac, Santo Domingo.[28] Another son, Paul, was a merchant at New Orleans. These businesses, founded with the help of brothers of Jacques who were long established on Santo Domingo, were complimentary to the family firm, yet independent. Investments were shared but the profits and losses were not. These firms were of great utility to the Rasteau firm in La Rochelle. Each port merchant worked through one or more correspondents located in the ports with which he traded. It was of the utmost importance that these agents be reliable and competent. Jacques Rasteau was fortunate in having brothers and sons who operated individual comptoirs in the islands and served as his correspondents. In later years, the sons of Pierre Isaac received the aid of their Santo Domingo uncles when circumstances brought the young men to that island. Belins, Giraudeaus, and Carayons used the Rasteau network while the Rasteau used the networks of families with whom they were intermarried in places where no Rasteaus lived.

Other Rochelais families set up sons in the Antilles, both as merchants and planters. Among them were the Bonfils, Belin, Bonneau, Charuyer, Garesché, and Goguet families. Charles Bonfils, brother of Trésahar, functioned as an agent for Delacroix & Bonfils in Santo Domingo.[29] Paul Belin de Marais, son of Ozée and cousin of Claude Etienne, had commanded vessels owned by the Belin family during the 1720s. Using his inheritance as well as profits from personal cargoes shipped on the vessels which he commanded, he purchased in the mid-1730s and thereafter managed a sugar plantation on Santo Domingo.

In the early 1760s, Paul retired to Paris, leaving the plantation in the hands of a salaried manager who shipped the sugars to the Belin firm in La Rochelle and to merchants in Nantes and Bordeaux. Paul was a commanditaire in Claude Etienne's firm, and the latter invested Paul's funds in shipping and insurance while managing his cousin's local real estate holdings.[30]

Paul, the Rasteau brothers, and others of their generation experienced a form of sponsored mobility. Class lines were not crossed but occupational advances carried Paul to the top of the middle class, a position he held in his own right. In contrast, Jacques Rasteau's passage from master to sugar refiner and armateur exemplified a different pattern of mobility, again within the same class. Unlike his sons or Paul Belin, Jacques earned his own capital. Although his marriage into the Seignette family must have aided him, he had no inheritence to work with as had Paul, his own sons, or the sons of Allard Belin. Had Jacques remained a captain or risen to but a minor armateur, positions of leadership in the city—syndic and director of the Chamber of Commerce as examples—would have evaded him. The older generation, Rasteau, Elie Giraudeau, Jacques Carayon, and others emerging during the last years of the seventeenth and early eighteenth century, comprised the generating entrepreneurs of La Rochelle.

The sons of the first generation initiated their careers from within the solid comptoirs built by their fathers. They inherited the name and the reputation, the contacts, the capital, and a supportive family structure. In return, they accepted the charge to preserve the family fortune and expand its base. While the career history of the second generation largely mirrored the first, it was undertaken at lesser risk, more likely pursued abroad, and the result of planning.

The needs of the individual family and kinship group and the social group of which they were a part circumscribed the autonomy of the sons. Claude Etienne's most private ambitions cannot be determined, but had they included early retirement to an estate and a comfortable life of leisure as a rentier, it was unlikely that they could have been fulfilled at the moment of Allard's preliminary division or even at his death. Claude Etienne was part of a larger family scheme, for which he had been carefully trained. Jacques Rasteau, with less luck and talent and ambition, might have ended his career as a ship's captain. Jacques was not part of a larger family scheme. His sons were, and he planned careers for them beyond that of a mariner, viewing that particular occupation as a preliminary step to something better.

Preparation for a career in business commenced at an early age. Jean Pierre Antoine Giraudeau, born in 1717, was sent at age twelve to Holland for training. His contemporary, Elie Nicolas Rasteau, born in 1714, went to sea at age eleven. Older sons such as Claude Etienne Belin, Pierre Jacques and Pierre Isaac Rasteau, François Gabriel Admyrauld, Etienne Van Hoogwerf, Jacques Carayon fils, among others, all became partners of their fathers before they reached the age of twenty. The businesses passed into their hands when the fathers died or retired, and in some cases younger brothers then entered the firm. A prolonged period of dependency upon the father, stretching into the late twenties, seems to have been avoided.

Ennoblement also served as a potential route of upward mobility, a path frequently characterized as a widely held class objective among the bourgeoisie. In La Rochelle, a few armateurs were ennobled: Jacques Carayon fils aîné in 1777, the Arnaud brothers in 1784, and Samuel Pierre Joseph David de Missy just prior to the French Revolution. A few other families were noble—the de Fredilly, de Butler, and Depont among the major armateurs. But noble status did not carry with it any economic advantages, nor did the noble families occupy a separate and higher stratum in the social hierarchy of La Rochelle. The de Butler, Depont, and others intermarried freely with the elite middle class négociant families, and in all respects led a bourgeois life. While one daughter of Paul Depont des Granges married a noble, other daughters married Carayons, Belins, and Morreaus. Deponts held high offices, one of Paul's sons being an intendant, but the Belins, Seignettes, and Delacroixs, too, held high prestige offices in La Rochelle and the généralité. At any rate, evidence is lacking that elite Rochelais families coveted noble status.

Rochelais négociants sought and held venal offices but few were functional and many were inherited through several generations. Knowing that Claude Etienne Belin held the office of "ouvrier à pleine part et ajuster à la monnaie de La Rochelle"—a position of some sort at the mint—and also served as "lieutenant de prévôt," or that Jacques Bernon held the office "maître de la monnaie de La Rochelle" or that Etienne Henri Harouard Dubeignon served as "seculaire du roy maison couronne de France et des Finances" tells us very little. Much more essential to them and to La Rochelle were the positions that they held in the La Rochelle Chamber of Commerce, the juridiction consulaire, and the municipal government. In the latter positions, such men debated questions and formulated policies directly related to the economy of the port.

Catholics did hold office more regularly than Protestants. Of the ninety families, seventy-five were identifiable by religion; Catholics numbered twenty-seven. During the eighteenth century, 44 percent of the Catholic families, compared with 27 percent of the Protestant families, possessed at least one venal office. Fifty-nine percent of the Catholic families seated at least one member on the juridiction consulaire while only 15 percent of Protestant families did so. Protestants, as noted earlier, occupied one-half of the directorships of the local chamber. For most Rochelais, Protestant or Catholic, mobility occurred within limits set by an unobtainable noble status at one end and an unwanted common status at the other end.

Instead of scrambling upward, the elite Rochelais on a number of occasions bent their collective efforts to repelling scramblers from below. One such incident, mentioned in Chapter 1, involved the resistance of the elite merchants, who controlled the chamber of commerce, to the seating of lesser traders in that body. Garnault's history of La Rochelle recounted in detail the efforts of Rochelais négociants to gain exemption from militia duty. Later authors have retold it to substantiate the existence of rigid social stratification in La Rochelle and other parts of France.[31] But further analysis of the militia and chamber of commerce situations suggests that négociant demands may have been induced as much by economic aims as by class consciousness.

In 1743 and intermittently thereafter, leading Rochelais merchants sought exemption from militia duty for their sons and principal clerks. To evade what might amount to an annual two-week tour of duty, the petitioners forwarded arguments to the crown based both on social class standing and economic considerations. A briefly stated objection alleged that the sons and clerks suffered humiliation through association with other classes in such a setting. Greater care and more space, however, was given the contention that militia duty seriously damaged the port's commerce by stripping the comptoirs of their personnel. Commerce depended, it was claimed, on the continuity of its operations. Younger associates in the comptoir maintained that regularity. Seasonality did not characterize merchant life. Investments, crediting and debiting, establishing contacts and negotiating contracts, financial exchange, the making of insurance, the armement and désarmement of vessels, all necessitated daily attention that militia duty disrupted. Moreover, such duty interrupted the education of the younger associates.

While social distinctions separated the classes in La Rochelle, the campaign for militia duty exemption did not derive from a threat to status perceived by the elite merchants. The elite, themselves, formed the senior officer corps of the units and their younger associates served as junior officers. Rochelais négociants did not seek exemption for themselves. Instead, they argued against spending time unproductively, emphasizing the essential duties of their junior colleagues, duties central to the functioning of the port. Obviously, the same points could have been advanced for the lower social orders but were not. Appeals founded on social distinctions represented, in this case, the couching of an argument in terms with which the crown might sympathize.

La Rochelle's Chamber of Commerce thwarted repeated attempts of ineligible merchants to gain admission to that organizaton. Chamber arguments rested entirely on economic distinctions between wholesaling and retailing, which did discriminate against members of the latter group. Retailers, manufacturers, and others could not, as a result of such distinctions, belong to the chamber or to the juridiction consulaire. Those seeking admission, largely retailers and artisans, attacked this distinction as spurious. To a degree the challengers were correct. Many of the merchants—armateur négociants—who monopolized seats in the chamber engaged in retailing, but few of those seeking entry were wholesalers. Among the excluded wholesalers were the *courtiers-d'eau-de vie,* middlemen in the brandy trade who were disliked by shippers.[32] In fact, the petitioners argued, the sole difference between the incumbents and the excluded was the connection of the former with shipping. This, too, was not entirely correct, for many of the aggrieved took shares in Rochelais ventures. More central, but unmentioned in the debates, was the greater wealth, power, and influence of chamber members as a group when compared to the nonmembers. This power basically derived from shipowning, the dominant industry of the city. While nonmembers may have invested in the armements of chamber members, the former were not directly engaged in shipping. The armateur négociants who controlled the chamber evinced a singular unwillingness to share power with groups whose interests were not directly consonant with their own. The chamber's argument that because of its membership, it alone best represented the economic interests of the city may have been a conceit, but the sentiment was expressed vigorously and regularly after 1765 as the efforts of the excluded intensified.[33] The persistent defense of self-interest and the exercise of chamber power during the last days of the Old Regime, combined with the accumulating resentment of the excluded, accounted for the chambers of commerce being among the early institutional victims of the Revolution.

Sharply defined social demarcations separating négociants or marchands en gros from the more affluent craftsmen-retailers became somewhat blurred during the eighteenth century. At the beginning of that century, the heads of both the Depont and Seignette families were apothecaries. Many artisans owned their own shops, and some of them, such as the Charuyers, who were master drapers, grew to a size justifying their operating at wholesale. Thus the Depont-Charuyer partnerships joined an armateur family with a craft family. Other cloth merchants dealing in both wholesale and retail include Jean and Barthelemy Ranson, Jean Isaac Raboteau, and Joseph Lefebvre, brother of Marc Antoine. André Benoist, a master baker, was also an armateur.

Neither the Ranson nor Raboteau families acted as armateurs or took shares in their vessels. The two families did intermarry and both married into the Seignette family. Jean Isaac Raboteau and Barthelemy Ranson married daughters of Jean Seignette fils aîné, while a sister of Barthelemy married Jacques Carayon fils aîné. Although the contractual details of the unions are unknown, they must have brought benefits to all concerned.[34]

No legal obstacles prohibited Ranson or Raboteau from acting as armateurs. The only requirement was the management of a vessel, and once the individual had performed that service, his admission to the status of négociant by the juridiction consulaire was a mere formality. Dozens of Rochelais, including some who operated in that gray area between wholesaling and retailing, took this step during the eighteenth century.

The status designation of négociant, however, promised little in the way of social acceptance. A highly selective process governed the social diplomacy of spouse selection and kinship group formation. Religion served as the primary criterion. But having passed the religious test, newcomers, unless well-connected by family and possessing some degree of or excellent prospects for wealth, were hardly more likely than a carpenter to gain admission into the closely-knit and socially exclusive groups of elite families. The social system created by the linkages among families and among kinship units was by nature reluctant to embrace the unfamiliar. Economic fortune and social status reinforced one another. From this system could be anticipated mutual support in time of need. The story of Pierre Isaac Rasteau's private anguish—*l'affaire Rasteau*—finely elucidates the sustaining qualities of the Rochelais kinship system.

Pierre Isaac Rasteau's business affairs were in serious disarray by the mid-1760s, partly as a result of the Rasteau family's propensity for taking risks. As a young man, Pierre's father, Jacques, had worked the interloping trade in the Spanish West Indies. In the 1730s, when Louisiana was ceded to the crown by the Company of the Indies, Jacques seized upon the opportunity to send vessels to New Orleans. Although this meant a voyage of high risk because of the dangers of navigating the treacherous currents of the Mississippi River, Rasteau sought to use that port as a staging point to prepare illegal armements for Spanish ports in Florida and Mexico. This traffic held even greater perils due to the unpredictable reception that vessels encountered from Spanish colonial officials. Nor did war deter Rasteau armements. During the War of the Austrian Succession, Pierre Jacques Rasteau, newly established as head of the family firm, had suffered the capture of four vessels by the English as of November 29, 1745, equivalent to 27 percent of all Rochelais losses. Before the war ended another four Rasteau vessels and cargoes fell into English hands. Rasteau losses during the conflict exceeded three million lt.[35] Pierre Isaac inherited the family's high tolerance for risk.

France officially declared war on England in June 1756, but hostilities had commenced in America and on the high seas as early as 1754. Three vessels dispatched by Pierre Issac in 1754 were seized by the English with losses amounting to 1.6 million lt. Another Rasteau ship was taken in 1756. During the height of the conflict, 1759–62, Rochelais armateurs ventured only twelve vessels, five outfitted by Rasteau. Three of these were captured.[36] By 1763, Pierre was deeply in debt, owing his brother-in-law Claude Etienne Belin 60,000 lt. and a comparable sum to others. Realizing that Pierre would go under if all debts came due simultaneously, Claude cancelled his debt. Rasteau pledged to seek recovery of funds owed him in the Antilles to which Belin had some claim.

Belin did more than cancel debts. Through the good offices of Pierre Jean Van Hoogwerf, Belin silently transferred funds to meet Rasteau's other obligations. Between 1769 and 1773, Rasteau struggled to pay his debts, but success eluded him; in 1771, in a letter to Pierre Joachim de Baussay (see figure 3.1, column 5), he despaired, believing that his sad position had brought dishonor to his wife and their children. In 1772, after years of effort, Rasteau's debts had increased. By 1773, Belin had advanced some 110,000 lt. to his friend and relative, and Rasteau was prepared to sell all of his property, including his vessels. But he survived and his fortunes improved. Pierre outfitted a vessel in 1773 and again in 1776. Both did well, greatly reducing his indebtedness, and he achieved some stability in his affairs for the first time in a decade. In 1777 his sons, Jacques fils aîné and Etienne Isaac, succeeded him in business

Pierre accepted the position as deputy from La Rochelle to the Council of Commerce in Paris, serving until his death in 1781. His sons continued the firm, repaid Belin, opened a house in Santo Domingo, and survived the Revolution and two decades of war.[37]

Secrecy shrouded the entire *affaire Rasteau*. Pierre's kin protected his solvency and his status. Belin, in addition to aiding a friend, relative, and long-time business associate, also protected his own family. Still another motive may have prompted Belin. Rasteau's time of troubles coincided with hard times for others in La Rochelle. Recovery from the Seven Years' War came slowly. Shipping losses had been heavy and Canada and Louisiana had been abandoned by France. The value of the city's external commerce only reached prewar levels during the mid-1770s. The city was falling behind its great Atlantic rivals. This was an unpropitious time for a great house to fall, perhaps dragging with it other, more solid firms.

CONCLUSION

The history of La Rochelle's négociant families elucidates the socio-cultural bases of capital formation and economic development. The history of the Charuyers and the Rasteaus reflect many of the particular themes of this evolution. Multiple family firms such as Delacroix & Bonfils or Charuyer & Depont bound together economically many of the families untied by marriage. Firms persisted; widows, widows and sons, or widows and other relatives assumed control upon the death of the male family head. Dowries, early estate divisions, and inheritance allowed children to purchase partnerships in the family firms or to establish themselves elsewhere. Belin money flowed into numerous families over three generations, not randomly, but rather in a pattern determined by marriage alliances with selected families of similar religion and status. Support in time of crisis could be expected from this cluster of négociant families. From an economic point of view, the Rochelais family of managers functioned efficiently. Children and children's children, old age and retirement, were all provided for. Businesses achieved flexibility and engaged in long-range planning. When death claimed the family head, the family and the business continued, even as new life cycles swung into full course.

FIVE

The Dominant Families
in La Rochelle

During the eighteenth century, leadership in economic and political affairs centered in a core group of ninety Rochelais families. Most of these families engaged directly in maritime trade. Their success in maritime affairs, the lifeblood of the city, led to formal positions of leadership. The ninety families furnished twenty-seven of the thirty-eight directors of the La Rochelle Chamber of Commerce, at least sixty-one of no more than a hundred chamber syndics, twenty-six of the thirty-nine members of the juridiction consulaire, a number of mayors, and an unknown but high proportion of city councilmen. Moreover, the crown bestowed hereditary offices, for a price, upon at least twenty-five of the families.

The leading maritime families have been identified in table 3.1. That table also designates twenty-six families as the economically most significant in the city. In most cases, dominance in the maritime sector also reflected a position of great general economic significance. But a high ranking in maritime activities did not necessarily mean an equally high general ranking, since activities other than the outfitting of vessels provided meaningful measures of economic dominance.

The following discussion of the methodology used to select and rank the families listed in table 3.1 will accomplish several purposes. First, it will identify those families with the greatest commitment to the maritime sector and measure the extent to which they dominated the port's shipping. Second, the significance of economic activities other than that of armateur—noneconomic indications of status such as office and membership in kinship groups—will be evaluated and utilized as indices of overall economic dominance. Thirdly, the weaknesses of this methodology will be assessed. A conspicuous shortcoming is the inability to measure failure as well as success. To remedy this defect, the chapter will conclude with a discussion of bankruptcy, the ultimate form of commercial failure which threatened all, and engulfed some, of La Rochelle's négociants. All of the above will explain why some families from among the ninety were more important to the economic life of the city than the others.

THE DISTRIBUTION OF SHIPPING OWNERSHIP

Ninety percent of the ninety families served as armateurs at one time or another during the eighteenth century, signifying at least part-ownership in the vessels that they managed. Capital investment in shipping accounted for a major portion of the capital outlay of the city. Rochelais armateurs readied in the 1780s on the average of thirty-five vessels le long cours annually (table 2.3). These vessels averaged some 425 tons each during the four years prior to the Revolution, with construction costing about 110 lt. per ton. During that period, the value of the Rochelais fleet, not including fishing or coasting vessels, must have exceeded 3 million lt. In an earlier period, 1750–54, the value had approached 2.5 million lt.

Control of shipping in La Rochelle, as measured by the number of armements, was concentrated in the hands of relatively few individuals. Indeed, the concentration of ownership in La Rochelle seems to have been more pronounced than in either Nantes or Bordeaux. At Nantes during the eighteenth century (1694–1792), 200 families outfitted 61 percent of all vessels with 76 of those families responsible for 40 percent of all armements. Twice as many armateurs operated at Nantes as at La Rochelle. Yet in the latter place, as data from table 3.2 indicates, between 11 and 18 armateurs accounted for some 36 to 59 percent of all outfits. At Nantes in 1772, 22 armateurs, composing 29 percent of the total, each of which dispatched at least two vessels, accounted for 47 percent of armements le long cours. At La Rochelle, as table 5.1 shows for four different time periods, five or six armateurs, or 15 to 23 percent of all shippers, outfitted from 33 to 49 percent of the ventures, those vessels contributing from 37 to 56 percent of total tonnage. While 54 Nantais sent out one vessel each in 1772, no more than 12 Rochelais outfitted only a single vessel during any of the four periods.[1]

Table 5.2 offers a precise comparison, of the distribution of shipping ownership in La Rochelle and Bordeaux.[2] The great difference in the respective size of the maritime sectors is immediately apparent. Bordeaux in two years outfitted 438 vessels compared with a five-year Rochelais total of 123. During the five-year period, however, each Rochelais dispatched proportionately more vessels than did Bordelais armateurs. Thirty-eight Rochelais armateurs averaged 3.23 armements during the five-year period, while 211 Bordealais shippers averaged 2.07 outfits. Expressed differently, Bordeaux, with five and one-half times as many armateurs as La Rochelle, outfitted only three and one-half times as many vessels. The degree of concentration of shipping among the largest Rochelais and the largest Bordelais firms was quite similar; 8 percent of Rochelais armateurs controlled 26 percent of all shipping, while 3 percent of Bordelais shippers controlled 12 percent of all armements (6 percent of Bordelais accounted for 21 percent of armements). In this upper category each armateur dispatched seven or more vessels. The most significant differences

Table 5.1.   The share of Shipping and Tonnage Controlled by Leading Rochelais armateurs, 1727–29, 1749–51, 1771–73, 1785–87

Armateur	% of all armateurs	% of vessels outfitted	% of tonnage dispatched
1727–29	18	49	52
Rasteau			
Belin			
Bonneau			
Delacroix			
Dujardin			
1749–51	15	36	37
Delacroix & Bonfils			
Blavout			
Rodrique			
Soubroum			
Belin			
Perdriau			
1771–73	22	49	56
Suidre			
Nairac			
Garesché			
Admyrauld			
de Saint Martin			
1785–87	23	33	47
Garesché			
Dumoustier de Fredilly			
Guibert			
de Missy			
Rasteau			
Weis			

between the two ports appeared among the smallest armateurs. One-half of all Bordelais shippers outfitted only one vessel each but accounted for 25 percent of all ventures; at La Rochelle, only 31 percent of the armateurs outfitted but a single vessel, and their efforts contributed only 10 percent of all voyages le long cours. A larger proportion of Rochelais were grouped within a middle level, outfitting from three to six vessels. That category, composing 34 percent of all Rochelais shippers, accounted for 48 percent of Rochelais outfits, whereas at Bordeaux that category encompassed 24 percent of all armateurs and 42 percent of armements. Bordeaux's maritime sector depended to a greater extent on the efforts of relatively small armateurs than did the maritime strength of La Rochelle.

A total of fifty families were involved in outfitting from three to six vessels during the four periods specified in table 5.1. Only eight did not fall within the core group of ninety families. Five of the families listed on table 5.1 outfitted from three to six vessels during time periods other than those under which they are listed. Only three families from table 5.1—Rodrigue, Blavout, and Soubroum—were Catholic. Of the forty-two core families outfitting at this

Table 5.2.   Number of armateurs and their Share of armements at Bordeaux, 1787–89, and La Rochelle, 1786–90

Order of vessels outfitted	No. of armateurs La Rochelle 1786–90	No. of armateurs Bordeaux 1787–89	La Rochelle % armateurs	La Rochelle % outfits	Bordeaux % armateurs	Bordeaux % outfits
1	12	111	31	10	53	25
2	10	42	26	16	20	19
3	3	27	8	7	13	18
4	3	18	8	10	8	16
5	4	3	10	16	1	3
6	3	4	8	15	2	5
7	0	3				
8	0	1				
9	1	1				
10	0	0	8	26	3	12
11	1	0				
12	1	0				
13	0	1				
Total armateurs	38	211				
Total outfits	123	438				

level, thirteen were Catholic. If other periods had been chosen for table 5.1, additional Protestant families would have been included among those outfitting seven or more vessels, but none of the Catholic armateurs would have been included (see also table 3.2). While the economic role of the Catholic families cannot be ignored, Protestants controlled the larger part of La Rochelle's shipping.

The relatively low number of small armateurs operating in La Rochelle reflects the difficulty that newcomers faced in obtaining backing for their ventures from within the city. Perhaps the supply of venture capital at La Rochelle was inadequate to sustain them; perhaps the Rochelais were unwilling to risk their capital on unknown armateurs. Whatever the causes, the addition of new blood and new family units was discouraged. Of the five leading armateurs in 1785–87 (see table 5.1), the Rasteaus and Gareschés were armateurs very early in the century; the Guibert and de Missy firms invested in vessels during the 1720s; the Weises were operating by the 1740s; and the de Fredillys, while only directly involved in the maritime sector in the 1780s, were an old Rochelais family.

The middle level armateurs managed a smaller proportion of shipping than their numbers warranted. In the three years 1727–29, they comprised 43 percent of all armateurs but accounted for only 36 percent of the port's departures. During the years 1749–51, the respective shares were 55 and 54 percent. The economy of La Rochelle seemed to be most open to penetration by new armateurs during those interwar years. But by the years 1771–73, the share of the middle level armateurs, forming 64 percent of that class, had fallen to 47 percent. The respective shares for the three years 1785–87 were 50 and 40 percent. Over the entire period, then, the contribution of the middle level armateurs to the maritime activity of the port increased at midcentury relative to earlier years and then declined, but their share of armements remained above that of the 1720s.

The share of armements attributable to the middle range of armateurs declined after midcentury, coinciding with the increasing importance of non-Rochelais investments in Rochelais shipping. While most of these men came from the core group of ninety families, few are included among the twenty-six dominant families identified in table 3.1. The uncertainties of the 1770s and the rising cost of armements in the 1780s may have taxed the capital resources of these individuals to the limit, allowing no room for further growth. The family connections and the non-Rochelais connections of these traders were inferior to those enjoyed by the leading armateurs.

A small group of armateurs dominated the maritime sector of La Rochelle. From 1730 to 1739, three families—the Belin, Rasteau, and Delacroix—prepared 115 vessels for le long cours while all other armateurs ventured 113 vessels (table 3.2). Between 1770 and 1789, Rochelais made 641 armements, of which the Gareschés, mostly David, made 74, or 12 percent of the total. During the 70 years 1720–90, 2,345 Rochelais vessels passed Île de Ré and gained the open sea. Eight families—the Belin, Rasteau, Vivier, Gareschè, Bonneau, Giraudeau, Delacroix, and Suidre—were each responsible for at least 50 ventures during those years. They outfitted 653 ships, or 28 percent of La Rochelle's total effort. Concentration of shipping at Nantes was less extreme; five kinship groups, consisting of about a dozen families, outfitted 4 percent of all ventures.[3] Figure 5.1 depicts the marital connections between the

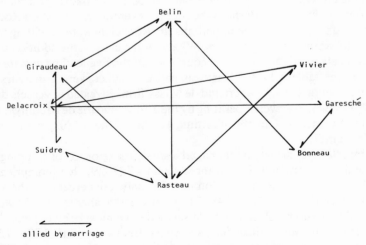

allied by marriage

Figure 5.1
Marital Connections between the Eight Largest Rochelais *armateur* Families

leading eight Rochelais families. Each family married into at least two of the remaining seven. A small number of kinship groups, owning and managing a disproportionately large number of La Rochelle's ships, controlled a major part of the city's most valuable fixed capital assets.

MEASURING THE RELATIVE ECONOMIC SIGNIFICANCE OF ROCHELAIS FAMILIES

The identification of economic dominants in communities has engaged the attention of numerous students of socioeconomic structure and political behavior. Basically, two methodologies have been suggested as efficient means for the definition and analysis of community notables (elites). In the reputational method, popularized by Floyd Hunter, individuals assumed to be leaders are asked to identify the most influential individuals in town. Those mentioned most frequently are judged to be the leaders. This methodology is highly supportive of elitist theories of political and economic organization. Advocates of a second method, emphasizing decision-making, have argued that since decision-making requires power and influence, those who can get things done are the true leaders. Reputation, as Robert Dahl and others pointed out, may not carry with it any real power. Advocates of the reputational approach generally have discovered coherent ruling cliques, while advocates of the decision-making methodology have found factionalism and an absence of cohesion among shifting power groups. The latter have preferred to explain politics in pluralist terms rather than in elitist terms. They have described a political system as one in which competing groups search for consensus through compromise.[4]

Replication of the investigatory techniques applied in the above studies was impossible. Unfortunately, the data base lacked such primary resources as newspapers, through which associational and other activities of La Rochelle's citizens could be followed. While the indicators used in the following analysis resemble those implicit in both the reputational and decisional methodologies, they were chosen because of their inherent utility rather than because of any congruence with measures used in other studies.

As a result of its possession of strategic resources, a discrete group of families, united by marriage into closely knit kinship groups and heavily involved in maritime trade, dominated the economic and political life of La Rochelle. While the power of the state forcefully intruded in all spheres, from religious life to the markets in which the Rochelais could operate, the ninety families exercised local supremacy within those externally created parameters, some of which could be covertly circumvented. For the most part, the resources emphasized to this point have been directly related to maritime activities. Other resources that the families controlled have been noted, particularly total wealth and appointment or selection to prestigious offices. By defining the resources crucial to the growth of a power base, by measuring the degree of control over such resources exercised by particular families, and by integrating those results with measurements of power and wealth amassed through maritime trade, the structure of socioeconomic power in La Rochelle can be reconstructed.

The ninety families supplied virtually all of the major négociant-armateurs operating in the city during the entire eighteenth century as well as virtually all of the leaders or manager-owners of the most significant economic institutions. Collectively, these prominent families took the lead in meeting situations threatening to the city and in initiating or providing necessary support for projects beneficial to both themselves and their city. As noted earlier, personnel from the 90 families organized and commanded the community's military defense in 1757, and the costs of those efforts were apportioned among 101 families, including 80 from the core group. In 1770, in order to initiate desperately needed port reconstruction, the Rochelais reluctantly agreed to contribute part of the cost through public subscription, an effort which yielded 108,794 lt. Fifteen families, including 13 of the 90, each subscribed over 2,000 lt. and accounted for 43 percent of the total. In all, 69 of the 90 families accounted for 75 percent of the funds raised.[5]

Four factors—maritime participation, office holding, participation in major economic institutions, and marriage ties—were selected as measures of general economic significance. Numerical weights were assigned to each factor or to its components according to my assessment of the importance of the activity. Table 3.1 ranks the twenty-six families with the highest scores. The absence of data resulted in the exclusion of several families of known prominence from the ranking; however, none of these families functioned as armateurs.[6] Sufficient data were available for most families.

Participation in maritime commerce encompassed a variety of functions. Values were assigned to activities directly related to the management of vessels, to longevity of operation, and to officeholding directly related to commercial affairs, the award of which also signified an honor bestowed upon the recipient. This index, then, included both active (management of a vessel) and passive (appointment to an office) qualities. In the latter case, reputation, implying the presence of power, was rewarded with an office carrying with it the guarantee of future policymaking functions.

To measure maritime significance, each individual undertaking an armement received one unit while each individual who invested in an armement received one-half of a unit. Armateurs accrued values for consecutive decades of maritime operation according to the following schedule: two units for the third consecutive decade, four for the fourth, eight for the fifth, and so on up to sixty-four for the eighth consecutive decade. Lesser values were assigned for three or more nonconsecutive decades of maritime operations. The factoring in of time endowed the measure with a dynamic quality. Individuals who served as syndics of the La Rochelle Chamber of Commerce received ten units per term; directors, fifteen units per term; members of the juridiction consulaire, twenty units per term; a deputy extraordinary to the Council of Commerce, twenty-five units; and a regular appointment as La Rochelle's deputy to the Council, thirty units. The specific numerical values assigned each function or role, while possessing no intrinsic or absolute meaning, distinguished between various functions and roles and in their sums permitted a relative ranking of individuals (see table 3.1).

As table 3.1 indicates, the Rasteaus ranked highest in maritime participation. They amassed points because they outfitted the most vessels over eight consecutive decades, invested in dozens of others, served as syndics and directors of the Chamber of Commerce, and provided a deputy to the Council of Commerce. The Belins were not far behind in maritime affairs. They scored higher than the Rasteaus in general economic significance, largely as a result of the venal offices they held. The Seignettes ranked considerably lower than the Rasteaus and Belins in maritime activities but were closer in general economic significance. Seignettes ranked second among the officeholding families of La Rochelle.

The measure for officeholding summarized in table 5.3 included venal offices whether functional or not, municipal offices, and designation by a foreign power as its resident official. Since there was no way of assessing the significance of one venal office as against another, each received ten units. Individuals holding municipal and foreign offices each received twenty units, largely because actual responsibilities devolved upon those positions.

Officeholding of this type, while apparently less functional than having positions in the Chamber of Commerce, presumed either high local status, sufficient wealth to purchase the office, or both. This index captured an important element in the life of the city, and the relevance of the measure rested in its utility as an indicator of status. As table 5.3 makes clear, officeholding promoted the status of Catholics more effectively than Protestants. While eleven Catholic and ten Huguenot families composed the leading officeholding families of the city, four of the top five were Catholic, and most Protestants

Table 5.3. *Rank of Leading Officeholding Families in La Rochelle*

Rank	Family	Religion	Score	Rank	Family	Religion	Score
1	Pascaud	RC	230	11	de Butler	RC	105
2	Seignette	P	215	12	Depont	P	95
3	Goguet	RC	205	13	Giraudeau	P	85
4	Bridault	RC	175	14	Leclerq	RC	85
5	Gastumeau	RC	165	15	Rasteau	P	85
6	Belin	P	160	16	Carayon	P	85
7	Legrix	RC	145	17	Surreau	RC	80
8	Papineau	RC	135	18	Bureau	RC	75
9	Claëssen	P	115	19	Bonneau	P	70
10	Vivier	P	110	20	Demontis	RC	65
				21	Dubeignon	P	65

ranked among the bottom ten. Order of rank in this table differs considerably from the two orders of rank presented in table 3.1

The significance to the community of the Catholic families Goguet and Pascaud, prominent among Rochelais armateurs but not among the leading ten, would not have been as apparent had maritime activities served as the single measure. Both of the Pascaud brothers, Antoine and Joseph Marie, represented La Rochelle in the Council of Commerce, served as mayors of the city, and held offices at the mint as well as other venal offices. Both had died by 1768. Pascauds did not appear on the port construction subscription list of 1770, and the subsequent fate of the family was not revealed in local documents. Goguets appeared in La Rochelle as armateurs during the 1750s, continuing in that capacity through the 1780s. The family had apparently returned to La Rochelle from Canada during the 1740s and rapidly established themselves among the leading négociants. All of their many commercial and noncommercial offices date from the 1750s. Denis Goguet held every chamber and juridiction consulaire position and served as mayor while his son held several venal offices, all previously occupied by Denis. Jacques, brother of Denis, was also elected to the chamber and sat on the juridiction consulaire.

Another Catholic family, the Bridaults, neither outfitted nor invested in the port's shipping. But Louis Benjamin (d. 1775) held virtually every commercial and municipal office at the disposal of the city. His sons, Augustin and François Jean Baptiste, succeeded their father in both the chamber and the juridiction consulaire, and continued the family brandy business. Without an officeholding factor—as much a measure of social as of economic significance—the Bridaults would not have been identified.

While Catholics predominated among noncommercial officeholders in La Rochelle and were more likely to receive appointments to the juridiction consulaire than Protestants, adherents of the reformed faith were well represented in both groups. Members from at least five Huguenot families—the Auboyneau, Belin, Dubeignon, Giraudeau, and Suidre—served on the juridiction consulaire prior to the selection of Etienne Jolly and Chanois in 1789.[7] Belins and Seignettes held an assortment of venal offices, and several other families, in addition to the Belins and Seignettes, held titles derived from purchased appointments to the royal mint in La Rochelle. Inclusion of officeholding as a factor in judging economic significance accentuated the role of members of Catholic families who pursued a vocation dominated by Huguenots, while also revealing the officeholding proclivities of Protestant families, a minority of the Rochelais population.

This measure added the leaven of status to the more functional measurement of maritime activities. Concluding the evaluation at this point, however, would have produced results biased in favor of the Catholic families. Investment and management opportunities other than those combined under the rubric of maritime activities were open to the Rochelais. Some families exploited those potentialities, while others did not. Since the opportunities were, in a sense, nontraditional, a measure was added which awarded scores to families who, through affiliation with major corporate institutions, demonstrated a willingness to venture beyond the traditional forms of enterprise.

Most Rochelais négociants affiliated with an individual or group in the formal or informal partnerships described in Chapter 4. This criterion did not recognize those connections. Doing so would not have differentiated among them but would have resulted only in adding *x* units to virtually each one of the ninety families. Instead, families who affiliated with corporate institutions such as insurance companies, refineries, or other businesses, either locally or nonlocally owned, in the capacity of incorporator (owner), director, or agent received credit for that attachment. Those involved with insurance companies or nonlocal firms received twenty units while owners of sugar refineries received thirty-five units. Later chapters describe the economic roles of sugar refining and insurance; here it is only necessary to identify participants in such businesses.

Twenty of the ninety families, sixteen of whom were Protestant, committed capital and managerial skills to corporations. Of the seventy-five families identifiable by religion, forty-eight were Protestant and twenty-seven Catholic. Thirty-three percent of the known Protestants participated in such institutions compared with 15 percent of the Catholics. While the latter displayed a greater propensity than Protestants for noncommercial officeholding and controlled most positions on the juridiction consulaire, Huguenots contributed the greater share of capital and management to such businesses as insurance and sugar refining.

Paul Depont des Granges, in addition to outfitting vessels on his own account during the 1720s, was the salaried resident agent of the Company of the Indies in La Rochelle. Depont managed the company's office and two stores. In 1721 and 1722, Depont handled company business valued at over 800,000 lt. Earlier, he had been the resident director of the La Rochelle branch of the Banque royale and had been responsible for the liquidation of its local transactions.[8]

At least thirteen Rochelais families, of whom ten were Protestant and all but one armateurs, owned sugar refineries. The refinery owners included such leading maritime families as the Rasteau, Belin, Delacroix, and Vivier.[9] Although the refining industry experienced hard times after midcentury, until that time the industry was able to supply large quantities of refined sugars to northern Europe, and La Rochelle ranked among the leading refining centers in France.

Beginning in the late 1740s, a number of Rochelais families established insurance companies or accepted positions as the salaried agents of non-Rochelais firms. Although joint stock maritime insurance companies appeared only on a large scale throughout France at that time, Rochelais had acted as independent underwriters of marine insurance during preceding decades and continued to write insurance independently even after the institution of the company had made its appearance.

Private underwriting may be considered as an alternative to direct investment in maritime ventures as an intéressé. Since underwriting involved most of the families engaged in shipping, and even some who did not invest as intéressés, it does not warrant inclusion as a factor in the index under discussion. However, the investment in and organization and management of a locally chartered insurance company or service as a resident agent of a nonlocal firm both demanded substantial administrative and promotional work. Such firms enhanced the economic strength of the city by increasing the efficiency of maritime operations and attracting outside capital. Agents and local owners assumed added and demanding responsibilities, which required complete knowledge of all facets of an insured venture and the willingness to make hard decisions—thus the inclusion of this activity in the measure of institutional affiliation.

Members of sixteen families were associated with insurance companies. With some exceptions, they have all been encountered before. Three of the families were Catholics—Brusle, Gastumeau, and Surreau, none of which were armateurs. Pierre Morreau l'aîné was the only other nonarmateur in the group of sixteen. Pierre's father, however, had been an armateur in association with his father-in-law Paul Depont and had been an investor in a Rochelais insurance company founded in 1695, about which nothing is known. Admyraulds, de Baussays, Gareschés, and Viviers served as agents of firms headquartered in other cities. Trésahar Bonfils, Théodore Delacroix, Jean Ezeckiel Couillandeau, Louis Perdriau, Pierre Isaac Rasteau, and Emanuel Weis formed a local company in 1751. Etienne Henri Harouard Dubeignon, a Protestant, and Jean Baptiste Gastumeau, a Catholic, jointly launched an insurance venture in 1750.

Insurance or sugar refining did not necessarily require a larger capital investment than shipowning, wholesaling, the commission business, or some combination of those operations. The fixed capital committed to shipping by such armateurs as the Rasteaus or Gareschés exceeded that required to operate a sugar refinery, whereas insurance required no fixed capital at all but merely greater premium receipts than allowable claims. The necessary ingredient of refining entered La Rochelle in great quantities, much of it on vessels owned by the refiners. They simply processed it further before reexport, thus enhancing the product's value and adding to the profits of the importer-refiner-exporter. Capital applied to sugar refining or venture capital, which sustained the insurance industry, might as easily have been committed to shipping or even diverted into rentes, thus essentially removing it from commerce. Instead, investment decisions were made which, by adding a new dimension to the port's functions, increased its attractiveness to outsiders. This criterion differentiates between those who introduced new industries to La Rochelle which attracted both capital and goods and those who, with comparable resources, elected to invest their capital more traditionally.

The final criterion selected, marriage ties, recognizes the role of the kinship group in conserving capital for use by successive generations in the maritime and other economic sectors. Five units were awarded each union after the first marriage; in other words, no units were given for the marriage of Allard Belin to Elizabeth Olivier (see table 3.3), but units did accrue as the children and grandchildren of Allard and Elizabeth married.

In general, the combined factors perform quite well as indicators of economic significance and socioeconomic notability. Discrimination between economic functions was achieved, and distinctions were drawn between positions carrying status and positions of authority. Families whose members appeared particularly enterprising were distinguished from those who pursued traditional routines. Criteria such as longevity in trade (perseverance) and marital alliances assured sensitivity to change over time. The marriage criterion gave weight to the economic functions and consequences of social mechanisms. The Admyraulds, identified in table 3.1 as among the most important families in the city, achieved their prominence through marital alliances, officeholding, investment in shipping, and participation in corporate businesses rather than as armateurs. Others who were leading armateurs during a particular decade, such as Jean Baptiste Nairac and Joachim de Saint Martin during the early 1770s, and Samuel Pierre de Missy and Conrad Achille Weis during the mid-1780s, appear in neither column of table 3.1. The limited scope and duration of their operations subjectively justified the attribution of less importance to them than to the merchants cited in table 3.1. The index corroborates this subjective conclusion.

Incomplete and missing data explain the most serious shortcomings of the index. Data on the intéressés for many vessels were lacking. But this was true for the armements of the Rasteaus, Gareschés, and Belins as well as for the ventures of lesser armateurs. Incompleteness did not skew the findings in favor of the larger armateurs; it simply means that the scores for all were lower, a fact of minimal importance. If a bias resulted it was probably in favor of Catholics. Had all intéressés been known it is unlikely that the Pascauds or Goguets would have ranked quite as high in the final tabulation. On the other hand, in all probability many of the noncommercial offices held by the families remain undiscovered. Since Catholics tended to hold more of those offices than Protestants, any missing data would bias this measure in favor of the Protestants.

The marriage factor might also be criticized for assigning equal value to each union. Certainly some unions provided greater advantages than others—but how to recognize the distinction? Had the size of the dowry been known for each alliance, a differentiation might have been possible, but since such data were lacking for most families, there seemed no alternative but to award equal value.

The absence of at least two crucial factors—real property ownership and failure in business (bankruptcy)—from this measurement of economic notability detracts from its usefulness. In both cases, abundant information was available regarding only a few families. The comparative qualities of the index would have been weakened rather than strengthened by the inclusion of criteria based upon fragmentary evidence. The sections that follow attempt a nonquantitative analysis of both factors.

At the risk of repetitiveness, some general, and perhaps obvious, conclusions about the economic leaders of La Rochelle can now be offered. A handful of families dominated the economic life of the city. Within the sphere of maritime affairs, virtually all of the leading families were Protestant. During the eighteenth century, the Catholic input to the maritime sector declined. By the 1780s, only seven Catholic families served as armateurs. From 1780 to 1789, they outfitted forty-five vessels le long cours, or 13 percent of the Rochelais total, compared with shares ranging from 20 to 25 percent during each of the three decades 1730–39, 1740–49, and 1750–59. Furthermore, during the 1780s, only one Catholic armateur ventured but a single vessel to the Indian Ocean.

Protestants thoroughly controlled the corporate economic institutions that evolved in the city. Of the families participating in corporate business, only four of the twenty were Catholic. Catholics contributed three of thirteen sugar refinery owners and only three of sixteen associates of marine insurance companies. During the 1780s, when scores of Rochelais underwrote insurance on their own account, Catholics provided only 8 percent of the total while underwriting only 5 percent of the risks taken in La Rochelle. Had participation in maritime affairs and involvement in corporate business been the only criteria applied in the index, virtually no Catholics would have appeared in the ranking. Within the Rochelais milieu, Protestants rather than Catholics composed the modernizing vanguard.

By and large, the Catholic families shared dominance as a consequence of their greater success in obtaining offices, both of the functional type such as the Chamber of Commerce or juridiction consulaire and such nonfunctional venal offices as could be purchased from the crown. Catholics, then, enjoyed a more substantial role in decisionmaking that affected commerce than their actual economic contribution to the port's economy warranted. Protestants, however, were by no means excluded from prestigious offices. In any event, Protestant and Catholic négociants, sharing similiar aspirations for their city, presented a united front in promoting the city's fortunes and in defending La Rochelle against the crown and competing ports.

THE PURPOSES OF PROPERTY OWNERSHIP

La Rochelle's négociants owned both local and colonial lands. As with the domestic estates of the Belin and Depont families, such investments directly supported their commercial enterprises through the production of marketable commodities. This is not to say that estate ownership did not satisfy whatever striving for status that may have motivated those families. Quite commonly, however, the desire for status and the quest for secure returns, among other motives, have been assigned primacy.[10] Indeed, Van Hoogwerf, responding to his sister's request to invest funds for her, suggested that they be placed in rentes or the purchase of land. Avoid exposure, counseled Odilé, to possible loss in commerce where investors are at the mercy of unforeseen events.[11] This was sound advice, offered to an individual in comfortable circumstances for whom Pierre Jean felt responsible and who sought only small but certain returns on the investment. It was not the course that Pierre followed when his own capital was involved.[12]

Rochelais négociants invested in rentes derived from lands. In 1753, Jacques Rasteau père purchased from Paul Vivier rentes hypothècaire capitalized at above 30,000 lt. These rentes on local vineyards produced an annual income in brandy of about 9 percent, a very acceptable return from an investment supportive of Rasteau's commerce. In 1774, the estate of Jean Denis le jeune consisted of 18,000 lt. in goods and shares of vessels, 15,000 lt. in mortgage interest on local agricultural lands, and 5,500 lt. in rentes from sources other than land; in other words, perhaps as much as 14 percent of his worth derived from noncommercial investments.[13]

Rochelais local real estate holdings consisted largely of brandy-producing lands and grain lands, salt lands, urban residences, and urban commercial buildings such as stores. The country properties supplied armateurs with produce necessary to their export trade and rental income, frequently paid in kind. The Depont and other Rochelais families owned large tracts of salt marshes on Île de Ré, Île d'Oleron, and to the south of the city. In 1773, veuve Delacroix earned a net income of 25,027 lt. from her salt lands. The Gastumeaus, Van Hoogwerfs, Goguets, and Deverignys, among others, managed wheat lands in Saintonge. Gastumeau, Brusle, Rasteau, and others owned vineyards. Lesser merchants also invested in vineyards. François Tourny, a master buttonmaker, and Julien Germane, a master baker, each owned vineyards worth over 5,000 lt.[14]

The proportion of total capital that La Rochelle's merchants committed to agriculture cannot be determined, but it is certain that Rochelais capital did flow into agricultural and salt lands in the region of the city. One of the serious weaknesses of the French economy, as P. Goubert has perceived it, was the failure to reinvest income from lands in agriculture. Rentiers, according to Goubert, were likely to be absentees who directed their income from lands into other locations and activities.[15] Rochelais négociants did return to the agricultural economy a portion of their profits from landholdings and commerce.

During the seventeenth and eighteenth centuries, numerous Rochelais families acquired plantations in the Antilles, and a few even had shares in Louisiana properties or owned lands in Canada. Merchants from Bordeaux,

Nantes, and other French cities also established plantations. As did the Nantais, many Rochelais purchased these lands in an effort to guarantee a minimal return for their maritime ventures, an objective explicitly stated in Van Hoogwerf's plans for a Cayenne plantation. As J. Meyer observed regarding Nantes's négociants, an untoward result of plantation ownership was the compulsion to continue the slave trade and to commit greater resources to that trade. While Meyer has produced statements by Nantais to that effect that were lacking for La Rochelle, there is every reason to assume that similar purposes motivated the Rochelais, especially after the War of the American Revolution.[16] Not only did the Rochelais invest a greater proportion of their resources in the slave trade—31 percent of their outfits from 1780 to 1789 compared to 20 percent from 1740 to 1749 and 25 percent from 1770 to 1779 (see table 2.3)—but during the early years of the French Revolution, Samuel deMissy stood alone among all Rochelais merchants in supporting the abolition of the slave trade.[17]

Plantation-owning families from among ninety families included: J. C. Garnier, who owned a refinery and coffee works as well as a plantation on Santo Domingo; the Auboyneaus, who owned four coffee plantations valued at 732,000 lt.; Jean Baptiste Charles Belin, who owned a plantation during the 1720s; Paul Belin Desmarais, who worked a large indigo plantation (with 169 slaves in 1763), as did Allard Belin fils; Daniel and Jacques Garesché, who possessed two sugar plantations valued at 1.2 million lt.; Jean Aubin and Jean Samuel Dumoustier de Fredilly, who each held extensive lands near Port-au-Prince during the 1780s; the Seignettes, who were proprietors of a coffee plantation; Jacques Bernon, who in 1744 inherited lands in Santo Domingo worth 51,600 lt.; the widow Labbé, who in 1748 received 21,000 lt. worth of indigo in one cargo from her estate on Martinique; and Pommier and Bonneau, who jointly owned an estate on Martinique during the 1720s and the 1730s. The Rasteau, Gastumeau, Poupet, Carayon, Guibert, and Paillet families also possessed colonial estates.[18] At least seven of the leading armateurs, then, operated colonial plantations that had demanded a substantial initial capital outlay.

In purchasing plantations in the West Indies, Rochelais merchants sought guaranteed markets for some of their African captives and assured cargoes of colonial staples for their vessels. At the least, produce from their plantations supplemented the colonial trade upon which the merchants depended; for some, perhaps the Garesché or others with large holdings, the guaranteed returns may have formed a major part of their cargoes. Other families, such as the Bernon, Rasteau, Belin, and Labbé who owned sugar refineries, probably utilized their own harvest.

In the aggregate, domestically owned lands probably contributed less to the total commerce of individual armateurs than their colonial holdings. Armateurs who owned both plantations and refineries managed economic operations that achieved some of the purposes sought by industrial firms through vertical integration more than a century later.

COMMERCIAL FAILURES IN LA ROCHELLE

Each of the factors utilized to identify the economic elite of La Rochelle and to measure their relative significance represents achievement and success. Vessels readied for departure, election or appointment to various functional offices, sufficient wealth to purchase an office or to initiate a business, perhaps even marriage, all connote accomplishment. The measure's bias toward success and its indifference to failure ought to be made congruent with life's actualities by the inclusion of a negative factor that would deduct units in proportion to the seriousness of the failure experiences. Not all armements returned a profit to the armateur or to the intéressés. Some, but certainly not all, of the less fortunate ventures were known. A sequence of individual failures could and did lead to bankruptcy, often prolonged and psychologically debilitating. Archival sources provided fairly detailed information on a minority of known bankruptcies, and the probability exists that many bankruptcies remain undiscovered. Since Rasteau's insolvency never surfaced publicly, all information concerning it remained in private hands (collections), where its discovery was a matter of chance rather than becoming part of the public record. Such uncertainties counsel against any arithmetical procedure purporting to measure failure. But the threat of bankruptcy loomed over La Rochelle's merchants and crashed down upon many. Failure was a fact of economic life.

When debts, large or small, could not be paid, the law required the merchant to sign and deposit a declaration of insolvency at the juridiction consulaire. After each creditor had received a financial statement detailing the total assets and liabilities of the bankrupt, the creditors or their representatives met to appoint a committee charged with the liquidation of the business and the distribution of assets. Rochelais frequently accepted commissions from nonlocal creditors to proceed against debtors. Jacques Bradshaw of Bordeaux commissioned Noordingh & Domus in 1745 to recover debts from Joseph Laurent Beltremieux.[19] Normally, outside creditors accepted the opinions of local agents on how best to proceed.

During this period, the bankrupt could not hold public office or dispose of any property. The bankrupt could apply to the comptroller general, however, through the office of the intendant, for a *lettre de réprit* or *arrêt de surcéance* (safe conduct) which granted the debtor a period of six months during which no proceedings could be taken against him or her. Even if the comptroller general approved the safe conduct prior to the meeting of all creditors, the debtor was legally obligated to notify them. The creditors could then meet and form a committee to supervise the bankrupt's operations. The committee possessed the authority to disapprove of particular ventures and to devise a schedule for the repayment of debts.[20]

Rochelais procedure adhered closely to the law. Much depended upon the general reputation of the bankrupt both in La Rochelle and elsewhere. The business of Rochelais négociants encompassed a good part of the Atlantic world, and the Pacific as well, with creditors and debtors scattered about from the Hanse cities to the Indian Ocean. In many cases of bankruptcy, the insolvent merchant stood creditor to others for sums more than sufficient to repay all debts. In the port cities, merchants with debts due in Europe experienced great difficulties in collecting from debtors in the colonies. Serious obstacles reflecting weaknesses in the structure of the colonial trade as well as slow communications impaired the quick collection of outstanding debts. All of these factors entered into the recommendation of the intendant, the closest royal official to the scene, to the comptroller general regarding the issuance of a safe conduct and the policies adopted by local committees of creditors. Each committee member must have been aware of his own vulnerability.

Bankrupt merchants in La Rochelle often resorted to arrêts de surcéance. Unless fraud was involved, it was likely that most merchants applied successfully for safe conducts. Freedom from civil action, permitting the insolvent to pursue his business and deal with his debtors, often proved the means of avoiding total failure and facilitated recovery. When the Lepage brothers failed in 1790, they frantically applied to the intendant for an arrêt de surcéance, informing him that their creditors hovered about, forcing them to remain at home instead of working at their shipyard.[21]

Sometime during the late 1760s, the La Rochelle Chamber of Commerce became formally involved in the procedure governing the application for safe conduct. Apparently, négociants habitually requested letters of recommendation from the chamber attesting to their good behavior and honesty. In 1770 the value of this was formally acknowledged and, thereafter, surcéances were issued only after the opinion of the chamber had been solicited. Bankrupts or merchants who feared its imminence regularly applied to the chamber for support and normally obtained it. Only one case of rejection came to light, and in that case the vote for and against divided so evenly that the intendant issued a stay after consultation with the comptroller general.[22]

If recovery followed, even after the passage of many years, the merchant applied to the crown for *lettres de réhabilitation*. These were issued only when the creditors attested that the bankrupt had honored all agreements relative to the payment of debts. In 1784, eighteen years after declaring bankruptcy, the onus of insolvency was lifted from Paillet & Meynardie, and they were freed from future suits against past indebtedness. As per agreement with their creditors, the firm had repaid 48 percent of their debts with 15 percent interest.[23]

The incidence of business failure in La Rochelle and in the rest of France accurately reflected extralocal pressures and crises, national and international. Prior to 1745, however, only fragmentary data survived concerning failure in La Rochelle. The brutal deflation of 1713–15 and the collapse of Law's company, followed by another period of deflation and monetary adjustments, caused failures throughout France. During the Regency years, eight to ten

Rochelais bankruptcies were reported annually while in Nantes many small merchants failed.[24] Perhaps major families in La Rochelle also experienced failure, but if so they must have recovered quickly because the dominant armateurs continued to make their outfits during those troubled times.

Severe economic dislocation accompanied the War of the Austrian Succession. From January 1, 1749 through June 9, 1753, twenty-one individuals and firms, including several of the city's larger comptoirs, declared bankruptcy, acknowledging debts that totaled 3.5 million lt.[25] Registrations of bankruptcy at the juridiction consulaire failed to include at least six additional failures, which occurred between 1749 and 1753. Of the twenty-seven known failures, eight—Pierre Blavout, Jacques Garesché, J. Arnauld, and Chabot l'aîné, all from the admiralty list, and Pierre Hardy, J. L. Beltremieux, Simon Lapointe, and Henri Brevet—were from among the ninety leading families; only Garesché, however, came from a family included in table 3.1.

Only the indebtedness of those listed in the admiralty records is known. Blavout suffered the largest failure, involving debts of over two million lt. while Arnauld's debts reached 415,000 lt., Garesché's, 288,000 lt., and Chabot's, 168,000 lt. All had suffered severe wartime losses. Hardy had lost two vessels to the English and died shortly after he declared bankruptcy, while Chabot lost a vessel worth 43,000 lt. and its cargo. Other merchants fell as a result of poor markets or defaulting debtors in the colonies and elsewhere. Unsettled times compelled each merchant to press his own debtors for payment, thus applying abnormal pressure all along the credit line. Garesché, caught in this bind, sold two of his ships at auction in order to meet the urgent demands of his creditors.

Blavout's failure resulted from poor management, overextension of his resources, and fraud. During the few years in which he operated in La Rochelle, 1745 to 1749, Blavout made fourteen armements, eight in 1749. He risked virtually no funds of his own in his ventures, even though the statements of intéressés indicated that he held sizable shares. Later investigations revealed inaccuracies in his accounts. Blavout used intéressé investments to meet personal obligations and charges against past armements. Giving the appearance of solvency, he deluded creditors and intéressés alike by shifting the same funds from account to account. Besides tampering with his accounts, his ventures were inefficiently organized and managed and normally suffered from very poor sales. Blavout covered up his poor returns by using funds from ongoing voyages to make nominal payments to intéressés of concluded voyages. His declaration of bankruptcy neglected over 300,000 lt. of indebtedness. The puncturing of the Blavout bubble caused great distress and consternation in the city, for many individuals stood to lose significant sums, including Garesché and Bessie de la Barthe, both of whom had extended credit for the outfitting of Blavout's ventures. His failure was the most serious in the city's history, precipitating a notorious scandal and a flurry of litigation, some of which remained unsettled as late as 1787.[26]

The good times of the 1750s rapidly healed the wounds of the struggling merchants. Jacques Garesché and Chabot recovered completely, and Pierre Hardy's widow and son made every effort to pay their debts. The economic difficulties of the late 1740s caused no permanent damage to La Rochelle. But the good times were all too fleeting. Severe economic dislocation occurred during and after the Seven Years' War, the crisis overlapping with and exacerbating the depressive effects of the War of the American Revolution and the troubled years that followed. Persistent economic instability punctuated by brief periods of acute crisis threatened the city's economic foundations during the period between 1756 and 1789, weakening many of the oldest and strongest family comptoirs and bringing total ruin to others.

While the peace of 1763 promised surcease from the heavy blows struck by England on the high seas and in the colonies, La Rochelle's merchants emerged but unsteadily to face an uncertain future. Shipping losses, especially during the first years of the war, had cost the city dearly—twenty vessels had been captured between 1755 and 1757, and armements had virtually ceased after 1758 (except for those of the Rasteaus, who paid heavily). Insurance covered only a small part of the losses because wartime premiums ranged from 30 to 50 percent of the amounts insured. More crippling, particularly for the Rochelais, and resulting in the loss of huge sums, were the policies of the royal government toward its debts in the colonies.

In 1759, the crown suspended payment on letters of exchange drawn by resident colonial agents of French merchants against the royal treasury. This repudiationist policy prevented merchants from collecting debts owed them by the royal government for supplies shipped to the colonies and for vessels leased to the crown. Suspension seriously depleted the supply of money in the colonies (inadequate even in the best of times), thus obstructing French merchants in the collection of colonial debts. Even planters who regularly met their obligations to Rochelais merchants lacked the ready cash to pay their creditors. With the English firmly in control of the sea lanes, payments in kind piled up uselessly in colonial ports or, in desperation, were sold to English and North American merchant vessels, which regularly plied French and Spanish colonial waters with impunity. Then, in 1765, came the crowning blow—the cession of Canada to England and Louisiana to Spain. In the long run, this abandonment boded great ill for La Rochelle; in the short run, the cessions brought disaster. The royal government partially repudiated its debts in those places and immediately ceased its financial backing of those economies. Not only were Canada and Louisiana removed from the French sphere of interest, but up to 50 percent of debts owed the Rochelais were simply erased, all of which struck heavily at Pierre Isaac Rasteau and other Rochelais who had actively participated in the trade with Canada and Louisiana.

Between 1769 and 1772, as the consequences of colonial losses, debt repudiation, liquidation of the war, and earlier failures (1762 and 1763) of commercial houses in London, Amsterdam, and Hamburg, impinged upon La

Rochelle, some thirty Rochelais merchants suspended payments. Polycarpe Bourgine, heavily committed in Louisiana; Paillet & Meynardie (their bankruptcy stemming directly from the partial repudiation of the Canadian debt); J. Manie; Jean Bedenc; Meschinet de Richemond & de Missy, all succumbed in 1771 and 1772. Within another year Thomas Delaire and others had fallen. Pierre Jean Van Hoogwerf in 1773 confided to his sister that business derangement and failures made him tremble for his own solvency. Hardly had a modicum of stability reasserted itself than another war erupted. By 1779, according to Van Hoogwerf, La Rochelle had been crushed by the war; its most substantial comptoirs lay in ruins or were seriously threatened.[27]

Each failure reverberated through the Rochelais economy as the effects of one merchant's downfall undermined the position of his creditors and associates. The creditors of Paillet & Meynardie, in agreeing to a repayment of 63 percent of the total debt, accepted a 37 percent loss. Isaac Garasché and Jacques Rasteau fils aîné, both intéressé for 24 percent in an armement of the bankrupts, each lost 8,800 lt. on the venture. Bedenc's failure caused J. Manie, who failed also, and J. B. Nairac to sustain large losses. Both Delaire and Manie were indebted to Claude Etienne Belin, who was also carrying Pierre Isaac Rasteau, the latter a major creditor of Paillet & Meynardie.[28]

By 1779, the shock waves of a new war had broken over La Rochelle, a war more severe in its consequences for the city than preceding conflicts. The Dutch were belligerents, and English cruisers mercilessly harassed traffic to northern Europe and the Baltic Sea. Dutch and Hanse purchases at La Rochelle during the four years 1777–80 declined by nearly 50 percent compared with their purchases from 1772 to 1775. Although Rochelais ventures to the Antilles declined slightly from peacetime levels, they remained far higher than during the last years of the Seven Years' War. But the risks faced by vessels moving to and from the north negated the advantages gained by means of French naval parity in American waters. Van Hoogwerf estimated in 1779 that 500 houses were for sale in the city but that no market existed for property and he implied that people were moving away from La Rochelle. In that year another round of failures commenced, continuing unabated during the 1780s and involving the fall of some of the city's most substantial houses.[29]

In 1777, Joanne de Saint Martin and Thiolliere Brothers & Company stopped payments. In the following year, Elie Vivier fils aîné avoided bankruptcy only by obtaining an agreement from his creditors to postpone collections until two years after the war. Augustin Bridault filed bankruptcy papers in 1779. An inflationary spiral, spawned by a new series of government loans occasioned by the declaration of war in 1779, forced Rochelais merchants to adopt a cautious posture toward maritime investments, especially with regard to supplying goods and services to the crown. As in Normandy, Rochelais merchants reduced their inventories, cut back on credits extended, and sent out ships with minimal cargoes. Van Hoogwerf sorrowfully reported in 1783 that such precautions enabled him to survive the war with losses of only 59,000 lt. If the war had kept him from achieving much, he hoped in 1782 that good times would soon return and restore his and the city's prospects.[30]

Peace came, only to be accompanied by even greater maladjustments and disappointments. Van Hoogwerf's losses staggered him. Failures were reported throughout France in 1783. The widow Admyrauld & Sons stopped payments in that year, with debts of over one million lt., a failure resulting from the fall of a Parisian firm speculating in joint stock company shares. By the end of 1784, Augustin Leclerq, de Richemond & Garnault, and Elie Seignette had declared bankruptcy. Disaster struck at all levels. Etienne Jousselin, a clothing merchant in La Rochelle for thirty-seven years, lost his business in 1784 at age 75, and begged the Chamber of Commerce for aid for his family of eleven children. The unemployed wandered through the streets.[31]

Some of the failures resulted from business miscalculations as much as from external pressures. Many merchants in the city viewed the United States as a market of great potential value, one that would more than compensate for the cessions of Canada and Louisiana. Relatives and friends of Rochelais conducted businesses in New York, Philadelphia, and elsewhere. But for some reason Rochelais armateurs ventured cargoes in total ignorance of actual market demands. Leclerq sent 80,000 lt. in fancy silks, candies, and other highpriced items in two vessels to New England, but the goods were so illchosen and sales so lethargic that the captain returned to La Rochelle with the cargo virtually untouched. Not until several other ventures to the United States met with similar discouraging results did enthusiasm cool toward that market.

Meschinet de Richemond & Garnault, too, plunged into the United States market but in addition ventured widely elsewhere. They attempted too much. In the four years 1781–84, they dispatched twelve vessels, two to Île de France, five to the Antilles, two to the Grand Banks, one to Angola for slaves, and one to New England. They also invested heavily in the armements of others, including Vivier's ill-fated *la Reine de Golconde,* and borrowed heavily, particularly from Garnault's father-in-law, P. C. Lambert of Paris, to purchase vessels and finance their operations. The New England armement failed totally. Slaves transported from Angola to the islands were all sold on credit, while their agent in Martinque turned out to be a thief. By 1784, owing Lambert over 100,000 lt. and others unknown sums, they stopped payment. By 1786, their debts had been reduced by over 200,000 lt., but Garnault prepared to move to Santo Domingo to start a business and further reduce their debts. Although several Rochelais creditors opposed the issuance of a third arrêt de surcéance, the intendant, cognizant of their unceasing efforts to pay their creditors, supported their application.[32]

As Garnault made his way to Santo Domingo in 1787, Dumontier & Dejarnac failed for 500,000 lt., Louis Vivier for 400,000 lt., Fleuriau Brothers & Thouron Co. tumbled, Benjamin Giraudeau failed for 600,000 lt., and

Jacques Carayon fils aîné, Weis & Sons, Dumoustier de Fredilly, and Wilkens Brothers also stopped payments. Not all creditors suffered total losses. Creditors of Weis & Sons took only a 10 percent loss and Carayon's debt only reached 40,000 lt. But creditors of Vivier and Dumontier & Dejarnac watched helplessly as 60 percent of their credits evaporated. The fate of the others and their creditors are not known.[33]

Many of the bankrupt armateurs had invested heavily in the slave trade, a traffic that commanded a rising proportion of La Rochelle's capital and accounted for 31 percent of the city's armements during the 1780s (see table 2.4). The Weis firm, as an example, had abandoned the commission business after the American Revolution and plunged into the slave trade. In the single year 1786, Weis & Sons prepared three vessels for Guinea, followed by two more in 1787. Dumoustier de Fredilly outfitted three slavers in 1786, two in 1787, and two in 1788. Dumontier & Dejarnac sent three slavers in 1786 and 1787.[34] The most treacherous and expensive of all the trades, slaving necessitated the granting of large credits in order to makes sales in the Antilles. Small returns drifted in slowly over long periods of time. Négociants, pressed by an inflationary spiral and dunned by their own creditors, suffered a scarcity of working capital because of uncollected colonial debts. Even when their assets exceeded their liabilities, they could go under as a result of this inability to turn credits into hard cash.[35]

During the 1780s, many of the older négociant-armateurs passed from the commercial scene. Death, retirement, and bankruptcy reduced their ranks. Two decades of war and radical economic fluctuations, the loss of Canada and Louisiana, repudiationist policies of the royal government and its obvious insolvency, all contributed to the erosion of the strength of La Rochelle's comptoirs. The exaggerated focus on the slave trade spread capital investments thin as did ventures to the Indian Ocean. Of all agricultural systems, none was as dependent upon credit as the plantation-slave system. Although a heightened demand for slaves in the Antilles (and in Spanish Louisiana) prevailed during the 1780s, payments stretched out over several crop seasons or longer. Rochelais merchants did not turn their attention to the potentials of northern European markets as destinations for their ships, nor did they attempt to gain a larger share of the petit cabotage. While some looked to the United States as a new market, early disappointment stifled that effort. La Rochelle's négociants, then, concentrated their attention on what they knew best. Times were hard but ships could not remain idle. Traditional trades had succeeded before.

CONCLUSION

The commerce of La Rochelle depended upon the activities of a proportionately smaller group of individuals and families than did the commerce of such major competitors as Marseilles, Bordeaux, and Nantes. The dominant families of La Rochelle, largely Huguenot, outfitted a high proportion of the high-seas vessels, monopolized such economic areas as insurance and sugar refining, and frequently owned agricultural lands in the vicinity of the city as well as in the colonies. Protestant and Catholic merchant families filled most of the critical offices in the chamber, admiralty, and municipal government. In addition, they possessed numerous venal offices of high prestige. Catholics held a higher number of offices, both functional and nonfunctional, than merited by their participation in the maritime sector. In this oligopolistic structure, the intermarriage of dominant families welded the parts together into powerful kinship groups dedicated to providing economic opportunity to succeeding generations.

The system performed well during good times and provided a buffer against the shock of bad times. But, beginning with the outbreak of the Seven Years' War and continuing through the War of the American Revolution into the 1780s, hard times prevailed. The economic repercussions of these crises, including the abandonment of Canada and Louisiana, sapped the strength of the Rochelais elite. Newcomers did not fill the vacuum. The Rochelais system effectively excluded them even during periods of prosperity. After the mid-1760s, numerous major comptoirs in La Rochelle succumbed. The 1780s were particularly harsh on many old and renowned Rochelais family businesses.

The Rochelais strove valiantly to recoup their losses and win the future. Great slaving ventures were launched and giant vessels sailed to the Indian Ocean. But, within a few years, these would be trades of the past, and La Rochelle would be a port of the past.

SIX

The Organization of the Colonial Trade: Preparation, Costs, and Participation in Maritime Ventures

Moving large cargoes, human and material, back and forth across the ocean was hazardous under the best of conditions. Armateurs in La Rochelle and elsewhere strove to minimize risks through the efficient organization and constant scrutiny of their affairs. Seaworthy vessels could be selected and the best of captains put under contract. The most suitable trade goods were obtained through correspondents of known reputations. Négociants guarded against overextension of their capital resources yet sought to utilize those resources to maximum benefit. Merchants realized that much remained beyond their control. Not only did storms, tropical disease, or slave mutinies cause delays, damage, destruction, and death, but the vessel, once at sea, passed beyond the effective control of its manager and owners. Once at sea a venture fell under the control of agents, and despite the most complete instructions furnished by the armateur concerning the ports to call at, the disposal of goods, and the procurement of a return cargo, much was left to chance.

News traveled only as rapidly as ships. Markets with high demand when the voyage commenced might be glutted when the vessel arrived; demand might have shifted from cloths to hardware. Poor crops lowered consumer demand and necessitated long credits. Fevers could kill one quarter of a slave cargo. Captains and correspondents might exercise poor judgment. A trusted agent might die or go bankrupt. Colonial officials might condemn the vessel. The sudden threat of war might fill the sea lanes with enemy privateers.

The Rasteaus, Bonneaus, and others, through long experience, broad contacts, reputation, and attention to detail, faced and surmounted recurring crises. Organization was the key. The recruitment and training of management personnel, from within the kinship network when possible, to serve both at home and abroad, the development of reliable sources of supply and credits, close attention to the procedures and costs of armement and désarmement, links with sources of information about prices, business conditions, and the commercial policies of France and elsewhere, all of these and other factors demanded the unwavering concern of the négociant.

SOURCES OF SUPPLY FOR EXPORTS TO THE COLONIES

Goods from France, northern Europe, and India flowed into La Rochelle for reexport to West Africa and the West Indies, Louisiana, and Canada. La Rochelle possessed neither a local manufacturing base of any real significance for the export trade nor a back country which contributed substantial quantities of goods for export. Local brandies comprised about 20 percent of exports during most years in the eighteenth century, but beyond that and small quantities of miscellaneous items produced in the immediate area, the Rochelais depended upon external sources of supply.[1]

Each sector of the overseas trade—the West African coast, the Antilles, the North American mainland, and the East Indies—required special assortments of goods.[2] Textile products composed the single most important category of trade goods to the West Indian and mainland colonies. Manufactured clothing, yard goods, draperies, handkerchiefs, linens, silks, and the like flowed into La Rochelle from Holland, the North, French textile centers such as Rouen, and, through French middlemen, from the Indian subcontinent and China. Imports of assorted manufactured cloth from Holland fluctuated in their value from year to year: in 1749, assorted cloths composed 28 percent of the total value of imports from Holland, in 1771, 7 percent, in 1774, 40 percent, and in 1776, 27 percent. French manufacturers and middlemen normally provided most of the textile products. During the first half of the eighteenth century, textiles often exceeded one-half of total exports to Africa and the colonies. The relative importance of cloth declined in later years, falling during the 1770s to under 50 percent in the colonial trade and below 40 percent in the African trade. Simultaneously, the export value of foodstuffs, wine and brandies, and other manufactured goods rose.

Brandy, the only major export that the Rochelais region supplied, composed roughly the same proportion of exports to Africa and to the Atlantic colonies during the first half of the century. By the 1770s, however, exports of brandy formed a greater proportion of cargoes made up for the slave trade than for the direct colonial trade. In 1776, for instance, brandies accounted for 21 percent of the value of all exports to Africa compared with 1 percent to the colonies.

Cauris (cowry), an item unique to the Guinea trade, consisted of strung seashells and served as a form of currency in West Africa.[3] The Rochelais obtained most of their cowry from Holland and it normally contributed between 5 to 10 percent of the total annual value of Dutch exports to La Rochelle. The declining role of cowry in the slave trade can be attributed to the rising demand of black middlemen for real goods and to the relatively weak position of the French along the African coast vis-a-vis English or Dutch, which frequently compelled French slavers to purchase their cargoes from Europeans.

Slaving vessels carried large quantities of cotton goods, originally obtained exclusively from India but quickly imitated by French and Dutch manufacturers. Indiennes, as the cloth was called—*rayées* (striped cottons) and *ramages* (prints)—were all manufactured in Rouen, Montpellier, and Nantes as well as in English, Dutch, and German cities.[4] In 1741, the Rochelais slaver *l'Aimable Esther* loaded a barter cargo valued at 66,495 lt. of which 25 percent consisted of goods from India and the East Indies, 18 percent originated in Holland, 17 percent were brandies for La Rochelle's immediate region, and the remainder consisted of manufactured items, gunpowder, and rifles from a variety of places, mostly in France. *Le Meulan,* embarking upon its first slave voyage in 1776, carried a cargo valued at 170,210 lt. Rouen supplied 21 percent of all goods, the rest of France, 12 percent, India, 10 percent, Holland, 30 percent, and the United Kingdom, 20 percent. Louis Vivier's venture to Angola in 1786 with *la Reine de Golconde* required a cargo worth 196,811 lt. Goods from India composed 17 percent of the cargo while 75 percent of the remainder originated in France.[5]

These cargoes reflected the importance of northern European and French manufacturing centers as suppliers of trade goods. Cargoes destined for the French colonies required no cowry, included greater amounts of foodstuffs, and utilized superior qualities of textiles products. In addition, they frequently included lumber and staves, pitch and tar, soap, lard, candles, and a wide variety of manufactured items.

Cargoes destined for the East Indies diverged markedly from the pattern of the Atlantic trade. While the composition of the trade goods resembled that sent to the other colonies, the value of the goods represented but a small portion of the value of the cargo. Since trade in India and China required cash payments for goods, specie became the principal cargo. Between 1772 and 1778, nine private French vessels carried cargoes to the Indian Ocean in which specie constituted 68 percent of total value and goods 24 percent. Eleven vessels belonging to the second Company of the Indies, which journeyed to the Indian Ocean in 1785 and 1786, carried 15 million lt. in specie and 895,000 lt. in goods. Rochelais armateurs engaged in trade to those waters followed similar practices. Jean Baptiste Nairac prepared during the 1780s a prospectus for a venture to India in which specie and letters of exchange for collection would make up to 80 percent of the cargo.[6]

Of necessity, La Rochelle's armateurs maintained extensive contacts throughout northern Europe and in Great Britain. Pierre Jean Van Hoogwerf's correspondence in 1785 may serve as one example. During that year he wrote at least 344 letters concerning the outfitting of five vessels among other business matters. He forwarded 22 letters to Amsterdam, 8 to German cities, 22 to other foreign cities, 16 to Paris, 16 to Rouen, 11 to Bordeaux, 11 to Abbeville, and so on through Rochefort, Saint-Malo, Dieppe, Lille, Nantes, and other French communities. Similarly, Meschinet de Richemond wrote hundreds of letters to Geneva, Lübeck, Hamburg, Bremen, Neuchatel, Amsterdam, Dijon, Amiens, Caen, and Bordeaux as he ordered goods for his overseas ventures, arranged for sales of colonial goods, negotiated exchange, placed goods belonging to other merchants on outbound vessels, made insurance, and pursued other routine business.[7]

The relationships between Rochelais merchants and their correspondents and agents were extraordinarily complex. Théodore Delacroix carried on an extensive import and export business with the Amsterdam firm Jean Cossart & Sons & Bouvier during the 1730s. The Amsterdam company filled Delacroix's orders for cowry, Russian furs, textiles, iron, and wooden products from Sweden and also ordered goods for German merchants to be placed on the Dutch account on Delacroix's vessels. Delacroix sold goods for the accunt of the Amsterdam firm, purchased colonial goods and brandy and wine for its account, and forwarded similar goods to it for sale on his account. Goods and services flowed back and forth, and both firms were debited or credited as operations terminated. But the monetary value of these transactions remains unknown, for the few pages of Delacroix's account book are indecipherable, kept as they were in some system of accounting that only he and his clerk understood.[8] The infrequent notation of transfers of money forms a striking feature of the whole process.

Earlier studies have demonstrated that specie transfer played a less central role in business transactions than that of exchange. In La Rochelle, as in other ports or manufacturing centers, merchants used the letter of exchange as their principal means of making payment for goods and services received. Letters served both for remittance and as instruments of credit, but some doubt exists as to which of those two functions was primary.[9] The Rochelais drafted or purchased letters both as a convenient form of remittance and as a credit device. Specie served as a means of making local payments for wages, salaries, désarmement, taxes, goods and services obtained locally, and of making extralocal payments only if specie was demanded or if payment in specie purchased superior terms. As in Marseilles, however, specie served principally as a commodity, to be bought and sold as any other commodity.[10] Only those armateurs involved in the trade with the Îles de France and Bourbon required large sums of specie for monetary purposes.

Rochelais merchants also bought and sold letters of exchange in an effort to turn a profit. Louis Charuyer purchased three letters in 1756 from de Richemond. These were letters drawn by unspecified third parties indebted to de Richemond upon other individuals, the drawees, who were indebted to the drawers. The letters were made payable to de Richemond, who, needing cash, sold them to Charuyer at a discount. He forwarded them to P. C. Lambert in Paris for collection. The difference between the price paid to de Richemond and the face value constituted Charuyer's profit. Cargoes to the Antilles and the Indian Ocean frequently included letters of exchange for collection, some of which had been purchased for speculation.[11]

Such operations and others—merchants functioning as local collection agents for non-Rochelais—sustain the observation that "in merchant capitalism banking was inseparable from trade."[12] Jean Bordier of La Rochelle dealt exclusively in the exchange market and was called a banker, but Belin, Rasteau, Depont, and virtually all other Rochelais négociants also operated in national and international exchange markets. It was merely a matter of degree and the shifting of roles as circumstances warranted. Paul Depont des Granges through the 1720s and 1730s, and Meschinet de Richemond and Van Hoogwerf during the 1770s and 1780s, managed the investment portfolios of investors throughout France and northern Europe. At those times they performed banking functions. Louis Vivier, Elie Seignette, Pierre Boudet, in need of specie for one purpose or another, negotiated letters of exchange through Bordelais bankers. Simultaneously, Vivier sold 1,000 piasters for Jean Pellet, merchant of Bordeaux. La Rochelle's specie needs were frequently filled by Bordelais merchants David Gradis, Pellet, Paul Nairac (brother of Rochelais Jean Baptiste Nairac), and the banker Da Silva. Banking and mercantile functions were indeed intertwined.[13]

BUSINESS SPECIALIZATION AMONG ROCHELAIS MERCHANTS

La Rochelle's dominant négociants performed a wide variety of business functions, acting sometimes on their own account and risk and sometimes as agents—brokers or commission agents—for other merchants or private individuals. During wartime, the négociants frequently served as agents of the crown, leasing vessels or readying freight or supplies for shipment to colonial posts. Specialists did exist in La Rochelle as some firms bought and sold solely on commission and some individuals functioned only as *courtiers de change* (exchange brokers) or dealt only in a single commodity, such as brandy or grain. By and large, these individuals did not rank among the leading merchants and rarely counted among the holders of prestigious local offices. In larger cities with great centers of international exchange operations such as Paris, Bordeaux, or Marseilles, specialists evolved more rapidly and were more visible in smaller places such as La Rochelle, Dieppe, or Saint-Malo. During the eighteenth century, Rochelais merchants more and more frequently hired their services. But Rochelais merchants also performed most of the specialty services in addition to carrying on the high seas trade.[14] Brokerage, insurance underwriting, and banking were dispersed throughout the entire business establishment of the city.

Specialization might also involve concentration on one trade more than another. It is well known that armateurs in La Rochelle and other major French ports committed their vessels to the slave trade, the colonial carrying trade, and cod fishing. Goods imported from and exported to Great Britain, Holland, and other northern European destinations traveled largely on foreign bottoms. Just as le grande cabotage utilized non-Rochelais vessels, so too did nonlocal vessels dominate le petit cabotage. But this does not mean that Rochelais armateurs, although not owners, were uninvolved in this shipping. During the 1720s, Abraham Delacroix, André Perdriau, Jean de Butler, and Paul Depont des Granges all managed non-Rochelais ships engaged in le grande cabotage, while during the 1780s, Daniel Garesché, Pierre Jean Van Hoogwerf, Jacques Carayon fils aîné, Nicolas Schaaft, and Jacques Gilbert did the same. But their actual financial investment, if any, is unknown. At the least, the armateurs received commissions for their services which may have formed a substantial part of their incomes.[15]

Tables 2.2 through 2.4 summarized the magnitude and general trade orientation of La Rochelle's high seas shipping. The discussion that follows shifts the focus from general trends to the specific trade concentrations of Rochelais armateurs. Three periods will be analyzed in detail, 1727–31, 1740–49, and 1780–89, in an effort to discover if some Rochelais armateurs favored one branch of trade over another and if trade with specific places tended to concentrate in the hands of a few armateurs. The gross data are presented in table 6.1.

Before probing the implications of the table, a supplementary point might be made. Table 2.3 indicates that the Rochelais outfitted 427 vessels from 1740 to 1749 and 345 from 1780 to 1789. The figures in table 6.1 for corresponding years are 370 and 282. The latter armements were owned in whole or in part by La Rochelle's négociants. The difference between the two sets of figures—57 in the first period and 63 in the second—reflects an approximation of the number of vessels outfitted at La Rochelle by Rochelais armateurs but owned by non-Rochelais.

Table 6.1. Number of Rochelais armateurs Engaged in Various Trades, 1727–31, 1740–49, and 1780–89

	1727–31		1740–49		1780–89	
	No. of departures	No. of armateurs	No. of departures	No. of armateurs	No. of departures	No. of armateurs
Santo Domingo	105	25	159	50	90	28
Cayenne	5	3	12	8	6	4
Martinique	2	2	36	21	13	12
Guadeloupe	2	1	1	1	3	2
Louisiana	1	1	46	24	0	0
Canada	28	9	45	16	0	0
Africa	12	8	71	26	100	22
East Indies	0	0	0	0	21	10
Grand Banks	?	?	?	?	46	16
United States	0	0	0	0	3	3
Total	155	30	370	64	282	49

Source: Registre des Sousmissions, ACM, Série B247, 250–51, 259–59bis.

It is obvious from table 6.1 that the Antillean trade (the first four places listed), of which the slave trade was a major part, dominated maritime activities in La Rochelle.[16] But within the general Antillean trade some islands counted more than others. In the direct trade, Santo Domingo continued as the favored destination, but by the 1780s, increasing numbers of Rochelais vessels trafficked for slaves prior to journeying to the Antilles. Most slavers headed for Santo Domingo upon obtaining their full complement of human cargo. Direct trade to Canada ceased after the Seven Years' War, and trade to Louisiana had disappeared by the 1780s. Simultaneously, while the East Indies claimed a greater share of resources, the promise of a vigorous trade with the newly independent United States failed to materialize.

Vessels prepared for direct voyages to the Antilles declined from 73 percent of all armements in 1727–31 to 56 percent in 1740–49 and to 40 percent during the 1780s. In each period a high percentage of all armateurs operating in La Rochelle participated in that trade. During the earliest period, seven shippers accounted for 80 of the 114 ventures to the Antilles, with Jacques Rasteau leading with 19 outfits. Of the seven leading armateurs, Depont des Granges, Delacroix, and Gareschè sent all of their vessels to Santo Domingo while Rasteau ventured five vessels to Africa, three to Cayenne, and one each to Martinique and Louisiana. Nineteen other Rochelais outfitted ships for the Antilles. From 1727 to 1731, only four armateurs did not dispatch vessels to the Antilles while 23 percent of all armateurs accounted for 70 percent of Antillean outfits.

Broad participation in the direct trade with the Antilles continued during the 1740s with 52 so engaged, or 81 percent of all armateurs, and in 1780–89 with 33 participants, or 67 percent. Still, the latter figure represents a diminished rate of involvement, caused by a heightened interest in fishing, the opening of the East Indian trade, and a shift from the direct trade to slaving. During the two later periods, the Antillean trade became less concentrated in the hands of a few armateurs than in the first period. From 1740 to 1749, eight leaders sent 42 percent of the vessels and from 1780 to 1789, eight leaders dispatched 51 percent.[17] During the eighteenth century, then, well over one-half of the armateurs operating in the city worked the island trade while the leading participants were all from the original group of ninety families.

During the two earlier periods used in table 6.1, only a few individuals, and those the least important, concentrated on a particular branch of the overseas trade. An exclusive focus occurred most frequently in the traffic with Canada, which engaged nine armateurs between 1727 and 1731 and sixteen armateurs between 1740 and 1749. During the former period, all nine were Roman Catholics. Of the thirty-nine vessels they outfitted, twenty-eight voyaged to Canada. Four individuals or firms—Bourgine, Pascaud Brothers, Lamarque, and Lapointe—outfitted 19 of the Canadian ventures, or 68 percent. The armements of Pascaud Brothers and Lapointe all traveled to Canada. During the 1740s, nine of the sixteen armateurs trading with Canada were Catholic. Pascaud Brothers and Lapointe persisted in their Canadian focus, outfitting nine and eight vessels respectively, or 37 percent of all outfits to Canada. But the Pascaud ventured two vessels to Louisiana, another two to Africa, and one to the West Indies. Of the remaining fourteen armateurs, only three focused entirely on Canada. By the 1750s, then, more individuals were participating in the Canadian trade, and the old Canadian hands had branched out into other trades.

The trade with Louisiana, which only became open to private merchants in 1731, was initially dominated by two merchants, Jacques Rasteau and Polycarpe Bourgine. Between 1731 and 1740, those two ventured eleven and eight vessels respectively to New Orleans, or 80 percent of the Rochelais effort. But in the next decade, as table 6.1 reflects, twenty-four armateurs ventured to the Mississippi. Only Pierre Hardy sent as many as six vessels; Bourgine sent four and Rasteau only one. The seven shippers sending at least three vessels to Louisiana accounted for 25 armements, but those armements composed only 23 percent of the total number of vessels managed by the seven. While the total shipping committed to Louisiana equaled that engaged in the Canadian trade, more armateurs participated in the former, each concentrating but a minor portion of his maritime resources on Louisiana. While under French hegemony, Louisiana served as a supplementary port of call for most shippers.

Although a few Rochelais (Paul Depont des Granges for one) ventured an occasional vessel to Africa for slaves during the 1720s, the Company of the Indies' monopoly of that traffic and the company's location in Nantes precluded broad Rochelais participation in the most difficult of all the trades. Only in the 1730s (see table 2.3), when the company opened the trade to private enterprise—for a price—did the Rochelais escalate their involvement. By midcentury, Nantes had become the premier French slaving port, normally accounting for above one-third of all French slave voyages, a position maintained until the end of the Old Regime. La Rochelle's slaving fleet exceeded Bordeaux's and Le Havre's through the first half of the century. Although La Rochelle slipped into fourth place after the Seven Years' War, the number of slavers outfitted by La Rochelle, Bordeaux, and Le Havre differed only slightly.[18]

By the 1740s, the slave trade at Nantes was concentrated in the hands of a few family comptoirs. As Pierre H. Boulle expressed it, by midcentury "a mere fraction of armateurs accounted for the majority of investments" in slaving.[19] Jean Meyer's count attributed two-thirds of all slaving ventures launched around midcentury to four families.[20] But Meyer also maintained that after the American Revolution, participation in the slave trade at Nantes became more widely dispersed among a greater number of armateurs.[21] Tables 6.1 and 6.2 and supplementary data will be utilized to determine if the same trends were descriptive of the slave trade at La Rochelle.

Table 6.2 compares the size of the high seas fleet and the number of slave armements at Nantes and La Rochelle. At midcentury the Atlantic fleet of Nantes was twice the size of La Rochelle's. Thereafter, the margin spread and,

Table 6.2.   Relative Importance of Slaving armements *at Nantes and La Rochelle, 1751–55,
1772–76, and 1783–90*

Year	Nantes high seas fleet	La Rochelle high seas fleet	Nantes slavers	La Rochelle slavers	% of slavers	
					Nantes	La Rochelle
1751	58	57	17	1	29	2
1752	78	53	35	6	45	11
1753	83	42	33	3	40	7
1754	79	37	34	10	43	27
1755	47	31	21	6	45	19
1772	107	28	16	5	15	18
1773	103	23	24	4	23	17
1774	93	37	18	13	19	35
1775	98	25	19	8	18	27
1776	112	33	20	9	18	27
1783	78	45	35	17	45	38
1784	126	44	20	14	16	32
1785	120	43	35	17	29	40
1786	90	47	37	24	40	51
1787	87	34	29	12	33	35
1788	106	21	34	9	32	43
1789	88	21	43	9	49	43
1790	88	24	42	13	47	54

Sources: Jean Meyer, *L'armement nantais dans la deuxième moitié du XVIIIe siècle* (Paris,
1969), pp. 83–86; Registre des Sousmissions, ACM, Série B251, 257, 259–59bis.

except for an occasional year during the 1780s, Nantes outfitted from three to
five times more vessels than La Rochelle. But the difference between the
slaving fleets of the two ports narrowed over time. Whereas Nantes outfitted
over five times as many slavers as La Rochelle between 1751 and 1755 and
two and one-half times more between 1772 and 1776, during the years 1783 to
1787 Nantes's slaving fleet was less than twice as large. La Rochelle's slaving
ventures fell off after 1787, but for the entire 1780s its fleet equaled 43 percent
of the fleet at Nantes. By the mid-1770s and thereafter, Rochelais armateurs
committed a greater part of their total fleet to slaving than did their counterparts at Nantes, Bordeaux, or Le Havre.

At La Rochelle, participation in the slave trade involved a sizable number
of armateurs during each of the periods covered in table 6.1. Eight of thirty
armateurs between 1727 and 1731, twenty-six of sixty-four between 1740 and
1749, and twenty-seven of forty-nine between 1780 and 1789 ventured to
Africa. According to Boulle, no more than fifty Nantais worked the slave trade
at midcentury. While Nantes's slaving fleet surpassed La Rochelle's by over
five times at midcentury, a greater proportion of armateurs participated at La
Rochelle than at Nantes.[22] In November 1785, de Richemond & Garnault
responded to an associate in Paris that they could interest no investors in a
venture from Le Havre to the Antilles. The Rochelais, they explained, had

renounced commerce with that area in order to concentrate on the slave trade.[23] While they exaggerated the situation, as table 6.1 and 6.2 make clear, a relative shift of interest from the direct island trade to slaving had occurred.

Armements to Africa reached a century high between 1783 and 1786, during which time 40 percent of all voyages originating in La Rochelle were destined for Africa. Moreover, the African trade commanded a greater proportion of the resources of those engaged in the trade than in earlier years. For example, in the period 1727–31, the African ventures of the eight arma-teurs involved composed only 16 percent of their total outfits. During the 1740s, those venturing to Africa committed 30 percent of their armements to that trade; in the 1780s, that commitment had risen to 51 percent.[24]

A broadening participation of armateurs in the slave trade, noted for Nantes during the latter half of the century, failed to transpire at La Rochelle. The social characteristics of the Rochelais slave trade remained consistent from the 1740s through the 1780s. The number of armateurs involved remained about the same, twenty-six in the 1740s and twenty-two in the 1780s, although in the 1780s that number represented a slightly greater proportion—45 percent—of all armateurs than were engaged during the 1740s—41 percent. The Protes-tant share of the traffic remained remarkably stable as did the share of leading slaving armateurs.[25]

Among the permutations in the character of the slave trade at Nantes, the appearance of new names among négociants dealing in slaves has been documented for the period following the Seven Years' War.[26] In La Rochelle, merchants registered as armateurs of slavers in the "Registre des Sousmis-sions" (La Rochelle "Register of Shipping") during the 1780s who had not previously organized slave ventures. But they were not necessarily new arma-teurs or new to La Rochelle. Between 1780 and 1789, forty-nine individuals or firms, representing fifty-three family names, registered vessels le long cours. Of those fifty-three families, at least seventeen had acted as armateurs prior to 1756, including the Vivier, Bernon, Rasteau, Giraudeau, Leclerq, Quenet, and Benoist, all active armateurs since the 1720s. Other families who first appeared as armateurs after 1770 but who had owned businesses prior to that included the Carayon, Van Hoogwerf, de Baussay, Fleuriau, Poupet, Weis, Bougereau, Dumontier, and Arnauld. Of the fifty-three families, then, at least twenty-six were old families, some—the Poupet, Vivier, and Fleuriau—having operated in La Rochelle since the end of the seventeenth century. Altogether, twenty-seven families appeared for the first time as armateurs in 1771 or subsequent years, but ten of those families had established themselves in La Rochelle between the War of the Austrian Succession and the outbreak of the Seven Years' War. Many of the new names that appeared as armateurs were not truly new. Of the seventeen new armateurs, nine outfitted only one or two vessels and then did not appear again in the register.

A similar pattern described the slave trade. Twenty-six family names appeared in the register as armateurs of slave ventures after 1771. Ten of those families had outfitted slavers prior to 1756. Another five had outfitted slavers during the years 1757–70. Among the twenty-six families pursuing the slave trade after 1771, the Rasteau, Giraudeau, and Vivier had plied that trade as early as the 1730s. Among twenty-four families engaged in slaving during the 1740s, the Bonfils, Belin, Delacroix, Depont, and Bonneau had ventured to Africa prior to 1720. The outfitting of a slaver after 1771 was the initial armement of any kind for eleven families, of which six had lived in La Rochelle since at least the 1750s.

New names, then, did appear in La Rochelle during the 1780s, some making their initial armements in slaving, some outfitting their first vessel for the island trade, and some shifting from the direct trade to slaving. Many of those making their first outfit were from old Rochelais families. While no Poupets had served as armateurs prior to 1787 when Michel Poupet entered both the direct trade and the slave trade, Michel's father had been born in La Rochelle in 1697 and had become a major brandy merchant by the 1730s. The lure of profits to be garnered in slaving attracted new faces to that trade, but many of those new slavers came from families with long histories of participation in the high seas trades of the city. Relatively few new individuals of non-Rochelais origin entered the trade during the 1780s.

Proportionately more Rochelais than Nantais outfitted for the slave trade. During the 1740s, 40 percent of all Rochelais armateurs tried their hand at it and in the 1780s, 45 percent did so. Still, close to 60 percent of slave armements at La Rochelle rested in the hands of a half-dozen families in both the 1740s and the 1780s. But the degree of participation in slaving relative to other ocean trades suggests that whatever obstacles—largely capital requirements—to becoming an armateur existed, they were operative with regard to outfitting in general rather than slaving in particular. In other words, an individual inclined toward and financially capable of outfitting a vessel for the high seas trade could organize a slaving venture if he had additional capital. Accumulating capital for the initial outfit proved more difficult than diverting capital from the direct trade to slaving once the initial outfit had been organized and had experienced financial success.

Following the Seven Years' War, a number of Rochelais armateurs availed themselves of the chance to trade with the French possessions in the Indian Ocean, an opportunity that accompanied the dissolution of the Company of the Indies. Of all the trades, that to the East required the heaviest capitalization since specie formed such a large part of the cargo. The voyage also took longer than even the typical slave voyage. But since a good portion of the return cargo was purchased with cash, the quick returns—relative to the slave or Antillean trades—counted among the tempting advantages of ventures to the Indian Ocean. Moreover, as noted previously, vessels frequently combined a slaving trip to East Africa either on the outbound voyage to the East Indies or the inbound voyage, the latter necessitating a journey to the Antilles before touching at the port of Lorient where Indian returns had to be made.

From 1770 to 1789, eleven armateurs directed their vessles to Île de France. Between 1770 and 1776, Admyrauld & Son outfitted eleven of the twelve Rochelais vessels engaged in the Indian trade. Following the conclusion of the American war, the Admyraulds—now widow Admyrauld & Son—sent only one vessel to the East as they transferred their primary attention to the slave trade with four armements. Of the twenty-one vessels outfitted for the East by Rochelais, Samuel de Missy fils outfitted nine. Only two firms sent as many as two, Fleuriau Brothers with two, and de Richemond & Garnault with three. Each of these merchants were at least third-generation Rochelais. Of the remaining armateurs for the East Indies, the Thouron, de Baussay, Seignette, and Weis families traced their Rochelais residence back many years. Only two individuals, Jean Baptiste Nairac and Bourrilon, were new to the city. Nairac moved to the port from Bordeaux in 1761 when he married Claude Etienne Belin's daughter Marie.[27] Bourrilon was never encountered in any other connection than a single armement in 1782 to Île de France. In the East Indian trade, as in all of the others, old Rochelais families predominated. Unlike the other trades, one or two firms contributed most of the armements.

Among the armateurs venturing to the East Indies, the two most important, de Missy and Admyrauld, enjoyed special advantages in this trade. Samuel de Missy, the most active of the East Indian armateurs, spent part of his boyhood on Île de France training in the comptoir of an uncle. He utilized these contacts and his knowledge during the 1780s, outfitting nine vessels for those waters.[28] Pierre Gabriel Admyrauld's oldest daughter married a merchant from Île de France, and the family exploited that association during the 1770s. But the troubled times caused by the American war put a stop to such lengthy trips. By the time peace had returned, Pierre Gabriel was dead and his widow and son François Gabriel decided to concentrate on the West Indian trade. De Richemond & Garnault outfitted three ships for Île de France, relying upon de Missy's contacts (de Richemond and de Missy were brothers-in-law). Whether the Fleuriau Brothers enjoyed expertise or contacts in that area was unknown. But de Missy and de Richemond & Garnault did invest in the East Indian ventures of the Fleuriaus.[29]

Financing East Indian armements probably prevented the infusion of new blood into the ranks of the city's armateurs via that trade. But such constraints did not exist for such major shipping families as the Garesché, Rasteau, Carayon, Giraudeau, or Van Hoogwerf. Their decision to eschew this trade may be explained, at least partially, by simple disinterest, unfamiliarity with its procedures and the absence of trusted agents, or the inconveniences entailed by the requirement that returns be made at Lorient. However, a more weighty reason might be suggested: their substantial financial stake in the West Indies, both in terms of credits which they had extended and sought desperately to collect and the ownership of island plantations. By the 1780s, the sucking force of colonial debts irrevocably trapped many Rochelais merchants in the Antillean trade.

PREPARING FOR THE VOYAGE

Armateurs, as we know, attended to the multiplicity of details required to ready a vessel for departure. In La Rochelle, the armateur usually owned at least part of the vessel that he prepared. But whether owning a share of the vessel or serving merely as the agent of other owners, the armateur charged a commission that was assessed against the costs of armement and that was shared among the intéressés in proportion to their investment. Costs of armement (involving the physical preparation of the ship for departure) together with the cost of the cargo constituted the *mise hors*. Commissions were levied against the cargo as well.

In 1780 Louis Vivier made the armement for *l'Elizabeth,* bound for Santo Domingo, and supervised the selection of the entire cargo. The vessel had been purchased by Vivier for 36,366 lt. Other costs included the ship's outfit (rigging, spare sails, surgical instruments, ship's stores) 8,508 lt., food and drink, 4,704 lt., advances on wages, 2,084 lt., and other miscellaneous expenses, 15,278 lt. Armement costs for the vessel amounted to 66,940 lt., added to which a cargo of 56,851 lt. brought total mise hors to 123,792 lt.[30] Vivier's commission of 2 percent netted him 2,475 lt. for his services as armateur. These fees, added to equivalent charges incident to the return and désarmement of the vessel, formed a substantial portion of an armateur's income. Fleuriau Brothers & Thouron, armateurs in November 1782 for the slaver *Het Kerperlick Zeepaert,* earned 8,735 lt. in commissions.[31]

While merchants in La Rochelle agreed in general upon the components of the mise hors and, thus, on those items or services subject to commissions, some variety existed. Few armateurs included insurance since individual intéressés assumed responsibility for covering the value of their shares. In the 1781 de Richemond & Garnault armement of *le Mars,* bound for Île de France, however, the insurance figured within mise hors and a commission was levied against it. But this action required the prior sanction of the intéressés. De Richemond & Garnault habitually reduced their normal commission of 2 percent to 1.75 percent when acting as armateurs for certain Parisian shipowners.[32]

An approximation of the income potential of the commissions earned by armateurs was possible for the period 1783–86, when the mise hors for a number of vessels were available. Jacques Carayon & Sons earned 12,699 lt. on two vessels, Louis Vivier, 13,040 lt. on three, Weis & Sons, 29,500 lt. on five, Dumoustier de Fredilly, 29,980 lt. on five, Rasteau Brothers, 31,500 lt. on six, and Daniel Garesché, 47,040 lt. on seven.[33]

Armateurs frequently included in the mise hors the purchase or construction cost of the vessel, greatly inflating the sum liable to commissions and increasing the likelihood that the vessel would be amortized in a single voyage. Indeed, it was assumed that ships would be amortized in a few voyages, if not in a single trip. In 1784, de Richemond & Garnault outfitted a new vessel, *le*

Montgolfier, for Cayenne. Included in the mise hors of 60,640 lt. was the 18,000 lt. cost of the vessel. The cargo, valued at 10,097 lt., was exchanged for colonial staples, which sold for 52,358 lt. in France. These returns were then divided by the intéressés after deducting the armateurs' commission. De Richemond & Garnault, holding two-fifths of the shares, received about 2,500 lt. in commissions, plus about 21,000 lt. from the division of returns. If the cost of the ship is deducted from their initial investment in the venture, the armateurs' investment amounted to 17,056 lt. De Richemond & Garnault cleared over 6,000 lt., one-third of the cost of *le Montgolfier,* in a small venture which barely returned the original investment to the intéressés. Similar procedures resulted in even more rapid amortizement for Vivier's *l'Elizabeth* and Fleuriau Brothers & Thouron's *Het Kerperlick Zeepaert,* both of which returned substantial profits.[34]

Although vessels were frequently amortized in a single voyage, many armateurs continued to add the original cost of the vessel to the mise hors of subsequent trips. Thus, in the next voyage of *le Montgolfier,* the armateurs included its full value, 18,000 lt., in the mise hors. Jacques Rasteau followed the same practice by including the original cost of *le Saint Louis* in the mise hors of each of three slaving voyages made between 1735 and 1743. All of the ventures in which Paul Depont des Granges invested during the 1720s were calculated in the same way. Rasteau and other armateurs of vessels that they owned in whole or in part, in following such procedures, had their vessels paid for several times over while assuring themselves of a sizable and steady income whether or not a particular venture returned profits.[35]

Armateurs and proprietors, obviously, could not long survive a run of profitless voyages; investors would soon look elsewhere. Chapter 4 analyzed the degree to which intéressés were kin, locals, or non-Rochelais. Many armateurs developed a stable group of intéressés, creating in effect a predictable capital supply, and thus extending the relationship of armateurs to intéressés beyond the final distribution of profits or losses from a given voyage to the next voyage.

Rochelais armateurs maintained extensive correspondence with their investors, apprising them of progress made in completing the outfitting, advising them as to the opportunities and problems that might be encountered, and accounting for all expenditures made in the name of the intéressés. As news of the vessel's progress came to the promoter, it was passed on even though it might be several weeks or months out of date. In this way investors in Rasteau's *le Saint Louis* or Brevent's *le Henoc* knew that those vessels reached the African coast, loaded so many slaves over a period of time, departed African waters for Santo Domingo, arrived at Léogané and experienced good (or bad) sales, loaded a return cargo, made collections worth x lt., extended credits for four, six, nine, or twelve months valued at y lt., departed Santo Domingo, arrived at La Rochelle, and sold its cargo for such and such prices. Finally, a statement showing the distribution of the returns reached the intéressés—first returns, second returns, and so on over a period of several years until the final liquidation of the affair.[36]

Between 1727 and 1729, Theodore Delacroix outfitted five vessels and bought shares in three of Isaac Garesché's vessels.[37] Others were concurrently armateurs and investors, promoting investment in their vessels while responding to similar blandishments from others. Armateurs with a reliable group of investors did not promote their ventures extensively, and the percentage share of intéressés remained remarkably constant over time. This was significant for it allowed an armateur to calculate closely his own capital needs. Since the investors normally paid for their shares in cash or trade goods acceptable to the organizer, and since, as figure 4.1 indicates, armateurs held on the average about one-half interest in vessels le long cours, capital equivalent to the mise hors of one vessel permitted the readying of two vessels.

During the last two decades of the Old Regime, armateurs were more likely to send out prospectuses or other promotional materials announcing their ventures than armateurs prior to the Seven Years' War. De Richemond & Garnault, J. B. Nairac, and Van Hoogwerf formally solicited investments from among non-Rochelais acquaintances. In earlier days, Delacroix simply informed Delaunay Montaudoin, a major Nantais armateur, that a venture was being prepared and that a share would be reserved if desired. Nairac prepared formal promotional brochures, Van Hoogwerf solicited widely in Paris, and de Richemond & Garnault advertised their ventures in cities throughout France and northern Europe.[38] Whether this apparent intensification of the search for outside capital reflected dwindling capital resources in La Rochelle will be left for consideration in Chapter 10.[39]

THE *MISE HORS* FOR MAJOR TRADES

Sufficient data exist for an analysis of the total cost of Rochelais armements during three periods: 1722–25, 1742–51, and 1780–88.[40] For the first two periods, the lack of sufficiently detailed information prohibits an analysis of cost and trade. Excellent data for the 1780s permits a comparative cost analysis of slaving voyages, direct trips to the Western Hemisphere, fishing, and somewhat less adequately, voyages to the Indian Ocean.

Table 6.3 summarizes changes in cost for the three periods.[41] Mise hors more than doubled between 1722–25 and 1742–51 and rose by another one-third by the 1780s. Costs rose by 193 percent over the sixty-six-year period. A general price inflation beginning during the late 1720s in France, but affecting most of Western Europe, produced a portion of the increase. One price index constructed for the period 1726–89 and including thirteen French agricultural commodities suggests a doubling of prices. Indexes of manufactured goods, however, reflected a much more gradual rise in prices, particularly in the commercially strategic textile industries. Woolen goods, manufactured cottons,

Table 6.3. Average Cost (mise hors) per armement at La Rochelle, 1722–25, 1742–51, and 1780–88

Year	No. of vessels in sample	% of sample to total departures	Average mise hors of sample (lt.)	Inferred mise hors of all departures (lt.)
1722–25	23	32	60,909	64,190
1742–51	78	17	136,281	126,237
1780–88	134	41	178,604	179,273

Source: See note 40.

and other cloths rose in price by less than 50 percent. However, that category of manufactured textiles known as *toiles,* including draperies and bed linens, which consistently formed a significant part of the cargoes shipped to the Antilles, increased in price by well over 100 percent after 1730.[42]

Prices at La Rochelle rose during the century as a result of inflationary pressures affecting the rest of Europe as well as the immediate area. The most significant price increases, however, occurred after the Seven Years' War. Average prices of imported raw sugar remained stable at La Rochelle between 1720 and 1753, rising thereafter from an average of 33 lt. per hundredweight in 1749–53 to 46 lt. in 1771–75. The price of flour exported to the Antilles displayed the same pattern of early price stability and later price increases. Both flour and sugar rose by less than 45 percent during the later period. Salt prices replicated that trend. Brandy prices began inching upward somewhat earlier, increasing by 12 percent between 1723–27 and 1750–54 and by another 26 percent by 1766–70. But iron bars, an important import from Holland, hardly fluctuated in price between 1720 and 1780.[43] Inflationary pressures, then, explained but a part of the appreciation in mise hors.

Rochelais armateurs turned increasingly to vessels of greater tonnage during the eighteenth century (see table 2.2). Since construction costs per ton rose, mise hors did also. Greater capacity allowed larger and more costly cargoes. But for such general statements to be meaningful, they require application to specific trades. Attention will focus first on the slave trade.

Reference to table 2.3 reveals that heavy Rochelais involvement in the slave trade commenced during the 1730s. Earlier, in 1720, the monopoly of the slave trade had been granted to the Company of the Indies. Between 1720 and 1725, the company attempted to exploit this monopoly by means of its own vessels. Recognizing its limited capabilities in this trade—forty-six company vessels carried only 16,000 slaves to the Antilles from 1723 to 1725—the company opened the trade to private individuals from ports privileged to trade with the colonies upon payment of 20 lt. per slave transported to the islands. Reduced to 10 lt. per slave in 1726, the fee system endured until the company lost its privileges in 1767.[44]

Most Rochelais and Nantais directed their vessels to Senegal, that coast between Cape Blanc and the Sierra Leone River, and to Guinea, stretching from the Sierra Leone River to the Niger Delta. Along this entire coast, strongly established Dutch and English forts and trading posts provided stiff competition to French traders, a competition that the English backed up with effective naval protection. French traders drew upon foreign intermediaries for most of their black captives.[45]

Death stalked the slavers. Fever and aggressive blacks struck down crew members while conditions aboard ship exacted a heavy toll of blacks. In 1749, contrary winds forced Henri Brevet's *le Noé* north along the coast of the Bight of Biafra. Captain Palmie dropped anchor and sent an officer and four men to search for wood and water. Although the vessel waited and continuously signaled, the party never returned. Days later heavy seas compelled the vessel to seek shelter off the island of Fernando Poo. Suddenly, 500 armed Africans appeared and threatened to cut off the ship's boat and its crew which had been put ashore. Captives accompanying the work party joined the attackers. Cannon fire drove off the blacks, who then prepared small vessels to launch a seaborne assault on the anchored *le Noé*. For a time it appeared as if the captives on board would revolt. Although only 151 slaves had been obtained, Palmie, with sick and wounded crew aboard, pulled up anchor and headed for Santo Domingo. All in all, the voyage was a disaster.[46]

Slave mortality of less than 10 percent represented a fortunate voyage. On Nantais vessels, mortality frequently exceeded 20 percent and normally surpassed 10 percent. During three voyages of Rasteau's slaver *le Saint Louis* from 1735 to 1743, slave mortality reached 22 percent, 6 percent, and 23 percent respectively. Of 1,020 blacks traded during those three trips, 175 died during the Middle Passage. Other slaving ventures had even worse records. The second voyage of *la Victoire*, 1737–39, lost 111 of 382 slaves, or 29 percent. Elie Vivier's *le Joly* lost 14 percent of its captives in 1774. In 1783, 31 of 175 blacks died aboard Fleuriau Brothers & Thouron's *la Creole*. Pierre Jean Van Hoogwerf, writing to his brother in 1785, bemoaned the loss of 111 of 408 slaves aboard his *la Pauline*. Three years later, Van Hoogwerf's *l'Aimable Suzanne* traded 454 blacks and arrived at Saint Marc with 361. Totaling the losses evokes a feeling of horror. One of five blacks ripped from Africa perished before encountering the slave block.[47]

Slaving voyages required a larger capital than direct trips to the islands. Death claimed 20 percent of the captives, all of whom had been paid for with cash or goods. Slavers demanded larger and better armed crews, more supplies and equipment, and required anywhere from 15 months to over two years to make the complete voyage. Vessels regularly engaged in slaving had a shorter life than other vessels.

None of the available estimates of the cost differences between slaving and island ventures were based upon a thorough analysis of mise hors. At Nantes, one estimate placed total costs of slavers at three to four times that of an Antillean venture, a differential also suggested for La Rochelle.[48] Too, some have maintained that the costs for slaving rose by as much as three to four times between 1715 and the 1770s. A Rochelais estimate of 1784 approximated the total cost of a slaver at 400,000 lt.[49] Table 6.4 indicates that these estimates were excessive for La Rochelle. Since the most complete evidence pertaining to total costs for particular trades existed for the 1780s, this period will be investigated first and then compared with earlier years.

The difference in mise hors between the average slaving voyage and the average direct voyage for the five years depicted in table 6.4 was 78 percent. However, a number of ventures combined two or even three vessels—a flagship and one or two vessels of slight tonnage carrying extra provisions or trade goods and returning directly to La Rochelle once the trade for captives was consummated. If these multiple-vessel ventures were counted as a single armement, then the difference between the two trades approaches 95 percent, still much less than the three to four times suggested elsewhere. Mise hors for multiple-vessel armements in La Rochelle rarely exceeded 500,000 lt.; at Nantes, total costs of this sort of venture occasionally approached one million lt. The typical Nantais slaver, during the 1780s, cost about 275,000 lt., compared to the Rochelais average of 272,102 lt. (see table 6.4).[50]

Total costs for slaving voyages in earlier decades cannot be calculated with equal precision. I uncovered no mise hors for slavers during the 1720s or the 1730s. A small sample of thirteen slavers and sixteen vessels to the Antilles and Louisiana found for the years 1742, 1743, 1748, and 1749, yielded average mise hors for slavers of 191,500 lt. while the others average 165,400 lt. The difference between the two trades, 16 percent, was considerably less than the difference, 78 percent, calculated for the 1780s. A sample of fourteen mise hors for vessels destined for Santo Domingo during the years 1722–27 and 1729, produced an average total cost of 87,217 lt. If the costs of ventures to Canada and other minor ports of call had been known and had been averaged in, these figures would approximate those presented in table 6.3. Mise hors, then, did rise during the eighteenth century, but more for slaving than for direct voyages. But neither the difference between the two trades nor the total cost of slave ventures were as great as has been suggested. If mise hors for the six voyages to the East Indies for which figures were available are added to the

Table 6.4. Mise hors *for Africa and the Western Hemisphere, 1783–87*

	Africa			Western Hemisphere		
	No. of vessels in sample	Ave. *mise hors* of sample no.	Value of vessel as % of *mise hors*	No. of vessels in sample	Ave. *mise hors* of sample no.	Value of vessel as % of *mise hors*
1783	6	282,796	28	3	136,917	41
1784	6	190,534	37	6	161,833	34
1785	8	275,750	29	6	170,667	30
1786	9	377,145	23	3	190,000	38
1787	5	162,240	31	3	73,770	32
Total	34	272,102	28	21	152,241	34

nonslave ventures, the mise hors average becomes 159,420 lt. This narrows the differential between slave and nonslave trades from an average of 78 percent to an average of 63 percent. The relatively narrow gap between the two trades may explain in part the ability of most Rochelais armateurs to participate in slaving. That most armateurs did not participate (see table 6.1) may have been the result of the length of the voyage, which tied up capital for considerable periods of time.

One last cost comparison is offered in table 6.4, that between the cost of the vessel and its outfit and the total cost of the cargo. Studies of this cost relationship have assumed that the value of the ship in the direct trade contributed a significantly greater portion of mise hors than in the slave trade. A further assumption posits an even larger vessel–mis hors disparity between these two trades and *terreneuviers* (fishing ships). At Nantes, the greater difference between the two major trades has been attributed to the relatively higher value of cargoes required for slaving. On direct trips cargoes often scarcely covered expenses, and profits resulted mainly from freights on the return voyage and from the sale of returns—colonial commodities—for the account of the vessel's intéressés. Goods purchased through the sale of slaves, which slavers could not carry back themselves, composed a portion of return freights for island traders.[51]

As table 6.4 indicates, vessels and their outfits formed a greater part of mise hors for direct voyages than for slavers, but the disparity was slight. Cargoes represented two-thirds of mise hors for the direct trade and just above 70 percent for slavers. The inclusion of costs for four East Indian ventures raised the relative value of the cargo to mise hors to an average of 68 percent for nonslavers. For eleven fishing voyages that average was 61 percent.

Perhaps necessary overhead expenses for slaving voyages—larger crews receiving salaries over a longer period of time, ship's stores, armaments, and so forth—maintained the cost of the outfit at a high and irreducible level, producing a ratio between the cost of a vessel and its outfit and the cargo quite comparable to that holding for direct voyages. High overhead costs compelled slavers to pack a maximum number of captives aboard each vessel in order to reduce overhead costs per slave. But for many ventures this strategy proved counterproductive because overcrowded conditions increased slave mortality to levels of 20 percent or more. Robert Stein maintains that at Nantes a relationship existed between size of vessel, slaves transported, and profits, "so in general the larger the ship the greater the possibility of success, if initial costs could be kept down."[52] In the 1780s, as table 6.5 shows, Rochelais armateurs turned to larger vessels.

Mise hors per ton, presented in table 6.5 along with average tonnage for the slave and direct trades, further suggests that the cost differential between the two dominant Rochelais trades varied less than others have asserted.[53] The ratio of the value of the cargo to mise hors, as we have seen, differed insignificantly, while slave voyages cost approximately 78 percent more than direct voyages. The tonnage of slavers, on the average, exceeded that of nonslavers (a comparison between the tonnage of Nantais and Rochelais slavers, presented in table 6.5, showed little overall difference for the 1780s), particularly during the 1780s when many Rochelais bought or built new vessels to replace those lost during the American war. But table 6.5, based upon the official registration of tonnage, exaggerates the size of slaving vessels.

Beginning in 1785, the French government paid a subsidy of 40 lt. per ton to vessels outfitted for the slave trade, resulting in a dramatic increase in the registered tonnage of slaving vessels. In 1783 and 1784, the registered tonnage of six Rochelais slavers—*le Comte d'Hector, le Comte de Forcalquier, le Tigre, l'Aunis, la Reine de Golconde,* and *le Loudunon*—was 2,330; by 1786 tonnage for the same vessels had soared to 5,108. Table 6.5 offers a correction of this tonnage inflation, bringing both average tonnage and mise hors per ton to more realistic levels.

Slaving vessels, using the corrected figures, carried an average tonnage of 377, 31 percent greater than the nonslavers. Mise hors for slavers averaged 666 lt. per ton, only 17 percent above the average for nonslave vessels. The Nantais slavers sampled by Stein and included in table 6.5 averaged 394 tons; Nantais armateurs also moved toward larger vessels.

In Stein's original table, the outfitters' cost per slave delivered was calculated, as were the net returns, in plus or minus percentages. Unfortunately, sufficient data—number of slaves sold, mise hors, and value of total sales—were found for only seven Rochelais slavers between 1735 and 1789 (see table 7.1). Five of those, however, were launched after 1776, four during the 1780s. While this sample lacks the necessary representativeness to allow a full comparison with Stein, the Rochelais data do suggest certain crucial differences in the conduct of the trade at the two ports. First of all, average mise hors per ton at La Rochelle over the five-year period 1783–87, based upon the much larger sample presented in table 6.5, was 666 lt., while at Nantes it averaged 780 lt. This variance suggests greater efficiency in the slave trade at La Rochelle than at Nantes. Second, outfitters' cost per slave delivered for Nantais vessels exceeded 900 lt. per slave in ten of twenty ventures studied by Stein. Eight of the ten suffered losses, one broke even, and the others recorded a plus 3 percent return. At La Rochelle, outfitters' cost per slave delivered never exceeded 850 lt. Moreover, Rochelais slavers received higher prices for their slaves than did the Nantais. *Le Meulan* (1776) received 1,651 lt. per slave; *la Belle Pauline* (1783), 1,753 lt.; *l'Aimable Suzanne* (1784), 2,345 lt.; *la Nouvelle Betsy* (1786), 2,227 lt.; and *la Nouvelle Betsy* (1789), 1,886 lt. In the twenty Nantais ventures, prices surpassed 1,000 lt. per slave in only four cases and fell below 900 lt. in ten cases. Thus, for the five Rochelais slaving trips, net returns, based upon the total sales price of slaves delivered, averaged 260 percent. This fantastic return was, as Chapter 7 will make clear, but a promise. In the last analysis, profits or losses depended upon the successful collection of outstanding debts. As table 7.1 demonstrates, those debts were substantial.

Table 6.5. *Average Tonnage and* mise hors *per Ton for Vessels to Africa and the Western Hemisphere, 1783–87*

| | Nantes | | | La Rochelle | | | | | |
| | To Africa | | | To Africa | | | To Western Hemisphere | | |
Year	No. of vessels in sample	Average tonnage	*mise hors* per ton (lt.)	No. of vessels in sample	Average tonnage	*mise hors* per ton (lt.)	No. of vessels in sample	Average tonnage	*mise hors* per ton (lt.)
1783	4	314	875	7	341	855	inadequate data		
1784	3	339	919	10	237	666	10	302	577
1785	4	397	695	8	515	535	4	280	651
1786	3	436	779	10	911 (455)[a]	395 (789)			
1787	4	482	589	7	691(345)	234 (468)	4	261	460

[a]Correction of artifically inflated tonnage registrations in ( ).
Source: Nantes figures adapted from Robert Stein, "The Profitability of the Nantes Slave Trade, 1783–1792," *Journal of Economic History* 35 (December 1975), table 2, pp. 786–87.

Stein's data substantiates his judgment regarding the positive relationship between size of vessel and profits. Seven of the Nantais vessels above the average tonnage recorded positive net returns, with the average net return for the eleven at 12 percent. For vessels under average tonnage, ten of the fifteen suffered negative net returns, with the average return for the fifteen at minus 4 percent.[54] If the same relationship held for La Rochelle—and I can think of no reason why it should not—then given the lower cost per ton of Rochelais slave outfits, more Rochelais vessels of smaller tonnage than the average probably enjoyed favorable returns.

Relative to the direct voyage, then, slaving ventures required greater initial capitalization, estimated at about 78 percent, and used vessels of superior tonnage. Cost analyses including the ratio of cargo cost to mise hors and calculations of mise hors per ton for slavers and island vessels suggest a gradual increase in the cost of preparing ventures that might be more properly attributed to the more common use of larger vessels than to general inflation.[55] Too, the cost analyses seem to indicate that vessels for both trades were used with about equal efficiency and that the cost differential between them probably exerted but a minor restraint on individuals who chose for some reason not to divert resources from the island traffic to slaving. It is likely, however, that although the costs of slaving were not too much greater, the length of time during which slaving tied up capital may have discouraged potential newcomers to the trade.

CONCLUSION

La Rochelle's négociants developed a worldwide commercial network that facilitated the accumulation and exchange of goods, services, and capital required for their various trades. The city's armateurs assumed the responsibility for accumulating the capital to form the mise hors, oversaw the armement, selected the cargo, hired the crew, and performed various legal and other duties while preparing the vessels for departure. The best of planning and the best of crews could not protect against such unpredictable misfortunes as plagued le Noé.

Most négociants pursued other endeavors even as they served as armateurs, making insurance, investing their own capital and the capital of others in various economic activities, acting as wholesalers, and even as retailers, and managing various properties that supplemented their trades. While they did not, then, specialize in a particular branch of commerce, they did tend to favor one or two trading areas over others. By far the most popular were the direct trade with the islands and its essential supplement, the slave trade.

Most Rochelais armateurs, at one time or another, engaged in the direct island trade, with Santo Domingo as the favored destination. Some, operating in the islands, also undertook trade with Louisiana or Canada. Very few armateurs concentrated all of their resources on the latter two colonies. The island trade composed the essential base of the city's economy and other trades such as the East Indian were of secondary importance. While open to all who could put together a vessel and cargo, the island and other trades were dominated by a small number of elite families.

Few new families appeared as armateurs in either the slave trade or the direct trade during the years following the War of the American Revolution. Although engaged in a much smaller overall trade than Nantes or Bordeaux, Rochelais committed a greater proportion of their resources to the slave trade than did their competitors. Participation was quite widespread among Rochelais armateurs through the 1750s, but then it contracted for the remainder of the Old Regime. The rising costs of all armements, length of the slaving voyage, lack of family connections, uncertain economic conditions of the 1780s, burden of a great colonial debt—all of these factors might have dissuaded merchants from entering the maritime trade at La Rochelle. In the 1780s as in the 1720s, the economic well-being of the city depended upon the ability of a few dominant families to cope successfully with a rapidly changing world economic order.

SEVEN

The Organization of the Colonial Trade: Routine and Extraordinary Difficulties

The success of a maritime venture reduces itself to a single measurement, the calculation of profit or loss. All of the armateurs' skills aimed at a single goal—returning more to the vessel's intéressés than their original investment. Thus, the armateur strove to keep costs of the outfit down, to select the most appropriate trade goods, to rent unused cargo space to others, and to retain efficient and trustworthy seamen. These objectives accomplished, heavy responsibilities then devolved upon agents or correspondents situated in the colonies who disposed of the cargo when it arrived at their ports and who supervised the gathering of a return cargo. The judgments of these agents, working within their own commercial networks, weighed heavily in determining the final results of a voyage.

Ships' captains might conduct a successful trade for captives in West Africa and, through proper planning, reach the colonies with minimal loss of life. Once anchored, agents normally assumed responsibility for the sale of the slaves—or goods, if a direct voyage—and made decisions regarding the extension of credits and the purchase of colonial goods for the return voyage. Excessive credits were burdensome, poorly selected staples, costly. Failure to order a vessel away from a slow or glutted market to one with more active demand could cause serious loss. But the best of agents commanded little leverage against oversupply or the normally severe scarcity of cash in the colonies. Shifting fiscal policies and the chaos accompanying war or even rumors of war exposed the vulnerability of agents and armateurs alike. And, given the weakness of French naval strength in Caribbean waters, particularly during times of peace, and the reasonable desire of colonists to purchase in the cheapest markets, colonial agents possessed few counters to the vigorous competition of interlopers. Indeed, from time to time, the royal government opened the colonies to foreign competition. From the perspective of the armateur, separated by thousands of miles from the individuals who handled his property and used his name, many phases of the trade were uncontrollable. Information traveled slowly; rarely were poor decisions revocable.

THE EXCHANGE OF GOODS

Family connections between Rochelais négociants and colonial merchants and planters received attention in Chapters 4 and 5. Sons were trained for positions in the colonies and kin and the relatives of kin were preferred to outsiders as agents. Bordelais and Nantais held similar preferences while even interior merchants from the Dauphine evolved kinship relations with planters and colonial merchants.[1] Each of the major Rochelais armateurs maintained regular agents in the important colonial ports. On Santo Domingo, numerous firms of Rochelais origins operated in Cap français, Port-au-Prince, and Léogané. Occasionally, Rochelais firms were found at Saint Marc, les Cayes, and Jérémie, the latter a center for Dauphinois merchants. On Martinique, which served as the *entrepôt* (warehouse) for Guadeloupe, Saint Pierre contained numerous Rochelais and Bordelais. New Orleans, Louisbourg, and Quebec served as the most important entrepôts on the mainland of North America.[2] The mainland ports were all lost to France by 1763. Only occasional intercourse maintained with Louisiana, while French commerce in Canadian waters, mostly fishing, centered on the small islands of Saint Pierre and Miquelon.

Pierre Garesché, brother of Daniel fils aîné, headed a typical kin-centered mercantile establishment—Garesché & Billoteau—during the 1770s and the 1780s at Au cap and Port-au-Prince.[3] Pierre's metropolitan correspondents included merchants at Le Havre, Bordeaux, Nantes, Marseilles, and Saintes, in addition to La Rochelle. Pierre served as Daniel's principal Santo Domingan agent, forwarding to La Rochelle the produce of two Garesché plantations on the island. In addition, Pierre managed the Antillean trade of Jacques Guibert (Jacques's brother Pierre Jean married Pierre Garesché's sister) and Jacques Carayon fils aîné, whose sister was the wife of Daniel. Another sister of Pierre and Daniel's, Marianne, was the wife of Meynardie le jeune, of Paillet & Meynardie. That firm cooperated with Garesché & Billoteau, handling the Au cap end of their affairs. Nicolas Paillet was the husband of Daniel and Pierre Garesché's aunt. Benjamin Giraudeau, Fleuriau Brothers & Thouron, and Elie Louis Seignette also availed themselves of Garesché & Billoteau's services. During the six years 1779–83, Garesché & Billoteau netted an annual average of 86,334 lt. in profits. They sold out to Meynardie & Picard in 1784 for 100,000 lt. in cash and other unspecified considerations.

Merchants in La Rochelle relied upon the judgment of such colonial firms as Garesché & Billoteau, Louis Charuyer & Company, and Rasteau & Company. Smaller traders or individuals shipping less than boat-load cargoes frequently consigned their goods to those firms. Others, shipping small assortments of goods—a *pacotille*—placed them in charge of passengers or ship's officers since they were carried freight free. Jean Mazin, ship's doctor on several Rochelais vessels, often served in this capacity during the 1740s, normally receiving one-half of the net profit but sometimes selling on commission. Pacotilles were found on virtually every vessel departing from La Rochelle, whether for Africa or the Antilles. In 1741, Desgaults, a Rochelais merchant, consigned 1,298 lt. in goods to the surgeon of *le Beril* for Guinea. With those goods, the surgeon purchased four slaves, who brought over 4,000 lt. in Santo Domingo. The surgeon then turned the proceeds into indigo and sugar, obtained space for them on his vessel, and received 50 percent of the net profits from their sale in La Rochelle by Desgaults.[4]

Larger merchants did not overlook this small parcel trade. Pierre Meynardie, Jean Labbé l'aîné, and Jean Vivier, among others, consistently sent pacotilles to the Antilles, generally consigned to their principal agents in one or another port. Viviers utilized Viviers who were ship's officers. Jean Vivier, officer of the vessel *la Marquise Surgère*, put together pacotilles, sold them to Rochelais merchants, and handled their sale for one-third of the net profits. Pierre Meynardie also assembled pacotilles and then sold interests in them, one-seventh to Jean Perry, three-sevenths to Jean Gerbel, and so on. He performed many of the same tasks as the armateur, instructing island agents as to the disposition of the goods, the commodities to be purchased with proceeds from sales, and where to send the colonial staples. Meynardie charged a commission against the intéressés of the pacotille.[5]

Planters and their establishments were at the center of the commercial process. They and their slaves produced the colonial staples that European consumers demanded and consumed the European goods sent in exchange. Harsh working conditions killed slaves quickly so that replacements were constantly required, and expanding plantation agriculture generated further demands for new labor. Thus, slaves were at once producers, consumers, and commodities, and the slave trade the kingpin of the entire system.

Planters disposed of their produce in one of two ways—either on the spot, in exchange for goods and slaves shipped in by a French armateur, or on consignment to an agent in a French port who sold the goods for cash and purchased supplies for the planter or sold for credit instruments, such as letters of exchange. The latter were then forwarded to the planters for use in slave, or other, purchases. Selling on consignment, rarely encountered in the Rochelais documents, delayed the use of returns, and most planters urgently needed to trade their harvests for goods.

Those few instances of planters selling in France on consignment involved plantation owners related by blood or marriage to Rochelais armateurs, such as Paul Belin des Marais, whose property was located in the vicinity of Saint Marc, Santo Domingo.[6] By the 1760s, Paul had left the plantation in the hands of managers and retired to Paris. In Santo Domingo, two firms marketed the produce of the plantation, receiving their orders from Etienne Belin in La Rochelle. While Etienne received the larger share of the production, significant portions were forwarded to merchants in other ports. Between October 1766 and December 1768, the Belin plantation shipped, at a minimum, 144,870 lt. of indigo and cotton. Etienne instructed the colonial agents to forward 49,606 lt. worth to Bordeaux, 9,500 lt. to Nantes, 8,500 lt. to Le Havre, and the remaining 77,263 lt. to himself. Between September 1777 and June 1778, the Belin plantation shipped 110,634 lt. worth of indigo and cotton to Etienne Belin, Elie Louis Seignette, and Pierre Jean Van Hoogwerf, all of La Rochelle. Paul had died by then and the proceeds were credited to the estate.[7]

Returns from this plantation composed part of the cargo of Belin's vessels. Securing such cargoes was a matter of great urgency to Rochelais armateurs. It was possible to turn a profit even with an outbound cargo of relatively little worth if a sizable inbound cargo, whether for the account of the intéressés or as freight, was procured. In order to guarantee returns, many Rochelais families, as noted in Chapter 5, established colonial plantations. Others in La Rochelle and elsewhere, attempted to conclude agreements with particular planters whereby the planter exchanged his crops at a predetermined value for wares, slaves, or credits.

A recent study has described the effort of the Bordelais firm of Romberg, Bapst, & Company, established in 1783, and a branch of a firm located in Brussels, to guarantee colonial returns by negotiating contracts with Santo Domingo planters. Under those contracts, the firm assumed the current debts of the planters at given interest rates, assured the planter of a constant supply of slaves, and received the entire crop of the plantation. Etienne Belin and Saintard, a Santo Domingan planter, had negotiated a similar contract in 1753. Saintard originally had offered his entire sugar crop to Belin in exchange for an open line of credit in France. Belin balked at that. When Saintard moderated his terms to credits based upon the value of his crop in France and agreed to purchase all of his supplies from Belin, the latter accepted. The arrangement was still operative in 1772. While this was the only documented agreement found in the Rochelais archives, it was likely that other armateurs and planters entered into similar arrangements.[8] It was one way to guarantee a return cargo; but if large credits were involved, it might also be burdensome to the creditor.

NORMAL RISKS OF THE TRADE

From time to time, nature and competitors conspired to deprive the Rochelais of the full cargoes that they sought in the islands. Human errors also posed a threat to the armateurs' profits. Occasionally, the commanders of merchant vessels disobeyed explicit orders regarding the ports to call at, the method of shipping home the returns, the freight rates to charge, or other matters. Deviance from the ship's registered itinerary jeopardized the insurance policies taken out, for they covered a preordained route. Unless the armateur could prove that unruly winds and seas had forced his vessel out of the prescribed route, he assumed full liability for losses resulting from the lapsed insurance or other extra costs charged to the vessel. Mathieu Benoist, owner of *l'Auguste,* registered a formal protest in 1730 against the captain of that vessel who returned to Bordeaux instead of to La Rochelle. Under Article II of the letters patent of 1717, the major piece of legislation governing French commerce during the eighteenth century, vessels were obliged under pain of a 10,000 lt. fine to return directly to the port of departure. As a result of his captain's actions, Benoist became subject to that fine.[9] Other instances of disobedience of written orders involved placing returns on other vessels at higher freight rates than instructions allowed, abandoning command without authorization, and making an unauthorized and uninsured voyage from Martinique to Port-au-Prince.[10]

Shipwreck usually occurred while entering or leaving a harbor. When news of such an accident reached the armateur, an act of abandonment of vessel and cargo was filed at the admiralty so that an insurance claim could be initiated and the cargo transferred to available shipping. But total loss through shipwreck was rare. More likely, a vessel would suffer reparable damage, the costs of which were charged against the vessel's intéressés.

More commonly, ventures turned out badly because of poor sales or inadequate returns. La Rochelle's armateurs received countless letters from colonial agents and ships' captains attesting to poor market conditions in the colonies. Severe hurricanes in 1737 and 1766 ruined plantations and destroyed vessels throughout the Antilles. At Saint Pierre alone, thirty-five vessels were lost in August 1766. Surviving vessels could locate little return freight since indigo plantations had suffered heavy losses. Rochelais indigo receipts in 1767, 55 percent of receipts in 1766, and 75 percent of receipts in 1768 reflected those losses. Drought, caterpillar blight, and other natural disasters also struck plantations and diminished returns.[11] Resulting losses exacerbated debt collection problems, which were serious enough even in the best of times.

Natural calamities, in the long run, posed less of a threat than oversupplied markets. Such conditions could occur at any time that a sizable number of French (or foreign) ships arrived simultaneously. J. Paillet, in 1752, informed Théodore Delacroix that his goods moved slowly at Saint Marc and Cap français because of the great abundance of available merchandise. Delacroix also learned that the arrival of two slavers at Cap français, both searching for return cargoes, had caused a general scarcity of freight. Paillet warned that anyone sending a heavily laden ship would suffer a ruinous voyage. Letters received by Etienne Belin between 1751 and 1753 from his agent in Martinique echoed Paillet's judgments about low island demand for goods and slaves. Slaves transported to Saint Pierre for sale in 1749 remained unsold in April 1751. Conditions had not improved two years later. Belin received word in 1753 that his goods were selling at a loss and that returns were not available for his vessel *la Thetis.*[12]

Belin's correspondents blamed depressed conditions upon the War of the Austrian Succession. Peace had inspired French shippers to outfit large numbers of vessels, charged with valuable cargoes, to supply colonists who had been all but isolated during the war. The vessels that arrived first normally did quite well, but those that followed encountered sated markets and depleted stocks of colonial commodities. A group of fifteen letters written by Beville, a merchant at Cap français, to his Rochelais partner, Molinier, documented the deteriorating condition of local markets. Many French merchantmen, as Beville reported it, arrived simultaneously. Competition among them for customers forced prices of French goods to very modest levels while bidding up prices for colonial products and depressing freight rates.[13]

Slavers encountered similar problems both in trading for captives in Africa and disposing of them in the colonies. Because of the war, no slavers departed from La Rochelle between February 1744 and June 1748. Nine left within the next five months and eleven more set sail in 1749. Through 1750, Rochelais slavers met heavy competition along the West African coast and paid high prices for slavers. Some slavers paid the prices demanded and headed for the Antilles, hoping to sell high there. Other prolonged their stays in African waters, waiting for prices to decline. Regardless of the strategy pursued, the slavers encountered glutted markets in the colonies.[14] Comparably saturated markets confronted merchants during the years immediately following the Seven Years' War and the War of the American Revolution.

The interwar period, 1763–78, posed more serious difficulties for La Rochelle's commerce than the preceding interwar period, 1748–55. Both Louisiana and Canada were lost to France and to the Rochelais as a result of the Seven Years' War. Difficulties in collecting colonial debts, the devaluation of colonial currencies, the massive penetration of colonial markets by the English and other foreigners, the solidification of English slaving posts along the African coast, and severe shipping losses during the war impinged heavily upon La Rochelle's armateurs and négociants. A spate of bankruptcies at La Rochelle attested to the failure of many merchants to adjust quickly to the new situation.[15]

Weaknesses in La Rochelle's economy, revealed during the early 1770s, had hardly been rectified when another war intruded. For the Rochelais, the last decade of the Old Regime must have been the most trying time of the eighteenth century. The usual postwar glut of colonial markets occurred in 1784 and 1785. Slavers fortunate enough to arrive at the islands in late 1783 and early 1784 conducted successful sales, but many on credit. The second wave of slavers that arrived made slow progress in selling the cargoes, and merchants were forced to extend longer and larger credits to buyers. Specie was scarce in Paris, Bordeaux, and other major commercial centers, and heavy speculation focused in the Paris bourse brought disarray to money exchange markets. These conditions, coupled with the financial weakness of the royal government, made it difficult for the Rochelais to pay for their trade goods, particularly in northern Europe, without collecting substantial sums from their colonial debtors. La Rochelle suffered from short supplies of specie during the 1780s, as did its primary supplier, Bordeaux. Royal efforts to stimulate the slave trade through subsidy programs, and other trades through tonnage subsidies, helped somewhat to protect a narrowing margin of profit as well as to pump specie money into the port. But these programs did little to alleviate Rochelais concern over the pronounced drift of the royal government toward free trade for the colonies. And then, in 1788, news of political unrest in the colonies filtered into La Rochelle. Four years later, the Belin plantation at Artibonnite and others in the vicinity of Cap français were sacked and fired by revolting slaves.[16]

Leaving aside the eruption of revolutionary disorders in both France and the Antilles, events certainly beyond the control of La Rochelle's négociants, none of the difficulties crowding the Rochelais weighed so heavily as debts outstanding (and not easily collected) in the colonies.

THE PROBLEM OF COLONIAL DEBTS

Négociants at La Rochelle (and presumably in other ports as well) devoted more space in their colonial correspondence to the question of the collection of debts than to any other phase of their businesses. Successful passages and good sales did not necessarily add up to a profitable venture. Returns were the key to success, and excessive credits which postponed those returns removed capital from circulation and denied funds to armateurs and intéressés. Benjamin Giraudeau, in 1781, urged Garesché & Billoteau to make strenuous efforts to collect debts of 110,000 lt. owed to the intéressés of two slaving ventures initiated in 1777 and 1778.[17]

Virtually every student of French maritime affairs has emphasized the centrality of the debt question to the commercial system. Garnault accused colonists of deceit and abuse of the good faith of Rochelais armateurs. Others, more sympathetic to the plight of colonists, legitimately emphasized the system of monopoly which legally compelled planters to purchase in the dearest market and to sell in the cheapest.[18] To compensate, colonists—both English and Spanish—not only repaid debts tardily but participated in contraband trade when opportunities arose. French merchants did mark up their goods from 100 to 150 percent and often more. Merchants and planters alike underpacked the sacks, casks, and barrels in which goods were shipped. While planters filled hogsheads with different qualities of sugar, merchants tampered with flour and watered brandy. Fraudulent practices on both sides of the Atlantic were not unknown, but they were not the rule. Many Rochelais négociants dealt year after year with the same businesses and planters in the colonies. Mutual trust in the exchange of commodities was the rule. So, too, were unpaid debts.

Debts embittered the relationship between French merchants and planters more than any other aspect of their relationship. Both sides accused the other of exploitation. Both sides were correct. Still, the fact remains that colonists owed sizable sums of money to French merchants for goods and slaves received. Long periods of time elapsed between the sale of goods and the liquidation of debts. Much money was never recovered. All of this imposed a great strain on the capital resources of armateurs and négociants and, from their point of view, justified the high prices charged. Planters, angered in their turn about exorbitant prices, were less than zealous in discharging their debt obligations. Without implying a judgment as to where the greater fault resided, I will adhere to the perspective of the armateur in this account.[19]

Armateurs relied upon their agents to sell for cash or goods and extend as little credit as possible. Cash was always scarce in the colonies, but normally at least a part of each cargo sold for money. Shippers, of course, preferred cash sales, for specie money purchased more goods for return cargoes than did barter. French merchants obtained much of their specie from Spanish sources, and Jacques Rasteau, among other Rochelais, made every effort to trade with the neighboring Spanish colonies. Indeed, as the Rochelais perceived it, a strategic advantage of Louisiana lay in its proximity to sources of Spanish silver. But the Spanish always bought more from England and its mainland colonies than from France. Moreover, specie in the French islands also slipped rapidly into English hands, especially during the years after the Seven Years' War. French shippers complained about the lack of cash in the colonies but, unable to correct the situation, begrudgingly extended further credits to the planters.[20]

Sales were not concluded solely by barter—exchanging a given value of French goods for an equivalent value of colonial products.[21] Specie, colonial money, and letters of exchange figured prominently in the transactions. Paul Vivier, in 1750, remitted 3,225 lt. in Spanish piasters to the Rasteau Brothers at Port-au-Prince for the purchase of colonial goods. Virtually every direct venture to the Antilles included some amount of letters of exchange in its cargo. Antoine Giraudeau's *la Sophia* carried, in 1781, 8,000 lt. in letters to purchase sugars for the account of the intéressés. Letters worth 100 lt. in the islands could be purchased for between 75 and 80 lt. in France. Rochelais merchants took advantage of this favorable exchange rate, which actually worked doubly to their advantage. Letters of exchange were also accepted by armateurs in payment for goods. Planters, however, had to pay 100 lt. in the colonies for letters, which would eliminate only 75 lt. of debt in France. Armateurs in La Rochelle normally accepted letters only from planters or agents with whom they were familiar. The Belins and Pierre Jean Van Hoogwerf readily accepted letters drawn on Paul Belin des Marais. Jean Charuyer, in Saint Pierre, screened letters prior to sending them to his brother Louis in La Rochelle. Such services accentuated the necessity of having trustworthy agents in the colonies.[22]

A precise measurement is not possible of the value of letters of exchange and cash relative to other goods exported from La Rochelle to the Antilles. While of secondary importance compared with goods, letters were not insignificant, and they were essential in the Louisiana trade. Regarding specie flow alone, there is no doubt that the proportion of specie to cargo was much smaller on a direct Antillean venture than on an East Indian voyage. Company of the Indies' ventures to the Indian Ocean during the 1770s and the 1780s had carried almost 90 percent of the value of their cargoes in specie. The cargoes of two Rochelais vessels departing for the East Indies in 1782 and 1783 had consisted of 60 percent specie. But evidence does not allow a comparison of this to the specie requirements of the Antillean commerce.[23]

Letters of exchange and cash often formed a significant proportion of returns from the initial sale of goods and slaves. Insofar as possible, both were turned into commodities for shipment to France, particularly the specie. A high value of letters, collectible in France, however, composed part of the return cargo to La Rochelle. As with outbound voyages, precision in this matter proved elusive. But the accounts of several voyages suggest the overall importance to armateurs of letters and specie receipts.

All of the ventures for which data allow some measurement of the magnitude of initial sales were slavers. Instructions written by armateurs to their agents indicated that preferred returns included one-quarter in cash, one-quarter in letters, and the remainder in goods. Cash, although normally employed immediately to purchase colonial products, frequently returned to France as part of the cargo and was utilized by the armateur to meet the expenses of désarmement. Cash remaining was distributed among the investors in the first division of the returns. Letters of exchange, preferably redeemable in France at sight but usually collectible only after a period of two or three months to a year, formed a sizable portion of the credits extended to the planter.

The best of these letters—those of Paul Belin des Marais, for example— were negotiable in Bordeaux, Nantes, and Paris. Armateurs holding these notes, initially discounted in the Antilles, negotiated them through *courtiers de change* (merchant bankers) who again discounted them. When Etienne Belin accepted a letter of exchange drawn on Paul Belin des Marais, it was discounted at a rate higher than the prevailing discount rate at La Rochelle. The difference between the two rates provided the margin of profit for Etienne, while Paul received an effective credit amounting to the difference between the face value of the note and the discount rate. When Etienne received notes from Paul for payment to third parties, Etienne charged a commission for negotiating the transaction. Armateurs retained many letters drawn by planters for future payment, sending them back to the islands for collection when they had matured. They formed part of the total colonial debt at any given time.

Cash and notes not turned into goods and the colonial goods themselves formed the returns. Armateurs provided their agents with specific instructions regarding shipment. Almost without exception, armateurs ordered a division of returns among a number of vessels, thus lessening the chances of total loss in case of some unforeseen accident. Shippers admonished their agents to select only reliable vessels in order to reduce insurance costs, and to notify the French shipper promptly about the vessel selected so that insurance could be taken on the inbound cargoes. Vessels making direct voyages to the Antilles or other colonies could, if goods were available, carry back the total return; not so for most slaving voyages. Proceeds from sales of 294 slaves carried to Santo Domingo in 1738 by *le Saint Louis* yielded 256,000 lt., requiring a division of returns among two vessels in addition to *le Saint Louis*.

A varying but sizable portion of the returns from slaving voyages consisted of cash and letters of exchange. Table 7.1 summarizes this and other information for eleven slaving ventures originating in La Rochelle.[24] Only in four cases—the first voyages of *le Saint Louis, le Meulan, la Belle Pauline,* and *la Nouvelle Betsy*—did the proportion of cash and letters to total sales fall under 20 percent, and in no case was it below 12 percent. This proportion reached as high as 70 percent in the ventures involving the vessels *la Petite Suzanne* and *le Joly.* In the remaining voyages, letters and cash formed between 30 and 42 percent of initial sales. In the voyages of *le Henoc,* initial payment in cash alone came to 24 percent of total sales; for *la Petite Suzanne* and *le Joly,* cash amounted to 29 percent of total sales; and for *la Nouvelle Betsy,* 12 percent.[25]

Since the ventures included in table 7.1 appear as typical as any other ventures for which similar details are unavailable, it might be inferred that payment in cash or letters was no less important in the aggregate than for the random sample. In the Rochelais trade, then, cash or letters of exchange composed a substantial fraction of the receipts from initial sales. In all probability, the same held true for the slave trade at Nantes, Bordeaux, and elsewhere. A disregard for the cash flow generated by the slave trade, combined with a justifiable emphasis on the difficulties of collecting outstanding debts within a reasonable length of time, results in a distorted view of the trade. In fact, it seems incredible that otherwise rational merchants engaged in slaving. The anticipated cash flow, either in specie or converted into goods, met the immediate costs of désarmement and, in the initial division of returns that followed, often provided the intéressés with funds that came close to repaying their investment.[26]

Much depended, of course, on the conditions encountered during the course of the voyage. *La Belle Pauline,* departing La Rochelle in 1783, apparently enjoyed a favorable market both in Africa and Santo Domingo. De Richemond & Garnault possessed a one-fortieth interest in that voyage, amounting to an investment of 14,915 lt. In late 1785, a first division of returns yielded 9,596 lt. and divisions through 1786 brought in an additional 15,015 lt. Pierre Jean Van Hoogwerf, however, had his high hopes of success for *la Nouvelle Betsy* dashed. In 1786, his ship arrived at Cap français with only 264 of 364 captives obtained in Africa, representing an immediate loss of 167,000 lt. before sales had even commenced. Within days of arrival, Poupet Brothers & Company reported sales of 106 captives. But then sales stopped. Two vessels had arrived

Table 7.1. *Accounts of Slaving Voyages Originating at La Rochelle, 1735–89*

Vessel	Date of departure	Number of slaves sold	Cost of *mise hors* (lt.)	Value of total sales (lt.)	Receipts in cash or letters (lt.)	To be collected (lt.)	As of—
le Saint Louis	1735	294	?	255,674	47,268	81,900	1738
la Victoire	1739	271	?	248,180	80,474	153,576	1740
le Saint Louis	1742	238	130,000	261,236	79,543	201,218	1743
le Henoc	1748	328	200,518	340,976	115,016[a]	85,244	1751
la Petite Suzanne and le Joly	1773	365	?	740,520	515,520[b]	527,567	1775
le Meulan	1776	304	240,640	505,155	57,817	294,414	1779
la Belle Pauline	1783	356	182,111	448,856	86,912	?	?
l'Aimable Suzanne	1784	344	180,050	806,710	336,426	115,685	1792
la Nouvelle Betsy	1786	264	177,000	587,996	199,211	262,102	1792
l'Aimable Suzanne	1786	354	?	900,450	300,000	230,787	1792
la Nouvelle Betsy	1789	353	300,000	666,217	80,030[c]	466,000	1792

[a] 81,834 lt. in specie, all turned into goods.
[b] 212,953 lt. in specie.
[c] All cash.
Source: See note 24.

with over 900 slaves, attracting buyers to them because of the greater choice available. Poupet Brothers decided to send the remainder of Van Hoogwerf's slaves to Martinique, where sales were concluded. While sales for cash in Santo Domingo amounted to 48 percent of initial receipts, in Martinique purchasers paid but 23 percent in cash. The additional expenses of the side trip from Au cap to Martinique and return—wages, supplies, etc.—plus the large credits extended to planters at Saint Pierre diminished immediate returns and negated the success that might have been anticipated from sales averaging 2,227 lt. per captive. By 1792, 45 percent of total sales remained uncontrolled (see table 7.1), and the returns of 323,397 lt. on a mise hors of over 200,000 lt. left little to be divided after meeting the expenses of désarmement.[27]

Whatever the prevailing market conditions and however much sales for cash, secure letters of exchange, and commodities provided some immediate cash flow for armateurs, uncollected debts posed a serious problem. As demonstrated in table 7.1, in only three of the ten voyages—*le Henoc,* 1748, and *l'Aimable Suzanne,* 1784 and 1786—were credits of under 30 percent extended. Debts amounting to one-third of total sales awaited collection three years after *le Saint Louis* sailed in 1735 from La Rochelle. Six years after *la Nouvelle Betsy* set sail in 1786, uncollected debts equaled 45 percent of total sales. Debts of such magnitude, borne by Rochelais armateurs and négociants, severely reduced the supply of investment capital in La Rochelle, where the maritime economy functioned virtually without support from industrial, agricultural, or service sectors.

The total value of the debt owed Rochelais by colonists cannot be precisely calculated. An approximation for one year, 1779, will be offered in table 7.4, but too few specific debts are known for other years to justify a similar effort. But evidence reflecting the credit position of individual armateurs and intéressés, including table 7.1, supports the contention that extraordinarily generous credits were granted the colonists and that collections dragged on over many years. Table 7.2 displays the investments of Paul Depont des Granges in 1722 in vessels outfitted by his father in partnership with Jacques Rasteau and Allard Belin. By 1727, five years after the ventures had been launched, Paul had received only 78 percent of his initial investment. Profits on his investments averaged only 4 percent per annum over the years 1722–29. By 1733, when all affairs had been liquidated, Paul had doubled his money while average annual profits ran at 10 percent. This was a good rate of return, but it took eleven years to materialize.[28]

With capital tied up in a voyage for an extended period of time, individuals found it difficult to launch their own expeditions without ample backing or a large capital of their own. In five of the seven armements itemized in table 7.2, returns failed to equal investments during the first five years. The break-even point for those ventures occurred sometime during the sixth or seventh year. In the meantime, the armateur readied other vessels for departure. During the period 1722–29, Depont père outfitted eleven vessels; Belin, twelve; and

Table 7.2.   Maritime Investments of Paul Depont des Granges, 1722, and Returns, 1722–33

Vessel	Date of departure	Initial investment (lt.)	Cumulative returns recieved from investments (lt.)			
			1722	1729	1731	1733
le Saint Philippe	1722	5,075	7,506	11,456		21,304
le Saint Paul	1722	4,691	5,612	8,378	10,127	11,598
le Paix Couronnée	1722	4,711		2,735		5,410
le Poste Gallere	1722	5,121	5,594	12,758	15,233	16,699
la Paix	1722	5,360	3,760	3,789		6,918
la Reine Esther	1722	5,025	2,810	5,740		9,347
l'Elizabeth	1722	5,214	2,315			3,199
Total		35,197	27,597	47,171	51,394	74,469

Source: Depont des Granges, Livre no. 1, 1722–63, Depont des Granges Papers, ACM, Ms. E483.

Rasteau, nineteen. Table 7.3, a theoretical representation of the magnitude of Rasteau's maritime investments, suggests that at any given time in the investment cycle an armateur had at least two times as much capital committed as he had capital to invest.[29] In real life, returns might equal investments within a shorter time span for direct voyages to the Antilles than for slaving voyages or ventures to the East Indies.

Random accounts of returns from different time periods corroborated the slowness of the entire process. Rasteau's la Fortune departed La Rochelle in 1733 for the Antilles with mise hors reaching 60,000 lt. As of late 1735, only 44,000 lt. had been collected. In 1743, Beltremieux & veuve Odet and Company outfitted le Roi Stanislaus for the islands and Louisiana at a cost of 243,000 lt. Six years later, returns—including the sale of the vessel—amounted to 153,000 lt., and all of the goods had yet to be sold. Returns from Delacroix's slaving venture in 1752 with la Marianne were still trickling in as late as 1777. In 1780, Benjamin Giraudeau was still owed 43,716 lt. from a venture launched in 1771. After three years, de Richemond & Garnault's investment of 52,000 lt. in Fleuriau Brothers & Thouron's les Trois Cousins, bound for Santo Domingo, had returned only 29,513 lt.[30]

Allard Belin died in 1747. The inventory of his estate, completed in 1749, included as assets 256,000 lt. in debts owed the estate by colonists as a result of credits extended during the course of thirteen voyages launched between 1739 and 1744. Belin had served as armateur for some of the trips and had invested in them all. Claude Etienne Belin, Allard's son and partner, assumed responsibility for collection, with unknown success.[31] In 1779, Claude Etienne died. The partition of Claude's estate indicated that some 209,000 lt. in debts remained for collection in the colonies. However, an independent calculation, presented in table 7.4, establishes a debt owed Belin of almost 259,000 lt. in the colonies for thirty-one armements with the total outstanding debt on those ventures falling just below three million lt.

Table 7.3. Estimated Rate of Return on Jacques Rasteau's Maritime Investments, 1722–33 (investment units)

Year	No. of armements	Inv. units	Cumulative units	Units recovered by												Cumulative units recovered
				1722	1723	1724	1725	1726	1727	1728	1729	1730	1731	1732	1733	
1722	1	100	100	0	40	30	20	10								0
1723	1	100	200		0	40	30	20	10							40
1724	2	200	400			0	80	60	40	20						110
1725	1	100	500				0	40	30	20	10					240
1726	1	100	600					0	40	30	20	10				370
1727	2	200	800						0	80	60	40	20			490
1728	5	50	1300							0	200	150	100	50		640
1729	6	600	1900								0	240	180	120	60	930
Total	19	1900														

By applying mise hors estimates of 260,000 lt. for slavers and 147,000 lt. for direct voyages (see tables 6.3 and 6.4) to table 7.4, an estimate of 6.7 million lt. can be suggested as approximating the total investment represented by these thirty-one voyages. Uncollected debts equaled 45 percent of the total investment. On the basis of material analyzed above and in tables 7.1, 7.2, and 7.3, it might be assumed that for the thirty-one armements the margin of profit anticipated consisted of the outstanding debts. It must also be remembered that France and England went to war in 1778, thoroughly disrupting collection efforts for the duration. In 1780, Daniel Garesché pleaded with his colonial agents to press his debtors energetically for the two million lt. owed him. Thus, by adding the debts owed this one armateur to the total presented in table 7.4 and assuming that little progress in collection occurred between 1778 and 1780, the debt owed Rochelais mushrooms to almost five million lt.

How much more must be added to reflect the total colonial debt owed the Rochelais? Any effort in that direction would be pure guesswork and the figure arrived at entirely conjectural. Suffice it to say that mise hors for Rochelais armements in 1784, the first full year of peace, amounted to a century high of six million lt. This effort followed an investment of three million lt. in 1783. For the two years, Rochelais had invested over nine million lt. in their ventures. Five million lt. in debts had been outstanding in 1780. Assuming that collections of old debts were at least matched by the extension of new credits, a debt outstanding of five million lt. seems not unreasonable to posit for 1784. In other words, in any given year, the debt owed Rochelais armateurs was equivalent to the total mise hors of the port's armements in that year, a conclusion consistent with the investment model presented in table 7.3. Moreover, all the evidence indicates that the burden became even heavier during the 1780s, reaching crisis proportions after 1789 when revolutionary tensions surfaced both at home and in the colonies.

Pierre Jean Van Hoogwerf's career as armateur encompassed the years of the American Revolution and the early years of the French Revolution. He organized the last four armements listed in table 7.1 and three included in table 7.4. Attention here will focus on the former, ventures launched during the twilight years of the Old Regime. In 1792, 1,074,574 lt. in debts remained uncollected from those voyages, to which must be added 102,271 lt. from la Pauline's voyage of 1777, or a total debt of 1,106,845 lt.

Van Hoogwerf's agents informed him in 1790 that colonists exploited the political crisis to avoid paying debts. Slave sales, he was informed, were dangerous to hold at Saint Marc due to the agitation of "free men of color." Indeed, whites and blacks had already clashed. Much was to be feared, they concluded, from the slave population. Unfortunately, Van Hoogwerf's slaver la Nouvelle Betsy arrived with 353 captives at that very time. Many years later, in 1828, almost 200,000 lt. in debts remained owing the estate of Van Hoogwerf.[32]

Table 7.4. *Colonial Debts Owed in 1779 to Rochelais and Claude Etienne Belin*

Armateur	Date of voyage	Vessel	Destination	Owed to Rochelais (lt.)	Owed to Etienne Belin (lt.)
Etienne Belin	1754	la Fidelle	Africa	27,775	12,151
Etienne Belin	1756	la Fidelle	Santo Domingo	80,127	15,171
Etienne Belin	1755	le Jupiter	Africa	187,374	31,429
P. J. Rasteau	1763	le Prince Noir	Martinique	50,187	6,273
J. B. Nairac	1767	la Mariette	Santo Domingo	19,425	2,356
J. B. Nairac	1768	la Mariette	Cayenne	8,747	2,186
J. B. Nairac	1770	la Mariette	Santo Domingo	2,950	737
J. B. Nairac	1771	la Mariette	Santo Domingo	1,061	265
J. B. Nairac	1772	la Mariette	Santo Domingo	14,508	3,627
J. B. Nairac	1769	la Suzanne Marguerite	Africa	29,905	1,869
J. B. Nairac	1772	la Suzanne Marguerite	Africa	17,521	1,095
J. B. Nairac	1774	la Suzanne Marguerite	Santo Domingo	5,770	360
J. B. Nairac	1775	la Suzanne Marguerite	Africa	64,085	4,005
J. B. Nairac	1777	la Suzanne Marguerite	Africa	20,831	1,264
J. B. Nairac	1779	la Suzanne Marguerite	Africa	285,043	17,815
J. B. Nairac	1769	le Nairac	Africa	23,923	1,495
J. B. Nairac	1771	le Nairac	Africa	23,685	1,480
J. B. Nairac	1773	le Nairac	Africa	64,640	4,040
Carayon & Fils	1770	le Saint Paul	Africa	26,600	1,662
Carayon & Fils	1772	le Saint Paul	Africa	18,000	1,125
Carayon & Fils	1774	le Saint Paul	Africa	45,699	2,856
Carayon & Fils	1773	le Duc de Leval	Africa	250,357	10,431
Carayon & Fils	1775	le Duc de Leval	Africa	506,031	21,084
P. J. Rasteau	1772	le Rasteau	Cayenne	398	132
P. J. Rasteau	1773	le Rasteau	Cayenne	1,051	350
P. J. Rasteau	1776	le Rasteau	Cayenne	6,844	2,281
Pierre Jean Van Hoogwerf	1774	la Betsy	Africa	194,615	24,326
Pierre Jean Van Hoogwerf	1777	la Betsy	Africa	290,529	36,316
Pierre Jean Van Hoogwerf	1777	le Hoogwerf	Africa	238,533	29,816
E. Vivier	1776	le Comte de Saint Germain	Africa	473,235	14,788
E. Belin	1777	la Menagère	Cayenne	8,189	6,142
Total				2,988,639	258,927

Source: Etat des fonds dans les collonnies provenant tard des navires appartenant à Monsieur Etienne Belin que dans ce dans les quelles il avoit intérêst, 1779, AMLR. Ms. 1962.

149

Armateurs and négociants found it imperative to extend credits to planters. Planters found it convenient to repay their debts slowly. Some portion of the debts were ultimately uncollectible.[33] All of the evidence marshaled to this point suggests that La Rochelle's armateurs possessed sufficient capital strength to carry their ventures for a period of up to five years. Thereafter, returns were an increment to capital supply unless the armement simply turned into a losing venture. Even then, as pointed out earlier, the mode of calculating mise hors influenced the picture of profits presented in the records. Commissions and fees for other services also formed a part of income and capital supply. Still, while an armateur might amortize a vessel in a single voyage, thus reducing distributable returns, and utilize the same procedure for that vessel's second, third, or fourth voyage, demands on capital were severe. Cash flow generated from sales of slaves for specie and negotiable notes offered some relief, sufficient probably to meet the immediate needs of armateurs. Realistically, however, an armateur required access to at least three times the amount of capital invested in any given year. Returns in 1788 from Van Hoogwerf's 1786 voyage of la Nouvelle Betsy (see table 7.1) failed to compensate for the cost of the outfit while désarmement charges, requiring cash, were still to be met.

Elapsed time between the payment of expenses and the initial returns, the need for cash to meet désarmement and other fixed charges, the dangers of winds and waves, and other difficulties characteristic of oceangoing commerce—all could at least be offset through high markups, insurance, and administrative efficiency. Other threats to maritime commerce were less easily guarded against.

WARS AND FOREIGN COMPETITION

From 1688 until the end of the Old Regime, war interrupted the free flow of Rochelais commerce with terrible regularity. Those engaged in maritime activities experienced, during the entire century, only one extended period of peace, from the conclusion of the War of the Spanish Succession until the entrance of France into the War of the Austrian Succession. Even those decades were not free of conflict, but the War of the Polish Succession affected the Rochelais but slightly.

La Rochelle's commercial strength peaked during the 1740s. While vulnerable to persistent and costly colonial debts and encountering heightened competition from other ports, Rochelais merchants adjusted to those threats by using larger vessels, charging higher prices, engaging more regularly in the slave trade, and seeking to exploit whatever benefits trade with Louisiana offered. But the Rochelais, seriously disadvantaged locationally, could not continuously adjust to the wars that punctuated each of the last six decades of the century. La Rochelle's commercial strength ebbed under the cumulative pressures exerted by those wars. The enervating effects of war inexorably drained the port's vitality and stripped it of its maritime significance.

Each of the last three prerevolutionary wars with Great Britain accelerated the erosion of the city's economic foundations. Some damage could be repaired—vessels captured or destroyed could be replaced. But other losses— Louisiana and Canada, insurance premiums costing one-third to one-half of mise hors, vessels idling in the harbor for years at a time—were irreplaceable. It mattered little that French armies enjoyed modest successes in land engagements fought on the European continent or even that French battle fleets fought English naval forces at least to a standstill during the War of the American Revolution. It mattered little that French naval defeats in Atlantic waters were compensated by victories in India or elsewhere. Each war promised immediate loss and threatened possible disaster for La Rochelle's merchants. War's aftermath aggravated these fears because of the predictable volatility of market conditions and the certainty that some portion of the colonial debt would never be paid.

For the Rochelais, each war precipitated an economic crisis, measured by captured merchantmen, kin and seamen killed or wounded in combat, unpaid debts, soaring costs, and the absolute cessation of the slave trade. The fear of capital and vessels resting idle for the duration prompted some armateurs to outfit and dispatch their ships regardless of risks. The gamble was magnified by the general inability of the French navy to provide adequate protection along the most traveled sea lanes, particularly off the Spanish Atlantic coast and the approaches to the islands.

Some risks of war were more easily avoided or minimized than others. War, however, caused certain irreversible consequences and prompted subtle and gradual changes in government policies toward the colonies, which threatened the foundation of the economies of the French ports, the monopoly of colonial commerce. Louisiana and Canada, essential to La Rochelle but considered expendable by the French government, were sacrificed at the peace table. The French government, under intense pressure from powerful colonial interests, first opened the colonies to neutral trade during wartime and then moved steadily toward authorizing foreign trade with the colonies during peacetime. Such drastic alterations of French policy, coupled with the immediate and cumulative effects of each war, boded ill for La Rochelle's economic future.

Any rumors, founded in fact or in fancy, of royal inclinations to compromise the strict prohibition of foreign trade in the colonies called forth energetic opposition from mercantile interests in La Rochelle and other ports. Both before and after the edict of October 1727 (the most explicit interdiction of foreign commerce with the colonies), merchants, individually and collectively, charged that colonial officials closed their eyes to or even encouraged traffic with foreigners. Complaints were leveled at the free ports, such as Saint-Malo, for introducing foreign goods into the colonies. Ship owners criticized fees and regulations that made French shipping more costly than Dutch or English and other competitive advantages allowing foreign merchants to pay higher prices for French colonial products while supplying colonial needs more cheaply. French officials assured the merchants that all went well. Cardinal Fleury informed the La Rochelle Chamber of Commerce of the seizure in 1727 of seventeen English interlopers off Martinique, while Minister of the Marine Maurepas denied that colonial authorities connived at smuggling that, he asserted, was insignificant in magnitude and sporadic in occurrence.[34]

The facts substantiated merchant apprehensions. Smuggling from the British West Indies, particularly Jamaica, and the New England region persisted and expanded during the eighteenth century. The French navy lacked the capacity to patrol adequately against interlopers. French colonial authorities, if not actually involved in smuggling, acted to prevent it only rarely and for appearance's sake. English and Dutch traders could supply French colonists for cheaper prices and pay higher prices for staples partly because of lower overhead costs on their vessels. Moreover, unlike French merchants, who were tempted by their position as monopolists to price goods at what the market could bear, foreign competitors sacrificed some initial gain in order to obtain cargoes of valuable colonial staples. Too, Dutch and English merchants, more successful in penetrating Spanish markets than were the French, came to the Antilles with cash, paid it out for crops, and earned it back, along with specie carried in by French vessels, in payment for their cheaper and better assortment of trade goods.

For a variety of reasons, largely related to excessive administrative control, inadequate capital investment, weak naval forces, and government policies toward emigration to the colonies (along with the general reluctance of the French to emigrate), French efforts to develop Louisiana and Canada as suppliers of the French West Indies failed. Canada was barely self-sufficient and French Louisiana never achieved that position. Neither were able to supply the islands with significant quantities of materials—stone and wood, livestock, or foodstuffs—upon which the hope of a mutually supportive intra-colonial trade rested. France remained the single legal source of island support, and all too frequently during the eighteenth century that source of supply failed the islanders.

The French government, responding to the inability of French merchants to supply the colonies during wartime, resorted to neutral shipping. As early as 1721, the royal Council of Commerce had threatened French shippers with this measure unless they committed greater resources to the colonial trade. And, in 1744 and again in 1756, the government did authorize neutral trade with the colonies.[35]

The protests of French merchants went unheeded. Neutral shipping did not meet colonial needs but English shipping did. In effect, Jamaica supplied Santo Domingo during the Seven Years' War. Rochelais négociants complained bitterly that foreign, mostly English, suppliers undercut the Rochelais slave trade. Joseph Pascaud, while deputy of commerce, informed the La

Rochelle Chamber of Commerce in 1761 that plantation pressure groups in Paris were prepared to demand a general extension of foreign trade privileges with the colonies once peace had been restored. He urged the chamber to mount a campaign which would convince the government that French shippers had the necessary capabilities to supply all colonial needs.[36]

War in 1778 resurrected the issue. According to Pierre Isaac Rasteau, colonial interest groups campaigned vigorously in favor of the use of neutral shipping. Indeed, the colonist wished the trade also opened to Americans. "It is ironic," mused Rasteau, "that while the Americans work with us to damage Great Britain, we are creating a strong competitor for our colonial trade in those same allies." In 1779, the admiralty offices in French ports began issuing permissions to foreign ships to trade with the colonies. These privileges were rescinded in 1783 but the pressures for free trade continued unabated, culminating in the arrêt du conseil of June 28, 1783, which allowed foreigners to carry slaves to the Windward Islands, and the arrêts du conseil published in August 1784.[37]

The regulations of August 1784 permitted colonists in the principal ports of Santo Domingo and Martinique and the other Windward Islands to import foreign goods carried in foreign bottoms. They recognized the developing commercial contact between the United States and the Antilles as well as the older surreptitious trade with Jamaica. The regulations did exclude both slaves and flour from the goods which foreigners could introduce to Santo Domingo. French armateurs concentrated their trade at northern Santo Domingan ports, paying little heed to the needs of Martinique or Guadeloupe. Martinique's requirements between 1763 and 1778 were met almost entirely via smuggling. "The consternation of all merchants against this blow at French commerce," as the Chamber of Commerce of Bayonne described it, and protests from merchant organizations at other ports, failed to shake the government from its decision.

In 1785, estimates put the foreign trade of the colonies at 33 million lt., about equal to the foreign trade at Marseilles or Bordeaux. During the first four months of 1788, arrivals at Santo Domingo numbered 470 ships, including 213 foreign. Officials in Santo Domingo in 1789, responding to serious crop failures in France and to the uncertainty of the times, unilaterally authorized foreigners to bring in slaves and flour. Royal annulments of the colonial decision were ignored. The system of *exclusivisme* had ended. Not that it mattered to La Rochelle by that time, since her days as a great entrepôt had also come to an end.[38]

Recurrent war afforded colonials and their supporters at Versailles the opportunity to apply continuous pressure for free trade. French naval power, generally inferior to that of England, was unable either to keep the sea lanes free from roving English squadrons and privateers or to efficiently convoy French merchantmen to and from the Antilles. Each of the Anglo-French wars between 1744 and 1783 elicited basically the same patterns of response and action. Armateurs, anticipating hostilities, would petition the minister of the marine for naval protection. The minister would assure each port of the crown's intentions to protect commerce. In the meantime, prior to the official declaration of war, English warships would begin to stop, search, and seize French vessels in French waters and on the high seas, while the French navy could deploy only token forces for short cruises along French coasts and could provide only partial convoys out of French or colonial ports. British privateers menaced the very entrances of French ports. In 1757, a large English fleet threatened La Rochelle, capturing Île d'Aix before departing. Shipping losses were so heavy that at the conclusion of each war, particularly the last two, many Rochelais armateurs had no vessels.[39]

France employed convoys extensively during the War of the Austrian Succession and subsequent wars. La Rochelle's island-sheltered waters provided a perfect roadstead for the organization of convoys. But such protection was costly to shippers who were charged an *indult* (fee) of 8 percent of the value of the cargo carried. Armateurs at La Rochelle, and presumably elsewhere, resented and protested the fee. They argued that the indult was a form of double taxation since the fees, tariffs, and charges, particularly the domaine d'occident, which they paid into the royal treasury, already paid for general services including adequate naval protection. The armateurs did not, however, advance that next logical step, at least publicly, to question the government regarding the uses to which their taxes were put. Lying dormant, issues so inherently threatening to the system of privilege surfaced only after the Revolution commenced. Moreover, the indult was assessed in full even though few convoys provided portal-to-portal escorts and even though the escorts were normally few in number. Convoys were frequently abandoned by their escorts or scattered by the strategy of penetration employed by awaiting enemy squadrons. Delays in the assembling of convoys off Île d'Aix increased operating expenses, while heavy fines threatened armateurs who struck out on their own despite the availability of a convoy.[40]

Large convoys with weak escorts predominated during the War of the Austrian Succession, the Seven Years' War, and the early years of the American war. In 1744, a single warship accompanied about 40 vessels from Rochefort to a point some 200 miles off Cape Finisterre where it turned them loose. A return convoy of 250 ships in 1746 depended upon the protection of 4 warships. In October 1747, 253 merchantmen, including 43 Rochelais ships, left Île d'Aix under the protection of 11 frigates. And in 1748, 45 Rochelais vessels joined a convoy of 253 merchantmen and 10 warships headed for the Antilles. English squadrons hovered off Cape Finisterre, scattering escorts and capturing merchant ships. Those vessels escaping the first assault then faced the perils of Antillean approaches, usually swarming with privateers and English patrols. Losses seemed to run at about 20 percent during the first quarter of the voyage and another 20 percent at the Antillean end—and only one-half of the voyage had been completed.[41]

During the first year of the American war, large convoys and small escorts prevailed. One French warship escorted 54 merchantmen from La Rochelle in 1778 and abandoned them to chase a single English warship, with the result that one-half of the convoy fell prey to nearby English ships. By late 1778, the government had finally decided to organize small convoys and escort them all the way to the Antilles or North America. A convoy organized at La Rochelle in 1778 and 1779, however, consisted of 100 vessels and was taken only 100 miles off Cape Finisterre when the escort suddenly dropped it. Daniel Garesché, Pierre Jean Van Hoogwerf, Pierre Hardy fils aîné, and Pierre Goguet all lost vessels after the warships turned back to France. The chambers of commerce of the Atlantic ports bombarded the minister of the marine with denunciations of the responsible naval commanders and forcefully urged the implementation of portal-to-portal escorts. Promises to improve convoying tactics apparently resulted in little change. One frigate escorted 42 vessels from La Rochelle in late 1781, while in 1782 10 warships accompanied 197 vessels. Only a convoy from Santo Domingo in 1780, consisting of 125 merchantmen and 28 warships, seemed adequately protected.[42]

La Rochelle's economy suffered heavy damage during each of the eighteenth-century wars. The port's high seas fleet declined from 65 vessels in 1687 to fewer than 20 by 1713. Relatively less severe, but still serious, shipping losses buffeted La Rochelle during the War of the Austrian Succession than during successive wars. French shipowners lost about 3,400 vessels of all types, only 200 more than the English, but this relative parity did not benefit La Rochelle, which outfitted few privateers. In two years, 1744–45, 30 vessels outfitted at La Rochelle and valued at over eight million lt. surrendered to English warships or privateers. At least another 15 ships fell into English hands by the end of the war. Wartime captures claimed about one-half of the Rochelais fleet.[43]

A succession of captures during the early stages of the Seven Years' War caused shipping activity to virtually cease at La Rochelle. The English seized eleven vessels prior to the declaration of war. By 1757, of 68 ships departing La Rochelle in 1755 and 1756, only three had returned. Many had been captured while others remained bottled up in friendly or colonial ports. Armements at La Rochelle declined from thirty-one in 1757, to twenty for Louisbourg and Quebec, to twenty in 1758, and twelve during the four years 1759–62. Pierre Isaac Rasteau, the Admyraulds, Paillet & Meynardie, Jacques Carayon, and Pascaud Brothers all lost heavily laden vessels.

Other ports shared La Rochelle's experience during the Seven Years' War. Saint-Malo's commerce was reduced by one-third. Bordeaux lost one-third of its tonnage during the first year of the war, losing altogether 236 vessels. Commerce at Nantes ground to a halt by 1759. Between 1754 and 1759, 109 Nantais vessels valued at 17 million lt. were captured, including a large number of slavers. At La Rochelle, nearly 100 vessels were leased to the crown during the war, a common practice in all ports, but as late as 1765 many of those vessels had not been returned to their owners. Moreover, the government had reneged on its lease agreements by reducing the charges originally negotiated with individual owners. Armateurs in France lost millions of livres tournois by this partial repudiation, and millions more when the government partially repudiated its debts in Canada and Louisiana. The experiences of this war produced few reasons that justified confidence in the royal government.[44]

Better convoys and French naval parity with the English somewhat diminished shipping losses between 1778 and 1783. Vessels did manage to reach the Antilles and return laden with colonial goods. Several factors, however, minimized the benefits of greater high seas security. As in earlier wars, the slave trade ceased. But this time potential losses were higher since current demands for labor on the islands had forced prices upward, prices that French slaving armateurs could not take advantage of. Similarly, plans for armements to the East Indies were postponed. But more critically, obstacles to the marketing of goods in Europe upset the Rochelais economy.

La Rochelle and other ports with a major reexport trade depended upon the shipping facilities of northern Europeans, especially the Dutch, for transportation to the north. Dutch vessels, in addition to Danish, English, and Hanseatic ships, carried the bulk of colonial goods to market. In earlier wars, although the English seized neutral carriers, available supplies of colonial goods were but a fraction of the norm and sufficient neutral shipping was available. But in the War of the American Revolution, the Dutch were belligerents and ingoing cargoes of colonial staples large. The English harassed neutral German and Scandinavian shipping, stopping and seizing many vessels. By 1780, few neutral ships touched at La Rochelle. Bordeaux and Nantes suffered from a similar interruption in the reexport trade.

Rochelais merchants soon discovered that returning convoys placed great lots of colonial goods on the market, at once deflating the prices of colonial goods and inflating freight rates. Serving as a staging ground for outgoing and incoming convoys also propelled the price of all services skyward. Harried citizens learned that the foodstuff demands of convoys of 50 to 200 vessels caused food prices to leap upward. To be sure, servicing the convoys injected money into the Rochelais economy, but from the perspective of the Rochelais armateur this brought few benefits if his imports, along with the goods from 50 other vessels, were dumped on a market without adequate grand cabotage.

Pierre Jean Van Hoogwerf's account book showed a loss of 59,000 lt. between 1777 and 1784, a figure that did not count the loss of several vessels. Nicolas Suidre lost all of his ships in 1779. De Richemond & Garnault turned to the salt trade in the belief that, of all commodities, privateers least coveted salt. Two vessels of Jacques Guibert were captured in 1780, and by 1781 he had no ships left. One, *la Nancy,* carried 450 slaves; another, *le Fort,* took heavy fire from an English frigate and sank in a Spanish harbor. With few sales occurring, all négociants experienced declining commission income. Van

Hoogwerf's claim that 500 houses were for sale in the city was probably quite accurate. All in all, it was the worst of times.[45]

CONCLUSION

The Seven Years' War battered the economies of France's maritime centers. But Le Havre, Bordeaux, and Marseilles demonstrated surprising powers of recuperation. Nantes recovered quickly enough but surged ahead less rapidly than the three other cities. Nantes's slower recovery and slower growth rate may be attributed to its intensifying concentration on the slave trade, at once difficult and costly to start up again and increasingly competitive. The other ports, less specialized and less committed to the slave trade, generalized trades more rapidly.[46]

La Rochelle lagged behind all the larger ports in rate of recovery and subsequent growth, experiencing great difficulties during the interwar years, 1766–78, in regaining her prewar capabilities. Legal foreign competition in the islands and the natural tendency of French merchants to ship large quantities of goods to the colonists during the immediate postwar years explain the glutted markets encountered by the Rochelais. The new system of free trade, which specifically excluded slaves, and the tonnage subsidy for slavers prompted Rochelais armateurs to shift resources from the direct trade to slaving. This certainly must be considered a rational response to changing conditions. But given the higher costs and higher value of the slave trade compared with the direct trade, the redirection of capital also exacerbated the critical problem of colonial debts.

Colonial debts imposed a heavier burden upon the smaller capital resources of the Rochelais than did debt servicing in the larger ports, especially those less focused on the colonial trade. Colonial debts mounting to millions of livres tournois compelled the Rochelais to sustain their shipments to the islands at high levels. To collect old debts, new debts had to be incurred. The direct competition of foreign merchant shipping, particularly English, forced the Rochelais to be ever more generous with their credit.

The city, ill-prepared in 1778 for another war, demonstrated little growth potential following 1783, focused excessively on the slave trade, sold too much on credit, suffered from a decline in both the salt and brandy trades, possessed no viable alternative and local resources to exploit, and failed to establish a trade with the United States as a substitute for Canada and Louisiana. By Thermidor, La Rochelle had lost forever her status as a *port du grand cours.*

EIGHT

The Commodity Trades in La Rochelle

Thousands of tons of manufactured and semimanufactured goods, processed foods, grain, and drink passed annually through La Rochelle. Most of the items, including commodities produced in the vicinity of La Rochelle, such as salt, grain, and brandy, entered the colonial trade and were sold or exchanged for sugars, indigo, coffee, cotton, tobacco, skins and other products of the forests and plantations. With the exception of sugar, colonial produce left La Rochelle in an untransformed state, entering the stream of trade to northern Europe and the interior of France. Local or regional needs diverted but a fraction of these items from the two main trade conduits.[1] The economy of the city ultimately rested upon the sale of imported colonial goods.

La Rochelle's sphere of commercial interest encompassed the colonies (including the West African coast), French Atlantic ports, English and Irish ports, and ports located on the North and Baltic seas. Whereas Marseilles developed its colonial commerce as an adjunct to the traditional trade with southern Europe and North Africa, La Rochelle's commitment to and dependence upon the colonial trade was unrelieved by a secondary focus. While Bordeaux exploited both a rich wine and grain producing hinterland and a dynamic riverine connection with France's southern provinces, La Rochelle's hinterland was less productive and, indeed, in decline as a center of grain, salt, and brandy production. Moreover, it shared the produce of that region with Nantes, Rochefort, and Bordeaux, as well as with small but competitive ports located on the Seudre and Charente rivers. Nantes's manufacturers supplied some of the city's exports, particularly textiles, while the Loire gave the city access to the wealthiest parts of France. Saint-Malo, Le Havre, Dieppe, and Dunkirk developed a substantial, if partially illegal, trade with England, and their proximity to Holland and the North afforded them swifter and cheaper access to goods from those areas used in the colonial trade.

La Rochelle's commercial interest groups, recognizing the geographic limitations of the port, sought to maximize the strength of La Rochelle not only by maintaining a high level of operating efficiency in the oceanic trade but by minimizing or neutralizing disadvantages or potential disadvantages of a political or fiscal nature. Each of the primary commodities in La Rochelle's commerce was subject to fiscal manipulation by the government. The Rochelais, sometimes successfully and other times unsuccessfully, attempted to ward off any and all fiscal exactions that reduced their margin of profit or placed them in a noncompetitive position relative to other ports. While on certain issues groups within the city divided into opposing camps, for the most part a united front prevailed against the attempts of other ports to gain some trade advantage and the persistent efforts of the government to increase its revenues at Rochelais expense.[2]

THE ENTREPÔT AT LA ROCHELLE

La Rochelle's imports from the colonies consisted of sugar, indigo, cotton, coffee, tobacco, and furs and skins. While the port's fishing fleet was small relative to that of other places and its fish imports mostly consumed locally, the city was an important source of salt for the French fishing fleet. Salt, along with grains and brandies, attracted foreign vessels and composed part of the exports both to the colonies and to northern Europe. This chapter will analyze first the characteristics of the import trade in colonial staples and then turn to the special trades conducted by Rochelais in grains, brandies, and salt. Emphasis will be placed on the impact of national trade policies on these commodities and on Rochelais efforts to protect such vital sources of local profit.

Sugar and Sugar Refining. Students of eighteenth-century colonial systems have long recognized the paramount role of sugar in the development of the plantation colonies, in stimulating a need for labor which the slave trade sought to fill, and in satisfying the rising European consumer demand for sweets and sweeteners. The total value of exported sugar far surpassed the value of any other colonial exports from the French and other foreign colonies in the Caribbean region. During the eighteenth century, superior French sugars won a preeminent position in European markets, and La Rochelle shared in the profits generated by a rising European demand.

La Rochelle received a much larger tonnage of sugar than of any other commodity, European or colonial. Sugars rarely contributed less than one-fifth of the total value of Rochelais imports, a proportion that frequently rose to over 30 percent. From time to time during the first half of the eighteenth century, imports of indigo or furs and skins surpassed the value of sugar imports. But in most years sugar remained the most valuable commodity entering the port. While the importance of coffee to the Rochelais trade heightened during the century, the value of that good did not, as occurred in Bordeaux during the 1780s, finally equal and then exceed the value of sugar.[3]

La Rochelle reexported in some form virtually its entire sugar import. An arrêt du conseil in 1671 prohibited the export of *sucre brut* (raw sugar) from

France and, since the colonies could export only to France, the mother country became the sole market for the islands and, consequently, the center of sugar refining. In 1714 and 1715, the French government permitted the reexport of raw sugars and semirefined *sucre terré*. During the years 1718 through 1744, the value of imported raw sugar greatly exceeded the value of other forms of sugar. Between 1746 and 1780, semirefined and refined sugars from the colonies surpassed raw sugar in value or at least equaled it in most years. This reflected the growing strength of colonial refining, a development upsetting to La Rochelle and other ports that had local refineries. Most of La Rochelle's reexports went to Holland and the Hanseatic cities. Refined sugars infrequently surpassed the value of raw sugar exported to the North. Indeed, after 1747 no refined sugars at all were exported to either the Hanse towns or to Holland. Of those two markets, the Dutch received the larger quantities until the 1750s; thereafter, sugar exports to the North were larger. A similar reversal in the sugar trade occurred at Bordeaux beginning in the 1740s, reflecting the declining role of Holland as a middleman in the trade between France and Hamburg, Bremen, and German ports on the Baltic Sea.[4]

Beginning in the 1680s, opposition emerged in the ports to colonial refining, and representatives of various interests debated the question of which types of sugar should be allowed into France. By this time, refining had assumed an important role in local economies, and some incompatibilities had surfaced between the economic needs of refiners and armateurs. The fact that certain of the leading armateurs in La Rochelle also operated refineries complicated the situation.[5]

Commencing during the period of Colbert's ascendancy and continuing into the eighteenth century, French policies supported the development of domestic refining by prohibiting the establishment of refineries in the Antilles. In 1683, twenty-nine refineries operated in France and five in the islands. An arrêt of 1684 prohibited the establishment of any new refineries in the islands. Although not entirely successful, this policy persisted until 1732, by which time refining in France had achieved significant size. Most colonial refineries had been small operations and had concentrated on the production of rum. Then, in 1732, colonists gained permission to manufacture their sugars.

Between the 1670s and 1730, La Rochelle's merchants developed one of the largest refining centers in France, one that dominated the otherwise small industrial sector of the city. From 1718 to 1728, exports of refined sugars to Holland and to the North contributed from 15 to 20 percent of the total value of all sugars forwarded to those places. Refined sugar, then, formed an important component of exports to northern European markets which absorbed, during those years, over one-half of all La Rochelle's exports. La Rochelle also forwarded refined sugars to various French markets.

The first refineries commenced operations in La Rochelle during the 1650s. By 1672, the city possessed five. Rouen led with eight while Bordeaux and Nantes each had three. By the end of the seventeenth century, refineries had sprung up in Angers, Saumur, and Orléans while Nantes had a dozen. In 1708, nine refineries worked in La Rochelle, including plants constructed between 1701 and 1708 by Adrian Delacroix, Pierre Hardy, and Louis Besnard. Between 1708 and 1713, an additional five, including a large factory constructed by François Fleuriau, began manufacturing refined sugars. By 1728, sugars from twenty-eight Rochelais refineries formed a significant portion of local exports to Norman, Dutch, and German ports. Bordeaux, at about that time, had twenty-two refineries, while in Nantes the number had declined to four.

Thereafter, the number of refineries, most owned by armateurs, declined at La Rochelle, falling to fifteen in the 1750s. The Belin family purchased two during the 1730s and 1740s. Other refining families included the Rasteau, Delacroix, Vivier, de Baussay, Fleuriau, Labbé, Papineau, Bernon, de Richemond, Dujardin, and Gilbert, all armateurs, and the Carré, a wealthy noble family. All but three families—the Papineau, Gilbert, and Carré—were Huguenots. On the eve of the French Revolution, only four refineries remained in operation at La Rochelle, while Bordeaux contained twenty and some twenty-three refineries at Orléans processed sugars imported via Nantes.[6]

Disagreements between refiners and armateurs surfaced during the first decade of the eighteenth century as did jealousy among refining centers. In 1699, for instance, Bordelais refiners sought and received permission to export sugars free of duty to markets in eastern France and foreign countries. La Rochelle's refiners petitioned the government for similar privileges. Then, in 1699, Nantes received permission to import sucres terrés destined for shipment to foreigners without payment of duties. La Rochelle's armateurs demanded similar entrepôt rights that would involve, if granted, the remission of 15 lt. per hundredweight duties on incoming sugars if reexported to foreign markets. However, refiners at La Rochelle opposed both the establishment of an entrepôt and the manufacture of sucre terré in the colonies. Simultaneously, the refiners demanded the free importation of raw sugar from Dutch and Portuguese colonies in whatever shipping happened to be available. Armateurs argued for the necessity of warehousing privileges for semimanufactured sugar in order to remain competitive with Nantes and Bordeaux. Moreover, because of the relatively small value of raw sugar compared to its bulk, shippers contended that the value of incoming cargoes of raw sugar fell below the cost of goods carried by their vessels to the colonies. Raw sugar simply took up too much space relative to its value, requiring shippers to hire space on other vessels or to operate more vessels than necessary. Allowing imports of sucre terré and other forms of manufactured sugar, according to the armateurs, would insure sufficiently valuable cargoes for their vessels to meet freight cost requirements. Theoretically, the value of incoming manufactured sugars would exceed the value of outgoing cargoes by a sufficient margin to make the trade profitable. Both sides warned that French commerce and, therefore, government revenues would seriously be injured if the other side had its way.

Armateurs predicted dire consequences for French maritime strength and for colonial economies should refiners be allowed to import foreign sugars on foreign vessels.

In this contest between industrial and commercial interests, the latter including colonial planters, the French government adopted policies beneficial to the commercial sector. Entrepôt privileges were extended to La Rochelle prior to the conclusion of the War of the Spanish Succession. The refiners, however, were not ignored. During the late 1720s, refiners at La Rochelle, Rouen, and Dieppe received an important concession, one already operative at Bordeaux, where import duties on raw sugar refined for reexport to foreign markets were rebated. Rochelais refiners thus enjoyed a significant cost advantage over Nantes in competing for foreign markets. Refiners at Saumur, Orléans, and Nantes cried out against this inequity but to no avail.

However, the favorable position achieved by refiners at La Rochelle by the 1730s lasted only until the outbreak of the Seven Years' War. Thereafter, the strength of the refining industry waned. In later years, Rochelais refiners blamed the industry's decline on the illicit competition in domestic markets of foreign refined sugars smuggled into Norman and Breton ports, the alleged ability of Breton refiners to avoid paying duties on exports to norther Europe, and the spread of refineries in the colonies. While all of these may have contributed to the subversion of La Rochelle refiners, more weighty factors bore down on the industry.

Competing refiners in Holland, the Loire valley, and Bordeaux slowly squeezed out the Rochelais. Dutch refiners, with assured supplies of raw sugars from English, French, and their own colonies, exploited their proximity to Scandinavian and other northern European markets and their ability to package and transport the finished product more cheaply than the French. A Rochelais mémoire on manufacturing written in 1789 estimated that Dutch access to cheap English coal—subjected to heavy import duties in France—combined with other production efficiencies reduced the costs of sugar manufacture in Holland to 70 percent of French production costs. Domestic refiners in the Loire valley, Bordeaux, and Marseilles utilized superior inland transportation routes to reach centers of population in and near Paris and in the south of France. Prior to 1740, La Rochelle sold large quantities of refined sugar in Lyons and Marseilles. By 1760, twelve Marseillais refineries shipped their goods up the Rhone River to Lyons, there encountering competition from sugars refined at Orléans. Bordeaux's inland connections with the south placed it in a better position than La Rochelle to reach buyers in Gascony and to compete with Marseilles for the market in Languedoc. Refiners in Rouen and Dieppe were heavy early eighteenth-century purchasers of Rochelais refined sugar, and, along with the Loire valley centers, they serviced demand in Brittany and Normandy. Thus, without attempting to assess the impact of the Seven Years' War and the War of the American Revolution upon La Rochelle, both of which damaged commerce at La Rochelle more severely than at Bordeaux or Marseilles, La Rochelle's competitive position after 1750 suffered serious erosion as a result of gains made elsewhere.

In 1786 the crown acted to stimulate refining in France by reducing duties and paying a premium on refined sugar exported to foreign markets. This move came too late to revive the industry at La Rochelle. Four Rochelais refineries produced less than one-half of the refined sugar that refineries manufactured in the early 1750s. Markets had been lost which could not be reentered since the quality of Rochelais sugars was no better than those of other refiners and their cost slightly higher when shipped long distances. In effect, La Rochelle's decline as a refining center anticipated its decline as a center of colonial trade and stemmed from the same basic cause—locational disadvantages.[7]

Indigo.   Until the Seven Years' War, the value of imported indigo roughly matched that of sugar. Santo Domingo's plantations supplied the larger part of French and Rochelais indigo, and only Guatemala surpassed the French possession as a New World producer of the dyestuff. While growers on Santo Domingo gradually shifted after 1730 to sugar, coffee, and cotton, indigo remained a major export crop. English textile manufacturers used Santo Domingan indigo in large quantities during the eighteenth century since harvests in India, Jamaica, and South Carolina, the leading English colonial producers, failed to meet English demand. By the 1790s, Brazil ranked behind Guatemala, Santo Domingo, and South Carolina as a source for Europe. During the 1780s, a fifth center of indigo cultivation, Louisiana, may have produced an amount equal to Brazil.

As with sugar, the bulk of Rochelais indigo imports were purchased by Holland and the Hanse cities, with German buyers receiving a larger proportion of diminishing total indigo exports after 1765. Unlike sugar, sizable quantities of indigo were occasionally forwarded to English, Danish, Italian, and Swiss buyers. Normally, during the first half of the century, Holland and the German cities placed orders for some 50 percent of Rochelais indigo imports. During the latter part of the century, exports to Swiss markets frequently equaled those sent to the north. Between 80 and 90 percent of indigo receipts at La Rochelle entered the entrepôt for reexport to foreigners.

Rochelais indigo resembled that available at any other French port. Prices at La Rochelle varied little from those at Nantes or Bordeaux. Indigo from Louisiana, reputedly of inferior dyemaking quality, supplied La Rochelle with a cheap grade that found a market in England. Only this minor and temporary advantage distinguished the indigo traffic at La Rochelle from that of other Atlantic ports. General supply and demand factors and annual negotiations with the Farmers General on the setting of the rate of the *domaine d'occident* (tax on the value of goods coming from the American colonies) comprised the routine concerns of armateurs and merchants dealing in indigo. Indigo receipts declined at La Rochelle, Nantes, and Bordeaux after 1765, partially as a result of the cession of Louisiana to Spain. Indigo gradually became of secondary importance in the colonial trade.[8]

Cotton. European demand for coffee and cotton rose dramatically during the eighteenth century, the former to satisfy a new taste and the latter to meet the ever-growing demand of textile manufacturers. Government policies affected the import-export trade in both commodities. Cotton figured but fractionally in the trade of La Rochelle even though its importance increased somewhat during the last two or three decades of the Old Regime. Following the Seven Years' War, the value of Rochelais cotton imports averaged 239,117 lt. for the five years 1764–68 and 288,533 lt. for the four years 1774–76, 1778. At Bordeaux, in 1778, cotton exports reached a value of 1.3 million lt., and in 1786 the value fell just short of four million lt., virtually all of which was reexported to England. While precise figures for La Rochelle's cotton receipts during the 1780s are not available, evidence fails to point to a marked growth in the trade.

Unlike sugar or indigo, only minor quantities of Rochelais cotton receipts were reexported. Prohibitive export duties on raw cotton, designed to assure a supply of the fiber to domestic cloth manufacturers, discouraged the foreign trade. As of 1749, export duties amounted to 24 lt. per hundredweight. Cotton prices averaged 185 lt. per hundred weight at La Rochelle for the three years 1749–51. Duties of 13 percent reduced reexport profits to practically nothing and pushed French cotton prices above those from other sources. Large supplies of cotton accumulated between 1752 and 1756, depressing prices to 100 lt. per hundredweight. Even a reduction in duties in 1751 from 24 lt. to 10 lt. per hundredweight did little to stimulate interest in the foreign trade, since duties of 10 percent still obstructed foreign demand.

Following the Seven Years' War, vastly higher reexport duties further discouraged cotton exports. Only after 1786 were they lowered to reasonable levels. Bordeaux, servicing a high demand in England, exploited the situation. Apparently, La Rochelle did not but rather continued to ship small quantities to Amiens, Le Havre, Rouen, and other textile manufacturing centers.[9]

Coffee. Coffee developed into a lucrative trade commodity during the 1740s and thereafter. At La Rochelle, coffee imports composed about 10 percent of the total value of colonial imports from 1740 through the end of the Old Regime. While of lesser worth than either sugar or indigo until 1765, after that year the value of coffee receipts almost equaled the value of indigo receipts. Of lesser value per unit than indigo, coffee in bulk provided two to three times the tonnage of indigo. A similar pattern described the development of the coffee trade at Nantes, where indigo remained the number two colonial import until the 1760s. Between 1763 and 1771, coffee and Indigo imports were of equal value, but thereafter, the value of coffee imports exceeded that of indigo by as much as six times. During the 1780s, coffee became the premier import at Bordeaux.

La Rochelle exploited only minimally the steadily rising European demand for coffee. Until 1736, the Company of the Indies held the exclusive privilege of importing and selling the bean. After that, the trade in coffee was opened to private merchants. Those who imported for domestic use paid a duty of six lt. per hundredweight. If destined for reexport within six months, the coffee was not taxed. By the 1740s, coffee culture had replaced cocoa on Santo Domingo, Martinique, and Guadeloupe after a blight had swept through the Antilles destroying the cocoa groves. Small quantities of coffee flowed into France until the conclusion of the War of the Austrian Succession, when imports began in earnest. Coffee exports from La Rochelle to northern Europe equaled 4 percent of total French shipments to those markets in 1750 and 5.7 percent in 1751.

Some two decades later, in 1775 and 1776, the Rochelais share of coffee exports had declined to under 3 percent, and only the outbreak of war and the availability in port of shipping from northern Europe pushed up the Rochelais share to almost 6 percent in 1779 and 1780. Annual Rochelais exports to the North during the period 1750–80, however, never reached 800 tons. At Nantes, coffee exports averaged some 5,000 tons yearly during the early years of the 1770s and contributed some 20 percent of total French coffee exports to the North. Evidence from the 1780s offered no reason to assume that La Rochelle's share differed substantially from that of 1775 and 1776. Rochelais armateurs had ready explanations for their inability to control a greater share of this profitable trade.

The six month entrepôt, according to the Rochelais, was too short a period since the bulk of exports went north where ports were frequently iced-in for four to six months during the winter. This serious inconvenience, however, hampered all the French ports, not only La Rochelle. Moreover, coffee importers complained that the regulations that required incoming coffee to be placed immediately in warehouses administered by the Farmers General resulted in much spoilage because of inadequate storage facilities and excessive dampness. The merchants accused the Farm of indifference to their grievances since the Farm received its dues and fees whether the coffee rotted or not. Thus, the Rochelais argued, the entrepôt period must be lengthened and the coffee left in the possession of its owners. Farm officials, of course, denied any culpability and, indeed, no proofs were ever offered by coffee importers to substantiate their charges. Merchants attacked the Farm whenever possible, for both small and large reasons, for reasons based on both fact and fancy. When the Farm was involved in an operation, it was second nature, an automatic reflex, for merchants to accuse it of cupidity, inefficiency, exploitation, or whatever seemed most appropriate. Entrepôt requirements remained unchanged through at least 1780, although from time to time temporary extensions were allowed by the Farm.

Heavy duties on exports from the colonies and payable there came under persistent merchant fire, as did the consumption tax and domaine d'occident rates. In 1774, the *droit d'octrois* (colonial export duty) amounted to 12 percent of the price of coffee in La Rochelle. Coffee sold for domestic consumption paid 6 lt. per hundredweight. Added to the colonial duty, tax charges equaled 24 percent of the price on the Rochelais market. If the coffee entered the warehouse in 1774, domaine d'occident duties skimmed off 8 lt. per hundredweight for a total tax rate of 28 percent. Either way, the importer bore a heavy tax burden. For a cargo of 300,000 pounds of coffee, worth 150,000 lt., the tax for shipment to domestic purchasers amounted to 36,000 lt., and for reexport, 42,000 lt. Rochelais armateurs warned in 1774 that if coffee prices in 1775 and 1776 continued to drop, as they had since 1770, and if tax rates remained the same, they would pay 40 percent of the commodity's value in taxes and would simply cease to import it.

Rochelais complaints about exorbitant taxation seemed well founded. But, high as taxes were—and domaine d'occident rates in 1789 were 80 percent higher than in 1774 while prices had risen but 30 percent—imports in Bordeaux and Nantes reached record levels. La Rochelle's merchants explained the lead of Bordeaux in the coffee trade by insisting that domaine d'occident rates were inequitable. Rochelais coffee, according to coffee merchants, paid over five lt. per hundredweight, whereas Bordelais coffee paid slightly over one lt. The Rochelais figure is correct; the Bordelais rate was not confirmed. Any tax differential favorable to Bordeaux, given the locational disadvantages of La Rochelle and the locational advantages of Bordeaux, would add to the attractiveness of the Bordelais coffee market and reduce the orders flowing into La Rochelle.[10] Weakening the force of the Rochelais argument, which emphasized unfavorable tax differentials between La Rochelle and other ports as an explanation for La Rochelle's slide toward obscurity, was the fact that Nantes paid higher duties on colonial goods—including coffee but particularly sugar—than La Rochelle. Yet Nantes's commerce in both staples expanded more rapidly after 1765 than La Rochelle's.

Tobacco. Tobacco, important as a source of revenue for the crown and the most profitable monopoly of the Farmers General, figured hardly at all in the commerce of La Rochelle. During the period 1718–30, when the Company of the West and its successors monopolized the tobacco trade, allowing private merchants to import for a fee, Rochelais merchants imported some tobacco.

In 1731, the company ceded Louisiana to the crown, having already leased the tobacco monopoly to the Farm a year earlier. In an effort to stimulate the economy of Louisiana, the crown offered certain incentives to armateurs who would dispatch vessels to the Mississippi, including the privilege of importing tobacco that then had to be sold directly to the Farm. Such Rochelais armateurs as Louis Vivier, Polycarpe Bourgine, and Jacques Rasteau initiated a trade with New Orleans. But the regulations of the Farm concerning the tobacco trade were onerous, the prices offered for tobacco low, production in Louisiana inconsequential, and the collection of debts in that colony most difficult. While the tobacco trade with Louisiana never amounted to much, Rasteau, Vivier, and a few others pursued it because the colony's propinquity to Spanish possessions fostered an interloping trade that brought some Spanish gold and silver to La Rochelle, and because the colony did provide a fair supply of furs and skins.[11]

Furs and Skins. Until the cession of Louisiana to Spain and the loss of Canada to England, furs and skins composed a substantial portion of Rochelais imports from the colonies. Canada supplied most of the beaver and other furs, Louisiana's forests contributed deerskins, and Santo Domingo provided cowhide and some horsehide. From 1718 through 1733, beaver pelts exceeded other pelts and hides in value in all but five years. During the next two decades, other pelts and hides surpassed beaver in value in all but two years. After 1765, the Rochelais virtually ceased plying this trade.

During the peak of the fur trade, imports valued in excess of two million lt. crowded La Rochelle's warehouses in 1727, 1744, 1749, 1752, and 1757. In 1754, almost four million lt. in furs entered the city, or 37 percent of total imports. The value of fur imports for most other peacetime years prior to 1765 normally approached one million lt. As indicated in table 8.1, while less than one-half of Rochelais imports were reexported, the reexport trade gained ground during the 1740s and 1750s. In 1744 and 1749, 21 percent and 16 percent, respectively, of imports were shipped to foreign markets. The value of reexports attained 30 percent of the value of imports in both 1752 and 1754, rising to 43 percent in 1757. Fur and skin buyers throughout continental Europe obtained goods at La Rochelle.

Rochelais merchants occasionally complained that local taxes on incoming furs exceeded those exacted elsewhere. But their active participation in the Canadian and Louisiana trades secured the city a preeminent role in the fur trade. Unfortunately, the trade shrunk after 1765 to but a fraction of its former magnitude. Niort, a nearby center of leather manufacturing, normally obtained all its skins from the Rochelais. After 1765, however, Niortais manufacturers were compelled to seek supplies elsewhere. Efforts made during and after the American Revolution to initiate a fur trade with the United States foundered on the inability of the French to supply Americans with goods competitive in price with those available in England. Also, in 1782, the Spanish government opened up the trade with Spanish Louisiana to selected French ports but unaccountably neglected to include La Rochelle. The Spanish corrected this oversight in 1785. Then, in 1786, the crown lowered import duties on hides while also remedying certain inequities in the levying of the domaine d'occident on furs and skins at La Rochelle. All of this occurred too late to benefit the Rochelais who, by then, had plunged heavily into the slave trade.[12]

Table 8.1. *Imports and Exports of Furs and Skins at La Rochelle, 1727–57 (lt.)*

Year	Value of imports	% of imports	Value of furs and skins exported to					Total value of exports
			Holland	the North	Spain	Italy	Switzerland	
1727	2,096,392	36	79,321	77,876	184,234	7,940	6,879	356,260
1744	1,854,605	33	20,995	93,959	7,216	0	58,835	381,005
1749	2,705,321	25	17,600	237,682	0	0	165,909	421,191
1752	2,693,290	23	3,700	565,437	90,708	138,581	0	801,541
1754	3,930,456	37	194,572	641,820	177,206	136,218	20,752	1,170,568
1757	1,979,459	27	43,680	336,683	71,183	49,194	385,060	851,800

Source: See note 12.

Fish. One sector of the Rochelais economy, fish and fishing, requires some attention even though the port ranked far behind Saint-Malo, Dieppe, Honfleur, Bayonne, or Granville in fishing armements. While the Rochelais dispatched an annual average of four to five terreneuviers to the Grand Banks during the 1770s and 1780s, compared with two or three in earlier periods, upward of twenty to twenty-five fishing vessels put in at the port each year to discharge their cargoes of codfish. Rochelais terreneuviers and those from other ports frequently carried their catch directly to the Antilles and returned laden with colonial produce. The catch that returned to La Rochelle found its way into local and regional markets.

The value of codfish deliveries to La Rochelle rose steadily during the 1740s and 1750s. Imports never reached 100,000 lt. in value prior to 1740 but, following the War of the Austrian Succession, averaged 327,080 lt. for the years 1747–49 and reached an annual average of 577,000 lt. for the years 1750–54. The Seven Years' War, unsettled conditions, British naval harassment of French fishing vessels in North American waters, and the American Revolution disrupted the trade, but it rebounded during the 1780s when one million lt. in cod was discharged at La Rochelle.

Revival of Rochelais interest in fishing ventures during the 1770s, reflected in table 2.3, followed government decisions to subsidize the trade. In 1767, the government granted a subsidy of 500 lt. to all terreneuviers fishing off the Grand Banks and a premium for codfish introduced into the Antilles. Higher premiums were authorized in 1785 for dried cod shipped to the Antilles, southern Europe and the Levant, and to northern Europe. Simultaneously, foreign cod imported by colonists paid increased duties. In 1787, both the premiums and the duties were raised again. These inducements offered sufficient advantages to the Rochelais to stimulate additional armements and even to convince such major armateurs as Meschinet de Richemond and Marc Antoine Lefebvre & Son to launch their own fishing ventures.

While entrepôt regulations and the domaine d'occident did not apply to codfish imports, the Rochelais were not without grievances. Each terreneuvier required large quantities of salt which La Rochelle, as a major center of salt production, was well equipped to supply to both local and nonlocal fishing vessels. But extremely high taxes were levied against salt.[13] Since the last part of this chapter analyzes the trade in locally produced commodities, including salt, further discussion of fishing will be coupled with the analysis of the salt trade.

THE SPECIAL TRADES OF LA ROCHELLE

La Rochelle developed a substantial market for certain products of its back country, which somewhat compensated for more general locational disadvantages. Although La Rochelle's hinterland produced insignificant quantities of grain, from time to time surpluses were harvested, which entered either the domestic or foreign trade. Of greater economic importance, La Rochelle's immediate back country produced essential supplies of salt. Moreover, the city was also central to a major brandy producing region, which stretched from the city's walls to Cognac on the Charente River and from there north along a crescent to Ruffec, Civray, and Parthenay, all within seventy-five miles of the port. The availability of these products attracted French and foreign vessels to La Rochelle and smaller neighboring ports and provided armateurs with valuable export cargoes. Of the two, brandy's economic value far surpassed that of salt, but among the advantages of the latter commodity was its essentiality to the fishing fleet. However, during the later half of the eighteenth century, falling production, high taxation, and competition from other producing regions reduced the value of these trades, in a sense stripping La Rochelle of its only natural advantages.

The Grain Trade. As a primary subsistence crop, cereals were essential to the city and its region. Local crop shortages demanded importation while surpluses allowed exports to both domestic and overseas buyers. Most Rochelais grain exports went to the colonies. Grain normally formed between 5 and 10 percent of the value of outbound colonial cargoes, but a varying quantity of that export—never exceeding one-half—derived from regional farms. La Rochelle's cereal exports, then, did not count heavily in the overseas trade and depended upon imports from nonlocal sources.

Few commodity trades were as firmly encased in regulations as grains. French cereal production became more stable during the eighteenth century and, after 1750, cereal production per capita rose. However, local fears of famine and transportation inefficiency frequently prevented the transfer of crops from regions of surplus to regions of scarcity. The magnitude of the grain trade at maritime centers depended upon local supplies and government assessment of national needs. Grain shortages to the north and south of La Rochelle in 1699–1700 prompted Rochelais merchants to apply for permission to export grains to Rouen, Bordeaux, and Libourne. Short crops in Brittany in 1694, 1696, and 1709 stimulated grain imports from foreign dealers and exports to Nantes. Rochelais merchants received permission to export cereals to Portugal in 1708 and also furnished grains to Guyenne. In 1709, however, the failure of crops in Saintonge and Aunis caused the intendant to prohibit exports, a condition that lasted through the poor crops of 1710. Rochelais grain dealers sought grains from northern Europe for local consumption.

Frequently during the first half of the century, and with distressing regularity prior to 1725, arrêts du conseil—1710, 1711, 1712, 1718, 1721, 1722, 1723, 1746, and 1747—interdicted all exports of grain to foreign markets. In 1744, La Rochelle and other nearby ports received special permission to export to foreign markets, a privilege suspended in 1746 and 1747. From 1764 to 1767,

France (with La Rochelle's participation) shipped large quantities of grain and flour to Spain and Portugal. Between 1767 and 1772, shortages in Normandy and Brittany prompted the suspension of the foreign grain trade. During that period, Rochelais shipments moved north. In 1773, a local crop failure caused grain to be imported from Holland. In 1774, excellent harvests in Aunis and Saintonge supplied needs in the southern provinces of France. Exports to foreigners were permitted in 1777, 1779, 1786, and 1787; prohibitions were in effect in 1778, 1781, 1784, 1788, and 1789. Thus the trade vacillated and its destinations shifted according to the supply of cereals locally, regionally, nationally, and throughout Europe.

Rochelais merchants moved in and out of the trade as conditions and regulations dictated. Those engaged in the colonial trade, either as armateurs or purchasers of cargo space, moved grain freely since flour destined for the colonies encountered no prohibitions other than those caused by supply. Flour was imported from foreign sources during years of short domestic supply, placed in entrepôt, and shipped free of duties. Greater risks faced merchants engaged in the foreign grain trade. Demand at foreign markets reacted sensitively to the ebb and flow of production throughout Europe. Information assessing that production moved but slowly and, as a result, was frequently out of date when acted upon. Grains were also liable to heavy import and export duties. In 1737, acting on the advice of Simonde Brothers in London, Théodore Delacroix shipped large quantities of grain to a Lisbon correspondent of that firm. At first the cargo met with slow sales; apparently, information describing a cereal crop failure had been exaggerated. The new crop did fail, however, and Delacroix's wheat and barley moved briskly at inflated prices Poor luck for the Portuguese turned potential losses for Delacroix into a neat profit.[14]

Rochelais grain dealers extolled the concept of free movement of cereals within the nation, accepted the necessity of controls on foreign exports, and lobbied for the designation of La Rochelle as the exclusive port of grain exports in the generality and immediate region. Arguing that all local cereals should be exported from their port, the Rochelais sought to undercut the grain trade of Marennes, a small mainland fishing village off the southern tip of Île d'Orleron and close to the Charente River. Marennes attracted coasting vessels of all nationalities because of its proximity to the salt flats, its rich oyster beds, and because fewer and lower grain taxes were levied than at La Rochelle. The Rochelais case made the most of inequitable tax rates. On the one hand, the Rochelais accused dealers at Marennes of avoiding the responsibilities of citizens to support their government through taxes; on the other hand, they requested that local duties at La Rochelle be revoked. The Rochelais also pointed to the lack of quality control at Marennes and the absence of adequate storage facilities, even though buyers of grain from Rochelais stocks often complained of inconveniences in loading grain due to the scarcity of lighter vessels and warehousing. The Rochelais displayed similar annoyance about the grain trade of Marans, a village to the north. At both Marans and

Marennes, Rochelais merchants employed agents to purchase grain and ship it to La Rochelle. They hoped to eliminate this costly step by concentrating the entire grain export trade of Aunis and Saintonge at La Rochelle. Their efforts to establish exclusivism in miniature failed and the cereal trade of their smaller competitors continued into the 1780s.[15]

Regulations impinged as tightly upon the local commerce in cereals as upon the foreign trade. A variety of regulations purportedly guarded local consumers against forestalling and monopoly while guaranteeing standard quality and accurate weight. Producers, bakers, wholesalers, retailers, and exporters submitted to controls, medieval in origin, designed to prevent artificial scarcities and inflated prices and to assure local residents an adequate daily supply. Thus, sales had to be transacted at stipulated times and places, public announcement of incoming shipments were compulsory, and sales at wholesale could occur only after local bakers had concluded their purchases.

The primary tax support for consumer protection was the *droit de ménage,* applied at La Rochelle since at least 1305. The receiver or collector of the ménage, prohibited from participating in the grain trade, collected the tax on grain put into storage. This official appointed assistants, who weighed and assessed the cereals as they arrived in the city whether by land or by sea. Initially administered by the municipality, the ménage was farmed to individuals until 1628. Following the conquest of La Rochelle, Louis XIII united this rente with his estate. Finally, in 1751, La Rochelle purchased the rente for 36,000 lt., adding the income from the lease or farm to the city revenues.

During the seventeenth and early eighteenth centuries, the coverage of the droit de ménage narrowed, circumscribing the rights of the tax farmers to collect the fees under certain circumstances. Exemptions from the duty applied to Rochelais importing grain at their own risk to be consumed in the city or province and to wheat grown on the property of Rochelais, regardless of the disposition of the wheat. In 1736, exemption from ménage was extended to wheat or flour destined for the colonies. And at some point, or so Rochelais armateurs maintained in their arguments against this tax, the ménage had been further narrowed by exempting transactions at wholesale. Considerable controversy arose between grain dealers and ménage farmers during the 1770s regarding that point, as the latter fought to protect their capital investment in their offices.

In 1771, Jacques Carayon fils aîné purchased several hundred tons of foreign grain for the account of a Limoges dealer. The collector of the ménage assessed the tax against the shipment, claiming that it applied to all grains entering the city and stored prior to export beyond La Rochelle. Carayon, supported by the La Rochelle Chamber of Commerce, asserted the exemption from the tax of grain purchased at wholesale. Carayon's argument also dramatized the fact that this shipment was destined for a region suffering from grain shortages. Dragging on into 1776, the dispute was finally settled by the Comptroller General, who concluded that wholesale transactions were exempt. He ordered the restoration of all taxes paid by Carayon and others in the interim.

As with many of the farmed taxes, the original protective goals of ménage had long since dropped from sight. Collectors viewed it as a means of livelihood, the crown and the municipality coveted its revenues, and merchants avoided payment. Merchants accused collectors of indifference toward the inspections designed to guarantee standard weights and qualities. Collectors countered with claims of gross tax evasion by dealers, pointing out in 1750 that wheat consumption in La Rochelle averaged about 7,200 tons annually while merchant statements admitted to receipts of under 6,000 tons. Successfully in 1739 and unsuccessfully in 1750 and 1751, the collectors defended their proprietary rights against proposals that the administration of the duty revert to the city. In their defense, the collectors advanced no arguments supporting the duty as an efficient regulator of the grain trade but rather only demonstrated the legality of their proprietary rights. Nor did the merchants in their critiques of ménage suggest an alternative method of control or an alternate source of revenue for the municipality. Instead, merchants ignored the regulation requiring the registration of their receipts, used grain and flour stored for export to the colonies for other purposes, and complained about all other taxes on the grain trade. Self-interest rather than concern for the public welfare prompted most of the contention.[16]

The Brandy Trade. A bewildering variety of regulations and taxes on brandy imposed so heavy a burden during the eighteenth century that the vitality of this essential Rochelais trade was sapped. Rochelais brandies lost their competitive edge over brandies from other places, forcing a shift in the focus of the trade from Europe to Africa. The politics of brandy, more complex than the politics of grain, pitted planters and armateurs against regional brandy producers and distributors and both of these groups against the government's venal officials, who considered brandy a secure source of personal income and state revenue rather than as the region's most valuable export.[17]

Rochelais wines enjoyed a good reputation in domestic and foreign markets into the early seventeenth century. However, at some time during the late sixteenth century, a serious plant disease invaded coastal Aunis and moved swiftly into the interior of the province. As the disease spread, affecting the quality of the wine, growers switched to grapes producing an inferior quality of wine and, by the early seventeenth century, some had commenced to distill the wine into eau-de-vie. By 1700, vineyards in the Charente and Boutonne river valleys as well as on Île de Ré and Île d'Orleron had turned to the production of brandies. During the same period, landowners in those areas turned wheat fields into vineyards, a development that increased the vulnerability of the region to cereal shortages and hastened the destruction of woodlands, but also provided farmers with a product superior in value to either wine or wheat. By 1700, brandy had become the major export commodity of local production.[18]

In 1720, brandy exports formed 37 percent of total Rochelais exports. While this share declined thereafter, it rarely dropped below 10 percent and normally rested between 15 and 20 percent. In 1773, brandy composed only 5 percent of a century-high total export of 20.4 million lt., but in absolute terms the value of brandy exports exceeded those of 1770 when it had formed 17 percent of the total (see table 8.2). In 1776, brandy constituted 14 percent of total exports of over 15 million lt., the second largest export year for eighteenth-century La Rochelle.

As table 8.2 indicates, the destination of brandy exports shifted markedly during the century. Holland and northern Europe had received well over 50 percent of the region's brandies before 1765; in some years exports to the North formed from 70 to 90 percent of the total. After 1765, brandy shipments to the North fell off sharply, more so to Scandinavian and German markets than to Dutch, but still replicating a pattern noticeable in exports of colonial staples. Although total exports to England were below exports to northern Europe, England received more Rochelais brandies after 1765, becoming the primary European market but a most unstable one because of Anglo-French hostility. The decline in brandy sales to European buyers was compensated by the dramatically enhanced use of brandy in the slave trade. As table 8.2 shows, Africa took 75 percent of all brandy exports in 1775 and 1776, years in which brandy formed 11 percent of total Rochelais exports. Brandy exports to the colonies normally contributed under 5 percent of the value of outbound cargoes and after 1750 were of lower value than wines.

Regulations subjected brandies, wines, and other alcoholic beverages to rigorous inspections at various points between manufacture and shipment. Complex and changing tax and pricing structures added to the mystery of the trade. A cadre of venal officers headed by *courtiers d'eau-de-vie* (brandy brokers), presumably expert in the rituals of the trade, presided over the traffic in brandy, acting as brokers and establishing the price paid for brandy by shippers. During the eighteenth century, brandy shippers leveled countless charges against the courtiers, claiming that the brandy marketing system not only obstructed growth but caused its decline.

The value of La Rochelle's brandy rested ultimately upon its reputation, its taste, and its bouquet. The distillation process and particularly the methods used to barrel and store the brandy before shipment determined the quality of the drink. To protect against improper or fraudulent packaging, local brandy producers and shippers in 1712 agreed upon the use of a standard liquid measure for brandy, the *velt* (about seven English quarts); thereafter the normal cask of brandy presumably contained twenty-seven velts. Then, to enforce conformity to the measure adopted, the municipality added a master cooper to the office of *d'Essayeur, marqueur, mesureur, et étalonneur des poids et mesures.* Only barrels marked by the cooper could be used for brandy and only coopers could make the barrels. An arrêt of 1743 prescribed the construction of the barrel down to the last stave. Few quibbled over the need for such standardization. A revised system was introduced in 1753, but as late as 1786 charges of dishonesty in the packaging of brandy elicited renewed efforts to devise a workable system. Despite inspections, casks of short weight,

Table 8.2. Brandy Exports from La Rochelle, 1720–76 (lt.)

Year	Total value of brandy exports	Holland and the North	England	Africa	The Antilles, Louisiana, and Canada	All other
1720	3,364,080	2,484,240	787,360	0	73,600	18,880
1730	1,521,250	1,140,350	344,700	0	36,200	0
1740	1,591,078	1,102,346	115,168	0	282,308	91,256
1750	851,175	428,433	232,380	45,450	93,780	51,132
1754	1,047,679	636,544	251,115	85,400	74,620	0
1765	1,424,555	1,296,455	35,550	57,690	34,140	720
1770	1,004,257	165,320	447,800	190,750	10,920	189,447
1773	1,116,170	231,770	420,585	426,346	0	37,469
1775	1,503,875	126,375	375,980	920,385	81,135	0
1776	2,173,130	72,243	184,072	1,825,690	33,075	58,050

Source: Récapitulation sorties, CCLR, carton 27.

poorly constructed casks, and casks made by unauthorized individuals continued to plague the trade.

In 1749, 120 casks of brandy readied for export to Dieppe were inspected by a *jaugeur* (gauger) and two *gourmetres* (tasters). These inspectors found some of the casks defective, giving the contents a bad taste, and they rejected 14. These offices, in 1753, were merged with the offices of *agréeurs à l'acceptation and agréeurs à l'embarquement,* authorized to inspect, taste, and mark each barrel of brandy as it entered or left the city. Four of the former and three of the latter officers were appointed by the lieutenant general of police at La Rochelle from nominations made by the city council and the chamber of commerce. Replacements were named alternately by those two bodies. Salaries of agréeurs came from fees per cask inspected.

This system produced better results than the earlier version. For one, individuals expert in the production and packaging of the beverage were appointed as agréeurs; agréeurs such as Jean Louis Gastumeau tended to be highly respected négociants. Arbitration in case of a disputed judgment was provided for. Merchants knew the tricks of merchants. In 1754, officials seized a large quantity of uninspected brandy just as the shipper prepared to load his vessel. Old barrels returned by the purchaser with the official stamp and marks had almost deceived the agréeur.

Once approved by the agréeurs, the brandy was purchased on order by the broker, who then transferred it to the shipper. Merchants, accepting the necessity of brandy inspectors, denied the need of the courtiers who performed no useful functions, added to the cost of brandy, and reduced local brandy's competitive advantages relative to the Portuguese and Spanish product. According to the regulations of 1753, courtiers received a fee per barrel from the buyer but were prohibited from dealing on their own account—as ménage officials were. Prior to that reform, however, courtiers not only received a fee, the *droit de courtage,* but purchased inspected brandy from producers and sold it at inflated prices to local merchants. Courtiers established an effective monopoly since all brandy passed through their hands. In 1749, several merchants accused the courtiers of monopoly, price-fixing, and collusion, charges that were substantiated and that prompted the intendant to sponsor the regulations adopted in 1753.[19]

Fees exacted by venal officials were but one form of taxation to which brandy and wine were subject. Other direct taxes raised their price for shippers. Rochelais marshaled arguments that demonstrated, at least to their own satisfaction, that such taxation increased production costs, fostered foreign competition in domestic markets, and weakened the competitiveness of French brandy in foreign markets. Thus, the Rochelais explained the decline in brandy exports which occurred during the 1780s.

Still other taxes and fees burdened the brandy industry. The *aydes* (excise or direct tax), farmed out in the manner of other taxes, were charged against brandy, wine, and ciders entering the city and sold at wholesale. In order to forestall private transactions at times and places other than those stipulated, the crown permitted tax farmers to organize unannounced search and seizure forays. Beverages for local consumption then paid the enormous sum of 70 lt. per ton (a ton equaled four barrels of 27 velts) to the *fermier des octroyer.* Wine and brandy of local production destined for foreign markets paid the *subvention par doublement* (surtax), at rates of 4 lt. per standard barrel of brandy. In 1728, the tax farm levied a surtax on brandy destined for Boulogne and Calais, justifying the assessment with vague references to unnamed merchants who shipped unspecified quantities of brandy under manifest to those places but in reality exported the brandy to Holland. The surtax doubled the subvention par doublement that had been increased in 1729 to five lt. per barrel. In all likelihood there was something to the farmers' charges, but merchants raised such a hue and cry that the Comptroller General ordered the revocation of the surtax and the return of all taxes collected.

In addition to the above taxes, an arrêt of 1722 imposed a new *droit d'inspecteur aux boisson,* separate from the fees already paid to agréeurs, amounting to almost two lt. per barrel of brandy exported abroad. Then, there existed local duties on river traffic: fourteen lt. per ton by the Boutonne River, eleven lt. on the Charente, Seudre, and Gironde rivers, plus one-half lt. if destined for foreign markets other than England, in which case one lt. was charged. In 1730, brandy sold at between fifty and sixty lt. per barrel while taxes, assuming a Charente River route, cost at least twenty-five lt., indeed a heavy burden.

These tax rates persisted until the very last years of the Old Regime. In 1784, an arrêt du conseil freed eau-de-vie from all export duties including the *droits d'aydes.*[20] But other problems had already pushed production costs upward and minimized the effects of this welcome relief. Wood, an essential resource in the brandy economy, had become extremely scarce in Aunis and Saintonge. Wood for barrel construction was purchased in northern Europe along with the iron and copper used for hooping and lining the containers. In 1775, Rochelais paid 1.3 million lt. for those items—39 percent for wood products—which, of course, served purposes other than brandy-making. Wood became so scarce and dear by the 1770s that distillers turned to coal. While French coal was cheap, distillers found it unsuited to their purposes because of its inferior heat-producing qualities. English coal was far superior, but high import duties made it very expensive. During the 1780s, distillers, in alliance with Rochelais brewers and sugar refiners whose operations also required the use of much fuel, lobbied in Paris in favor of reduced duties on English coal. But their efforts to stem the tide of rising costs of production yielded no benefits. French coal miners, many operating mines financed by noble investment, opposed any reduction in the tariff. The French government feared a loss of revenue. Coal duties remained high.[21]

To an outsider from another age, the diversity of beverage taxes appears as a bewildering collage. Had their purpose been the suffocation of the brandy trade, it might be said that the taxes bore the mark of bureaucratic genius. Taxes, duties, fees, and soaring production costs so weakened the competitive strength of Rochelais brandy that cheaper Spanish and Portuguese brandies replaced the French product in Dutch and German markets (see table 8.2). To be sure, the increasing use of brandy in the slave trade compensated for the loss of markets in Europe in terms of the total value of brandy exports. But this new turn carried with it grave disadvantages, amounting to the substitution of colonial buyers, who were poor credit risks, for European buyers, who paid promptly in cash or manufactured goods. Some part of the value of the brandy shipped to Africa for the purchase of slaves was swallowed up in uncollectible debts. Too, the use of cheaper brandy in the slave trade tarnished the reputation of all Rochelais brandies and in all probability contributed to the decision of European buyers to seek the Spanish and Portuguese product.

Government recognition, however tardily, of the artificially high price of Rochelais brandy led to the arrêt of 1784. Unfortunately, it came too late; markets had already been lost and the arrêt did not prevent the continued introduction into France, especially at Calais and Dunkirk, of foreign brandy. Two decades earlier, in 1763 and 1764, the cities of La Rochelle, Nantes, Bordeaux, Saintes, Tours, Bayonne, Orléans, Angers, Rochefort, Cognac, and Saint-Jean-d'Angely had cooperated successfully to stiffen prohibitions against the introduction of rum into the country and to interdict the export of Norman cider and peach and pear brandies. A similar campaign against foreign brandy imports failed to materialize during the late 1780s. By the conclusion of the Old Regime, the brandy industry in Aunis and Saintonge was ailing, having exchanged its solid base in European markets for the flimsy support of the colonial trade.[22]

The Salt Trade. Rochelais négociant families such as the Gastumeau and Rasteau invested a portion of their wealth in agricultural lands in the region. Rasteaus owned and managed both wheat lands and vineyards and used the product from their fields in domestic and foreign commerce. The Rasteau family also held extensive tracts of salt marsh near Rochefort, as did the Depont and Charuyer families. Rochelais owned and farmed salt marshes on Île de Ré and Île d'Orleron and as far south as Rochefort and Marennes. Rochelais merchants owned an estimated 25 percent of the salt farms on Île de Ré. In the 1750s, the Delacroix family added 50,000 lt. of salt marsh to prior holdings on the two offshore islands. In 1773, the Delacroix marshes on Île de Ré yielded 25,000 lt. worth of salt. Merchants from Bordeaux and Rochefort also owned marshes north of the Gironde estuary, particularly on Île d'Orleron. Most of this salt was shipped to La Rochelle for sale.

Salt provided Rochelais merchants with an important export commodity. Along with brandy, it attracted both foreign and domestic shipping and was, of course, essential in the preparation of a variety of foods like meat and fish. But during the latter decades of the eighteenth century, the value of Rochelais salt exports declined. Sales to the Dutch, averaging 303,284 lt. for the five years 1718–22 and 446,213 lt. for the five years 1737–41, fell to an average of under 100,000 lt. annually during the 1750s and 1760s and under 25,000 lt. annually during the years 1774–78. Exports to English, German, and Scandinavian markets also dropped off, although less precipitously. Large quantities of salt, estimated in the neighborhood of 30,000 to 40,000 *muids de Brouage* (one muid equals about 24 bushels) annually during the 1780s, were required by the terreneuviers. During a peak export year such as 1741, La Rochelle exported almost 53,000 muids to Holland and northern Europe. Fishing requirements for salt, then, composed a significant portion of total demand at La Rochelle.

A number of factors intervened during the eighteenth century that damaged the Rochelais salt trade. In 1340, Philip VI (1328–50) instituted the *gabelle* (salt tax), which made the sale of salt a state monopoly. The most hated of all taxes, the gabelle provided the most stable source of government revenue during the Old Regime. In 1765, the gabelle consumed one-fifth of the value of salt produced in Aunis and Saintonge. Other taxes, transportation charges on local rivers, and various fees extracted another 10 to 15 percent of its value. Furthermore, the salt tax farmers attempted, from time to time, to inflate prices—already high because of charges against the commodity—by artificially limiting the supply of salt that reached the wholesale market.

Rochelais salt marsh owners contracted with peasants who, in return for a share of the salt, harvested and packed it. Owners somewhat blunted the effects of taxation upon themselves by reducing the shares, or in case of lease arrangements, increasing the rent, sometimes paid in cash but normally paid in salt. While this strategy shifted some of the tax burden to the lower classes, tax exactions remained so high that foreign salts could undersell Rochelais salt in foreign and domestic markets.

Regulations governing the use of salt in the fishing industry both benefited and harmed the Rochelais trade and the fishing fleet. Prior to 1680, terreneuviers paid the gabelle, but after that date that tax was not applied to fishing vessels. La Rochelle and ports in its vicinity benefited by regulations requiring terreneuviers to purchase their salts in that area. While La Rochelle's fishing fleet was always small, this requirement offered it some cost advantages over vessels from north of the Brittany peninsula, compelled to head south for salt before heading northwest for the fishing grounds. La Rochelle's advantage here was endangered when the government, responding to the artificial scarcities engendered by the salt farm, authorized the importation of cheaper and higher quality salt from Spain and Portugal and permitted fishing vessels to purchase salt at Nantes. Salt at Nantes, not subject to the gabelle, was cheaper than the Rochelais product. To counter the turn of events, the Rochelais obtained exemption in 1731 from the gabelle on all salt used to prepare provisions for crews and for export to the colonies. Another small victory was gained in 1779 when an arrêt formally suspended permission to draw salt from Spain and Portugal for use in codfishing.

While a segment of the salt trade survived because of various regulations, the foreign trade continued to suffer from taxes that priced Rochelais salt out of Dutch, Danish, and German markets. The import of Spanish and Portuguese salt at Dunkirk and other channel ports also reduced domestic demand. When, in 1786, an arrêt lowered the gabelle on salt destined for the foreign trade to two lt. per muid, the La Rochelle Chamber of Commerce protested the inadequacy of the reduction. With the price of salt only eleven to twelve lt. per muid, the chamber pointed out, the tax rate remained above 15 percent. But the government, according to Torterue Bonneau, would wait and evaluate the effects of the arrêt before doing any more. As with other tax and tariff reductions formulated by the government during the 1780s, the arrêt of 1786 provided too little relief and came too late to stimulate new endeavors in the trade. According to the Rochelais, the decay of the brandy and salt trades could be attributed directly to stifling taxes and the unstinting efforts of a legion of tax collectors to squeeze maximum profit from their offices.[23]

CONCLUSION

La Rochelle distributed hundreds of valuable products to the colonies, to much of northern Europe, and to many regions of France. While its commerce included such commodities as Charente paper and rocou, and its function as a center of distribution assured its position as a wholesaler of pharmaceuticals from Montpellier, La Rochelle's economy essentially depended upon the movement of relatively few products. Sugar, indigo, coffee, cotton, furs and skins from the colonies, and grain, brandy, and salt from the immediate hinterland sustained the high-seas trade of the port. The Rochelais enjoyed nothing approaching a monopoly in any of its major trade goods. Colonial staples flowed into many ports. Nantes and Bordeaux trafficked in salt. Brandy from the Charente River valley—Cognac, Pons, or Jarnac—was available at Bordeaux as well as La Rochelle, and was sold directly, along with salt and grain, to small Dutch or English coasters that navigated the Charente.

La Rochelle, then, faced competition in all its trades. As a distribution center patronized by merchants throughout Europe who trusted and relied upon their Rochelais counterparts, La Rochelle required large quantities of goods of assorted grades or qualities at competitive prices. Any factors that raised prices at La Rochelle and not elsewhere or reduced the variety or quantity of goods at La Rochelle and not elsewhere harmed the city's economy. Virtually without exception, each of the principal trade goods at La Rochelle, and particularly the regional products, bore tax and tariff burdens that in the long run reduced the magnitude of trade. Tax farmers, whether in tobacco or salt, preferred a stable volume of trade, which could be taxed at a high rate and thus assuring a stable revenue, to lower taxes, which might stimulate sufficient new sales to increase total revenues. The government, too, subscribed to this policy. Each war intensified the financial problems of the government, prompting it to initiate a new round of tax increases by either raising existing rates or selling new venal offices.

The Rochelais were correct in attributing the loss of European markets for brandy and salt to the fees of venal officials, high taxes levied on both goods, and in the case of brandy, high taxes on such necessary supplemental products as wood and coal, and government trade policies. All of these factors greatly increased production costs and priced the La Rochelle products out of traditional markets. Coupled with the diminished capacity of Rochelais sugar refineries, resulting from competition from other refining centers, these trends reduced La Rochelle's attractiveness as a port of call. English, Dutch, Danish, and German vessels—which in earlier years ascended the Charente, sent lighters into the canals that crisscrossed the salt marshes, and put into La Rochelle for mixed cargoes of salt, brandy, and colonial staples—were conspicuously absent during the 1780s. Similarly, coasters from Saint-Malo or terreneuviers from Granville, seeking salt and other goods, appeared less regularly.

That goods might be carried to customers in the North in their own vessels occurred to the Rochelais. They recognized the high price of reliance upon foreign shipping. They discussed the possibilities of a larger coasting trade under Rochelais registry. But they did not act, save to petition the government for free port status and tonnage subsidies for le grand cabotage. When, during the mid-1780s, the French government initiated a series of tax and tariff reductions, and in addition negotiated in 1786 a new commercial treaty with Great Britain which promised to increase French brandy and wine exports, the eleventh hour for Rochelais commerce had already struck.[24]

NINE

Marine Insurance
Industry in Eighteenth-Century
La Rochelle

 Merchants at La Rochelle and other ports during the seventeenth and eighteenth centuries developed the habit of insuring their ventures against the hazards of the sea by taking out insurance policies. By the end of the Old Regime, it was an unusual merchant who failed to insure a major part of his shipments. La Rochelle, by that time, had become one of the most important insurance centers in France. Rochelais armateurs were among the most active insurance underwriters in the community, covering risks on vessels and cargoes of both Rochelais and non-Rochelais ownership.

As the magnitude of the insurance business grew, insurance companies appeared in La Rochelle. Some were established by Rochelais, and others, with their headquarters elsewhere, operated branches in the port which were managed by Rochelais. These firms, and underwriting by individual Rochelais, quickened the pace of capital circulation and fostered capital formation in the city.

Capital in the form of premiums and claims payments flowed between major insurance centers. Determining the desirability and the capability of Rochelais capitalists to cover the insurance needs of the local maritime sector will be useful in assessing the overall economic strength of the port. Identifying the prominent Rochelais underwriters and measuring the magnitude of their insurance business will supplement the data already presented regarding investment patterns. Attention to the institutionalization of the insurance industry will further elucidate the structure of business organizations in the city.

GENERAL MARINE INSURANCE PRACTICES

Scholarship on insurance traces the origins and development of insurance from the middle ages through the sixteenth century much more adequately than its maturation during the seventeenth and eighteenth centuries. Available eighteenth-century studies have focused almost exclusively on the legalistic and contractual aspects and upon the origins of certain insurance companies. While insurance during the eighteenth century became a major investment area and, of course, an absolute necessity in carrying on a vastly expanded maritime trade, few studies have investigated the general economic characteristics of insurance. Even less is known of the routine practices of insurance underwriting in France: about coverage, peacetime or wartime premiums, claims adjustments, or about the individuals who insured the risks of others. Nor has the insurance business been studied from within the context of a commercial city and its economic structure.[1]

The earliest cities with significant underwriting capabilities were situated on the Italian peninsula. As the center of economic strength in Europe shifted to the north and west, so too did the insurance industry, first to the Iberian Peninsula and, by the mid-seventeenth century, to the Low Countries and England. Earlier customary practices had been codified in Barcelona in 1435, in Florence in 1523, again in Spain in 1556, and in Antwerp in 1563. Governments attempted to exercise some control over the business through the licensing of brokers, who brought underwriters together with those seeking insurance. Chambers of insurance were established and legally recognized by the state in Amsterdam in 1598, London, 1601, Rotterdam, 1614, Marseilles, 1669, and Paris, 1671 and served as insurance policy registrars and as regulators of insurance practices.

By 1600, general agreement prevailed regarding the format of a policy and its coverage. Insurance protected both vessels and cargoes along predetermined routes from dock to dock, with policies normally terminating twenty-four hours after a vessel achieved secure anchorage or upon the safe unloading of the cargo. Rules for the abandonment of a vessel or cargo varied slightly from state to state as did the procedures to be followed for submitting claims. The rules of simple and gross averages applied to claims adjustments also differed in detail from place to place, but their essence was agreed upon.[2] Deductible clauses were also common, although the deductible percentage, too, varied from nation to nation.[3]

Certain insurance practices, common at one time or another, were gradually prohibited. Both England and France adopted the compulsory registration of policies in order to prevent multiple insurance—the writing of two or more policies on a certain piece of property which provided coverage in excess of its value. Policies taken on ventures in which the insured held no property interest were common into the eighteenth century. Referred to as "interest no interest" policies and recognized as simple speculation, England and France declared them illegal during the 1740s. In England, legislation passed in 1746 also prohibited reinsurance, the practice of insurers taking insurance on the premium or on the solvency of the insurer. French legislation permitted insurers to apply to the admiralty office for permission to make reinsurance. Thus in 1766, the widow Legriel & Son sought and received permission to reinsure risks of

12,250 lt. underwritten in 1764 by Boiven, a Parisian merchant, who had stopped payment in 1765. The Legriel firm wished to cover the risk of Boiven's failure since the ventures originally covered by him had not been concluded.[4] While French and English legislation made overinsurance illegal, it remained legal in Hamburg, Amsterdam, and Stockholm.

Since it was patently impossible to foresee all eventualities, a necessary flexibility existed in the actual practice of making insurance. For example, Joseph Pascaud took out a 10,000 lt. insurance policy on goods arriving from Canada and paid premiums on that sum. When the vessel arrived with 4,745 lt. in goods, his premium payment on 5,255 lt. was refunded. Since Pascaud had made the policy in good faith, acting on the latest information available to him, practice allowed the nullification of the inapplicable portion of the coverage. When Jean Ezeckiel Couillandeau took out a policy of 27,500 lt. to cover his five-sixths interest in a venture and his agent took out a similar policy at Bordeaux, cancellation of the duplicate policy was mandatory and premiums were returned.[5] In France, an ordinance published in 1681 spelled out the basic outlines of insurance practices. Certain changes in detail occurred during the eighteenth century, but in most essentials the rules of 1681 prevailed during the remainder of the Old Regime.

COMPANIES OF INSURANCE

During the eighteenth century, the insurance business assumed its corporate form. Attempts to establish monopolistic companies in England, Holland, and France were defeated, while a number of private insurance corporations were established in northern Europe. Amsterdam and London competed for primacy, with the Dutch maintaining a superiority until their entry into the War of the American Revolution. France did not develop the insurance capabilities of either Holland or England. French armateurs regularly sought to cover a part of their ventures in London or Amsterdam. So lucrative was French patronage that coverage was extended by the English even when at war with France, a practice that generated heated debate in Parliament during the wars of the 1740s and the 1750s.

After the War of the Spanish Succession, successful insurance companies emerged throughout Europe. In 1719 and 1720, partly as a result of the speculative fever unleashed by Law's schemes in France and the English South Seas Company, a number of English insurance companies attempted to gain charters. Only two survived the economic collapse, the Royal Assurance Exchange and the London Assurance Company. The first Dutch company also became operational in 1720, with offices in Rotterdam and twenty-six other cities. Other companies opened their doors in Copenhagen (1727), Anvers (1754), and elsewhere in northern Europe.[6]

In France, a number of companies were established in Paris and the major maritime centers, particularly during the latter half of the eighteenth century.

Two large companies had their headquarters in Paris. One, the Chambre d'assurance et grosse aventure, chartered in 1750, was capitalized at 4.5 million lt., soon raised to 12 million. A second, the Compagnie d'assurances générale, received its charter in 1754 and was capitalized at nine million lt. At Nantes, the oldest known company dated from 1739. Others entered the industry in 1742, 1750, 1763, 1767, 1782, and 1787. At least three were actually writing insurance at any given time following the 1750s. Rouen, with seven functioning companies, and Le Havre, with two large organizations, emerged as important insurance markets. Following the American Revolution, three insurance companies entered the trade at Marseilles. Individuals at Bordeaux and Dunkirk, too, founded insurance companies.[7]

In 1695, a group of Rochelais négociants, complaining of the difficulty of obtaining insurance in Paris, London, and Amsterdam because of the war, requested and received permission to organize a local company. Nothing is known of its history and no references to it were encountered in my research. Presumably, if ever operational, it fell victim to the War of the Spanish Succession. The next effort occurred in 1751. In that year, Weis & Sons, Trésahar Bonfils and Théodore Delacroix, en société, Louis Perdriau, Pierre Isaac Rasteau, Pierre Gabriel Admyrauld, and Jean Ezeckiel Couillandeau entered into an agreement to form the Société d'assurances at La Rochelle. This company operated until the 1760s when it apparently ceased operating. After its demise, there is no evidence that another locally owned company operated in the city.[8]

Compared with the Parisian insurance firms, the Rochelais venture was small. Indeed, it had no capital at all. Its incorporators intended to pay immediate claims, divided equally among them, out of their private capital, which stood as the collateral. With each adjusted claim against the company, all the incorporators were obligated to bank their share of the loss, and penalties were imposed should an incorporator be unable to put up his share. This corporation possessed neither capital nor stock. Its acceptance in the city depended entirely on the business reputations of the incorporators. Most of the other insurance companies were organized as typical joint-stock operations, the larger among them employing agents (frequently stockholders) in other port cities. Companies for which information was available were capitalized anywhere from 40,000 lt.—a company chartered in Nantes in 1782—to 900,000 lt. for a company formed in Marseilles in 1788. None of the provincial companies approached the capital strength of the Parisian competitors.[9]

In most cases, the capitalization determined the size of the risk that the company would underwrite. The Rochelais company limited its policies to 40,000 lt. per vessel. Other companies underwrote individual risks that frequently matched initial capital up to about 150,000 lt. Thus, the Nantes company chartered in 1783 authorized insurance of up to 40,000 lt. per vessel, while the Parisian company formed in 1750 allowed policies of up to 150,000 lt. per ship. But the Parisian company chartered in 1754 would only permit policies of up to 30,000 lt. per vessel and another 30,000 lt. on the cargo—this despite a large capital. A low ceiling was probably adopted because the firm also wrote fire insurance on buildings. The charter of incorporation clearly identified the individual or group that determined the total value of policies written in any given year. As a general rule, companies seem to have limited the value of total policies to a sum that, multiplied by average premium rates, equaled the working capital plus the premiums earned during the current year.

Companies that accepted risks of under 100,000 lt. during the latter half of the eighteenth century denied armateurs the possibility of insuring an armement in one policy (see table 6.3). *Armements pour le long cours* cost more than the 40,000 lt. insurance available through La Rochelle's company. It was, then, usual for armateurs to make several policies on a single venture without disobeying the law prohibiting multiple policies. For the Rochelais, this meant purchasing a policy through the branch office of an outside firm or through a correspondent in another city, foreign as well as French, or through any one of dozens of independent underwriters in La Rochelle.

Each of the large French insurance companies maintained a branch office in La Rochelle, managed by an agent who might receive both a salary and a commission. One of the first acts of the Parisian Chambre d'assurance et grosse aventure and the Compagnie d'assurances générale was the appointment of agents in La Rochelle and other commercial centers. The Chambre, in 1750, appointed Paul Vivier and Pierre Jacques Rasteau fils aîné, while the Compagnie appointed Charles Sureau and E. Boursalt. Thus, one Rasteau brother served as agent for an outside firm while another participated in a firm of local origin. In 1754, both Rasteau and Vivier resigned their agency and were replaced by Pierre Gabriel Admyrauld and Jean Baptiste Rocault fils. By 1768, Sureau and Boursalt had been replaced by Nicolas Weis and Louis Fort. During the period 1760–89, the Admyraulds continued as agents of the Chambre, the widow Admyrauld & Son carrying on for the deceased Pierre Gabriel, Vivier accepted an agency from the Nantes firm of Bernard & Company, and Pierre Jacques and Pierre Isaac Rasteau managed the affairs of another Nantes firm, as did Etienne Belin. Louis Ranjard fils and Joachim de Baussay served firms located in both Nantes and Rouen, Nicolas Suidre made insurance for firms located at Saint-Malo, Le Havre, and Rouen, and Dumoustier & Dejarnac became agents of the Nantes firm chartered in 1782.

Agents received specific instructions: abide by the maximum coverage prescribed, avoid making insurance on ventures in which they had an interest, offer the company insurance to prospective customers before underwriting on their own account, and make insurance only on vessels of Rochelais registry and only on those known to be in good condition. The parent firm expected its agents to send daily reports of business conducted and take swift action when news of a shipwreck reached them so as to obtain the maximum salvage possible. Agents received authority to draw on the company treasury to pay debts and adjust claims, after recourse to binding arbitration if necessary. Debtors were to be pursued with diligence. For these services Admyrauld and Rocault received several shares of company stock and 5 percent of all premiums. Other agents received salaries ranging from 300 lt. to 600 lt. annually and lesser commissions.[10]

The establishment of insurance companies in La Rochelle reduced the number of underwriters required when intéressés sought full coverage of their shares. Before insurance companies became common, an armement might carry policies written by several dozen underwriters. Even large ports such as Nantes, Bordeaux, Le Havre, or Marseilles, did not have enough underwriters to cover a single venture to Africa or the colonies, thus compelling armateurs and intéressés to seek insurance in other cities.

Each private underwriter provided only a small part of total coverage. In 1720, thirteen Rochelais underwriters supplied less than 30 percent of the insurance on the Nantais vessel *le Victorieux*. In that same year, the Rochelais vessel *la Royalle* received some 30 to 40 percent of its coverage from eight Nantais. Henri Brevet, in 1748, took out 168,000 lt. of insurance on the body and cargo of two vessels dispatched to Africa. Forty Rochelais underwrote this venture. One policy reached 9,000 lt. None of the remainder exceeded 4,500 lt., and policies averaged 2,595 lt. Policies worth 64,000 lt. were made in other cities. Insurance taken out by Théodore Delacroix on his interest in vessels outfitted between 1730 and 1768 reflects a decline in the number of separate policies, an increase in the average value of each policy, and more frequent use of insurance companies.[11]

If the number of policies per armement declined during the eighteenth century, the number of places providing coverage did not. While evidence from the period prior to 1783 is fragmentary, it suggests that insurance on a venture might normally be obtained in three or more cities, frequently including Amsterdam and London. Insurance claims following the loss in 1708 near Havana of the Rochelais *le Lion d'Or,* Jacques Rasteau, captain, were forwarded to Amsterdam, Nantes, and Rouen. When, in 1732, *le Saint Pierre* foundered on its return from Santo Domingo, underwriters at Bordeaux, Amsterdam, and La Rochelle covered the loss. Following the capture by the English in 1757 of *l'Aimable Catherine* as it headed for Louisiana, claims were filed in Paris, Marseilles, and La Rochelle. Cargoes shipped to and from northern Europe on foreign vessels for the account of Rochelais were likely to be insured by underwriters at London, Amsterdam, or Hamburg in addition to La Rochelle. These policies were negotiated on the spot by correspondents of the Rochelais. If the goods were addressed to a Rochelais merchant but for the account of a northern merchant, insurance might be made in La Rochelle and other French cities.[12]

Data covering the 1780s enable more precision in analyzing insurance practices in La Rochelle. For twenty-eight armements launched in 1786, or 60 percent of total departures, Rochelais underwriters covered 854,100 lt., and non-Rochelais assumed a risk of 845,800 lt., for a total of 1,699,900 lt. of insurance. Insurance made at Le Havre accounted for 20 percent; Nantes, 13 percent; Rouen, 6 percent; Paris, 1.2 percent; and La Rochelle, 50.2 percent. Seventeen of the ventures carried policies made in at least four places in addition to La Rochelle.[13] Surprisingly, Marseilles did not provide any insurance for these or any other Rochelais ventures made between 1783 and 1787. Armateurs and intéressés from Marseilles did seek insurance at La Rochelle during those years.[14]

According to the registered policies for 1786, most of the non-Rochelais insurance belonged to insurance companies. Much of this could be handled in La Rochelle through agents of the companies. Since Nicolas Suidre underwrote on his own account as well as in the name of companies located in other cities, insurance policies written by him might be included in the totals for La Rochelle and for Le Havre, Rouen, and Saint-Malo. Insurance policies for the vessel *le Réparateur* amounted to 64,300 lt. Suidre participated for 1,000 lt. on his own account but made an additional 3,000 lt. insurance for other parties, probably including Quentin & Company of Saint-Malo. Le Havre's total contribution was underwritten by a single insurance company as was Nantes's. In addition to Suidre, 16 other Rochelais made insurance for their own account on *le Réparateur* in 1786. Several of these underwriters also made insurance for the account of non-Rochelais insurance companies.[15]

An estimate of the net profitability of the Rochelais insurance business can be arrived at inferentially. The vessels insured in 1786 paid an average premium of 5.3 percent. Non-Rochelais insurers, then, collected about 44,900 lt. in premiums from the 28 armements. In a two year period, 1784–85, Quentin & Company of Saint-Malo received premiums of 20,651 lt. and paid claims of 13,093 lt., leaving net profits of 37 percent. For the five year period 1783–87, Nicolas Suidre received premiums of 29,920 lt. from insurance written for his own account and paid out 14,737 lt. in claims, for a net profit of 51 percent. In 1783, de Richemond & Garnault netted 6,258 lt. from 13,678 lt. in premiums, or a profit of 46 percent. Net profits of 45 percent seemed reasonable enough to apply to the 44,900 lt. in premiums which Rochelais paid to non-Rochelais for coverage, largely on vessels, worth 845,000 lt. At that rate the companies netted 20,205 lt. on the vessels alone on the outbound voyage. Since the value of the vessel contributed but 30 percent of mise hors (see table 6.4), another 40,000 lt. in net profits derived from insuring the cargo. Double the 60,000 lt. to account for incoming vessels and their cargoes, and a total net profit in the neighborhood of 120,000 lt. might be suggested for division among some six to ten maritime insurance companies.[16] The company at Le Havre realized 24,000 lt. from insurance made at La Rochelle and the company at Nantes made 16,000 lt., while the other companies earned lesser amounts.

Rochelais underwriters, providing an equivalent amount of insurance, can be assumed to have netted an equal profit, for a total return of 240,000 lt. on twenty-eight armements. In 1786, La Rochelle outfitted forty-seven vessels le long cours. It might be assumed that the insurance account for each of the nineteen vessels for which no information is available replicated that of the twenty-eight. If it did, the annual net return from insurance approached 400,000 lt. at La Rochelle. Such profitability from the smallest of the major ports suggests a business of significant magnitude on a national scale. Without comparable data from other cities, however, regarding the total premiums paid to and the total net profits of the insurance companies, the role of insurance in an emerging corporate capitalism in France must remain unknown.

During the course of the nineteenth century, individual underwriters passed from the scene, superceded by the great commercial insurance companies. In the previous century, companies and individuals had competed for the expanding patronage of merchants. At the beginning of the eighteenth century, an unorganized insurance market had prevailed. Centralization had occurred during the eighteenth century. But as highly centralized as the insurance industry had become in England, centered in London at Lloyd's Coffee House in the Royal Exchange in 1774, independent underwriters continued into the nineteenth century to write insurance while coverage was available at Liverpool, Bristol, Hull, and other places. London probably accounted for at least three-quarters of the total coverage and perhaps a greater proportion in the foreign trade.[17] In La Rochelle, by the 1780s, companies and individuals seem to have divided about equally the available business. De Richemond & Garnault replied, in 1783, to a Nantais request for 60,000 lt. of insurance that only 33,000 lt. could be obtained. La Rochelle's underwriters, according to the firm, had taken the full amount of risks that they wished.[18] If de Richemond & Garnault were correct, the companies were not depriving Rochelais underwriters of insurance sales on Rochelais armements. An equal division of available business reflects the unwillingness of Rochelais to underwrite larger amounts rather than financial inability or superior company marketing.

Insurance companies provided necessary services efficiently and cheaply to Rochelais négociants. The companies simplified the entire process of premium payments and claim adjustments.[19] In providing 100,000 lt. in insurance on a venture, a company substituted for twenty to thirty individual underwriters, each of whom would require separate payment and separate notification and documentation of a claim against the policy. At the least, the insured must have saved considerable time. The companies offered competitive peacetime insurance rates and, during wartime, individuals—mostly armateurs in their own right—eschewed underwriting even though rates soared, leaving the field to the companies. While relationships between the insurer and insured were not notably contentious during times of peace, the outbreak of war and the rate decisions of the companies fostered hostile attitudes among the insured, encouraged cooperation against the companies, and provoked long and bitter legal strife between the two parties.

PEACETIME AND WARTIME PREMIUM RATES

Peacetime insurance rates during the eighteenth century gradually declined for all maritime routes. Premiums from London to La Rochelle, at 4 percent in 1620, fluctuated between 1¼ and 2¼ percent in 1753. In 1700, rates from Saint-Malo to the Antilles ranged close to 10 percent; fifty years later they had fallen below 4 percent. From Saint-Malo to Le Havre, the rate of 2½ percent prevailing in the early 1700s had declined to 1½ percent by 1750. During the mid-fifteenth century, a premium rate of 14 percent bought coverage for ventures from La Rochelle to the Low Countries. By 1715, that particular rate exceeded the rate charged a round trip voyage from La Rochelle to the Antilles and, by the 1780s, 14 percent was more than two times the going rate for voyages to Africa and the West Indies.[20]

A number of developments combined to lower insurance rates during the eighteenth century. Improved charts and reliable pilots reduced the dangers of port entry and exit. Increasingly stringent packaging regulations protected certain kinds of goods more adequately against damage from storms or wrecks causing leakage in the holds. Salvageable goods lowered the losses to underwriters. Except during hostilities, the major sea lanes were reasonably safe. Piracy slackened and became insignificant during the eighteenth century. In the Mediterranean, plagued by the depredations of North African pirates and privateers throughout the seventeenth century, greater safety prevailed as the maritime states either bought off or cowed with superior force the coastal warlords. While the forces of nature assured that no voyage could be assumed routine, at least the element of lawlessness on the high seas became less of a concern.[21] Insurance rates fell as it became apparent that a high percentage of vessels reached their destinations without incident.

Prevailing rates at La Rochelle differed little from rates for the same routes available elsewhere, although rates sometimes varied among different cities for the same venture.[22] Le Saint Louis, bound for Africa and the Antilles in 1743, obtained rates of 11½ percent at Nantes and Bordeaux and 10 percent at La Rochelle. Following the same route in 1748, le Noé paid premiums of 7¼ percent at Bordeaux and 9 percent at La Rochelle. During the 1770s, vessels returning to Le Havre and Bordeaux from the Antilles paid rates of 2¼ to 44.7 percent, similar to rates available in La Rochelle. Eleven expeditions to Île de France launched by the Company of the Indies in 1785–86 paid an average of 8 percent, a rate also available in La Rochelle for armements to the Indian Ocean.[23] Rochelais rates were as frequently lower as higher than those offered elsewhere for journeys between the same points.

The reasons for the differences are difficult to explain. Each underwriter, whether an agent or an independent, made a judgment regarding the insurability of a vessel and adjusted rates according to seasonal determinants and current information. These separate evaluations might partially explain the port-to-port differential in rates. The current demand on the available supply of coverage might also inflate or deflate rates. The paucity of information about insurance procedures in other ports precludes any useful comparisons about rate-making practices.

While insurers protected themselves against potential loss by charging higher rates on policies written for vessels in poor condition, they were unable to inspect ships with any regularity. No lists rating the seaworthiness of vessels are found in Rochelais archives and studies of other ports make no reference to such lists. Presumably, insurers acted individually in this important matter. But a spate of insurance claims in 1776 and 1777, initiated by owners and intéressés of allegedly unseaworthy vessels, spurred the insurance companies to press for legislation tightening up the inspection requirements for vessels making ready to depart. This effort reveals the increasing power of the companies.

Ship inspectors did exist in most metropolitan and colonial ports.[24] Occasionally, vessels were condemned and their exit prohibited. But for the most part, the inspection system operated perfunctorily. Legislation developed in 1778 promised a more efficient system. Inspection by a ship's carpenter and a shipbuilder was mandated in the port of departure; another inspection was required after the vessel had unloaded its cargo at the port of call; and still another visit would occur when new cargo was loaded and departure was imminent. The vessel's intéressé paid for these inspections. Abandonment of a vessel by the insured to the insurer as a result of damage incurred during the voyage was contingent upon the certification by the inspectors of the vessel's seaworthiness. Any failure by the captain or the armateur to follow these procedures made abandonment impossible, thus precluding a claim against the insurer. Heavy fines were also imposed if vessels lacked certification.

Debate on this proposal in the Council of Commerce revealed a division between proponents—Le Havre–Rouen and Marseilles—and opponents—La Rochelle, Amiens, Lyons, Paris, and the representatives from the French islands. Nantes and Bordeaux maintained a neutral stance. In 1778, La Rochelle's concern reflected that of a port city without a local insurance company. While numerous independent underwriters functioned in the port, they were also armateurs and intéressés. Opposition from the deputies from interior cities and the Antilles also mirrored the interests of those investing in the colonial trade—as colonial landowners, as exporters to the colonies, or as shareholders in armements to the colonies. Advocates represented the position of major insurance companies, companies by then large enough to have developed interests distinct from those of the armateur-négociant. The companies at Nantes and Bordeaux, less powerful than those at Rouen and Marseilles, were important nonetheless and sufficiently influential to neutralize opposition in those cities to the inspection procedure. In the past, on issues pitting the welfare of armateur-négociants against corporate interests, La Rochelle, Nantes, and Bordeaux had usually adopted a common posture. The rise of corporate insurance weakened that ad hoc alliance.[25]

Loans à la grosse aventure. Declining insurance rates at La Rochelle somewhat diminished the use of bottomry loans or sea loans or armements. During the seventeenth and early eighteenth centuries, bottomry loans, variously called in France *prêts de la grosse aventure, emprunts à la grosse,* or *contrats à la grosse,* were very common. Disagreement exists regarding their essential purpose, with some scholars viewing them as high interest capital loans and other defining them as an early form of insurance. Depending upon the needs of the borrower, a loan *à la grosse* could serve both purposes.[26]

The bottomry loan was a transaction in which the lender advanced a sum of money, at interest rates between 15 and 30 percent during the eighteenth century, to a borrower for use in a specific venture. If the voyage was completed, the lender received, normally within thirty days, the principal plus the interest. Damage to the vessel or the cargo, however, reduced the borrower's obligation. For example, damage of 2,000 lt. to a vessel valued at 10,000 lt. discharged the borrower's obligation. Creditors, in proportion to the sum advanced, shared in losses of all general or gross averages. Bottomry loans did not share in simple averages unless stipulated in the contract. French law prohibited the insurance of bottomry loans.

Loans à la grosse served a dual purpose when insurance was difficult to obtain or when rates were high, for the borrower received in advance the full amount of the loan. In effect, the lender covered the risks of the voyage while advancing the amount insured. If the borrower deposited that sum, making no use of it, and returned it with interest at the conclusion of the voyage, then the transaction served primarily as insurance. If the borrower used the loan to finance a voyage or to purchase a share in a venture, then the loan also functioned as a form of capital advance. When Jean Gitton advanced 10,000 lt. to Bonfils Brothers & Company in 1715 for use in the armement of *l'Aimable Marie,* the borrowers simply held on to the money. This was an insurance loan. A loan à la grosse made by Alexandre & Rabatteau, Jean Vivier, Jean Bruslé, and others in 1715 to Louis Allaire for use in the voyage of *le Neptune* was a capital advance, for Allaire turned part of the cash into cargo and spend another part of it for désarmement. In effect, however, this loan of 4,700 lt. insured Allaire to that amount against damage to or loss of the vessel and cargo—but, at 26 percent, it was an expensive transaction.

As insurance became more readily available and cheaper, sea loans lost much of their earlier significance. La Rochelle's armateurs and négociants during the first half of the eighteenth century made sea loans to non-Rochelais as well as to Rochelais. Loans were frequently made to armateurs of terreneuviers. By the mid-eighteenth century, however, most of the bottomry transactions, other than for fishing, involved relatively small sums advanced to officers of vessels who were offered a share in the venture or who wished to ship a small cargo. Etienne Belin advanced in 1767 a loan à la grosse of 1,000 lt. to Jean Frémon, captain of *le Saint Joseph,* who purchased goods for his account. Armateurs without large capital resources, such as Jacques Gillet in the 1780s, or armateurs temporarily suffering from a dearth of ready capital, continued to make use of bottomry loans during the latter part of the century. Large operators rarely appeared as borrowers. Frequently, they appeared as lenders. For the larger capitalists, sea loans provided another, and potentially lucrative, investment opportunity. Insurance companies, too, were authorized to lend à la grosse, but the extent of their business is unknown.[27]

Bottomry loans have been described as an archaic and inefficient use of capital for both borrower and lender.[28] For the lender, they were a species of speculative investment that, while carrying greater risk than alternative forms of investment, resulted in handsome returns. Armateurs and négociants at La Rochelle accepted measured risks. It seems unlikely that a significant portion of working capital was used to make such loans which represented the outer limit of risk-taking investment that the Rochelais indulged in.

For the borrower, loans à la grosse provided capital and insurance simultaneously. When insurance became easy to obtain, bottomry loans, always functioning as insurance whatever the real purpose of the loan, assumed the characteristic of a quick, medium-term loan. Entrepreneurs caught short of capital at a moment when an opportunity to engage in a profitable venture presented itself might justifiably have recourse to a high interest loan. Rates in the 1780s of 15 to 20 percent were not that much higher than rates on money lent for industrial purposes which cost 12 to 15 percent during the 1770s.[29] Since the loan à la grosse also served as insurance, there was no need to take out insurance on the capital obtained in that way which reduced the actual cost by a few percent.

In 1750, Jacques Garesché received a sea loan of 18,000 lt. from widow Labbé to be used in the outfitting of *l'Achille,* bound for Santo Domingo. Eight days after the vessel's return to La Rochelle, Garesché promised to repay the 18,000 lt. plus 17 percent interest, for an interest cost of 3,060 lt. Had Garesché put up his own 18,000 lt. and insured it from La Rochelle to the Antilles at 4 percent and then made another policy for the return trip at 4 percent—the typical pattern—the premium would have been 1,480 lt. Garesché, in effect, paid 1,580 lt. for the use of 18,000 lt., a loan of 8.7 percent—not an unreasonable rate considering that during the 1780s the *Caisse d'Escompte* of Paris, a banker's bank, lent money at 4 percent to other bankers, who then made loans at 5 to 6 percent.[30] For Garesché and widow Labbé, the loan à la grosse served as an efficient mechanism to obtain and to use working capital.

Wartime Premium Rates. The serious threat or actual outbreak of war sent premiums soaring. Rates on the La Rochelle-Antilles route, for example, rose to as high as 30 to 50 percent. Each policy contained a provision for *augmentation* (increase in rates) in case of war. A group of policies taken out by Théodore Delacroix in 1754 and 1755 with Dangiraud & Company of Rouen, covering 236,724 lt. of risk on vessels and cargo, stipulated that increases of 20 to 25 percent would be levied in case of war. Similarly, twenty-five policies taken by Paul Depont des Granges between 1707 and 1709 carried attachments indicating that augmentations of 10 to 15 percent had been made.[31]

French wartime rates exceeded those in England by from 5 to 10 percent. English insurees received rebates of 5 to 7 percent when their vessels were convoyed. Lower outbound than inbound rates reflected the greater availability of convoys for the outbound passage. French rates, regulated unlike the English, did not reflect such a differential nor were premium rates lowered for vessels receiving convoy protection. The rate differential between England and France during wartime, from the 1740s through the 1780s, developed in part because the English convoy system was more efficient than the French, and in part because French insurance companies possessed sufficient political power to raise rates to high levels.

Two questions fomented controversy: on what date should the increases take effect, and what should be the rate of increase? During the War of the Austrian Succession and the two conflicts that followed, formal discussions in each of the ports between the insured and the insurers resulted in a schedule of augmentation. These separate proposals were then forwarded to the central government which, in consultation with the Council of Commerce, issued a final regulation. Defining the date that hostilities on the high seas actually began proved the major point of contention. That date need not have coincided with the date on which war was officially declared. When did the enemy—England—act in a consistently hostile manner toward French shipping? The insurers, particularly the companies, pressed for the earliest possible date while the insured sought the latest possible date.

In 1757, the Chamber of Commerce of La Rochelle adopted a schedule of augmentation which had been agreed upon by local underwriters, including the agents of non-Rochelais companies, and armateur-négociants. Through 1762, both corporate and independent insurers levied rates according to the Rochelais schedule, reproduced in table 9.1, with increases taking effect only during the last week of August 1755. Between the 1757 publication of the Rochelais schedule and 1762, the central government worked on its own schedule, beseiged by advocates of the insured to accept the Rochelais version and pressured by the representatives of insurance companies to accept an earlier date of augmentation. While the official French declaration of war against England was announced in June 1756, hostilities had commenced in America in July 1755. At what point hostilities began on the seas was at issue.

An arrêt in 1762 established June 8, 1755, as the date maritime hostilities commenced. This was based upon the attack and capture of two royal naval vessels on that date. The insurance companies vigorously supported this date and diligently sought to compel policyholders to pay the augmentation on ships that departed after June 8. The insured at La Rochelle resisted these demands and a large number of court cases resulted, some still unsettled when another war erupted in 1778.

For armateurs and other policyholders, large sums of money were at stake. Not only did the companies dispute the calendar suggested by La Rochelle, but

Table 9.1. *Rochelais Schedule for Increases in Insurance Rates, 1755 (by route)*

Destination	Departing from	If arrive between	If leave between	Augmentation
French ports, Brest to Bayonne	America	Aug. 28–31		6%
French ports, Brest to Bayonne	America	Sept. 1–15		20%
French ports, Brest to Bayonne	America	after Sept. 15		27.5%
Santo Domingo and America	French ports, Brest to Bayonne		Aug. 24–Sept. 1	20%
Santo Domingo and America	French ports, Brest to Bayonne		after Sept. 1	27.5%
Africa and America	French ports, Brest and Bayonne	Aug. 28–Oct. 29		24%
Africa and America	French ports, Brest and Bayonne	after Oct. 29		34%
Quebec	French ports, Brest and Bayonne	Aug. 28–Sept. 27		15%
Quebec and return voyage	French ports, Brest and Bayonne	Aug. 28–Sept. 27		25%
Louisbourg	French ports, Brest and Bayonne	Aug. 28–Sept. 27		27%
America via English Channel	Bay of Biscay	Aug. 23–31		20%
America via English Channel	Bay of Biscay	after Aug. 31		40%

Source: Règlement fait à La Rochelle, entre les Assurés et Assureurs soussignes, pour l'augmentation des Primes sur les assurances faite à Prime de Paix, 1757, CCLR, carton 17.

they demanded larger augmentations during the initial stages of hostilities. Denis Goguet, insured in May 1755 the vessel and cargo of *la Reine des Anges,* bound for Quebec, for 40,000 lt. at 5 percent in a policy taken out at the Rochelais branch of one of the Parisian companies. The vessel arrived safely in the Saint Lawrence River on June 22, 1755, well before the date for increases adopted in La Rochelle (see table 9.1). In 1757, the company accepted Goguet's payment of 2,000 lt. Then, in 1762, the company ordered Goguet to pay at 25 percent. With 8,000 lt. at stake, Goguet carried the case through four different courts. Others also filed suit, including Jean Baptiste Soumbrum, Etienne Belin, Pierre Boudet, and the company's agent, Pierre Gabriel Admyrauld. In 1768–69, Goguet served as the attorney for a group of eight armateurs, including Belin, who brought suit against the Compagnie d'assurance of Paris.

Using basically the same arguments, the insured centered their defense on the erroneous selection of June 8, denying that English commanders sought individual merchant ships as prizes until well into August. The capture of the royal vessels was portrayed as an isolated incident. Belin introduced evidence proving that England had not authorized the capture of merchantmen until August 27 and that English admiralty courts had declared illegal any seizures made prior to that date, ordering the return of the vessels with damages to French armateurs. All of the insured also criticized the company for refusing to heed comparable schedules prepared by other ports and for arbitrarily raising rates to exorbitant levels.

In Boudet's case, the vessel in question had arrived in Santo Domingo in April 1756, long after the Rochelais schedule had provided for an augmentation. He argued, unsuccessfully, that since *le Robuste* encountered no danger, he should not be assessed at the wartime rate—35 percent. The company case, in this instance, was upheld in all courts. The company argued that after June 8, French vessels ran considerable risks; that Boudet's contention that a 35 percent rate was exorbitant was nonsense since he gained profits three times the norm for a voyage to Santo Domingo; and that since the company ran a great risk, it deserved an augmentation to 35 percent. But the company's only evidence that risk increased after June 8 remained the capture of the two French frigates. While the insured also proved that the agents of the company had signed the schedule of 1757, accepting payments according to its rates, and that the company made no move to contest those rates until 1762, the strength of the case lay in the absence of risk between June 8 and August 27. On that basis the courts gradually ordered the reimbursement of policyholders who had paid according to the schedule of 1762. Goguet's clients received 49,147 lt. in rebates in 1768 and Belin received another rebate in 1773.[32]

Hardly had this issue been resolved when it raised its head again in 1778. Many of the questions debated during the prior conflict generated heated controversy during the War of the American Revolution. But a major new factor intruded to shape the course of the argument and determine its outcome.

Whereas most of the ports had supported the Rochelais schedule of 1757, this time several, including Le Havre, Rouen, Bordeaux, and Marseilles, supported the schedule adopted in 1783 by the crown. The Compagnie d'assurance of Paris, its agents in Marseilles, Bordeaux, and Le Havre–Rouen, and the stockholders of other companies in those cities orchestrated support for the crown's schedule which confounded the efforts of La Rochelle, Nantes, interior cities, and the smaller ports. The political power of the insurance companies, intimated during the struggle to institute a rigid system of ship inspection, reached maturity in the fight over augmentation. Pierre Isaac Rasteau reported to the Rochelais chamber in 1779 that the situation looked bleak as directors of the Compagnie d'assurance had left for Le Havre–Rouen to drum up support for the crown's schedule. In effect, he pointed out, the royal schedule had been devised by the insurance company. The company proposed June 17, 1778 as the date of hostilities and an immediate increase of premiums to 20 percent without regard to route, rising shortly thereafter to 45 percent. The Rochelais adopted July 28. French Atlantic port vessels arriving in the Mediterranean between July 28 and August 15 would pay a premium of 12 percent. Vessels arriving in the colonies or returning from the colonies between those dates would pay 17 percent. An ascending scale of augmentation would then take effect during two successive time periods until October 14. Thereafter, premiums would be assessed from 43 to 47 percent.[33]

By the end of April 1779, the issue had been referred by the crown to the deputies of the Council of Commerce for their advice. According to Rasteau, the great majority of deputies favored the Rochelais schedule or a similar one from Nantes. Moreover, dissidents at Marseilles and Le Havre, opposing the official position of their chambers of commerce as too favorable to the insurance companies, sent special representatives to Paris to support the Rochelais scheme. The insurance companies, however, exerted superior influence in official circles, as predicted by the juridiction consulaire at Nantes. In January 1783, letters patent officially fixed the date of augmentation at June 17 and the first increase at 20 percent.[34]

Armateurs at Le Havre, Nantes, and La Rochelle, pained and surprised by the progovernment stance adopted at Bordeaux, could not understand why a community of merchants would adopt a position so damaging to commerce. They did not perceive that the interests of the armateurs and négociants at Bordeaux were no longer synonymous with the commercial interests of that city. Just as the economic structure of Le Havre and Nantes reflected the infusion of corporate industrial and commercial organizations, so too did the Bordelais position reflect the power of corporate insurance. Specialization of economic functions and the rise of corporations proceeded less rapidly at La Rochelle, and its dominant armateur-négociant class remained more buffered, more isolated from the consequences of such developments. In La Rochelle, the merchant elite could and did adopt traditional positions without challenge from newer economic elites.

THE SIZE AND CAPABILITY OF
LA ROCHELLE'S INSURANCE INDUSTRY

Despite regulations in 1681, and again in 1763, compelling the registration of all insurance policies, noncompliance was so general that it is impossible to gain a clear idea of the magnitude of insurance activity at La Rochelle until the 1780s. During that decade, the secretary of the La Rochelle Chamber of Commerce reported that few policies made in the city went unregistered. Most of the discussion that follows, then, focuses on the mid-1780s.[35]

At one time or another many of the port's armateurs engaged in underwriting. Théodore Delacroix's accounts record insurance policies made between 1730 and 1754 with Pommier, Labbé l'aîné, Jean Seignette, Rasteau fils aîné, Schellebeck fils, de Richemond, and de Missy. Between 1736 and 1739, armateurs such as Perdriau, J. Chaudruc, J. Vivier and E. Vivier, Jacques Carayon, and Jacques Leclerq all made insurance. More than thirty individuals or firms participated in providing 113,000 lt. of coverage for two vessels outfitted by Henri Brevet for Africa in 1748. Among them were some of the most active armateurs in the port. During the decade 1740–49, Rochelais outfitted 427 vessels le long cours (see table 2.2). Eleven of the underwriters for Brevet's ventures accounted for 124 armements, or 29 percent. During the four years 1784–87, thirty-nine individuals or firms made insurance in the city either on their own account or for the account of other individuals or insurance companies. Of those thirty-nine underwriters, only twelve did not act as armateurs during the 1780s. Five outfitted terreneuviers. The remaining twenty-two outfitted 225 of the 345 Rochelais armements, or 65 percent.[36]

Rochelais underwriters insured the vessels of La Rochelle and vessels from other ports both on their own and for others' accounts. The volume of that business, as entered in the chamber's insurance register for the years 1784–87, is depicted in table 9.2. Insurance made for the account of others, 70 percent of the total, fell largely into the hands of insurance company agents. Unfortunately, underwriters did not consistently identify the parties whom they represented or even their residence when registering the policies, frequently using only initials—H. L. or M.A.B.—or simply referring to "les autres." Still, the city of residence is known of some of the non-Rochelais underwriters who made insurance by means of Rochelais representatives and the value of the risk. These data, corresponding in the aggregate to the last column of table 9.2 are elaborated in table 9.3. The unknown totals are very large, and the significance of Parisian investments stands out. Most of these were made through the agency of Pierre Jean Achille Maubaillarcq. Policies registered by him referred only to "amis en pays de Paris." No evidence links him to a Parisian insurance company, so the presumption must be that he managed insurance investments for individuals. His discretion is to be marveled at. Not one of the 167 policies that he wrote identified a single individual by name.

Table 9.2. *Value of Insurance Made by Rochelais Underwriters, for Own Account and for Account of Others, April 1784–August 1787 (lt.)*

Underwriters	Total insurance made	Insurance for own account	Insurance for others' accounts
Daniel Garesché	1,767,400	192,300	1,575,100
Pierre Jacques Achille Maubaillarcq	1,233,730	21,000	1,212,730
Dumoustier & Dejarnac	921,000	223,200	697,800
Marc Antoine Lefebvre	505,700	263,200	242,500
Louis Vivier	428,700	58,500	370,200
Nicolas Suidre	297,400	101,000	196,400
Jean Perry	273,250	0	273,250
Joachim Debaussay	260,200	0	260,200
Etienne Jolly	246,700	245,200	2,000
Dumoustier de Fredilly	221,300	209,300	12,000
Jacques Gilbert	219,700	100,400	119,300
Ranjard fils & cie.	177,400	155,400	22,000
Louis Fort	160,800	114,800	46,000
Weis & fils	150,000	0	150,000
G. Souchet	117,600	91,600	26,000
Thouron Frères	115,500	94,200	21,300
E. & J. Rasteau frères	111,150	99,150	12,000
Fleuriau frères & Thouron	105,540	63,540	42,000
DeStockar & D'Ébert	79,500	17,500	62,000
D. Boulanger	66,100	66,100	0
Pierre Bordé	65,400	21,800	43,600
J. Denis	62,000	5,500	56,500
P.J. Van Hoogwerf	60,100	60,100	0
Donneadieu	44,500	43,700	800
Nicolas Schaaf	40,000	40,000	0
Jacqueline & fils aîné	30,000	30,000	0
David Roy	24,400	700	23,700
Wilkens frères	22,200	22,200	0
10 others (each under 20,000 total)	55,900	47,700	8,200
Total	7,863,670	2,388,090	5,475,580

Source: Registre des policies sur navire Commencée le 7 avril 1784 à fini le 6 août 1787, CCLR.

A large part of the unknown total resulted from a similar discretion practiced by Daniel Garesché, the largest underwriter-agent in the city. Garesché handled 1,575,100 lt. worth of insurance for non-Rochelais but only 433,640 lt. was identified by place of origin, all from Le Havre. Garesché accounted for 42 percent of the missing data. Dumoustier & Dejarnac made insurance for firms at Nantes and Rouen. Of the total insurance made for non-Rochelais by that firm, only 39 percent was identified. The bulk of the unknown portion should probably be added to the Nantes and Rouen columns on Table 9.3.

For all the shortcomings of the data, the significance of non-Rochelais participation in the insuring of Rochelais ventures should be clear. To analyze

Table 9.3. Residence of Underwriters and Value of Insurance Made by non-Rochelais at La Rochelle, 1784–87 (lt.)

Year	Paris	Nantes	Le Havre	Rouen	Saint-Malo	Unknown	Total insurance for others' account
1784	173,800	371,300	168,500	45,000	59,500	773,000	1,591,100
1785	472,360	204,184	156,423	5,054	64,300	643,359	1,545,680
1786	407,721	167,200	195,830	14,000	70,400	961,149	1,816,300
1787	195,500	10,000	6,600	4,050	19,000	287,350	522,500

Source: See table 9.2.

other aspects of the Rochelais insurance industry, conjecture, based however on rather solid data, must be employed. How much insurance did La Rochelle's commerce require? How much insurance did Rochelais merchants actually purchase? What proportion of actual coverage was obtained outside of La Rochelle? How much insurance did Rochelais underwriters make on the shipping of other cities? Did the Rochelais pay more for insurance to non-Rochelais than was received from them in premiums? Answers to these questions will be inferred from data available for the three years 1784–86.[37]

In order to determine the insurance requirements of Rochelais shipping, it is necessary to know the total value of outgoing ships and cargoes and the proportion of the total value that armateurs normally insured. Table 9.4 presents this data.[38] Some part of the difference between insurance made and total value of armements was probably accounted for in loans à la grosse. Next, the insurance written at La Rochelle on local armements for the account of Rochelais and non-Rochelais was derived from the "Registre de policies. . . ." That record provided the value of the policy and identified underwriters precisely enough to distinguish between Rochelais and others. Policies were discovered for 104 of the 134 armements launched during the three years. Since it is unlikely that the full value of insurance on the 30 missing vessels was taken elsewhere, an insurance value was derived for them. That value appears in parentheses ( ) in table 9.4 and formed part of the total value of insurance taken at La Rochelle on Rochelais ventures.[39]

As the material presented thus far indicates, the value of Rochelais armements rose much more rapidly following the American Revolution than did the value of insurance made in the city. The latter provided 60 percent of the coverage in 1784, 49 percent in 1785, and 40 percent in 1786. Moreover, during the three years in question, insurance made for the account of Rochelais covered a declining proportion of the requirements of local shipping—22 percent in 1784, 18 percent in 1785, and 14 percent in 1786. The significance of this decline will be addressed shortly.

Underwriters in other cities, whose policies were presumably registered in those cities, supplied a rising share of La Rochelle's insurance needs. The total value of those policies, obtained by subtracting the amount made at all places (see table 9.4), is presented in table 9.5. To determine the total amount of insurance underwritten by non-Rochelais, whether the policies were made locally or elsewhere, the value written for the account of non-Rochelais at La Rochelle must be added to the value of policies written in other cities. This, too, is summarized in table 9.5, along with the percentage of total insurance attributable to non-Rochelais. The cost of premiums paid by Rochelais to non-Rochelais, derived by using the average premium rates prevailing in La Rochelle during each of the three years, completes table 9.5.

Balanced against the sums paid in premiums by Rochelais to non-Rochelais was the income earned by Rochelais underwriters. One component of this

Table 9.4. *Total Insurance Taken on Rochelais armements and Insurance Made at La Rochelle, 1784–86 (lt.)*

Year	Number of *armements* le long cours	Total value of ships and cargoes	Total insurance made at all places	For account of Rochelais	For account of non-Rochelais	Total insurance made at La Rochelle
1784	44	6,238,452	4,991,817	1,089,393 (183,750)	1,916,483 (325,383)	3,005,876
1785	43	7,511,025	6,008,820	1,091,978 (171,290)	1,833,248 (287,568)	2,925,226
1786	47	11,447,930	9,158,344	1,322,177 (286,427)	2,318,581 (502,281)	3,640,758

Source: See note 38.

Table 9.5. *Value of Insurance Attributable to Non-Rochelais and Its Cost to Rochelais, 1784–87 (lt.)*

Year	Insurance on Rochelais ventures made elsewhere	Insurance for account of non-Rochelais	Total insurance underwritten by non-Rochelais	% underwritten by non-Rochelais	Average premium rate %	Cost of premiums
1784	1,985,941	1,916,483	3,902,424	78	.0465	181,462
1785	3,083,954	1,833,248	4,917,202	82	.0498	244,876
1786	5,517,568	2,318,581	7,836,149	86	.0536	420,017

Source: See table 9.2.

income, drawn from table 9.4, is repeated in the first column of table 9.6. The premium rates cited in table 9.5 were employed to calculate the income from this insurance. Still another component, income from insurance made by Rochelais for their own account on non-Rochelais ventures, not included in any of the tentative figures offered thus far, must also be added to the insurance income account.[40]

Rochelais underwriters regularly covered the maritime risks of armements initiated in other ports. In 1764, M. Boivon of Paris insured at La Rochelle his interests in ventures outfitted elsewhere. Armateurs from Nantes in 1785 solicited the services of de Richemond & Garnault to secure Rochelais underwriters for a voyage to Martinique. In 1787 and 1788, Dumoustier de Fredilly underwrote 130,000 lt. in risks on three Marseillais armements to the East Indies, or 7 percent of the total risk covered on those voyages.[41] Unfortunately, not all of these policies were registered. References were discovered to policies on non-Rochelais vessels that do not appear in the insurance register. Moreover, the registered policies lack precise dating. The cumulative value of all of these policies written in 1784, 1785, and 1786, covering 30 ventures outfitted in Bordeaux and 61 ventures organized in at least 15 other ports, totals 2,024,850 lt. As the policies did not specify in which of the three years the insurance was made, the three-year average of 674,950 lt. was added to table 9.6. Premium rates on the above policies averaged 4.83 percent for the three years. That rate was used to derive the second premium column in table 9.6.

What remained was the need to present an estimate of the income received by Rochelais on the insurance that they wrote elsewhere on non-Rochelais armements. To produce this essential figure, the insurance accounts of Pierre Jean Van Hoogwerf for the years 1784–86 and of Nicolas Suidre for the years 1784–87 were used.

Suidre underwrote 679,000 lt. in risks on vessels and cargoes. Insurance made in other cities and on non-Rochelais ventures formed 85 percent of his business. Van Hoogwerf's total insurance business amounted to 265,000 lt. Of that, 77 percent consisted of policies written on non-Rochelais shipping in cities other than La Rochelle. Adopting a ratio of insurance made on Rochelais ventures at La Rochelle for the local account to insurance made on the shipping of other ports that approximated the Suidre and Van Hoogwerf ratios would probably be excessive. It was assumed, subjectively to be sure, that for each livre tournois of protection offered in La Rochelle for the account of Rochelais, another livre tournois of insurance covered the risks of some other port's shipping. This approximated the practice of de Richemond & Garnault in 1783.[42] Thus, the last two entries in table 9.6 simply repeat the first two columns.

A final balance was then struck in table 9.7 between incoming premium payments and outgoing premium payments. This balance against La Rochelle is only suggestive, based as it was on the inferential use of incomplete data. The degree to which the negative balance reflects Rochelais inability to protect

Table 9.6. *Insurance Income at La Rochelle, 1784–86 (lt.)*

Year	Insurance made in La Rochelle by Rochelais for Rochelais	Premium income	Insurance made in La Rochelle on non-Rochelais ships	Premium income	Insurance made for Rochelais account elsewhere on non-Rochelais shipping	Premium income
1784	1,089,393	50,656	674,950	32,600	1,089,393	50,656
1785	1,091,978	54,380	674,950	32,600	1,091,978	54,380
1786	1,322,177	70,869	674,950	32,600	1,322,177	70,869

Source: See table 9.2.

Table 9.7. The Balance of Insurance Trade at La Rochelle, 1784–86 (lt.)

Year	Total insurance made for account of Rochelais	Total premium income	Total insurance made for account of non-Rochelais	Cost in premiums	Rochelais deficit in premiums
1784	2,853,736	133,912	3,902,424	181,462	47,550
1785	2,858,906	141,360	4,917,202	244,876	103,516
1786	3,319,304	174,338	7,836,149	420,017	245,679

their own commerce and, by implication, the absence of adequate local capital will be elaborated upon in the concluding pages.

CONCLUSION

Demand by armateurs for insurance on their shipping increased at a quicker pace than the total value of armements prepared at La Rochelle. Until the 1750s, insurance normally covered less than 70 percent of the actual value of individual ventures. Twenty-five policies taken out by Paul Depont between 1707 and 1709 covered slightly above 55 percent of the full value of his interest in the vessels and goods. Even during the 1750s, with insurance more readily available and premium rates falling, the policies on Théodore Delacroix's l'Infante Victoire covered less than 65 percent of its value. Much to Delacroix's dismay, the vessel burned and sank in a Santo Domigan port.[43] For most armateurs, however, cheapness and accessibility prompted them to purchase more complete coverage of their shipments, reaching 80 percent during the 1780s. The establishment of insurance companies at La Rochelle and other cities facilitated this trend.

At no time during the eighteenth century did Rochelais underwriters fully cover the insurance demands of local shippers. During the first quarter of the century, the bottomry loan provided an important alternative to a regular policy. La Rochelle was a major source of such loans. To an unknown extent, the loan à la grosse narrowed the insurance deficit at La Rochelle. But large amounts of insurance were made elsewhere. More than 65 percent of the value of Depont's policies had been made at Amsterdam, and Delacroix purchased some 70 percent of the insurance taken on l'Infante Victoire at Rouen. Until the conclusion of the War of the American Revolution, it was likely that some 40 to 50 percent of La Rochelle's insurance needs were met in other cities.

Following the American Revolution, the West Indian trade of France entered a new period of expansion. French armateurs engaged heavily in the East Indian trade, and hopes were raised, particularly in La Rochelle, that the newly independent United States would offer a market replacing those lost by the cession of Louisiana to Spain and Canada to England. While Bordeaux and Marseilles surged ahead more swiftly than La Rochelle, the latter kept pace with Nantes. In all of the ports, wartime shipping losses were quickly replaced, contacts with northern Europe and the colonies renewed, and preparations made to reap a postwar bonanza. For a time, La Rochelle received its full portion from the revitalization of the Atlantic trade. Beginning in 1783 and lasting for a few years, La Rochelle's maritime trade expanded rapidly. By 1786, the total value of departing Rochelais vessels and cargoes exceeded by 83 percent the magnitude reached in 1783. The volume of insurance made by Rochelais for their own account on Rochelais shipping, however, rose by only 21 percent. In 1786, only 40 percent of La Rochelle's insurance coverage was carried locally. La Rochelle's négociants and armateurs functioned only as part-time underwriters, devoting a minor portion of their working capital to insurance. They received in return but a small increment to their incomes. After claims were paid, de Richemond & Garnault divided 12,499 lt. in profits from risks assumed in 1780, 1781, and 1782. Suidre's recompense for his underwriting activities between 1783 and 1789 amounted to 19,142 lt., not of great moment to a man with over one million livres tournois invested in various armements in 1786.[44]

La Rochelle's insurance deficit meant little. The city's merchants possessed more than sufficient capital to meet local insurance demands without recourse to underwriters located elsewhere. As individuals, however, they chose not to emphasize that aspect of their business. Armateurs and shippers in search of insurance, unable to obtain it locally, secured it elsewhere at rates comparable to those available at home. Merchants at Bordeaux, Nantes, and Marseilles also made insurance extralocally. The somewhat surprising absence of a locally owned insurance company resulted from individual decisions of Rochelais capitalists to limit to relatively small sums their investment commitment to insurance. Perhaps the experience of several important Rochelais in a local company during the 1750s had been unsatisfactory since the Seven Years' War had erupted so soon after its inception. More likely, the intense Rochelais involvement in the slave trade and a lesser emphasis on the East Indian trade, both requiring large capital inputs, accompanied by the further accumulation of colonial debts, determined the Rochelais to invest no more in insurance than small-scale underwriting required.

A full understanding of the maritime insurance industry in France depends upon detailed studies of the major insurance centers, interior cities as well as ports, and probably some knowledge of the volume of insurance purchased in foreign cities. La Rochelle alone, during the 1780s, generated at least 400,000 lt. annually in premium income. Much of that accrued to the profit of non-Rochelais. Capital flowed into La Rochelle for insurance purposes, as did capital specifically designated for direct investment in the port's armements. A far-flung capital investment network linked together the major ports as well as the ports with interior cities. Insurance investments composed part of the capital flow. Considerable organization occurred in the insurance industry in many French cities, but little information exists regarding the degree to which companies superceded independent underwriters or the aggregate value of the business.

La Rochelle's commerce was much smaller than Bordeaux's or Marseilles's. Annual premium income in those ports must have reached five to ten million livres tournois. This was big business, business with significant political clout, and business which, to some degree, was dependent upon the gross capital strength of western Europe, of the "Atlantic economy." The full story of French capitalist development during the Old Regime must remain incomplete until the maritime (and other) insurance industry has been studied. Such investigations may then offer new perspectives by which to evaluate the tentative findings of this chapter.

TEN

Sources of Capital
for the Maritime
Trade

The magnitude of La Rochelle's commerce and the size of its ocean-going fleet required the port's armateurs to have access to sizable amounts of capital. At any point in time, vessels being readied for departure represented one portion of capital outlay and voyages in progress another, while ventures just concluded replenished capital resources. These outlays and inputs subsumed all credits extended to the Rochelais or granted by them. Two distinct sources of capital supplied Rochelais enterprise: Rochelais investments in their own shipping, and non-Rochelais investment in Rochelais armements. Capital also moved outwards as Rochelais investors participated in ventures outfitted at other ports. In this chapter, the total value of capital invested in outgoing shipping—*le long cours*—will be measured, and the share of total investments provided by the port's dominant families will be analyzed.

A measurement of the amount of capital which Rochelais committed to their shipping and the amount non-Rochelais invested in the port's ventures will permit a discussion of the capital self-sufficiency of the city and the significance of self-sufficiency, whether achieved or not. Available data will be utilized to identify the cities and areas within France and western Europe from which capital flowed into La Rochelle. When possible and appropriate, the investment patterns of other ports in maritime commerce will be compared with those of the Rochelais.

ROCHELAIS INVESTMENTS
IN LOCAL ARMEMENTS

Column two of table 10.1 estimates the total value of outgoing vessels le long cours and their cargoes for selected years during the eighteenth century.[1] While these sums do not include such essential factors as depreciation in the value of vessels, the value of individual *pacotilles* (small shipments of goods), or the capital outlay for the fishing and coasting fleets, the table does

Table 10.1. Rochelais Investment in La Rochelle's Ocean-going Shipping, 1722–87 (lt.)

Year	Total value of ships and cargoes	Value and % of Rochelais investment		Value of non-Rochelais investment
1722	1,543,392	933,752	60.5	609,640
1723	1,279,122	933,759	73.0	345,363
1724	721,110	519,199	72.0	
1742	7,706,370	4,585,290	59.5	3,121,080
1743	6,506,304	4,261,629	65.5	2,244,675
1744	3,418,968	2,085,570	61.0	1,333,398
1748	5,379,416	2,931,781	54.5	2,447,635
1780	2,189,620	1,215,239	55.5	974,381
1782	5,650,018	3,022,760	53.5	2,627,258
1783	10,673,190	4,909,667	46.0	5,763,523
1784	6,238,452	3,337,571	53.5	2,900,881
1785	7,511,025	3,492,627	46.5	4,018,398
1786	11,447,930	5,094,328	44.5	6,353,602
1787	6,619,731	3,442,259	52.0	3,177,472

achieve as complete an accounting as possible of the annual capital require-ments of the port's maritime sector. The third and fourth columns of table 10.1 estimate in lt. and percent, respectively, the direct capital investment of Rochelais in the armements of their port. The last column suggests that the remainder originated elsewhere.[2]

Table 10.1 depicts a commerce in which the share of investment attribu-table to Rochelais declined while the proportion of capital derived from nonlocal sources rose. Although the percentage capital contribution of the Rochelais diminished, a comparison of the absolute value of investments made during the 1740s and the 1780s reveals a moderate increase in the value of local investments. Rochelais investments in their own shipping, then, ad-vanced at a slower rate than did the capital requirements of their ocean-going commerce, thus duplicating the Rochelais investment pattern in meeting the insurance needs of the port's shipping.

The Rochelais, as Chapter 9 suggested, chose not to increase the insurance coverage they provided at a rate proportionate to the rise in the total value of ships and cargoes; instead, Rochelais armateurs elected to purchase coverage elsewhere. That conclusion rests on the assumption that the Rochelais possessed the capability to provide for their total insurance needs, an assump-tion supported by the activity of many Rochelais underwriters in insuring risks on the shipping of other ports. While Rochelais invested directly in the shipping of other ports, a point to which I will return, the line of reasoning rele-vant to insurance may be less applicable to direct investment in shipping. Whereas the difference between locally provided coverage and total insurance needs amounted to 246,000 lt. in 1786 (see table 9.7), the annual differential between local and nonlocal investment in shipping involved several million lt. (table 10.1).

The magnitude of non-Rochelais investments in Rochelais shipping reflected the opinion of outside investors that the city's maritime commerce offered opportunities for acceptable returns. But the question remains as to why the Rochelais failed to increase their investment commitment in their armements. Why did they permit the diversion of profits to other places? One answer may be that Rochelais investors during the 1740s and 1780s had reached the limit of their capacity to invest. Another answer may be that significant numbers of the city's wealthiest négociants diverted a larger part of their wealth to such nonmaritime purposes as offices, land, rentes, residential housing, and consumer goods. Both Jean Périer and Henri Robert believed the latter to be the case and attributed the decline of the port during the 1780s to enhanced conspicuous consumption by the leading families.[3] But the analysis in Chapter 3 of the passage of wealth through the Belin and Depont families, as well as supplementary evidence presented in Chapters 4 and 5, offers little evidence indicating an augmented use of capital for such purposes. Instead, a substantial share of the earnings of the elite families flowed directly into commerce or enterprises supportive of commerce.

During the eighteenth century, then, direct Rochelais investments in shipping provided between one-half and three-quarters of the financing necessary for ocean-going commerce. The data in table 10.1 and in figures 4.1, 4.2, and 4.3 are congruent, the latter three suggesting that armateurs in La Rochelle held over 50 percent of the shares in local armements.[4] The figures were based upon a larger sample than table 10.1, and the vessels were not the same in each case. In 1724, for example, the percentage of shares held by each intéressé in *la Reine Esther* was known but the value of the armement was not. In the same year, a total mise hors and the names and shares of each intéressé were known for *le Saint Phillippe*. *La Reine Esther* composed part of the sample in figure 4.1 while *le Saint Phillippe* formed part of the sample for table 10.1.

Nantes was the only other port for which comparable data exists, but the data cover only two or three years. Students of Saint-Malo, Le Havre, and Bordeaux have remarked upon capital movement between those and other ports but did not calculate its volume. Without explaining his reasoning, R. Richard has contended that the investment of outside capital in locally organized ventures amounted to a form of capital drainage from Le Havre. The author of the most recent study of Marseilles has insisted upon the capital self-sufficiency of that port but has offered no analysis of known outside investments in Marseilles's commerce. Self-sufficiency, according to Carrière, reflected the strength of Marseillais capitalism. However, a major Marseillais firm, Solier & Company, utilized large amounts of Swiss capital in its ventures. Swiss relatives supplied Solier & Company an estimated 55 to 60 percent of total investment capital. Shareholders in the firm's armements to the East Indies included individuals from Leghorn, Geneva, Cadiz, Bordeaux, La Rochelle, Nantes, and Paris. Dumoustier de Fredilly and other Rochelais participated in Solier & Company voyages.[5]

Capital moved freely from one port to another and from the interior of France to the seaports. Findings from Nantes and La Rochelle support the conclusion that local capital was never adequate to finance the expeditions launched at those places. A thorough investigation of investment connections between Marseilles and the interior would probably arrive at the same conclusions. The ability of a port to attract outside investors reflects the confidence of participants in the port's armateurs rather than being symptomatic of structural weaknesses in its economy. Had armateurs at La Rochelle consistently failed to turn a profit, investments would have ceased quickly enough. A steady inward flow of capital supplementing a major local commitment of funds was a measure of strength. The question to ask of a port that attracted little or no outside capital is, Why?

It seems likely that the larger ports drew significant sums of outside capital for use in trade. Conversely, it is probable that ports smaller than La Rochelle—Bayonne, Honfleur, Rochefort—appearing minimally attractive to outside investors, functioned with local capital. If growth was desired by the merchants of those ports, capital self-sufficiency would not be a goal to strive for but rather a condition to avoid.

It might be hypothesized that during the 1780s, the failure of La Rochelle to grow at a rate comparable to that of its larger competitors reflects a judgment made by local and outside investors that the city had achieved its maximum size. La Rochelle's shrinking port area, its isolation, its reduced brandy and salt trades—all these troublesome factors were well known. Nonetheless, its commerce was of sufficient size and attractive enough to outsiders to allow the city to maintain a stable state until the revolutionary upheavals. Whether or not this suited the Rochelais cannot be known with any certainty. La Rochelle's armateurs did engage in advertising during the 1780s in order to promote their ventures among outside investors. There was no way of determining, however, if a significant number of prospective armements failed to materialize due to insufficient capital. If the Rochelais perceived growth potential to which outsiders were blind, then the Rochelais experienced serious frustration. More likely, the Rochelais recognized their own limitations. While striving to reverse the downward trend in brandy and salt, improve facilities in the port, develop a trade with the United States, and counter the efforts of competitors to enhance their positions, they harbored no grandiose notions about their own future.

CAPITAL SUPPLY AND THE LEADING ROCHELAIS FAMILIES

In La Rochelle, as in Nantes, relatively few families during the eighteenth century accounted for a disproportionately high percentage of total armements. At Nantes, seventy-six families organized 65 percent of the armements (totaling 6,300 from 1694 to 1792) for which the armateur could be identified. Five family groups served as armateurs for 6 percent of the port's ventures.[6] In La Rochelle, eight families outfitted 28 percent of armements le long cours between 1720 and 1790 (figure 5.1). Table 3.2 indicates that the dominant twenty-six Rochelais families still accounted for 37 percent of armements during the decade of the 1780s, a share that had declined from over 50 percent during the period 1720–39.

Investments in the outfits of others further enhanced the centrality of the families who served as armateurs. While the Carayon family, as an example, outfitted only 17 vessels during the period 1720–89, they owned shares in at least 59 other vessels. Similarly, in addition to serving as armateur for 162 ships, the Rasteaus invested in at least 132 other ventures. The Rasteaus, then, participated as investors or armateurs in 13 percent of La Rochelle's armements le long cours.[7] While available data does not allow the translation of the number of vessels outfitted or invested in by the leading maritime families into a lt. value, table 10.2 attests to their high rate of participation in the commerce of the port.

During the decade 1720–29, the Rasteaus outfitted or invested in 21 percent of the port's departures. Over the seven decades, that family invested in 13 percent of total armements. The Gareschés, dominant after 1770, had a stake in one of every twelve departing vessels, and the Belins were not far behind. Complete data on the shares owned by armateurs in 91 of 101 vessels departing La Rochelle in 1748 and 1749, summarized in table 10.3, indicates that ten families provided almost 23 percent of the capital invested in the port's armements. Rochelais investors contributed 56 percent of the total, of which the ten families produced 40 percent.[8]

The investment share of the families composing tables 10.2 and 10.3 had declined by the 1780s. Of the sixteen families in table 10.2, only six continued to outfit or invest in the port's shipping between 1784 and 1787. A new group of families had emerged following the War of the American Revolution. While the maritime commitment of the Giraudeau, Rasteau, Guibert, Vivier, Gareschés, and Carayon families persisted, new men such as Pierre Jean Van Hoogwerf, Samuel de Missy, and the Fleuriau Brothers achieved high status as négociant-armateurs. A number of the newcomers—Van Hoogwerf, Nicholas Suidre, Jean Baptiste Nairac, among others—were related by marriage to the older families. The businesses of both Van Hoogwerf and Suidre received large capital inputs through dowries as a result of marriages into the Rasteau, Belin, and Giraudeau families, and both men ultimately benefited from substantial inheritances. In addition to providing capital resources to the armateur generation of the 1770s and 1780s, the Giraudeau, Rasteau, Guibert, Vivier, Gareschés, and Carayon families accounted for 13 percent of total direct investment in shipping and 22 percent of the Rochelais share.

Moreover, the influence of the older families suffered no eclipse. Pierre Gabriel Admyrauld served as director of the La Rochelle Chamber of Commerce in 1781 and 1782, while his son François held an admiralty

Table 10.2. Percentage of Total Departures Outfitted or Invested in by Sixteen Rochelais Families, 1720–89

Family	1720–29	1730–39	1740–49	1750–59	1760–69	1770–79	1780–89	1720–89
Rasteau	21	14	13	11	16	6	9	12.5
Garesché	6	4	4	5	6	18	22	8.9
Belin	19	11	9	5	7	5	0	7.5
Vivier	4	8	9	3	1	4	6	5.2
Giraudeau	2	5	5	4	4	3	4	4.0
Delacroix	11	28	0	1	2	0	0	5.7
Carayon	3	–1	3	2	–1	3	10	3.2
Bonneau	14	8	7	4	–1	0	0	4.4
Bonfils	2	–1	6	8	6	0	0	3.5
Seignette	–1	–1	2	–1	6	1	1	1.8
Perdriau	4	–1	5	11	2	0	0	3.5
Depont	18	8	2	0	0	0	–1	3.2
Suidre	0	0	0	1	6	17	4	3.8
Goguet	0	0	–1	5	3	7	6	2.9
Pascaud	4	6	5	3	0	0	0	2.5
Guibert	–1	–1	0	0	1	11	9	3.0

position. Jacques Carayon fils aîné, representing the third generation, was elected to syndic and director of the chamber. Jean Elie Giraudeau guided chamber affairs in 1778 and 1779 and during the 1780s held a seat on the juridiction consulaire. Jacques Guibert fils and Louis Elie Vivier, son of Jean, both won election during the 1780s as chamber syndics. From 1778 to 1781, Pierre Isaac Rasteau represented La Rochelle as the first Protestant deputy to the Council of Commerce. Daniel Garesché served as mayor of the city during the difficult years 1791–92. Thus, several of the older families retained and indeed added luster to their traditional status as political and economic leaders in La Rochelle.

An estimate of the investment capital required at La Rochelle to support its commerce must account for the elapsed time between the commitment of capital and the amortization of the investment. Evidence from La Rochelle, summarized in tables 7.1 and 7.2, establishes that amortization of investments stretched out anywhere from three to seven years for direct voyages and perhaps longer for slave expeditions. In any given year, the capital commitment of La Rochelle's armateurs and intéressés represents a magnitude considerably larger than the total annual value of ships and cargoes presented in table 10.1.

The model developed in table 7.3 to calculate the rate of return on Jacques Rasteau's maritime investments will be applied in the following measurement of the port's capital requirements. That model makes no distinction between direct voyages and slaving ventures, but instead adopts a rate of return which reflects the general average of all voyages le long cours. For present purposes the model must represent more accurately two variables: (1) the longer period

Table 10.3. Investment Shares of Ten Families in La Rochelle armements, 1748–49

Family and/ or company	No. of vessels outfitted by or invested in	No. of Shares	Estimated value of investment (lt. value)	Investment as a % of total value of outbound vessels and cargoes
Rasteau	9	239	295,100	2.3
Garesché	10	381	470,422	3.7
Belin	15	413	509,943	4.0
Vivier	4	44	53,093	0.4
Giraudeau	4	75	92,604	0.7
Delacroix & Bonfils	10	280	345,724	2.7
Carayon	12	154	190,148	1.4
Bonneau	4	233	287,692	2.2
Seignette	2	100	123,473	1.0
Perdriau	9	382	471,667	3.6
Total			2,839,866	22.7

of time required for the amortization of a slaving voyage compared with a direct voyage, and (2) the shifting proportion over time of investments in direct and slaving ventures. At La Rochelle, slaving armements comprised 20 percent of all ocean-going ventures from 1740 to 1749 and 37 percent from 1783 to 1792 (table 2.3).

The time periods selected for analysis, 1748–51 and 1783–86, represent the most active commercial years of the eighteenth century. Table 10.4 contains investment data for the earlier period, while table 10.5 covers the 1780s. Each table distinguishes between investments in direct voyages and investments in slavers.[9] Evidence from the accounts of armateurs indicates that the rate of return for slavers differed from direct voyages and from the earlier to the later period. During the 1780s, the crisis in credits intensified, compelling armateurs to commit proportionately greater amounts of capital to trade and for longer periods of time than was the case during the years 1748–51. Taken together, the tables disclose the impact over time of changes in the cost of outfits and an augmented demand for credit in the colonies upon the invest-ment patterns of Rochelais merchants, and thus on the capital supply necessary to sustain the city's commerce.[10]

The total cost of both direct and slave armements averaged 7,390,650 lt. for each year during the 1740s and 7,378,400 lt. for the relevant years during the 1780s. However, the relative emphasis given to each branch of commerce differs substantially. In the earlier period, slave armements cost 25 percent of total mise hors, whereas in the later period they consumed 56 percent of invest-ments. Although the initial annual investments in each period were similar, the intensified focus on the slave trade, the higher cost of slave ventures, and the extended period of time before accomplishing full amortization meant that Rochelais capital needs would be greater during the 1780s than during the 1740s.

In 1748 (see table 10.4), Rochelais capital investment in both branches of

Table 10.4. *Investment Capital Needs of La Rochelle, 1748–51 (lt.)*

Year	Total cost of direct voyages	Total capital recovered by								Capital outstanding
		1748	1749	1750	1751	1752	1753	1754	1755	
1748	5,458,200	2,456,190	1,910,370	1,091,640						3,002,010
1749	5,789,000		2,605,050	2,026,150	1,157,800					4,275,590
1750	5,458,200			2,456,190	1,910,370	1,091,640				4,159,810
1751	7,112,200				3,200,490	2,489,270	1,422,440			5,003,350
	Total cost of slave voyages									
1748	1,723,500		689,400	517,050	344,700	172,350				1,723,500
1749	2,106,500			842,600	631,950	421,300	210,650			3,140,600
1750	1,340,500				536,200	402,150	268,100	134,050	3,121,450	
1751	574,500					229,800	172,350	114,900	57,450	2,183,200

trade reached 7,181,700 lt., 76 percent directed into direct trade and 24 percent into slaving. Within that year, 2,456,190 lt. in returns were distributed among the intéressés or expended to liquidate other obligations. A sum of 4,725,510 lt. remained to be collected, 36 percent attributable to the slave trade. In 1749, a new capital investment of 7,895,500 lt. launched 35 direct and 11 slaving armements. By the end of that year (figuratively speaking), returns from the two years 1748–49 had yielded 7,661,010 lt., leaving uncollected 7,416,190 lt. Debts owed by colonists who had purchased slaves and the value of slaves still unsold composed 42 percent of the capital yet to be remitted to the armateurs. For the two years, then, the Rochelais required capital resources of 22,493,390 lt. to finance ventures worth 15,077,200 lt. Over the four-year period, the Rochelais must have commanded 37,741,750 lt. in capital in order to invest 29,562,600 lt. in the colonial trade. In effect, the Rochelais disposed of capital resources that would be the equivalent of five years' worth of armements in order to make armements for four years.

Note that investment in slaving consumed between 20 and 27 percent of the capital for the years 1748–50 but had fallen to 7 percent by 1751. Had the pattern of the first three years persisted into the fourth, the Rochelais would have required control of capital the equivalent of six years worth of armements to support shipping actually launched in four years. That the Rochelais reduced the number of slaving outfits, undoubtedly influenced by specific market conditions, conveys their reluctance at that moment to pour additional capital into a trade that taxed their resources so heavily.[11]

Despite the negligible difference in the total cost of armements between the two periods, the demand upon Rochelais capital resources intensified during the 1780s as the port's armateurs focused their efforts more sharply on the slave trade. Antillean and slaving armements in 1783 cost the Rochelais 7,901,056 lt., 59 percent channeled into slavers (see table 10.5). In that year, remittances to La Rochelle reached 1,454,003 lt. The slave trade accounted for 6,447,053 lt. or 72 percent of the unreturned capital. During the following year, armateurs launched twenty-two direct and fourteen slave ventures capitalized at 6,863,292 lt. Slaving required 53 percent of the investment. At the end of 1784, returns for the two years had yielded 5,906,872 lt. while the unamortized capital totaled 8,695,098 lt., 74 percent carried by the slave expeditions. As a direct result of armements expedited over the two-year period and worth 14,764,348 lt., the Rochelais carried a debt and investment burden of 23,495,446 lt. By the end of the fourth year, total investments had reached 29,513,761 lt., of which 16,994,240 lt. remained uncollected. Over the full four years, Rochelais armements valued at 29,513,761 lt. actually demanded capital resources of 46,212,607 lt. Phrased differently, to ready outfits during a 48-month period, La Rochelle's shipowners committed a capital equivalent to the cost of armements of seventy-eight months. If projected further, say over a ten-year period, Rochelais armateurs assumed a liability of 200 lt. for each 100 lt. actually invested in an outfit.

Table 10.5. Investment Capital Needs of La Rochelle, 1783–86 (lt.)

Year	Total cost of direct voyages	Total capital recovered by								Capital outstanding
		1783	1784	1785	1786	1787	1788	1789	1790	
1783	3,231,118	1,454,003	1,130,891	484,667	161,566					1,777,115
1784	3,231,118		1,454,003	1,130,891	484,667	161,566				2,261,781
1785	2,203,035			991,365	771,062	330,455	110,152			2,018,449
1786	1,909,297				859,183	668,254	296,394	94,465		1,661,276
	Total cost of slave voyages									
1783	4,669,938		1,867,975	1,167,484	933,987	466,993	233,497	181,609		4,669,938
1784	3,632,174			1,452,896	908,043	726,435	363,217	441,050	220,525	6,434,127
1785	4,410,497				1,764,199	1,102,624	882,099	1,245,317	622,658	10,092,256
1786	6,226,584					2,490,633	1,556,646			15,332,964

This estimate of Rochelais capital needs substantiates the more general conclusions reached by Jean Meyer regarding the capital required in Nantes in 1727 and 1728—and applied to later years as well—to outfit 108 vessels. Meyer estimated the total cost of armements at six million lt. and assumed a two-year turnaround. Nantes disposed of a capital of 12 million lt. by 1790; the value of Nantes's shipping was worth 25 million lt. Thus, the city required at least 50 million lt. in available capital.[12] In all likelihood, Meyer's two-year turnaround underestimated the time actually required to amortize the initial investment. Still, this analysis of the rate of return at La Rochelle and the estimates of Meyer accentuates the great sums necessary to support the Atlantic trade. How much greater must have been the capital resources of Bordeaux and Marseilles?

Meyer has asserted that the Nantais in 1790 possessed a greater capability than the Nantais of 1725 to finance their maritime sector with local capital. The fortunes of the port's négociants, according to Meyer, reached 120 million lt. in 1725.[13] Did a similar improvement in Rochelais capabilities occur during the eighteenth century?

At La Rochelle, the number of armateurs remained fairly stable during the eighteenth century, with the exception of a sizable increase during the boom years of the 1740s. The dominant Rochelais families maintained unchallenged supremacy in the port's maritime sector during the 1720s and the 1740s. By the 1780s, they had monopolized it almost entirely (see tables 3.2, 5.1, 10.2, and 10.3). It had become difficult for other merchants to enter the field. The costs of outfitting had risen, and the time during which capital was tied up had lengthened. All merchants knew of the seriousness of the debt situation in the colonies. Individuals with small capital and few contacts might have been discouraged. La Rochelle might have been viewed negatively. Individuals contemplating careers in shipping may have perceived greater advantages in other ports or in other avenues of investment. But since little is known of the composition of the armateur class in other ports and the degree of mobility or entry into the field that prevailed, it may be that in those ports, too, the older families retained and strengthened their ascendancy.

Armateurs provided over 50 percent of the financing for La Rochelle's expeditions. In each of the above three decades, another group of 20 to 40 individuals—kin and other Rochelais who were not armateurs—contributed an additional 30 percent of the cost of the city's armements (see figures 4.1, 4.2 and 4.3). Thus, an investment group of from fifty to eighty families, most included among the nuclear group of ninety, were responsible for the greater part of local investment in shipping. The investing group at La Rochelle, then, did not expand markedly during the eighteenth century. Did the wealth of this group grow sufficiently over the century to enable its members to invest more heavily in the city's shipping?

A precise rendition of the wealth of the ninety families is impossible. Chapter 3 contains descriptions of the estates of a few families—Belin, Rasteau, Depont—and suggests that the dominant Rochelais families owned estates ranging in value from 200,000 lt. to one million lt. A few families are known to have possessed estates in excess of the latter sum. Both the Belin and the Depont families seem to have committed 60 to 70 percent of their total wealth to commercial pursuits. To estimate the total wealth of the ninety families, inference and assumption must be employed to supplement the sparse data available. At least one basic assumption seems justified: that the estates of the wealthiest were more valuable during the 1780s than during the 1740s. This seems clear from estate documents discussed in Chapter 3 as well as from the enlarged capital requirements of the port's commerce during the 1780s. Tables 10.4 and 10.5 suggest that capital demand in the 1780s exceeded by 22 percent the demand of the 1740s, whereas the number of active Rochelais investors had actually declined.

La Rochelle's commerce required 37.7 million lt. during the four-year period 1748–51 and 46.2 million lt. for the four years 1783–86. Armateurs regularly supplied one-half of mise hors, and kin, in the 1740s, at least another 20 percent. During the earlier period, then, forty-six families, accounting for 79 percent of all armements, carried an investment burden of 20.8 million lt., or a four year average of 453,000 lt. for each family. The Rasteaus, investing or outfitting 13 percent of all ventures during the 1740s, would have a capital commitment exceeding that of the Gareschés, who participated in 4 percent of all armements. In the later period, thirty-five families outfitted 97 percent of all ventures. Their investment contribution (figuring 10 percent participation for kin) amounted to 26.9 million lt., or a four-year average of 768,000 lt. for each family. Here, the capital commitment of the Gareschés, participating in 22 percent of all ventures, would have greatly surpassed that of the Rasteaus, who participated in only 9 percent of all armements. Capital demands on the primary armateurs in the 1780s had risen by 70 percent since the 1740s. Such a sharp increase, largely attributable to the intense focus on slaving, may have exerted severe pressure on the investment capabilities of the city's maritime families.

During the 1720s, thirteen of the twenty-six notables listed in table 3.2 outfitted vessels. Many of these men had just initiated their careers as armateurs, so it may be assumed that their estates fell at the lower end of the scale, say 200,000 lt. The thirteen would command a total capital of 2.6 million lt. An additional fifteen families, all from among the ninety notables, functioned as armateurs. Assume their estates to have been worth 100,000 lt., or in the aggregate, 1.5 million lt. The remaining outfitters might have possessed estates of 50,000 lt. each, for a total of 750,000 lt. Estates worth some 4.8 million lt. financed ventures that averaged 1.7 million lt. in outfitting costs during the 1720s. Meyer's ratio of maritime investment to wealth for Nantes in 1725 was 1:3; at La Rochelle, for the 1720s, it was 1:2.1.[14]

By the 1780s, eleven of the twenty-six notables listed in table 3.2 outfitted vessels. Of the eleven, the Rasteau, Vivier, Seignette, Garesché, Giraudeau, Carayon, Admyrauld, and Bernon families were entering their seventh consecutive decade of maritime activity. Assume estates of one million lt. for each, or a total of eight million lt. Three other elite families—Van Hoogwerf, Goguet, and Suidre—might have possessed estates of 500,000 lt., or 1.5 million lt. Twenty-four additional families from among the ninety outfitted vessels. Assuming estates of 250,000 lt. for each, the yield would be six million lt. If the nine remaining armateurs disposed of 100,000 lt. each, or 900,000 lt., the estates of all armateurs would reach 17.4 million lt.

During the 1720s, kin provided almost one-quarter of the necessary maritime investment. In the present calculation, their share is included in the general estimate of armateur family wealth. The portion provided during the 1720s by Rochelais who were not kin to the armateurs was relatively slight. But by the 1780s, the share of nonkin investment had expanded to almost 25 percent of local contributions. About twenty families or individuals, including five of the notables, participated as intéressés. Assuming estates of 200,000 lt. each for these families, or a total of four million lt., the addition of this sum to the above estimate of 17.4 million lt. produces a total of 21.4 million lt. to finance a local cost of armement, which averaged 6.4 million lt. during the years 1780 and 1789. Meyer's ratio of maritime investment to wealth for Nantes in 1789 and 1:5.2; at La Rochelle, the ratio was 1:3.4.[15] While this signifies an increase of disposable wealth relative to annual costs of armements at La Rochelle, the increase was less dramatic than at Nantes.

The annual cost of armements represents but a portion of the actual capital necessary to sustain commerce for a period of years. At Nantes, the increase in capital worth of merchant families may have enhanced their ability to finance armements more completely from local capital, but such was not the case of La Rochelle.

The actual capital needs of La Rochelle from 1783 through 1786 exceeded the four-year total of direct annual investments in voyages le long cours. During those four years, the Rochelais required a capital of 46,212,607 lt. to sustain armements valued at 29,513,761 lt. The average annual capital commitment for the four years equaled 11,553,151 lt. Using this figure instead of annual costs of armements produces a ratio of maritime investment to wealth of 1:1.8, a substantial reduction from 1:3.2. Thus, during the 1780s, the Rochelais approached the upper limits of their capacity to invest in maritime commerce.

Some 20 percent of maritime investments derived from non-Rochelais sources during the 1740s and the 1780s (see figures 4.2 and 4.3). An expanding commerce during the 1740s welcomed such investment. In the later period, the maintenance of commerce at fairly high levels demanded increasing draughts of outside capital. Non-Rochelais investors alleviated a severe local shortage of capital.

NON-ROCHELAIS INVESTMENT IN ROCHELAIS COMMERCE

Some part of the money directed into the maritime sector of each French port originated elsewhere. Little is known regarding the paths that intercity investments followed or the magnitude of those investments. During the eighteenth century, significant amounts of Swiss capital flowed into France, directed largely to Protestant comptoirs. The merchant house Christophe Bourcard of Basel participated in East Indian ventures launched by Solier & Company of Marseilles; invested in the armements of Honfleur, Saint-Malo, and Bordeaux; purchased shares in the ventures of the Admyraulds and Meschinet de Richemond of La Rochelle; and operated a branch establishment at Nantes. That the Swiss connection and others assumed a significant role in French commerce is well known; remaining unknown is the total value of direct investments made by foreigners and nonlocal French.[16]

Just as each French port attracted some of its capital from foreign locales and the interior of France, so too did the négociants of one port frequently invest in the armements of other ports. At La Rochelle, scattered evidence documents the movement of Rochelais capital to other ports, a propensity that, ideally, should be accounted for in the analysis of the capital strength of the city. Data simply do not allow an exhaustive investigation but it is clear that important investments were made. Between 1720 and 1722, Paul Depont regularly invested in the fishing vessels of Sables d'Olonne. During the same years, Belin capital flowed into Nantes, and other Rochelais purchased shares in vessels belonging to armateurs in Rochefort and Rouen. André Chabot, Rasteau fils aîné, and Perdriau, in 1751, participated in nine terreneuviers outfitted at Saint-Malo and Granville. Numerous Rochelais, including Weis & Sons, Robert father and son, Jacques Gilbert, and Trésahar Bonfils, took shares during the 1750s and 1760s in ventures organized at Hamburg, Cherbourg, Marseilles, and Saint-Malo. De Richemond & Garnault spread their investments widely: in fishing at Dunkirk, in four slavers sent out from Nantes between 1779 and 1784 and one from Saint-Malo in 1785, and in other vessels dispatched from Brest, Rochefort, and Marseilles. In 1783 and 1784 a group of Rochelais invested 400,000 lt. in a three-vessel expedition to the East Indies, which was capitalized at six million lt. and prepared at Marseilles.[17]

The cumulative impact of outward capital flow on the ability of Rochelais to finance their own armements must have been substantial. The estimates of Rochelais wealth presented above suggest that the Rochelais could not have supported a maritime commerce much greater than that achieved during the 1780s. But here we see Rochelais diverting an unknown part of their assets into the shipping of other seaports. Obviously, the port's merchants knew what they were doing. If the Rochelais recognized the limitations of their port, venture capital would naturally seek other and outside opportunities for gainful employment. The desire to spread risks would also support the wisdom of outside investments. Balanced against this would be the inward flow of capital which may have functioned to provide just that margin necessary to maintain armements at desirable levels, thus permitting the Rochelais to speculate in enterprises organized elsewhere. All of this accentuates the usefulness of port studies that, in addition to counting ships and quantities of goods, attempt a quantitative measurement of capital needs and the magnitude and directions of capital flow.

Investors in La Rochelle's shipping lived throughout France and western Europe. Available data for the period 1720–89 suggested a preponderance of investors from Paris, Bordeaux, and Nantes. Since information is most complete for the two two-year periods 1748–49 and 1784–85, attention will center on those years.

In 1748 and 1749, non-Rochelais were known to be intéressés in 37 of the 101 vessels outfitted at La Rochelle, while for 1784 and 1785, non-Rochelais participated in at least 19 of 87 armements. Each vessel, as explained earlier, consisted of 100 shares (1 share=1 percent of total mise hors). At a minimum, outside investors, holding 1,079 known shares in 1748 and 1749, contributed capital sufficient to outfit almost 11 vessels, and in 1784–85, almost 5 vessels. The reduction from the earlier to the later period reflects the size of the sample rather than an actual decline in outside investment.

Total shares, all held by Rochelais, were also known for another 22 ships in 1748 and 1749, and 22 ships for 1784 and 1785, amounting to the equivalent of 2,200 shares in each period. That leaves 42 vessels in the earlier period and 46 vessels in the latter period for which the division of shares is unknown.

If the ratio of wholly Rochelais-owned vessels (22) to all vessels for which intéressés are known (59) is applied to the armements for which no intéressés are known (42), it might be tentatively suggested that 15 of the latter were also wholly owned by Rochelais, yielding a total of 37 home-owned vessels (consisting of 3,700 shares). In the sample of 37 vessels for which non-Rochelais intéressés are known, the number of outside-owned shares totals 1,079, or 29 percent of the shares. If nonlocals also owned 29 percent of the unknown outfits (42), or 1,216 shares, the total shares owned by non-Rochelais in 1748 and 1749 equals 2,297, or 22 percent (2,297÷10,100) of all shares in Rochelais shipping. The application of the same method to the years 1784 and 1785 yields an estimate of total non-Rochelais ownership approximating 19 percent. These findings are congruent with the estimate found in figures 4.2 and 4.3.

Less compatibility prevails between these conclusions and those suggested in conjunction with table 10.1, which presents data revealing that approximately one-half of Rochelais capital needs originated outside the city in 1748 and during the 1780s. The different samples explain part of the divergence; even more germane are the hidden components in the shares registered in the name of the armateur.

The registered share of an armateur, whether 100 percent or less, quite possibly included the investment of parties unnamed, particularly foreigners and individuals associated as *commanditaires* in a comptoir. In 1721, Vincent Bureau registered as "seul proprietaire" of the vessel *l'Union*. In fact, the Parisian banker Jean Cottin and unnamed Dutch associates owned the vessel. Numerous examples in 1748 and 1749 and again in the 1780s replicated the Bureau example. Foreign investors in de Richemond & Garnault's ventures during the 1780s subscribed through the office of P. G. Lambert of Paris, Garnault's father-in-law. Lambert's interests and those of his foreign associates were subsumed within the shares attributed to the Rochelais partners. Delacroix & Bonfils during the 1730s and 1740s, and Weis & Sons, Stockard & d'Ebert, Nicolas Schaaft, and Pierre Jean Van Hoogwerf during the 1780s, represented intéressés residing in Holland, the Hanse cities, and England, although the names of these investors never appear in the registrations.[18] The value remains unknown, but the investments were common and their effect would be to lower the estimate of Rochelais investments presented above to a level more compatible with the data in table 10.1.

CONCLUSION

La Rochelle attracted venture capital from places scattered widely about in France and western Europe. The volume of risk capital annually directed to La Rochelle, averaging over four million lt. during the 1740s, and the unknown but substantial funds that Rochelais invested in the shipping of other ports presupposed the existence of and Rochelais participation in a far-flung network of commercial capitalism. La Rochelle received investment funds from communities as near as Saint-Jean-d'Angely and Niort, from places in the general region such as Poitiers and Loudoun, from those more distant places such as Basel and Geneva. With the exception of funds channeled to the ports through Paris, the most active segment of the network linked the ports together. For La Rochelle, the most active competitors—Nantes, Bordeaux, Le Havre, Marseilles—as well as such lesser ports as Bayonne or Rochefort provided during the eighteenth century the most constant source of risk capital. Investors in foreign cities—London, Amsterdam, Hamburg—also bought shares in Rochelais armements.

Whether the pattern attributed to La Rochelle diverged significantly from that prevailing in the larger entrepôts cannot be known with any certainty. Henri Sée has noted that Magon de la Balue of Saint-Malo drew investment funds from Nantes, Paris, Rennes, Marseilles, and Dijon. Other studies, too, attest to the wide-ranging net flung out by armateurs in their quest for capital.[19] With the exception of Nantes, the total capital needs of French ports have not been estimated. While Nantes offered some basis of comparison with La

Rochelle, that analysis could not be pursued because Meyer did not attempt to distinguish local investors from non-Nantais investors.

If the Rochelais pattern resembles that of other ports, the extraordinary growth of French commerce during the eighteenth century derived substantial support from individuals throughout France and western Europe who looked to the maritime centers for profitable use of their surplus. Those investors may have earmarked their funds for specific ventures, managed by specific arma-teurs. Solier & Co. of Marseilles drew from a fairly stable group of outsiders. Meyer has described similar practices in Nantes. Intéressés in Van Hoog-werf's expeditions during the 1780s normally consisted of the same people. Similarly, Dumoustier de Fredilly's armements included the same share-holders from Marseilles, Bordeaux, and Paris.[20] Armateurs tended to develop a stable of investors, not all of whom were identifiable. Still other sums from unnamed third parties passed through intermediaries to the armateurs. P. Giradot of Paris regularly invested others' funds in the outfits of Théodore Delacroix. Shares were registered in Giradot's name and Delacroix had no knowledge of the original source. Delacroix, too, served as broker for D. Dubrocq, merchant of Bayonne, who entrusted funds to Delacroix for invest-ment in armements in La Rochelle and Nantes. Antoine Guymonneau of Rouen performed similar functions.[21] It seems likely, then, that capital flow into and out of French ports structurally resembles that described for La Rochelle.

La Rochelle, the smallest of the major French ports, annually committed to commerce a capital greater than the capitalization of all but the largest indus-trial establishments in the realm.[22] By the 1780s, outside capital was essential if the port was to function at full capacity. The city's armateurs provided one-half of the required capital. Other Rochelais, relatives and nonkin, contributed from 20 to 40 percent and a similar, shifting proportion came from outside of the city. Evidence suggests that the Rochelais could not have raised more capital than they did. The trade of the port had achieved its maximum size in the last decade of the Old Regime.

With expansion no longer an option, fewer individuals unattached by mar-riage to the elite families sought entry into the armateur class. The share of arme-ments attributable to the dominant families rose to monopolistic proportions. Concentration on the slave trade and the persistent burden of colonial debts, coupled with the stagnancy of hitherto important staple trades, taxed the capital resources of the city's entrepreneurs. Even without the Revolution, La Rochelle would have experienced rapid decline in her maritime fortunes.

ELEVEN

Conclusion

An American visitor to La Rochelle in 1807 described the port as "not susceptible of great and extensive commerce."[1] Its days as a dynamic Indian port had ended. Today, its harbor offers shelter to pleasure craft and a fishing fleet exceeding 16,000 tons. Berths for ocean freighter traffic have been constructed at La Palice, some five and one-half kilometers west of the old port, at the end of the peninsula that faces the eastern tip of Île de Ré. Since World War II, industrial plants have located at La Rochelle and large housing projects have been constructed to the east and west of Vieille Ville. But the city is by no means central to the economy of France. Le Havre, Bordeaux, and Marseilles maintained their predominance through one-quarter century of revolution and war against the armed might of Europe. La Rochelle did not.

La Rochelle's experience during the eighteenth century encompassed decades of vitality and expansion commencing in the 1720s and lasting until the outbreak of the Seven Years' War, and decades of decline thereafter. If a single cause had to be assigned for the deterioration of the Rochelais economy, war would serve the purpose. The process was more complicated, however, for the pressure of war impinged more severely upon La Rochelle than upon her rivals. The city's economy proved less capable of shaking off the damaging consequences of war than did the economies of her competitors. Nantes and the other great ports suffered serious losses during wartime, but in those places the losses proved temporary, were rapidly overcome, and left fewer permanent scars.

Despite serious natural disadvantages, debilitating intervention on the part of the crown, and in the face of persistent and vigorous competition, La Rochelle managed to maintain its status as a major port until the French Revolution. Locational inferiority and the steady deterioration of a restricted port area proved unamenable to improvement. The city lacked convenient access to the interior of France and the national consumer market, and its immediate hinterland produced neither diverse nor particularly valuable goods. Such factors tended to exaggerate La Rochelle's dependence upon the sea and its concentration on the reexport trade, as did the absence of a diversified industrial base. The inconveniences of the roadstead and inner port at La Rochelle—small size and silting of the channels—reduced the amount of traffic the port could manage and added to the costs of conducting business.

La Rochelle's port could have been improved, but the city's leaders failed to win sufficient support from the government to pay for renovation. The state not only compelled the Rochelais to spend local tax monies on such unessentials as the construction of an arsenal but so burdened the municipality with fiscal levies that it was perpetually in debt to the crown. Indeed, of all the threats to the vitality of the port, none impinged with more harsh consistency than the power of the state.

One characteristic of an underdeveloped economy is a central government that commits a relatively high proportion of taxes to purposes neither productive of social overhead capital nor growth-promoting. Such states may support elaborate bureaucracies staffed with legions of civil servants or ridiculously large military establishments, as do numerous Third World countries today. Or, as was the case in eighteenth-century France, vast sums may be spent on maintaining the court, protecting privilege, and waging basically dynastic wars. In either case, the state functions as a "universal sink" into which private funds are poured and out of which flow few of the developmental supports necessary to promote economic growth. The government is a competitor for capital in all states whose economies are dominated by the private sector. Generally, however, state exactions represent but a moderate share of the total wealth—despite protests to the contrary from individual and corporate taxpayers—and the government normally reinvests a large portion of taxes in projects and programs that serve the public interest.

In France, three economies functioned. The rural economy consisted largely of peasants living at a subsistence level in small communities engaged, at most, in regional market systems. With the majority of French consumer units rural and composed of low income families, who spent 50 to 70 percent of their total income on food, the potential for contact between this sector and the commercial sector was quite limited.[2] If the focus of the subsistence economy was survival, that of the commercial economy was exchange for profit. With the weakness of the national consumer market, however, the coastal and interior river cities which formed the second economy of France looked abroad for trade and gain. Each component of the private sector, then, had its own focus and complementariness was minimal. Evidence from La Rochelle and other ports failed to support the contention that prosperity in the seaports ebbed and flowed with the production of grains. The antenna of the ports pointed overseas toward the colonies, northern Europe, the north African coast, and other points. The ports were attuned to an Atlantic, if not quite global, economic system.

Astride the two private sectors sat the crown, insatiable in its fiscal demands, unrelenting in its search for new and larger sources of revenue. Employing an army of tax gatherers, the crown ripped capital from the private sectors to perpetuate itself, the court, and the system of privilege. Royal interests differed from those of the rural and port worlds and the crown's fiscal decisions, rooted in considerations that reflected its own needs, made it a consumer of vast amounts of capital and an obstruction to economic growth. The self-serving intervention of the central government in the economy transformed the potentially growth-inducing Company of the West into the Company of the Indies, a fiscal machine so burdened with royal obligations that it collapsed. The crown's role transcended that of a state that sought to impose its policies on the nation through the control of the decision-making process by competing directly with the productive sector for the wealth of the nation. By means of its support of privilege and the social environment which privilege sustained, the royal government denied the private sectors the use of necessary capital and turned productive capital to nonproductive purposes. The crown formed the most powerful sector in the tripartite economy of France.

In the competition for economic gain that raged among the ports of France and, occasionally, among ports and interior cities in such industries as sugar refining, growth potential depended upon relative economic advantages. Ports vied with one another for political preference and protection in trades considered essential to their viability. Ports such as La Rochelle contributed to the strength of privilege by seeking the status for themselves and attacking it only selectively. La Rochelle, Nantes, Bordeaux, and other seaports persisted during the eighteenth century in their condemnation of monopolistic companies, particularly the Company of the Indies; at the same time, they defended the French monopoly of the colonial trade, sought to deny to unprivileged ports the right to conduct colonial trade, and criticized privileges that they did not enjoy and that they perceived as productive of unfair competitive advantages.

The La Rochelle Chamber of Commerce acted as the primary institutional defense of the maritime interests of the city. The chamber marshaled arguments against policies of the state or its representatives, especially the tax farm, believed damaging to the interests of the city's commerce. Similarly, the Chamber of Commerce of Rouen believed its major function to be the defense of commerce against onerous taxation.[3] Through instructions to the Rochelais deputy to the Council of Commerce in Paris, the chamber orchestrated support from other ports against monopolistic trading companies, insurance companies, and foreign trade in the colonies. The chamber, and secondarily the juridiction consulaire and the municipal government, protected the vital interests of La Rochelle by selective support or opposition to privilege. These institutions manifested parochial rather than national interests as did the Council of Commerce, composed of individuals responsive to the needs of their communities rather than to the more amorphous needs of the nation.

La Rochelle's chamber was the most prestigious forum for the elite armateur-négociants. As a bulwark of elite supremacy in La Rochelle, the body sought to avoid sharing power with lower economic orders, whose interests might deviate from those of its elite constituency. During the eighteenth century, the chamber successfully resisted efforts of retailers and other merchants to gain seats in the body while concurrently extending its areas of responsibility over the commerce of the city.

While religious persecution and emigration had transformed the Huguenot majority in La Rochelle to a minority, Protestants dominated the city's economy and shared power with Roman Catholics in the chamber. Vestiges of religious controversy persisted in the juridiction consulaire, whose members unsuccessfully opposed the admission of Huguenots into the chamber. But in the latter body, the urgency of presenting an united front to the crown and its officials overwhelmed whatever latent antagonism may have existed. During the eighteenth century, few examples of internal divisions emerged that pitted elite against elite.

Huguenot and Catholic armateur-négociant families shared common assumptions concerning the economic requirements of their city. Protestant families exerted much more influence than their numbers warranted, but this did not irritate their Catholic peers. Shared leadership between the two religions worked smoothly. Viewed collectively, certain divergent patterns were visible. Catholics tended to hold royal offices more frequently than Protestants, but the Belin, Seignette, Depont, and Carayon families, among other Protestants, did hold venal office. Protestants participated more frequently than Catholics in large scale, corporate organizations, but the Catholics Jean Baptiste Gastumeau and Théodore Charles Surreau both participated with Protestants in the insurance business. More Protestants than Catholics served as armateurs and Protestants outfitted more vessels, but the Catholic Pascaud, Goguet, Lefebvre, and de Butler families were all deeply involved in maritime affairs. Convergent patterns rather than divergent practices best describe the public political and economic lives of Protestants and Catholics.

Consensus regarding broad policy issues shared by the adherents of both faiths partially stemmed from the similar ways in which they organized their family and kinship groups of their comptoirs. Rochelais family networks, similar in structure to those evolving much earlier in Venice, Amsterdam, and other European cities, perpetuated the clan and its wealth and assured that the bulk of the family fortune worked actively in commerce.

Elite Rochelais families employed a variety of traditional mechanisms to achieve their goals. Most young Rochelais married other Rochelais of their class and religion. Through dowries, the early partition of estates, and inheritance, the wealth of allied families flowed through the generations in waves similar to that described for the Belins. Marriage contracts minimized the possibilities that wealth would be withdrawn from commerce, while dowries and funds gained by early partition and final inheritance were quickly turned into working capital. Assiduous attention to the education of young Rochelais, in comptoirs both at home and abroad and on the high seas, provided management personnel. Rochelais women, too, frequently assumed managerial responsibilities and even if their roles were limited while their husbands lived, they were knowledgeable about business affairs.

Not all sons could become partners of or successors to their fathers or associates of other Rochelais, generally kin. There were simply not enough jobs to go around. Parents had to plan for the probability that one or more sons would have to make their careers elsewhere, frequently in the colonies. Catholic youth enjoyed many more potential career lines than their Huguenot contemporaries. Proscriptive laws closed many professions to Protestants. But Catholic sons as well as Protestant followed their fathers into comptoirs or struck out on their own, perhaps in association with a brother, uncle, or cousin. Not a wisp of evidence suggests that Huguenot youth were forced into vocations that they did not wish to enter or that as adults they resented their occupations and the society that had "forced" it upon them.

During the eighteenth century, Rochelais spouses limited the size of their families. La Rochelle offered restricted opportunities for growth, and an excessive number of children would have rapidly depleted the family wealth and endangered the stability of the family.

Each Rochelais négociant family operated in the capitalist mode: they took risks and spread them out over a variety of enterprises, reinvested returns in the business, sought to parlay short-term changes in prices to advantage or to minimize losses, engaged in long-term planning, maintained channels of communication, and performed specialized functions. Family comptoirs offered sufficient flexibility and merchants moved easily into and out of other forms of organization.

During the early eighteenth century, independent entrepreneurs dominated the local business scene. They joined together regularly with other négociants for specific purposes, some of which were short-term ventures and others that lasted for a long period of time. Armements brought together an organizer—the armateur—and investors—the intéressés. While each armement represented a venture and the association of armateur and intéressé ended with the final distribution of profits or losses, in fact associations between particular armateurs and the same group of investors continued through many voyages. Armateurs with a fairly stable investment group were better able to predict their future capital needs. Relatives composed an important part of the intéressé group, thus forming an interlocking network of investment among the armateur-négociant families. Nonkin, both Rochelais and non-Rochelais, also invested significant sums in Rochelais commerce.

Partnerships became more common in La Rochelle as the second generation entered into management roles alongside their parents or kin. Such firms frequently endured into the third generation, although the personnel might change. Thus, Charuyer & Depont, organized in the 1750s, continued as widow Charuyer & Sons and then, during the 1780s, became Charuyer Brothers. A portion of the capital of Charuyer Brothers derived from Van Hoogwerf wealth, part of which originated with the Belin family.

Rochelais merchants, Protestant and Catholic, displayed an active capitalist spirit. They labored long hours in the pursuit of profit, and the reinvestment of most of their wealth in the family business or the establishment of sons in business manifested their dislike for idle capital. While many Rochelais families invested in lands, rentes, and offices, and some few sought ennoblement, most Rochelais wealth was committed to enterprises directly related to maritime commerce. Numerous families owned salt marshes and brandy or grain lands. Ownership of colonial plantations was not uncommon. These operations were integrated into the primary endeavor, maritime trade.

Survival and prosperity depended upon skillful organization and management. Deciding the precise time to divide the family patrimony or charting the training program of a young son required careful attention. So, too, did the process of armement, beginning with the ordering of goods from correspondents and suppliers throughout France and Europe and including outfitting of the vessel and conveying precise instructions to the captain (who might be a son or relative) and to correspondents in the colonies. Great responsibility rested with the agents, the best of whom were rendered impotent by glutted markets and declarations of war.

Special considerations ruled each of the major trade routes—to Africa and thence to the Antilles, direct voyages to the West Indies or to Louisiana or Canada, and to the Indian Ocean. Slaving, the riskiest of the trades, tied up capital for a greater duration and, because of longer voyages and larger ships, cost more to prepare than direct voyages. Yet during the eighteenth century, slaving consumed a growing share of Rochelais capital resources until, in the 1780s, slave voyages composed 35 percent of all armements and over one-half of capital commitments. At La Rochelle, slaving involved a greater proportion of all armateurs than at Nantes, and this traffic took a proportionately greater part of Rochelais shipping and capital than at Le Havre, Bordeaux, or Marseilles. In the aggregate, however, shipping concentrated in fewer hands at La Rochelle than at either Nantes or Bordeaux. From 1720 to 1789, eight Rochelais families—each married into at least two of the other seven—accounted for 28 percent of all Rochelais armements le long cours.

Concentration on the colonial trade at La Rochelle intensified during the eighteenth century, yet the port's share of French trade with the colonies declined in the face of vigorous competition from Bordeaux, Le Havre, and Marseilles. The economies of both La Rochelle and Bordeaux were more closely meshed with the Atlantic world than with the French economy, but to La Rochelle, lacking the rich hinterland and excellent interior connections of Bordeaux, the colonial tie meant more. Thus, the steady and debilitating swelling of colonial debts caused greater difficulties at La Rochelle than at some larger ports.

The Rochelais, as well as the Nantais, were tightly locked into the colonial trade by the 1750s. To conduct the trade, credits had to be extended to planters. Planters repaid their debts but slowly, and the Seven Years' War and the War of the American Revolution further complicated the collection of debts. These wars nurtured no interests at La Rochelle, or for that matter at the other ports. Although France may have achieved certain goals on the Continent, for the maritime centers each war resulted in defeat. Certainly this was the case at La Rochelle, which suffered from the cessions of Louisiana and Canada. The Rochelais were always on the losing side and planters seized the advantage of wartime chaos to renege on debts.

Inadequate convoys and superior British naval strength along colonial routes resulted in severe losses at the beginning of each war and the virtual cessation of armements at La Rochelle during the latter stages of the Seven Years' War. The crown responded to colonial complaints about the absence of French shipping not by improving the convoy system but by allowing neutral trade in the colonies. The next logical step, free trade in the colonies, followed during the 1780s, exacerbating problems of debt collection and marketing. In order to keep the collection process in motion, additional credits had to be extended. As a result of that unbreakable cycle, in any given year after the Seven Years' War the colonial debt probably exceeded the total *mise hors* for that year.

Visible manifestations of Rochelais patriotism never waned during the eighteenth century; but expressions of unswerving loyalty to the crown were coupled with vigorous criticism of the policies of government officials. If colonial debts sorely burdened the Rochelais while the apathy and inefficiency of French naval officers resulted in the destruction or incapacitation of the local merchant fleet, so too did the fiscal needs of the state, inflated by the exigencies of war, press heavily on the city. High tax rates and augmented numbers of venal offices ate into the margin of profit that Rochelais extracted from the salt and brandy trades.

Rochelais stores of coffee, indigo, cotton, or sugars enjoyed no superiority in quality or price to those offered at other French entrepôts. The availability of salt and brandy had attracted hundreds of foreign coasting vessels to La Rochelle, enhancing the sale of colonial staples. But from the mid-eighteenth century on, taxes and fees on salt (the equivalent of 35 percent of its value) and on brandy (equal to 40 to 50 percent of its value) destroyed the competitive advantages of the Rochelais products. As a result of those charges and cheaper Spanish and Portuguese varieties, fewer and fewer northern European coasters anchored at La Rochelle and smaller nearby ports.

Efforts of the La Rochelle Chamber of Commerce to obtain tax and fee reductions met with stiff opposition from tax gatherers and little enthusiasm from the crown. Nominal tax and tariff reductions and some subsidization of fishing and slaving offered inadequate compensation for the loss of Canada and Louisiana, the destructive competition of foreigners in the Antilles, the heavy tax on English coal which raised production costs in the brandy and sugar refining industries, and the unwillingness of the crown to support the merchants in their efforts to reduce the size of the colonial debt. During the Seven Years' War, and again during the succeeding war, the crown adopted the position of corporate insurance at the expense of the shipping interests in the debates over *augmentation,* attesting to the evolving political strength of corporate organizations. The crown normally sustained the views and interests of monopolistic companies against individual entrepreneurs. While the identification of government support structures that aided the Rochelais is difficult, itemizing damaging government policies is a simple task.

La Rochelle's armateur families maintained a commerce that grew less rapidly than that of their rivals. As at other ports, venture capital from nonlocal sources provided a portion of the necessary financing. La Rochelle's negative balance of trade in insurance did not reflect inability to finance the coverage of local shipping but rather decisions of independent underwriters to limit their insurance investments. The capital resources of La Rochelle were inadequate, however, to fully finance its armements.

Armateurs at La Rochelle and other ports depended upon outside investment in their ventures. Their ability to attract outside capital demonstrates the strength of their comptoirs and of their home port. During the eighteenth century, a moderate increase occurred in the capital committed by Rochelais to their shipping, yet the proportionate amount declined relative to the total value of ships and cargoes. Moreover, from the 1740s to the 1780s, the total amount of capital required to support a static unit value of cost rose by as much as 70 percent. If the Rochelais had had access only to local capital, their commerce would have been much smaller.

Non-Rochelais investors provided at least 20 percent of capital needs. Most important were investors in other maritime centers; Paris, too, was significant. But it was the intermaritime city connection that accounted for most inbound capital while Rochelais funds flowed outward along those linkages. This was the dominant economic axis for La Rochelle. International contacts, particularly the Protestant network, joined together La Rochelle, Amsterdam, London, and Geneva. A similar network facilitated the financial operations of Languedocien bankers.[4] For La Rochelle and other ports, the Atlantic formed the central operational universe.

La Rochelle, by the 1780s, had achieved its maximum growth and reached a stable state. Rochelais capital worked at capacity, and investment from outside became a more critical need. Local and nonlocal investors recognized La Rochelle's limitations. True, the port's commerce remained sufficiently attractive to maintain itself at a relatively stable level—but signs of decay were visible.

Physical facilities at the port had deteriorated and the commodiousness of the harbor reduced by the winds and tides. Access to the interior had improved little over two centuries. Commerce in traditionally profitable regional products had been damaged by government policies. Major armateurs turned toward the slave trade in increasing numbers as the crisis of colonial debts worsened. Merchant failures increased after 1765, and several dominant families struggled thereafter merely to survive.

Rochelais merchants confronted these challenges as best they could, within the context of their times. Kinship support shored up Pierre Isaac Rasteau, saving him from disaster. The relatives of other threatened merchants agreed to sustain serious losses rather than press their kin to the wall. Family wealth continued to pour into commerce. Armateurs advertised prospective ventures throughout France and western Europe. Some turned to the East Indian trade. Partnerships flourished.

Certainly, unwise decisions were made. Efforts to develop trade with the United States failed because of unsuitable cargoes. De Richemond & Garnault overextended itself. The slave trade was overemphasized. But many of these decisions resulted directly from the consequences of the last two pre-revolutionary wars. Merchants attempted to recoup losses suffered during those wars as quickly as possible, causing glutted markets and swollen debts. The inability to turn credit into cash precipitated failures even when book assets exceeded liabilities.

In the final analysis, the last two wars were destructive of the Rochelais economy. While the outbreak of revolution in France and in the Antilles administered the coup de grace, La Rochelle's decline was inevitable. The French Revolution merely fixed the precise date.

Notes

Chapter One

1. Among the secondary works that describe the port are M. Arcere, *Histoire de la ville de La Rochelle et du pays d'Aunis,* 2 vols. (La Rochelle, 1756–57), 2:456–57; P. Boissonnade, "La marine marchande, le port, et les armateurs de La Rochelle à l'époque de Colbert (1662–1683)," Comité des travaux historiques et scientifiques, *Bulletin de la section de geographie* 37 (Paris, 1922): 6–8; Emile Garnault, *Le commerce rochelais au XVIIIe siècle d'après les documents composant les anciennes archives de la chambre de commerce de La Rochelle,* 4 vols. (La Rochelle, 1888–98), vol. 2; Henri Robert, *Les trafics coloniaux du port de La Rochelle au XVIIIe siècle,* Memoires de la société des antiquitaires de l'Ouest, 4th ser., vol. 4 (Poitiers, 1960), pp. 31–33; [François Marlin], *Voyages en France depuis 1775 jusqu'à 1817,* 4 vols. (Paris, 1817), 4:65–66. See also the following archival collections: Correspondance des ministres, intendants, ou autres dignitaires, AMLR, Ms. 341, 369, 430; ville de La Rochelle, Archives Bibliotheque Municipale de La Rochelle (hereafter cited as AMLR), Ms. BB8; Correspondance des députés du commerce, Archives de la Chambre de Commerce de La Rochelle (hereafter cited as CCLR), carton 4; Chambre du Conseil des juges consuls, 1717–46, Juridiction consulaire de La Rochelle, Archives de la Charente-Maritime (hereafter cited as ACM), La Rochelle, Ms. Series B339.

2. Arcere, *La ville de La Rochelle,* 2:456–57; Robert Forster, "The Noble Wine Producers of the Bordelais in the Eighteenth Century," *Economic History Review* 14 (August 1961): 18 (hereafter cited as *EHR*); Marlin, *Voyages,* 1: 310–11.

3. Gaston Martin, "Nantes et la Compagnie des Indes, 1664–1769," *Revue d'histoire économique et sociale* 15 (1927): 44–45 (hereafter cited as *RHES*); Jean Meyer, *L'armement nantais dans le deuxième moitié du XVIIIe siècle* (Paris, 1969), pp. 66–69; J. Letaconnoux, "Les transports en France aux XVIIIe siècle," *Revue d'histoire moderne et contemporaine* II (1908–9): 274–88, 290 (hereafter cited as *RHMC*); Roger Dion, *Histoire de la vigne et du vin en France des origines au XIXe siècle,* (Paris, 1959), pp. 379–91; François-George Pariset, ed., *Bordeaux au XVIIIe siècle,* vol. 5, *Histoire de Bordeaux,* ed., Ch. Higounet (Bordeaux, 1968), pp. 206–10.

4. The salt and brandy trades and sugar refining are discussed in detail in Chapter 8; J. J. Garnault á M. de Richemond, Brest, 8 octobre 1779, AMLR, Ms. 2247; Réponse de la Chambre de Commerce de La Rochelle aux demandes de Messieurs les Députés extraordinaires de manufactures et du commerce de France, 7 octobre 1789, CCLR, carton 20; L. J. Nazelle, *Le Protestantisme en Saintonge sous le régime de la Révocation, 1685–1789* (Paris, 1907), pp. 13–16; Jean Périer, *La prospérité rochelaise au XVIIIe siècle et la bourgeoisie protestante* (Mesnil, n.d. [c. 1899]), pp. 1–3; Henri Sée *Le commerce maritime de la Bretagne au XVIIIe siècle, d'après les papiers des Magon, Mémoires et documents pour servir à l'histoire du commerce et de l'industrie en France,* ed. Julien Hayem, 9th ser. (Paris, 1925), pp. 56–59.

5. Louis Péronas, "Sur la démographie rochelaise," *Annales Economie, Société, Civilisation,* 16 (November-December 1961); 1131–40 (hereafter cited as *Annales ESC*); Emile Levasseur, *La population française: Histoire de la population avant 1789 et démographie de la France,* 3 vols. (Paris, 1889), 1: 225–27; J. C. Toutain, *La population de la France de 1700 à 1959,* vol. 3, *Histoire quantitative de l'économie française* (Paris, 1963), pp. 9–17.

6. Péronas, "La demographie rochelaise," pp. 1132–36; *Bulletin de la société de l'histoire du Protestantisme français* 44 (1895); 372; 104 (1958): 15.

7. For the preceding three paragraphs, see Piganiol de la Force, *Nouveau voyage de France,* 2 vols. (Paris, 1755), 2: 93–94; Marlin, *Voyages,* 1:160; [J. B. Nairac], On the Taxation of Incoming Colonial Products and on Property Taxation, ca. 1780, [untitled document], AMLR, Ms. 1417; Account of Wages, 1750, [untitled document], AMLR, Ms. 2646; Ordinance de police concernant les ouvriers et compagnons et de l'obligation de maîtres à leur regard, 16 février 1786, AMLR, Ms. 329; M. Genain, subdélégué de l'intendant de La Rochelle à M. Griffon, maire de la Rochelle, La Rochelle, 23 février 1768, AMLR, Ms. BB8; Arrentement des maisons situées à La Rochelle, 1782, ACM, Ms. 4J958; Van Hoogwerf à P. G. Van Hoogwerf, La Rochelle, 6 décembre 1785, and à Odelie Stuart, La Rochelle, 31 juillet 1787, Pierre Van Hoogwerf Papers, ACM, Ms. 4J2847 and 4J2848.

8. Henri Hauser, *Les débuts du capitalisme* (Paris, 1927), p. 125.

9. Many municipalities, including La Rochelle once its municipal government was restored in the early eighteenth century, resisted the tendency of royal government to weaken municipal independence through the office of the intendant, created during the reign of Louis XIII. While not entirely successful in their resistance, most cities retained certain financial authority, provided services, and were partly responsible for charity and education. Pierre Goubert, *L'Ancien Régime,* vol 1. *La Société* (Paris, 1969), pp. 191–95, contains the best brief discussion of municipal privileges.

10. Garnault, *Le commerce rochelais,* 3:58–69; 4:256–62; Charles de la Morandière, *Histoire de la pêche française de la morue dans l'Amérique septentrionale: Des origines à 1789,* 3 vols. (Paris, 1962), 2:546–47; J. T. Viaud and E. J. Fleury, *Histoire de la ville et du port de Rochefort,* 2 vols. (Rochefort, 1845), 1:322–23; for mémoires and arrêts, see CCLR, cartons 14 and 15; for an expression of concern from Nantes over the pretensions of Saint-Malo, see Delaunay Montaudoin à Théodore Delacroix, Nantes, 31 janvier 1737, Théodore Delacroix Correspondence, AMLR, Ms. 2645.

11. John G. Clark, *New Orleans, 1718–1812: An Economic History* (Baton Rouge, La., 1970), p. 63; Laurence C. Wroth and Gertrude L. Annan, comps., *Acts of French Royal Administration Concerning Canada, Guiana, the West Indies, and Louisiana, prior to 1791* (New York, 1930), no. 1155; Henri Wallon, *La Chambre de Commerce de la province de Normandie (1703–1791)* (Rouen, 1903), pp. 302–10. The titles of the protests from La Rochelle, Dunkirk, Bayonne, Marseilles, and *les six corps des Marchands de Paris* are too long to reproduce here. They are located in CCLR, carton 15. See Chapter 7 for a more detailed account of the Rochelais response to foreign trade with the colonies.

12. Mémoires supporting the suspension of the regulation from Saint-Malo and Brest, and La Rochelle's counterresponses, are located in CCLR, carton 14.

13. Paul Logié, *Les institutions du commerce à Amiens au XVIIIe siècle: Juridictions consulaire et chambre de commerce sous l'Ancien Régime et pendant la période revolutionnaire* (Amiens, 1951), pp. 102–5; see also above citations of material from CCLR.

14. Traité d'amitié et de commerce conclu entre le Roi et les Etats unis de l'Amérique septentrionale, ratifié le 16 juillet dernier 1778, CCLR, carton 17; Meschinet de Richemond à M. Franklin, La Rochelle, 14 décembre 1776, ACM, Ms. E446; Torterue Bonneau à la Chambre de Commerce de La Rochelle, Paris, 8 mars 1783, 9 septembre 1783, 21 novembre 1786, and 3 mars 1787, CCLR, carton 4.

15. See Albert Babeau, *La ville sous l'Ancien Régime,* 2 vols. (Paris, 1884), 1: 4, 347–48; Phillipe Sagnac, *La formation de la société française moderne,* 2 vols. (Paris, 1945–46), 2:216.

16. Benjamin Ippolito, *Les chambres de commerce dans l'économie française* (Bordeaux, 1945), pp. 6–9; Félix Olivier Martin, *L'organisation corporative de la France d'Ancien Régime* (Paris, 1938), pp. 288–90; R. B. Grassby, "Social Status and Commercial Enterprise under Louis XIV," EHR 13 (August 1960): 26–27.

17. The paragraphs on the Rochelais chamber were derived from Emile Garnault, *Livre d'or de la chambre de commerce de la Rochelle contenant la biographie de directeurs et présidents de*

cette chambre de 1719 à 1891 (La Rochelle, 1902), pp. 4–5, and idem., *Le commerce rochelais,* 1: 20–27, 184, 235–40; Robert, *Trafics coloniaux,* pp. 184–88; Arie Théodorus Van Deursen, *Professions et métiers interdits: Un aspect de l'histoire de la Révocation de l'Edit de Nantes* (Groningen, Neth., 1960), p. 338; Wallon, *Chambre de commerce de Normandie,* p. 6; F. O. Martin, *L'organisation corporative,* pp. 290–91; Ippolito, *Les Chambres de commerce,* pp. 9–11. The Chamber of Commerce and the *juridiction consulaire* at Rouen were also completely dominated by merchants; see Dale Miquelon, *Dugard of Rouen: French Trade to Canada and the West Indies, 1729–1770* (Montreal and London, 1978), pp. 14–15. See also, Chambre du conseil des juges consuls, 2 octobre 1719, ACM, Ms. B339; [Minister of the Marine] à la Chambre de Commerce de La Rochelle, Versailles, 13 janvier 1770, CCLR, carton 10.

18. The Rochelais deputies were F. Mouchard (1715–23), Jean Moreau (1719–29), Nicolas Claëssen (1729–46), Antoine Pascaud (1746–58), his brother, Joseph (1758–67), Théodore-Charles Surreau (1767–76), Pierre Isaac Rasteau, the first Protestant (1777–81), and another Protestant, Jacques Torterue Bonneau (1781–91). Bonneau was in office when the Constituent Assembly abolished all chambers of commerce.

19. The correspondence of the deputies of commerce is located in CCLR, carton 4. See also Léon Biolly, *L'administration du commerce,* Etudes économique sur le XVIIIe siècle (Paris, 1885), pp. 285–339; Pierre Bonnassieux, *Conseil du Commerce et Bureau du Commerce, 1700–1791: Inventaire analytique des procès-verbaux* (Paris, 1900); Warren C. Scoville, "The French Economy in 1700–1701: An Appraisal of the Deputies of Trade," *JEH* 22 (June 1962): 231–52.

20. For the discussion of the municipal government, see Babeau, *La ville,* 1: 4, 95–102, 347–48; Henri Mariage, *Evolution historique de la législation commerciale de l'ordinance de Colbert à nos jours, 1673–1949* (Paris, 1951), pp. 11, 50–63; Nora Temple, "The Control and Exploitation of French Towns during the Ancien Régime," *History* 51 (February 1966): 16–34. The original sources used include Administration communale, Brevets de nomination des Maires et Echevins, 1717–43, AMLR, Ms. BB4; and, for 1743–89, Ms. BB5, and Offices municipaux, Ms. BB15. Also Ville de La Rochelle, États des charges ordinaires et extraordinaires duër par le corps de ville, 1765–89, AMLR, Ms. CC79; Bignon à corps de ville, Saints, 19 décembre 1733 and de Pleuve à Mss. les maire et échevins à La Rochelle, La Rochelle, 8 décembre 1748, AMLR, Ms. CC79.

21. AMLR: for wheelwrights, Ms. 324; for drygoods merchants, Ms. 325; for potteryware merchants, Ms. 326; for bread vendors, Ms. 329; for firewood monopoly, CCLR, carton 13.

22. The Law era has generated a large body of literature; for brief summary of the evolution of Law's company, see Clark, *New Orleans,* pp. 16–20. For other accounts of this company and earlier companies, see Boissonnade, "Marine marchande de La Rochelle;" Pierre Bonnassieux, *Les grandes compagnies de commerce: Etude pour servir à l'histoire de la colonisation* (Paris, 1892); Jean Canu, Claude-Joseph Gignoux, and André Gobert, *Le commerce du XVe siècle au milieu de XIXe siècle,* vol. 4, *Histoire du commerce,* ed. Jacques-Lacour Gayet, 6 vols. (Paris, 1951); H. Carré, *Le règne de Louis XV (1715–1774),* vol. 8, *Histoire de la France depuis les origines jusqu'à la révolution,* ed. Ernest Lavisse, 9 vols. (Paris, 1909–11); Charles Woolsey Cole, *Colbert and a Century of French Mercantilism,* 2 vols. (New York, 1939); Earl J. Hamilton, "John Law of Lauriston: Banker, Gamester, Merchant, Chief," *American Economic Review* 57 (May 1967): 273–82; P. Harsin, *Les doctrines monétaires et finacières en France du XVI au XVIIIe siècle* (Paris, 1928); Dom H. Leclerq, *Histoire de la Régence pendant la minorité de Louis XV,* 3 vols. (Paris, 1921), vol. 2; Herbert Lüthy, *La Banque protestante en France de la Révocation de l'Edit de Nantes à la Révolution* 2 vols. (Paris, 1959–61); G. Martin, "Nantes et la Compagnie des Indes," pp. 25–65, 231–53; Léon Vignols and Henri Sée, "Les ventes de la Compagnie des Indes à Nantes (1723–1733)," *Revue de l'histoire des colonies françaises* 13 (1925): 489–550 (hereafter cited as *RHCF*).

23. The privileges of the Company of the Indies and its major areas of trade will be treated at appropriate points in following chapters.

24. For the above five paragraphs, see G. Martin, "Nantes et la Compagnie des Indes," pp. 42–43, 65, and idem., *Nantes au XVIIIe siècle: L'ère des négriers (1717–1774), après des docu-*

ments inédits (Paris, 1931), pp. 181–83; Garnault, *Le commerce rochelais,* 3:13; Wallon, *Chambre de Commerce de Normandie,* pp. 111–12; Louis Dermigny, *Cargaisons indiennes: Solier et Cie., 1781–1793,* 2 vols. (Paris, 1959–60), 2:154–55; André Ducasse, *Les négriers, ou le trafic des esclaves* (Paris, 1948), pp. 164–65; M. J. Conan, "La Dernière compagnie française des Indes . . . ," *RHES* 25 (1939): 37–58, 159–85, 293–312. For Depont's activities as company agent, see Depont des Granges Papers, ACM, Ms. E486. For the Rochelais response to monopoly, see CCLR, cartons 4 and 15.

25. Studies that describe an essentially dual economy include Lüthy, *La banque protestante,* 2:13–14; Sée, *Le commerce de la Bretagne;* Henri Hauser, "The Characteristic Features of French Economic History from the Middle of the Sixteenth Century to the Middle of the Eighteenth Century," *EHR* 4 (October 1933): 257–73; Edward Whiting Fox, *History in Geographic Perspective: The Other France* (New York; 1971), p. 68; Bert Hoselitz, "Entrepreneurship and Capital Formation in France and Britain since 1700," in *Capital Formation and Economic Growth,* ed. Moses Abramovitz (Princeton, N.J., 1955), pp. 292–300. Historians of port cities are generally found in this camp. Crouzet's chapters in the multiauthored history of Bordeaux, Pariset, *Bordeaux* chaps. 2–4, more or less reversed the position he had earlier assumed (see note 26). Meyer, *L'armement nantais,* pp. 70–71, and Charles Carrière, *Négociants marseillais au XVIIIe siècle,* 2 vols. (Marseilles: Institut historique de Province, 1973), 1: 43, described ports attuned to an international and oceanic, rather than national, economy. In both groups of studies, the state appears as a force retarding economic growth.

26. A second group of scholars depict a developing economic unity in eighteenth-century France: Sagnac, *Société française moderne,* 2:194–99, and François Crouzet, "Angleterre et France au XVIIIe siècle: Essai d'analyse comparée de deux croissances économiques," *Annales ESC* 21 (March-April 1966): 265–74. Ernest Labrousse, *La crise de l'économie française à la fin de l'Ancien Régime et au début de la Révolution* (Paris, 1944), pp. xv, xxxiv–vi, argued for the dominance of the agricultural sector. Rural depression after 1778, according to Labrousse, dragged down the entire economy. The dominant impacts of the agricultural sector were also argued by Labrousse in his sections of Ernest Labrousse et al., *Histoire économique et sociale de la France,* vol. 2, *Des derniers temps de l'âge seigneurial aux préludes de l'âge industriel (1660– 1789)* (Paris, 1970), pp. 530, 545, 563. Sagnac and Crouzet spoke of rising strength through integration. Labrousse viewed interrelatedness as a source of weakness because most agrarians were at a subsistence level. Goubert, *L'Ancien Régime,* 1: 42–43, emphasized the vulnerability of most of France to crop failures.

27. George V. Taylor, "Types of Capitalism in Eighteenth-Century France," *EHR* 79 (July 1964): 478–97, suggested that four types of capitalism existed, each exploiting different kinds of wealth. In his scheme, the economy was pluralistic rather than unified. Merchant capitalism, court capitalism, early industrial capitalism, and proprietary capitalism defined discrete categories of economic activity. I have attempted to extend his structural analysis to one emphasizing function and interpenetration.

28. Chapter 7 will treat this in more detail.

29. The pattern of noble participation in commerce—either as noble *négociants* or as investors—is described in George V. Taylor, "Noncapitalist Wealth and the Origins of the French Revolution," *American Historical Review* 72 (January 1967): 488–89. While not absent from La Rochelle—Paul Depont des Granges and a few others were nobles, and some nobles took shares in Rochelais ventures—the contribution of the nobility remained an insignificant part of the investment flow in the city. This flow is discussed in Chapters 9 and 10.

30. Garnault, *Le commerce rochelais,* 2:41–74, 84–115, 229–75; Arrêt du conseil d'état du roy pour l'entretien du logement de troupes destinées pour travailler au curement du Havre de La Rochelle, 1 août 1730, AMLR, Ms. 341; Nicolas Claëssen à la chambre de commerce de La Rochelle, Paris, 15 mai 1730, CCLR, carton 4; Mémoir de la chambre de commerce de La Rochelle, 4 août 1764, AMLR, Ms. 369; Pierre Isaac Rasteau à la chambre de commerce de La Rochelle, Paris, [n.d.], CCLR, carton 4; Marlin, *Voyages,* 4:65–66.

31. Mémoire d'observations adressé à M. Le Controlleur général par les officiers municipaux de La Rochelle, and Supplément au mémoire . . . La Rochelle, 1765, AMLR, Ms. CC79.

32. Chapters 9 and 10 will analyze the sources of capital for the maritime trade.

33. L'Affaire de grande et petite traitte, 1706–30, ACM, Ms. B4197; Droits que se levent dans la ville de La Rochelle, 1706, AMLR, Ms. 318; Chambre du conseil des juges consuls sur le droit du doublement, 15 septembre 1717, ACM, Ms. B339. For an analysis of the financial system emphasizing its individualistic and entrepreneurial characteristics, see J. F. Bosher, *French Finances, 1770–1795: From Business to Bureaucracy* (Cambridge, 1970), pp. 6–9, 277–80.

34. The controversy over the *taille* was documented from AMLR, Ms. CC159. Among the most important documents were Arrêt du Conseil du Roi remplaçant la taille réelle par un abonnement municipal de 4000 livres, 1 juin 1634; Pelletier à M. Billaud, La Rochelle, 1 janvier 1765; Mémoire des habitants de la paroisse de la Jarne contre Sr. Rondeau et autres Bourgeoise qui ont de dormainer à la Jarne, 1775; Précis pour la ville de la Rochelle contre les Habitans des Paroisses circonvoisines, par Raoult, Député de la ville de La Rochelle, 1781; Arrêt du conseil d'état du roi, 18 août 1785; Taille, 1786, Ville de La Rochelle, listed the following families, all of whom were prominent *négoçiants,* as exempt: Bonneau, Brevet, Giraudeau, Hardy, Pelletau, Gigoux, Ranson, Carayon fils aîné, Rasteau, Legrix, Bougereau, Seignette, Jenner, Belin, and Guyon.

35. The special trades of La Rochelle—brandy, salt, and grain—will be covered in Chapter 8.

36. Réné Josúe Valin, *Commentaire sur l'ordonnance de la marine du mois d'août 1681, avec des notes par V. Bécane,* 2d ed., (Paris, 1841), p. 19. H. du Halgouet, *Nantes: Ses relations commerciales avec les îles d'Amérique au XVIIIe siècle* (Rennes, 1939), pp. 6–10; Droits que se levent dans La Rochelle, 1706, AMLR, Ms. 318.

37. Rates were set for raw sugar, semirefined sugar, sugar from Cayenne, and for indigo, cotton, cacao, and coffee from Santo Domingo, Cayenne, and Martinique.

38. CCLR, cartons 4 and 20 contain most of the material on the *domaine d'occident.* The most important documents include M. le Controlleur Général aux Directeurs de Commerce de Bordeaux, 15 janvier 1725, carton 20; Joseph Pascaud à la Chambre de Commerce à La Rochelle, 1758–64, carton 4; Pierre Isaac Rasteau à la Chambre de Commerce de La Rochelle, 28 février 1778 and 14 mars 1779, carton 4; Torterue Bonneau à la Chambre de Commerce de La Rochelle, 6 janvier, 9 septembre 1783, carton 4; M. le Directeur des Fermes du Roi à la Chambre de Commerce à La Rochelle, 25 février 1784, carton 20.

39. Tax costs for the four commodities were calculated as follows: known total imports × assessed value × .035 percent. Annual figures of total imports were kept by the Chamber of Commerce and were found in Récapitulation des toutes les marchandises entrées dans le royaume par les divers ports de la direction de La Rochelle venant des pays étrangers pendant l'année [1718–80] (hereafter cited as Récapitulation entrées), CCLR, carton 27. The method by which outward bound value was calculated will be explained in Chapter 6.

40. Paul Walden Bamford, "French Shipping in Northern European Trade, 1660–1789," *Journal of Modern History* 26 (September 1954): 208–9; Périer, *La prospérité rochelaise,* pp. 24–26; Copie de la lettre écrite par la compagnie [des Indes] à Monsr. Deselicouis, Fermier général, Paris, 7 février 1722, CCLR, carton 20; Droits d'entrée sur les pelleteries, La Rochelle, 1778, CCLR, carton 21.

41. Edouard Dupont, *Histoire de La Rochelle* (La Rochelle, 1830), pp. 504–5; Extrait des Registres du conseil d'état, 26 mai 1693, AMLR, Ms. 325: Arrêt du Conseil d'état du Roy, 23 décembre 1704, AMLR, Ms. CC16; Mémoire pour les habitants de la ville de La Rochelle et du pays d'Aunis, contre Jacques Hué, fermier des droits de Courtiers Jaugeure et Inspecteur aux boissons de la généralité de La Rochelle, 1749, AMLR, Ms. 430; Information de vie moeurs et capacité su Sieur Peronne, agréeur de l'eau-de-vie, 1754, AMLR, Ms. 326; Arrêt du conseil d'état sur le charbon de terre, 13 septembre 1763, CCLR, carton 20.

42. George V. Taylor, "Noncapitalist Wealth and the Origins of the French Revolution," pp. 477–79.

43. Chapter 2 analyzes the value and composition of La Rochelle's exterior trade, while

Chapters 6 through 8 discuss its organization. Chapters 9 and 10 trace the inward and outward capital flow at La Rochelle.

44. Chapters 3 through 5 identify the members of the négociant elite of the city, tracing their origins, analyzing the socioeconomic characteristics of their kinship systems, and measuring their economic significance.

Chapter Two

1. Arthur M. Wilson, *French Foreign Policy during the Administration of Cardinal Fleury, 1726–1743: A Study in Diplomacy and Commercial Development* (Cambridge, Mass., 1936), p. 316; J. Saintoyant, *La colonisation française sous l'Ancien Régime (du XVe siècle à 1789),* 2 vols. (Paris, 1929), 2: 11; G. Lacour-Gayet, *La marine militaire de la France sous le règne de Louis XV* (Paris, 1902), p. 103; P. J. Charliat, "L'économie maritime de la France sous le règne de Louis XV: Notes historiques et statistiques," *RHES* 34 (1956): 172–80; Jean Meyer, *L'armement nantais dans la deuxième moitié du XVIIIe siècle* (Paris, 1969), p. 77. After November 10, 1785, the government paid a subsidy per ton for vessels outfitted for particular destinations. More will be said of this in subsequent pages.

2. Paul Walden Bamford, "French Shipping in Northern European Trade, 1660–1789," *Journal of Modern History* 26 (September 1954): 207–19; for the preponderance of foreign vessels at Bordeaux at the beginning of the eighteenth century, see Christian Huetz de Temps, *Géographie du commerce de Bordeaux à la fin du règne de Louis XIV* (Mouton, 1975), pp. 26–27.

3. The primary sources for Rochelais shipping data are Etat des vaisseaux partis pour les îles françaises de l'Amérique et Canada, depuis le premier octobre 1713 jusques et compris le 26 mars 1717, appartenant à Messieurs les marchands de La Rochelle (hereafter cited as Etat des vaisseaux), ACM, Ms. B4197; and Registre des Sousmissions, ACM, Série B247 (1727–33), B248 (1733–39), B250 (1739–48), B251 (1748–52), B257 (1752–56), B259 (1756–84), and B259bis (1784–92). These records list the registrant of the vessel, the name of the vessel and frequently its tonnage, the destination, the anticipated date of departure, and the reported date of return. Some registered vessels did not depart, while some departed that were never registered. Actual destinations often differed from those given. Normally only those vessels engaged in le long cours were registered. The Rochelais did not possess a large coasting fleet, but the figures mentioned are still too low. Fishing vessels frequently departed without registering, so those figures are too low also. However, my figures do reflect the size of La Rochelle's high seas fleet with greater accuracy than estimates in other studies. For other French ports see Meyer, *L'armement nantais,* 61; Jean Delumeau, "Le commerce malouin à la fin du XVIIe siècle," *Annales de Bretagne* 56 (September 1959): 264; Jean Delumeau, *Le mouvement du port de Saint Malo, 1681–1720: Bilan statistique* (Rennes, 1966), pp. 277–78; Wilbert Harold Delgliesh, *The Company of the Indies in the Days of Dupleix* (Easton, Pa., 1933), pp. 130–31; Maurice Begouen-Demeaux, *Memorial d'une famille du Havre: Stanislas Foäche, 1737–1806* (Paris, 1951), pp. 13–15; Pierre Dardel, *Navires et marchandises dans les ports de Rouen et du Havre au XVIIIe siècle* (Paris, 1963), pp. 681–85. Rouen, without a harbor, depended upon Le Havre. The two are treated as a single export-import unit; H. du Halgouet, *Nantes: Ses relations commerciales avec les îles d'Amérique au XVIIIe siècle* (Rennes, 1939), pp. 12, 18, 46, 97; Théophile Malvezin, *Histoire du commerce de Bordeaux depuis les origines jusqu'à nos jours,* 4 vols. (Bordeaux, 1892), 3:204; Francisque Michel, *Histoire du commerce et de la navigation à Bordeaux,* 2 vols. (Bordeaux, 1866–70), 2:286–88; Jean Tarrode, *Le commerce colonial de la France à la fin de l'Ancien Régime: L'évolution du régime de l'exclusif de 1763 à 1789,* 2 vols. (Paris, 1972), 2: 730–33, presents shipping figures for La Rochelle that are much too low.

4. These figures were derived from the two basic sources used in constructing table 2.2, cited in note 3. The tonnage figures are inferences based upon the known tonnage of departing Rochelais vessels. For each year between 1720 and 1791 the tonnage was known for more than one-half of

departing vessels. Average tonnage per vessel represents the known tonnage of departing vessels. Total average tonnage was obtained by multiplying the number of vessels outfitted by average tonnage per vessel.

5. The above two paragraphs were based upon Etat des vaisseaux; P. Harsin, *Les doctrines monétaires et financières en France du XVI au XVIIIe siècle* (Paris, 1928), pp. 135–36, 166–72; Herbert Lüthy, *La banque protestante en France de la Révocation de l'Edit de Nantes à la Révolution*, 2 vols. (Paris, 1959–61), 1:281–89; Hiroshi Akabane, "La crise de 1724–1725 et la politique de deflation du Controlleur-générale Dobun," *RHMC* (July-September 1967), pp. 266–83; H. Carré, *Le règne de Louis XV (1715–1774)*, vol. 8, *Histoire de la France des origines jusqu'à la Révolution*, ed. Ernest Lavisse, 9 vols., (Paris, 1909–11), pp. 34–38; Henri Sée, *Le commerce maritime de la Bretagne au XVIIIe siecle, d'après les papiers des Magon, Mémoires et documents pour servir à l'histoire du commerce et de l'industrie en France*, ed. Julien Hayem, 9th ser., (Paris, 1925), pp. 50–53.

6. For the last four paragraphs, see Registre des Sousmissions; Emile Garnault, *Le commerce rochelais au XVIIIe siècle d'après les documents composant les anciennes archives de la chambre de commerce de La Rochelle*, 4 vols. (La Rochelle, 1888–98), 4:331; John G. Clark, *New Orleans, 1718–1812: An Economic History* (Baton Rouge, 1970), pp. 82–83; Francois-Georges Pariset, ed., *Bordeaux au XVIIIe siècle*, vol 5, *Histoire de Bordeaux*, ed. Ch. Higounet (Bordeaux, 1968), pp. 210–23, 236–37; Malvezin, *Commerce de Bordeaux*, 3:193, 204; Meyer, *L'armement nantais*, pp. 175–76; Halgouet, *Nantes*, pp. 12–18; Louis Dermigny, *Cargaisons indiennes: Solier et Cie., 1781–1793*, 2 vols. (Paris, 1959–60), 1: 76–77; Dardel, *Les ports de Rouen et du Havre*, pp. 49, 60–61, 640–41, 681–85; Thomas M. Doerflinger, "The Antilles Trade of the Old Regime: A Statistical Overview," *Journal of Interdisciplinary History* 6 (winter 1976): 409–10.

7. The Company of the Indies fully monopolized trade with Louisiana, West Africa, Santo Domingo, and the East Indies, and held the tobacco monopoly as well.

8. The above four paragraphs were derived from the following: Raymond Mauny, "Le déblocage d'un continent par les voies maritimes: Le cas africain," in *Les grandes voies maritimes dan le monde (XVe-XIXe siècles)*, ed., Michel Mollat (Paris, 1965), p. 177; Clark, *New Orleans*, pp. 18–19; Gaston Martin, *Nantes au XVIIIe siècle: L'ère des négriers (1717–1774), après les documents inédits* (Paris, 1931), pp. 74–78, 177–83; André Delcourt, *La France et les établissements français au Sénégal entre 1718 et 1763*, Mémoires de l'Institut français d'Afrique noire no. 17 (Ifan-Dakar, 1952), pp. 70–73; Simone Berbain, *Etudes sur la traite des noires au golfe de Guinée: Le comptoir français de Judah (Ouidah) au XVIIIe siècle*, Mémoires de l'Institute français d'Afrique noire no. 3 (Paris, 1942) pp. 1–8, 31–33; Ducasse, *Les négriers, ou le trafic des esclaves* (Paris, 1948), pp. 162–63.

9. Registre des Sousmissions; Garnault, *Le commerce rochelais*, 3:72–75; Philippe Barrey, "Le Havre et la navigation aux Antilles sous l'Ancien Régime: La question coloniale, en 1789–1791," in *Mémoires et documents*, ed. Julien Hayem, vol. 5 (Paris, 1921), pp. 227–28; Berbain, *Le comptoir français de Judah*, pp. 43–44; G. Martin, *Nantes au XVIIIe siècle*, p. 64; Jean Meyer, "Le commerce négrier nantais (1774–1792)," *Annales ESC* 15 (January–February 1960): 122–27; Malvezin, *Commerce de Bordeaux*, 3:35, Pariset, *Bordeaux*, pp. 238–39; Robert Stein, "The Profitability of the Nantes Slave Trade, 1783–1792," *JEH* 35 (December 1975): 779–93. According to Jean Mettas, "Honfleur et la traite des noirs au XVIIIe siècle," *Revue française d'histoire d'outre mer* 60 (1973): 6, 8, Honfleur ranked fifth, behind La Rochelle, as a slaving port during the latter part of the eighteenth century. From 1763 to 1792, at least 114 slavers departed Honfleur. From 1760 to 1792 at least 214 Rochelais vessels departed for Africa.

10. G. Martin, *Nantes au XVIIIe siècle*, pp. 17–21.

11. De Richemond & Garnault à Texier à Paris, La Rochelle, 15 mars 1785, ACM, Ms. E450.

12. Copie de la lettre écrite par M. le Controleur Général à M. Senac de Meilhan, Intendant de la Généralité de La Rochelle, 16 août 1769, CCLR, carton 15. This letter contained the arrêt suspending the privileges of the Company of the Indies and establishing regulations for trade to the East Indies. Among the regulations were: (1) the crown reserved the right to freight 10 percent of

each vessel either in men or goods, (2) the import duty on Indian goods was set at 5 percent, (3) in issuing permissions preference would be shown to those armateurs employing at least two ex-officers of the Company of the Indies.

13. Ch. Lanesse à la Chambre de Commerce de La Rochelle, Bordeaux, 21 mai 1785, CCLR, carton 15.

14. These figures are from Dermigny, *Cargaisons indiennes,* 1:98–102. He counted ten Rochelais vessels but the actual number was fifteen. Pariset, *Bordeaux,* p. 243, states that Bordeaux sent twenty-nine vessels in the single year 1788. So it would seem that Dermigny's figures are quite low.

15. For the East Indian trade, see Pierre Creppin, *Mahè de la Bourdonnais, Gouverneur général des Îles de France et de Bourbon (1699–1753)* (Paris, n.d.), pp. 20–21, 39–45; Albert Lougnon, *L'île Bourbon pendant le Régence: Desforges Boucher les débutes du café* (Paris, 1956), pp. 14–18, 57–62; Dermigny, *Cargaisons indiennes,* 1:88–90, 96–105; Conan, "La dèrniere compagnie française des Indes," pp. 39–57, 163–85, 293–301. For the Rochelais response to the new company, see Chapter 1.

16. Michel Mollat, ed., *Le rôle du sel dans l'histoire* (Paris, 1968); Robert de Loture, *Histoire de la grande pêche de Terre-Neuve* (Montrouge, 1949), pp. 205–28; Charles de la Morandière, *Histoire de la pêche française de la morue dans l'Amérique septentrionale: Des origines à 1789,* 3 vols. (Paris 1962), 2:520–23, 595–96; Henri Robert, *Les trafics coloniaux du port de La Rochelle au XVIIIe siecle,* Mémoires de la Société des antiquitaires de l'Ouest, 4th ser., vol. 4 (Poitiers, 1960), pp. 95–96; Georges Musset, *Les rochelais à Terre-Neuve, 1500–1789* (La Rochelle, 1899), pp. 3–4.

17. Observations sur le commerce du nord relativement à la France, [probably written by de Baussay and Gareschè], 1783, CCLR, carton 18; Paul Walden Bamford, *Forests and French Sea Power, 1660–1789* (Toronto, 1956), pp. 160–66.

18. Danish vessels calling at ports within the jurisdiction of the admiralty of La Rochelle, 1742–55, [untitled ms.], ACM, Ms. B5593; Garnault, *Le commerce rochelais,* 2:173; P. Desfeuilles, "La navigation à travers le Sund en 1784, d'après les registres de la douane danoise," *Annales ESC* 14 (July–September 1959): 492–520; Pariset, *Bordeaux,* pp. 257–60.

19. Garnault, *Le commerce rochelais,* 2:173; Visites du vaisseaux, 1779–84, ACM, Ms. B5788.

20. This is based upon a rule of thumb derived from the length of voyages. Monthly arrivals and departures were about equal in most years. Direct trips to and from the West Indies, Louisiana, or Canada took about one year. For each vessel leaving, another was about to return. In 1750, forty-eight Rochelais vessels departed the port, of which forty-three went to the above destinations. Thus, some 86 Rochelais vessels were engaged in that trade at that time. Another five ships went to West Africa. Those voyages required at least eighteen months and frequently more than two years. For every two slavers departing, a third was about to arrive. In 1750, the Rochelais had some eight slavers in operation, and in that year operated some ninety-four vessels. The functions of the armateur will be discussed in Chapter 6.

21. Seconde déclaration des Srs. Rasteau pour le vaisseau le Bellamy, 24 février 1748, and déclaration du Andre Chabot l'aîné, 17 août 1748, and other documents attesting to the purchase of a vessel, in ACM, Ms. B5738 and B5739. These notices provided the name and tonnage of the vessel, the place of purchase, the individuals holding shares in the vessel (*intéressés*), and the proportion of their interest. The term *intéressés* will be used in the text when reference is made to the shareholders of vessels; A Messieurs les directeurs et sindics de la Chambre de Commerce de La Rochelle, La Rochelle, 17 décembre 1762, in which several Rochelais purchased vessels in Brittany and sought permission to outfit the vessels in the port of purchase rather than, as required, in their home port. The chamber endorsed the request and forwarded it to the minister of the Marine, who extended the necessary authority, CCLR, carton 17.

22. Vente du vaisseaux le St. Charles, 9 juillet 1749, and documents for other sales at auction are scattered throughout ACM, Ms. B5738 and B5739.

23. Actes de propriété, 1784–85, ACM, Ms. B5786 and B5794. Other notices of Lepage

Brothers construction are dispersed throughout B5787, B5789, and B5791–92; for a prospectus describing a speculative construction venture, see AMLR, Ms. 2286–88.

24. Data on construction and purchase costs were derived from virtually every ACM collection cited in this study. These estimates do not reflect such additional costs as the making of needed repairs on purchased vessels.

25. Etat des navires du port de La Rochelle et du montant de leurs chargements, pris par les Anglois, 29 novembre 1745, CCLR, carton 7; Etat des navires qui ont chargés à La Rochelle d'eau-de-vie, sucre [ms. torn] pour les ports de Manche, lesquels ont été arrêtes par les Anglois avant la guerre déclarée, 9 octobre 1756, CCLR carton 17; Etat des navires de La Rochelle arrêtés par les Anglois soit en Europe ou en Amérique, avant la guerre déclarée, 18 septembre 1756, CCLR, carton 17; Meyer, *L'armement nantais,* p. 81; Martin, *Nantes au XVIIIe siècle,* pp. 266–68; Pariset, *Bordeaux,* pp. 290–93; Garnault, *Le commerce rochelais,* 4:188–89; Charles Frostin, "Les colons de Saint-Domingue et la metropole," *Revue historique* 237 (April-June 1967): 396. The armements of small operators were compiled from Registre des Soussumissions. Further discussion of the distribution of shipping ownership among Rochelais armateurs appears in Chapter 5.

26. Unless otherwise noted, the basic sources for this discussion and the tables that follow are: Récapitulation entrées, and Récapitulation de toutes les marchandises sorties du royaume par les divers ports de mer de la direction de La Rochelle allant aux pays étrangers et les colonies, 1718–80 (hereafter cited as Récapitulation sorties), CCLR, carton 27. These figures do include the external commerce of ports on nearby islands and the small mainlaind ports in the vicinity. The trade of those places contributed but a few percent to the totals of the district. In the salt and brandy trades, however, the deduction of their contribution from the Rochelais figures might alter the tabular figures significantly. There was no way of calculating the volume of that trade.

27. Emile Levasseur, *Histoire du commerce de la France,* 2 vols. (Paris, 1911), 1:*Avant 1789,* 511–12; Dardel, *Les ports de Rouen et du Havre,* p. 59; Pariset, *Bordeaux,* p. 197. A recent effort to construct a series representing the annual value of French colonial commerce appears in Tarrode, *Le commerce colonial,* 2:739.

28. The colonies included Guinea and the East Indies as well as the North American and Caribbean possessions; Dardel, *Les ports de Rouen et du Havre,* 63; Pariset, *Bordeaux,* pp. 197–98; Doerflinger, "The Antilles Trade," pp. 413–14.

29. Dardel, *Les ports du Rouen et de Havre,* p. 55; Pariset, *Bordeaux,* 198–99; Doerflinger, "The Antilles Trade," pp. 407–9; Ernest Labrousse, *La crise de l'économie française à la fin de l'Ancien Régime et au début de la Révolution* (Paris, 1944), p. xxxvii.

30. Armement du Meulan, premier voyage de Guinée, 1776, AMLR, Ms. 1977.

31. Récapitulation entrées, and Récapitulation sorties.

32. For the above four paragraphs, see Paul Butel, "Bordeaux et la Hollande au XVIIIe siècle: L'exemple du négociant Pellet (1694–1772)," *RHES* 46 (1967): 58–86; Michel Morineau, "La balance du commerce franco-néerlandais et le resserrement économique des Provinces-Unis au XVIIIe siècle," *Economisch-Historisch Jaarboek* 30 (1963–64): 170–233; Pariset, *Bordeaux,* p. 197, passim; Dardel, *Les ports de Rouen et du Havre,* pp. 64, 83–93, 117–18; Clark, *New Orleans,* chap. 9.

33. Halgouet, *Nantes,* p. 126; Dardel, *Les ports du Rouen et de Havre,* p. 59; Pariset, *Bordeaux,* pp. 193–99, 256; for a series of articles on various aspects of French commerce in the Mediterranean, see J. P. Filippini et al., *Dossiers sur le commerce français en Méditerranée orientale au XVIIIe siècle* (Paris, 1976).

Chapter Three

1. Pierre Goubert, *L'Ancien régime,* vol. 1, *La société* (Paris, 1969), pp. 228–29; George V. Taylor, "The Paris Bourse on the Eve of the Revolution, 1781–1789," *American Historical*

Review 67 (July 1962): 953–55, and idem., "Types of Capitalism in Eighteenth-Century France," *English Historical Review* 90 (July 1964): 489.

2. Many of the best social and economic studies of French communities have treated places in which *rentier* and administrative bourgeoisie were dominant. See Marcel Couturier, *Recherches sur les structures sociales de Châteaudun, 1525–1789* (Paris, 1969); Pierre Goubert, *Beauvais et le beauvaisis de 1600 à 1730: Contribution à l'histoire social de la France du XVIIe siècle* (Paris, 1960); Olwen Hufton, *Bayeaux in the Late Eighteenth Century: A Social Study* (Oxford, 1967); Marcel Lachiver, *La population de Meulan du XVIIe au XIXe siècle (vers 1600–1870): Etude de démographie historique* (Paris, 1969). The most recent study of a French port, Charles Carrière, *Négociants marseillais au XVIIIe siècle,* 2 vols. (Marseilles, 1973), neither identifies the elite group in its totality nor constructs samples representative of the group. This chapter and those which follow rest upon what I believe to be the first effort to identify and analyze the whole class of négociants in a major French port.

3. Other scholars have treated family networks that resembled La Rochelle's. See Violet Barbour, *Capitalism in Amsterdam in the Seventeenth Century* (Baltimore, 1950) and Frederic C. Lane, *Venice: A Maritime Republic* (Baltimore, 1973). Less systematic analyses of merchants in French ports are found in Carrière, *Négociants marseillais* and Jean Meyer, *L'armement nantais dans la deuxieme moitîe du XVIIIe siècle* (Paris, 1969).

4. In 1757, when an English fleet menaced the city, the négociants were responsible for the maintenance and management of the defense batteries. Costs were apportioned among 116 individuals belonging to 101 families. Eighty of the 90 families appeared on this list. In 1770, a second subscription to raise funds for work on the port yielded 108,794 lt. from 125 donors. Sixty-nine of the 90 families contributed 75 percent of total donations. The 90 families also provided 27 of the 38 directors of the La Rochelle Chamber of Commerce between 1719 and 1789, *Liste des négociants qui ont Payés les fraix des Batteries dressés sur le havre et murs de cette ville lors de sèjour des Anglois dans nos rades, 1757,* AMLR, Ms. EE16; Emile Garnault, *Le commerce rochelais au XVIIIe siècle d'après les documents composant les anciennes archives de la Chambre de Commerce de La Rochelle,* 4 vols. (La Rochelle, 1888–98) 2:198:200; Emile Garnault, *Livre d'or de la chambre de commerce de La Rochelle contenant la biographie des directeurs et présidents de cette chambre de 1719 à 1891* (La Rochelle, 1902).

5. Sufficiently detailed information existed about the economic activities and kinship connections to allow a ranking of families in terms of their overall economic importance in La Rochelle. From this general ranking, the leading sixteen armateurs and the leading twenty-six families in all factors were separated out and identified in table 3.1. While the methodology and the criteria used to rank the families will not be explained until Chapter 5, it was thought that a list of the most significant families and their religion would be helpful at this point.

6. P. Boissonnade, "La Marine marchande, le port, et les armateurs de La Rochelle à l'époque de Colbert (1662–1683)," Comité des travaux historiques et scientifiques, *Bulletin de la section de géographie* 37 (Paris, 1922):18, 42, Louis Péronas, "Sur la démographie rochelaise," *Annales ESC* 16 (November-December 1961):1136–40; Louis Delmas, *L'église réformée de La Rochelle: Etude historique* (Toulouse, 1870), p. 287; *Bulletin de la société de l'histoire du Protestantisme française* 104 (January-March 1958): 15 (hereafter cited as *BSHPF*).

7. Ozée and Allard both married into the Yuommes family, all of whom fled La Rochelle during the late 1680s, AMLR, Ms. 1054; Belin Papers, ACM, Ms. E291.

8. Depont des Granges Papers, ACM, Ms. E489, pp. 491–92; AMLR, Ms, 1910–13; Georges Musset, *Les rochelais à Terre-Neuve, 1500–1789* (La Rochelle, 1899), p. 89.

9. For the Bonneaus: Bonneau Papers, ACM, Ms. E313–17; Marcel Delafosse, "Les rochelais au Maroc au XVIIe siècle: Commerce at rachat de captifs," *RHCF* 35 (1948): 72–79; Simone Berbain, *Etudes sur la traite des noirs au golfe de Guinèe: Le comptoir français de Judah (Ouidah) au XVIIIe siècle,* Mémoires de l'institut française d'Afrique noire no. 3 (Paris, 1942), p. 44: For the Delacroixs: AMLR, Ms. 1961, 2644–46; *BSHPF* 63–65 (1914–15):429.

10. For the Seignettes: Arie Théodorus Van Deursen, *Professions et métiers interdits: Un*

aspect de l'histoire de la Révocation de l'Edit de Nantes (Groningen, Neth., 1960), pp. 120–21, 130, 195. Other data on the Seignettes are scattered throughout the archives used in this study.

11. For the Rasteaus: John G. Clark, *New Orleans, 1718–1812: An Economic History* (Baton Rouge, La., 1970), 77, 99–102, 137, 144–45; AMLR, Ms. 1054, 1424, 1933, 1960–61; ACM, Ms. B5717. For the Giraudeaus and Viviers, information is located in numerous collections used in this study; See also Garnault, *Livre d'or*, pp. 17–18.

12. The eighteenth-century phase of the history of the Pascaud and the Goguet families originated in Canada during the late seventeenth century. Both established comptoirs in La Rochelle shortly after 1700. Family members held various royal, commercial, and municipal offices during the eighteenth century. Material on these families is found throughout the collections consulted. Jean de Butler, from a family of ancient and noble standing in Kilkenny, Ireland, arrived in La Rochelle around 1655. His son Jean de Butler fils aîné held many offices in La Rochelle, and in 1814 a son of Jean fils aîné served as a staff officer in the French Imperial Army. See Genealogy of Jean de Butler, [untitled document, n.d.]. de Butler Papers, ACM, Ms. 4J1580; Delafosse, "Origine géographique et sociale des marchands rochelais au XVIIe siècle," *Actes du 87e congrès des sociétés savantes* (Poitiers, 1962, Paris 1963), p. 665; Garnault, *Livre d'or*, pp. 20–21.

13. Rasteau to de Baussey, La Rochelle, n.d. [probably 1769 to 1772], AMLR, Ms. 1918.

14. Sources for the above three paragraphs include Boissonnade, "La marine marchande de La Rochelle," pp. 40–42; Jean Périer, *La prospérité rochelais au XVIIIe siècle et la bourgeoisie protestante* (Mesnil, n.d. [c. 1899]), p. 30; Van Deursen, *Professions et métiers interdits*, p. 325; Péronas, "La démographie rochelaise," p. 1138; L. J. Nazelle, *Le Protestantisme en Saintonge sous le régime de la Révocation, 1685–1789* (Paris, 1907), pp. 54–55, 83–84, 117–19, 222–25; *BSHPF* 10 (1861): 195, and 39 (September 1890): 479; Michel Richard, *La vie quotidienne des Protestants sous l'Ancien Régime* (Paris, 1966), pp. 202–6; Delmas, *L'église réformée de La Rochelle*, pp. 295–99.

15. Delmas, *L'église réformée de La Rochelle*, pp. 343–45; Nazelle, *Protestantisme en Saintonge*, pp. 46, 259.

16. Richard, *La vie des Protestants*, pp. 256–57; Documents mise en défense de la ville contre l'attaque probable d'une flotte angloise, 1757–58, CCLR, carton 17.

17. Périer, *La prospérité rochelais*, p. 30, and Henri Robert, *Les trafics coloniaux du port de La Rochelle au XVIIIe siècle, Mémoires de la société des antiquitaires de l'Ouest*, 4th ser., vol. 4 (Poitiers, 1960), p. 186, advance this explanation while Garnault, *Le commerce rochelais*, denies it but presents no evidence for his case. The Roman Catholic bourgeoisie of Beauvais, and presumably the rest of France, did enjoy greater career options than Protestants. In Beauvais many sons were placed in church positions, a prized route of upward social mobility. Daughters were placed in convents, but that was hardly cheap since the parents paid full support, Goubert, *Beauvais*, pp. 325–26, 340–42. J. G. C. Blacker, "Social Ambitions of the Bourgeoisie in 18th-century France and their Relation to Family Limitation," *Population Studies* 11 (July 1957): 59–60, points to the greater financial burden that having daughters imposed on families, and suggests that this may have contributed to the decline in fertility rates. There is no evidence that daughters were considered burdensome among the Rochelais merchants. Dowries promoted and sustained family alliances. Given the endogenous nature of négociant marriages, the dowry was not lost to the family providing it. The convent was no less expensive and, unlike the dowry, served no economic functions. Marriage also brought sons-in-law into the family comptoir.

18. The following offer such a characterization of the middle class: Robert Mandrou, *La France au XVIIe et XVIIIe siècles* (Paris, 1967), pp. 94–95; Joseph Aynard, *La bourgeoisie française: Essai de psychologie* (Paris, 1934), pp. 396–410; Goubert, *L'Ancien régime*, pp. 229–32; John B. Wolfe, *The Emergence of the Great Powers, 1685–1715* (New York, 1951), p. 101. Elinor G. Barber, *The Bourgeoisie in Eighteenth-Century France* (Princeton, N.J., 1955), pp. 57–62, and Bernard Groethuysen, *The Bourgeois: Catholicism vs. Capitalism in Eighteenth-Century France*, trans. Mary Ilford (New York, 1968), are examples of studies of the bourgeoisie which

fail to select representative examples for analysis and base their generalizations upon such elite observers as Madame d'Epinay, Voltaire, and Bousset. Both Barber and Groethuysen virtually ignore the hard-working middle and upper ranks of the bourgeoisie, who were dominant in the ports.

19. Pierre Jean Van Hoogwerf à Odelie Van Hoogwerf à Edinbourg, La Rochelle, 16 janvier 1776, mai 1776, and à Matheus Van Arp & Cie à Amsterdam, La Rochelle, 30 août 1778, Van Hoogwerf Papers, ACM, Ms. 4J2847; Trésahar Bonfils à mon cher oncle, Venise, 31 mars 1753, Geneva, mai 1753, Paris, 17 juin 1753, Delacroix Papers, AMLR, Ms. 2645; de Richemond à de Machey à Abbeville, La Rochelle, 29 juin 1780, Meschinet de Richemond Letterbook, March 1780–September 1780, ACM, Ms. E447.

20. Van Deursen, *Professions et métiers interdits,* pp. 50–54; M. Richard, *La vie quotidienne des Protestants,* pp. 210–12; Périer, *La prospérité rochelais,* pp. 44–46; Déclaration d'Elie Giraudeau, 25 juin 1729, 17 juin 1732 and Déclaration de Jacques Bernon, 3 juin 1730, ACM, Ms. B225. Carrière, *Négociants marseillais,* pp. 741–43, 753–56, speaks in general terms about young Marseillais taking long trips as part of their training, but their connections with local comptoirs are not pointed out.

21. Robert, *Trafics coloniaux,* p. 190–94; Garnault, *Livre d'or,* p. 17–18; Etat des biens de Isaac Garesché à Nieulle, 1769, Garesché Papers, ACM, Ms. 4J1610–14; Contrat de mariage du Henri Bonneau et de la Jeanne Belin, Bonneau Papers, ACM, Ms. E313.

22. Meyer, *L'armement nantais,* pp. 171–72, 181–88. The Vivier estate was worth £56,000 or 438,000 Dutch guilders or florins. In Hull, England, a port somewhat smaller than La Rochelle and engaged largely in domestic and foreign coasting, an estate of £20,000 was considered immense. Sir Samuel Standidge, founder of Hull's whaling industry and one of its wealthiest citizens, left an estate valued at £76,000 or 1.1 million lt., Gordon Jackson, *Hull in the Eighteenth Century: A Study in Economic and Social History* (London, 1972) p. 105. At Liverpool, the greatest slavers left personal estates averaging approximately £13,000, Francis E. Hyde, *Liverpool and the Mersey: An Economic History of a Port* (Newton Abbot, 1971), p. 33. A source used by Charles Boxer, *The Dutch Seaborne Empire: 1600–1800* (New York 1965), p. 39, defined the upper middle class as possessing estates worth 40,000 florins or 60,000 to 70,000 lt.

23. Pierre Jean Van Hoogwerf à P. G. Van Hoogwerf à St. Petersbourg, La Rochelle, 28 avril 1781 and 8 septembre 1789, à Odelie Stuart à Edinbourg, La Rochelle, 23 janvier 1790, Van Hoogwerf Papers, ACM, 4J2848.

24. J. B. Nairac, On the taxation of incoming colonial products and property taxation, [untitled mémoire], c. 1780, AMLR, Ms. 1417.

25. For the sketch in the above paragraphs: Registre pour reçevoir la déclarations des Negrès, négresses, mulâtres et mulâtresses qui sont dans cette ville de La Rochelle suivant les lettres de M. L'Intendant, 1763, 1770, 1776, AMLR, Ms. 352.

26. M. Moheau, *Recherches et considérations sur la population de la France, 1778* (Paris, 1778) in *Collections des économistes et des réformateurs sociaux de la France,* vol. 10, with an introduction by René Bonnard (Paris, 1912). Moheau, a psuedonym used by M. de Montyon, who served as intendant of Aunis during the early 1770s, found that only 67 families had above five children in a sample of 3900 families residing in unspecified parishes.

27. Louis Henry, "The Population of France in the Eighteenth Century," trans. Peter Jimack, in *Population in History: Essays in Historical Demography,* edited by D. V. Glass and D.E.C. Eversley (London, 1965), pp. 446–47; Couturier, *Structures sociales de Châteaudun,* pp. 91–92; Lachiver, *Population de Meulan,* p. 210.

28. Paul Butel, "Le trafic europeen de Bordeaux de la guerre d'Amérique à la Révolution," *Annales du Midi* 78 (1966): 38–82; Thomas M. Doerflinger, "The Antilles Trade of the Old Regime: A Statistical Overview," *Journal of Interdisciplinary History* 6 (winter 1976): 397–415; Robert Stein, "The Profitability of the Nantes Slave Trade, 1783–1792," *JEH* 35 (December 1975): 779–93.

29. Récapitulation entrées, and Récapitulation sorties, Registre des Soumissions, ACM, Ms. B247–59bis.

30. The decline in fertility rates among Rochelais négociant couples conformed to patterns noticeable among the bourgeoisie throughout France. Explanations for the gross patterns are offered by Blacker, "Social Ambitions of the Bourgeoisie," pp. 46–63, and John Hajnal, "European Marriage Patterns in Perspective," in *Population in History: Essays in Historical Demography,* edited by D. V. Glass and D.E.C. Eversley (London, 1965).

31. Pierre Goubert, "Historical Demography and the Reinterpretation of Early Modern French History: A Research Review," in *The Family in History: Interdisciplinary Essays,* edited by Theodore K. Rabb and Robert I. Rotberg (New York, 1971), p. 25.

32. Some of the more notable outside marriages included the marriage in 1739 of Marie Madelaine Belin to Nicolas Guyon, a Bordelais merchant. Guyon moved permanently to La Rochelle shortly after the wedding. Another Bordelais merchant, Pierre Rocault, married Marie Delacroix in the 1750s. Pierre's brother, Jean Baptiste, was an established merchant-banker in La Rochelle whose two daughters both wed Viviers. Gabriel Rasteau, son of Jacques, married the sister of the powerful Parisian banker, Jean Cottin. In the 1770s a sister of Jean Isaac Raboteau (see figure 3.1) married the partner of Samuel Rother, Swiss manufacturer of indienne cloths and who was located in Nantes. At about the same time, a daughter of Pierre Gabriel Admyrauld and Marie Marguerite Giraudeau Admyrauld married Benoit Bourcard. He was a partner in the large Nantes firm of Christopher Burckhardt Co., manufacturer of indiennes and a branch of the Swiss house of Burckhardt.

Data on the connections of each family were derived from hundreds of separate manuscripts, making citation of each item impractical. Only the most general will be noted, including secondary sources with relevant information. Herbert Lüthy, *La banque protestante en France de la Révocation de l'Edit de Nantes à la Révolution,* 2 vols (Paris, 1959–61), p. 306, n. 6; Louis Dermigny, *La Chine et L'Occident: Le commerce à Canton au XVIIIe siècle, 1719–1833,* 3 vols. (Paris, 1964), 2:609–10; Contrat de marriage du Nicolas Guyon et de la Marie Madelaine Belin, 8 aôut 1739, AMLR, Ms. 1932; Pierre Jean Van Hoogwerf à Odélie Van Hoogwerf à Edinbourg, La Rochelle, 7 mai 1776. Van Hoogwerf Papers, ACM, Ms. 4J2847.

33. Similar practices among the bourgeoisie have been established in other local studies; see Goubert, *Beauvais;* Couturier, *Structures sociales de Châteaudun,* p. 133, estimated that between 1724 and 1789 only 17 percent of the females married outside of the city; and Martine Segalen, *Nuptialité et alliance: Le choix du conjouint dans une commune de l'Eure* (Paris, 1972), pp. 75–83, observed only a slight decline in the proportion of intermarriage in the commune during the eighteenth century. Professionally and occupationally endogenous marriages predominated as in La Rochelle. In an interesting study of seventeenth-century financiers, Julian Dent, *Crises in Finance: Crown, Financiers, and Society in Seventeenth-Century France* (Newton Abbot, 1973), p. 210, found that the daughters of financiers were much less likely to marry the sons of financiers than the sons were likely to marry the daughters of financiers. Daughters married up in the social scale. In La Rochelle, both sons and daughters married horizontally.

34. Chapter 4 investigates the origin of funds invested in Rochelais armements and Chapters 9 and 10 analyze the aggregate flow of capital into and out of the city.

35. Contrat de mariage du Nicolas Guyon et de la Marie Madelaine Belin, 8 août 1739, AMLR, Ms. 1932; Contrat de mariage du Pierre Isaac Rasteau et de la Suzanne Belin, [n.d.], ibid., Ms. 1424; Contrat de marriage du Henri Bonneau et de la Jeanne Belin, 1729, Bonneau Papers, ACM, Ms. E313; Contrat de mariage du Pierre Morreau et de la Françoise Depont, 22 décembre 1710, Depont des Granges Papers, ACM, Ms. E472. Morreau was the son of Pierre Morreau, an elder of the Protestant church in 1685. Other marriage contracts involving the Bonneau, Paillet, Delacroix, and Van Hoogwerf families cite dowries of between 10,000 lt. and 25,000 lt. in cash and property. A dowry of 45,000 lt. came to Pierre Jean Van Hoogwerf by his marriage to Elizabeth Belin, daughter of Claude Etienne.

36. In French law the dowry is exclusively the responsibility of the female. Males do not bring dowries to a union. The portions carried by males in the cases involving Rochelais marriages were earmarked for immediate use, either in commerce or in the household. In either instance, the contribution became part of the joint estate.

37. Contrat du mariage du Louis Torturue Bonneau et de la Marie Besnard, 1688, ACM, E313; Contrat du mariage du Gerard Van Hoogwerf et de la Marie Fleurance Delacroix, 17 février 1727, AMLR, Ms. 1946; Contrat du mariage du Nicholas Paillet (veuf Jeanne Gareschê) et de la Jeanne Suzanne Bonneau, 1756, ACM, E313; Contrat du mariage du Etienne Charuyer et de la Suzanne Van Hoogwerf, 12 juillet 1791, AMLR, Ms. 1947.

38. H. J. Habakkuk, "Marriage Settlements in the Eighteenth Century," *Transactions of the Royal Historical Society,* 4th Ser. 32 (1950): 22–33. As with the arrangement of marriages, no information was discovered describing the courtships preceding these marriages or the negotiations establishing the terms of the dowries. Nor does any empirical evidence exist which exposes the relationship that developed between the spouses. The records are not sufficiently complete even to establish the ages of the newlyweds. In the case of the Belin-Rasteau union, it was Suzanne's second marriage, her first husband having died. Both Suzanne and Pierre Isaac were apparently in their mid-thirty's when they wed. They must have known each other since childhood; the same would be true of the Belin marriages with Seignettes and Bernons and Françoise Depont's marriage with Pierre Morreau. Only Guyon, a Bordelais, was an outsider.

39. J. J. Garnault à de Richemond, Paris, 29 octobre 1782, Garnault Correspondence, AMLR, Ms. 2248.

40. Pierre Dardel, *Navires et marchandises dans les ports de Rouen et la Havre au XVIIIe siècle* (Paris, 1963); Meyer, *L'armement nantais,* pp. 64–65. Pierre Léon, *Economies et sociétés préindustrielles,* vol. 2, *1650–1780; Les origines d'une accélération de l'histoire* (Paris, 1970), pp. 364–65, and Ernest Labrousse et al., *Histoire économique et sociale de la France.* vol. 2; *Des derniers temps de l'âge seigneurial aux préludes de l'âge industriel* (1660–1789) (Paris, 1970), pp. 613–15. The latter two works focus on the exceptionally wealthy in the largest urban centers.

41. George V. Taylor, "Noncapitalist Wealth and the Origins of the French Revolution," *American Historical Review* 72 (January 1967): 479–80, offers definitions of the types of rentes common in France. In general, rentes were "an annual revenue that was received for having transferred something of value to someone else."

42. Bernard Farber, *Guardians of Virtue: Salem Families in 1800* (New York, 1972), pp. 92–96, is the only study with which I am familiar that deals explicitly with the question of inherited wealth in a mercantile setting. At Salem, contentiousness over inherited wealth divided shipowning and merchant families into hostile factions. As in La Rochelle, family partnerships were of great economic significance. Disputes over family wealth frequently weakened Salem's business organizations. Research at La Rochelle uncovered no evidence of wills or divisions being contested by disgruntled heirs. The declining fortunes of a Rochelais comptoir were invariably the result of economic causes rather than internal divisiveness.

The division of the Charuyer estate, discussed in Chapter 4 relative to the management responsibilities of widows, illustrates perfectly the expedience of an early division.

43. Information on the estate of Allard Belin was derived from Documents divers concernant les affaires de Allard Belin, 1724–59, AMLR, Ms. 1932; Inventaire du meubles et effets du Sr. Allard Belin, 20 janvier 1748–10 septembre 1749, Belin Papers, ACM, Ms. E291.

44. Partage de la communauté et succession de M. Etienne Belin entre Madam Carayon sa veuve et les dames ses filles, 23 juillet 1779, AMLR, Ms. 1933. A different investment pattern is depicted in Goubert, *Beauvais,* pp. 330–33, in that land and rentes and mortgages contributed a major part of local bourgeois income.

45. [Untitled manuscripts], AMLR, Ms. 1993; Renunciation of the inheritance by Jacques Allard Belin, 17 March 1781, AMLR, Ms. 1993; Statement of Joseph Lefebvre Dufresne, 21 July and 5 August 1778, in which Joseph renounced his rights to the estate of his father, Marc Antoine Lefebvre, ACM, Ms. B1882; Etat des biens de Sr. Robert Laurant Beltremieux, 7 juillet 1778, ACM, Ms. B1882, in which the six children of the deceased waived their inheritance rights and turned over all assets to his creditors after the judicial inventory.

46. Power of Attorney granted by Pierre Jean Van Hoogwerf, executor of last will and testament of Marie Madelaine Belin to Charles Tressier and Stephen Tressier, London, April 5, 1781,

and Etat des biens que Pierre Jean Van Hoogwerf à reçu de Elisabet Belin sa femme décédée la quatre novembre 1786, AMLR, Ms. 1946.

47. Paul's son, Pierre Paul François, apparently withdrew from commerce between 1744 and 1755, investing his inheritance from Paul and from his mother, who died in 1754, in rentes while living on and managing the estate of des Granges. In 1755, however, he returned to business en société with his brother-in-law Louis Charuyer. Between 1755 and 1776, Depont operated with the Charuyers or on his own account. He then withdrew from commerce permanently, becoming a noted Rochelais philanthropist. He may even have converted to Catholicism, for one of his charities supported perpetual masses at the cathedral.

48. Testament de M. Paul de Pont des Granges et de Dame Sara Bernon son épouse, 8 novembre 1712, 2 juillet 1715, Depont des Granges Papers, ACM, Ms. E472; Codiciles du 1 juillet 1723, 1 décembre 1726, 19 décembre 1732, 12 janvier 1733, 13 mai and 2 juin 1737, 13 mars 1743, ibid.; Sale of seigneurie d'Argrefeuille to Paul Depont, Seigneur des Granges, 12 June 1776, [untitled ms.], ibid., Ms. E492; Depont des Granges, Livre No. 1, 1723–63, ibid. Ms. E483; Estimate of value of seigneurie des Granges, 1788, [untitled ms.], ibid. Ms. E491. All of the Depont wealth was sequestered during Thermidor, by which time many members of the family had emigrated, ibid.,Ms. 475.

49. Petitions of Pierre Jean Chauvet, 1736, of Jacques Chauvet, 1764, of Jean Pierre Chauvet, 1786, [untitled documents], AMLR, Ms. 324; Inheritance of Jean Denis le jeune, 1780, [untitled document], AMLR, Ms. 1587; Marchandes drapiers à La Rochelle, AMLR, Ms. 325.

Chapter Four

1. Charles Carrière, *Négociants marseillais au XVIIIe siècle,* 2 vols. (Marseilles, 1973), 2:883–85; Jean Meyer, *L'armement nantais dans la deuxième moitié du XVIIIe siècle* (Paris, 1969), pp. 103–6; Jacques Teneur, "Les commerçants dunkerquois à la fin du XVIIIe siècle et les problèmes économiques de leur temps," *Revue du Nord* 48 (January-March 1966): 21; George V. Taylor, "Some Business Partnerships at Lyon, 1785–1793," *JEH* 23 (March 1963): 50; Henri Sée, *Le commerce maritime de la Bretagne au XVIIIe siècle, d'après les papiers des Magon, Mémoires et documents pour servir à l'histoire du commerce et l'industrie en France,* ed. Julien Hayem, 9th ser. (Paris, 1925), pp. 152–53.

2. Max Weber, *The Protestant Ethic and the Spirit of Capitalism,* trans. Talcott Parsons (New York, 1958), pp. 21–22; David S. Landes, "French Entrepreneurship and Industrial Growth in the Nineteenth Century," *JEH* 9 (May 1949); François-Georges Pariset, ed., *Bordeaux au XVIIIe siècle,* vol. 5, *Histoire de Bordeaux,* ed. Ch. Higounet (Bordeaux, 1968), attributed structural weaknesses in the economy of Bordeaux to the predominance of family firms and the lack of liquid capital aggravated by the flow of funds into lands.

3. For Pierre Goubert, *L'Ancien Régime,* vol. 1; *La Société* (Paris, 1969), pp. 68–69, the notion of armateurs dabbling in insurance and doing a little banking while essentially engaged in commerce attested to their nonspecialization and the narrowness of their temporary associations. Thus, Goubert posited a mediocrity of techniques and organization that weighed heavily on the Old Regime. I view the armateur-négociant as having worked in a vocation of great complexity, requiring astute decisions based on considerable knowledge if success was to be achieved. Rochelais practices resembled those of merchants in other parts of the Atlantic world.

4. Jean Cavignac, *Jean Pellet, commerçant de gros, 1694–1772: Contribution à l'étude du négoce bordelais au XVIIIe siècle* (Paris, 1967), pp 38–44; Henri Levy-Bruhl, *Histoire juridique des sociétés de commerce en France aux XVIIe et XVIIIe siècles* (Paris, 1938), p. 30; Judah Adelson, "The Early Evolution of Business Organization in France," *Business History Review* 31 (summer, 1957): 231; Henri Mariage, *Evolution historique de la législation commerciale de l'ordinance de Colbert à nos jours, 1673–1949* (Paris, 1951), pp. 19–21.

5. Adelson, "Evolution of Business Organization," pp. 237–38; Levy-Bruhl, *Sociétés de commerce,* pp. 44–47, 183, 250–51.

6. Chapter 10 attempts to measure aggregate capital investment in Rochelais shipping and to identify its sources.

7. In the first period, 1719–21, 1723–24, intéressés were known for 35 of the 121 vessels outfitted at La Rochelle, or 29 percent. Since shares were most frequently designated in percentages, 100 shares per ship became the total investment unit. Thirty-five vessels produced 3,500 shares, of which 3,308 were accounted for, or a sample of 95 percent. In the second period, 1748–49, the relevant armateurs managed 27 of the 101 vessels le long cours departing La Rochelle, or 27 percent. Those vessels consisted of 2,700 shares, of which only 33 were unattributable. For the last period, 1784–87, in which all armateurs were included, the intéressés were identified for 62 of the 168 ships outfitted in the city, or 37 percent. Owners of 5,747 of 6,200 shares, or 93 percent, were accounted for.

8. Taylor, "Business Partnerships at Lyon," pp. 61–63, 65; Levy-Bruhl, *Sociétés de commerce,* pp. 30–31; Meyer, *L'armament nantais,* pp. 101–2.

9. Documents conçernant les Belins et aussi, par alliance les Van Hoogwerf, Rasteau, et autres, 1766- An IV [1796], AMLR, Ms. 1933; Documents relatifs aux terres et autres matières aux familles Bonneau, Bonfils, et autres, XVI–XVIII siècles, AMLR, Ms. 1419; Jean Perier, *La Prospérité rochelais au XVIIIe siècle et la bourgeoisie protestante* (Mesnil, n.d. [c. 1899]), p. 42.

10. The Huguenot Charuyer family did not outfit vessels (they did invest in the armements of others) and thus do not appear on table 3.1. They did, however, form one of the most important kinship groups in the city and conducted a large brokerage, commission, and wholesale business.

11. Documents detailing the course of the Charuyer firm are listed below. To document each other firm or informal business association mentioned would require the separate notation of a similar number of documents, making the notes longer than the narrative. The following documents can be found in Documents de famille concernat les familles Charuyer et Depont, AMLR, Ms. 1910–17: Mémoire à consulter, Charuyer et Depont, 1777, Ms. 1913; Compte générale de ce que La Veuve Charuyer doit à moy P. Depont, 30 mai 1776, Ms. 1913; Inventaires des biens du S. Louis Charuyer, 7 mai–30 mai 1760, Ms. 1917: Comptes de famille et commerciaux de la famille Charuyer, 1760–88, Ms. 1928–29, included Inventaire générale, Veuve Charuyer, 1777; Act des société, Jean et Etienne Charuyer, 1777; Inventaire des affaires en société de Jean et Etienne Charuyer frères, 26 décember 1782; Inventaires des biens de la veuve Charuyer, 1777; Inventaire fait par nous frères et soeurs des tous les meubles et effets que nous avons trouver après le déces de la veuve Charuyer, 23 juin 1782; Inventaire fait par nous Jean et Etienne Charuyer frères des nos affaires en sociétés jusqu'à ce jour 1 avril 1786; Act de société, Etienne et François Charuyer frères. For the Charuyer-Van Hoogwerf relationship, see Documents de famille concernant la famille des Van Hoogwerf, Contrat de mariage, Etienne Charuyer et Suzanne Van Hoogwerf, 12 juillet 1791, AMLR, Ms. 1947; Acte de société de Pierre Jean Van Hoogwerf & fils, AMLR, Ms. 1946.

12. Procès verbal chez M. Admyrauld, 14 mai 1783, ACM, Ms. B1771 (Présidial de La Rochelle); Delacroix Papers, AMLR, Ms. 2645; Acte de société, Jean et Jacques Chaudruc et Alexandre Dumas, 8 juin 1751, ACM, Ms. B6086.

13. Meyer, *L'armement nantais,* pp. 98–100; Acte de société entre nous soussignes Pierre Garesché et Charles Billotteau 1778, Garesché Papers, ACM, Ms. 4J1610. During the late 1780s, one of the largest firms in Hull, England, Wilberforce & Smiths, managed a capital of £15,000, or some 240,000 lt., Jackson, *Hull in the Eighteenth Century: A Study in Economic and Social History* (London, 1972), pp. 108–9.

14. Déclaration de M. Van Hoogwerf, 6 mars 1784, ACM, Ms. B5786; P. Giraidot à Théodore Delacroix, Paris, 2 juin 1753, AMLR, Ms. 2645; Meyer, *L'armement nantais,* pp. 101–2; Taylor, "Business Partnerships at Lyon" pp. 59–60; Léon Vignols, "Le commerce maritime et les aspects du capitalism commercial à Saint-Malo de 1680–1792. Simple aperçu d'après des textes inédit," *RHES* 19 (1931): 10–11.

15. Levy-Bruhl, *Sociétés de commerce,* pp. 136–38.

16. George V. Taylor, "Types of Capitalism in Eighteenth-Century France," *EHR* 79 (July 1964): 483.

17. Déclaration du S. Jean Vivier et du Jacques Rasteau père, 1748, ACM, Ms. B228; Déclaration du Jean Vivier, 19 mars 1748, and Facture des marchandises pour la Louisianne, 1751, ACM, Ms. B229.

18. Guy Richard, "La noblesse de France et les sociétés par actions à la fin de XVIIIe siècle," *RHES* 41 (1962): 492–93.

19. Acts of proprietorship, [untitled ms.], ACM, Ms. B5756–59.

20. Pierre Jean Van Hoogwerf à Déshommet à Paris, La Rochelle, 18 mai, 1 juin, 16 juin 1773, Van Hoogwerf Papers, ACM, Ms. 4J2487; Déclaration de M. Van Hoogwerf, 6 mars 1784, ACM, Ms. B5786.

21. Henri Robert, *Les trafics coloniaux de La Rochelle au XVIIIe siècle,* Mémoires de la Société des Antiquaires de l'Ouest, 4th ser., vol. 4 (Poitiers, 1960).

22. Taylor, "Types of Capitalism," p. 483; H. du Halgouet, *Nantes: Ses relations commerciales avec les îles d'Amérique au XVIIIe siècle* (Rennes, 1939), pp. 122–23.

23. Chapter 6 details these procedures and specifies the total costs (*mise hors*) of an armement.

24. Taylor, "Business Partnerships in Lyon," pp. 59–60. Taylor's findings concerning the flexibility of the large Lyonnais firms are applicable in La Rochelle to small and large partnerships of both short and long duration.

25. Van Hoogwerf accounts, [untitled document], AMLR, Ms. 1946.

26. These themes were implicit in Cavignac, *Jean Pellet*; Pierre Dardel, "Importateurs et exportateurs rouennais au XVIIIe siècle: Antoine Guymonneau et ses opérations commerciales (1715–1741)," *Etudes d'histoire économique* 4 (Dieppe, 1954): 83–150; Delumeau, "Le commerce malouin à la fin du XVIIIe siècle," *Annales de Bretagne* 56 (September 1959); Maurice Begouen–Demeaux, *Mémorial d'une famille du Havre: Stanislas Foäche, 1737–1806* (Paris, 1951); Emile Gabory, *La marine et le commerce de Nantes au XVIIe et au commencement du XVIIIe siècle (1661–1715)* (Rennes, 1901); Pierre Léon, *Marchands et speculateurs dauphinois dans le monde antillais du XVIIIe siècle: Les Dalle et les Raby* (Paris, 1963); Herbert Lüthy, *La banque protestante en France de la Révocation de l'Edit de Nantes à la Révolution,* 2 vols. (Paris 1959–61); Gaston Martin, *Capital et travail à Nantes au cours du XVIIIe siècle* (Paris, 1931); Meyer, *L'armement nantais;* Robert Richard, "Le financement des armements maritimes du Havre au XVIIIe siècle (Position des problèmes)," *RHES* 47 (1969): 5–31; Sée, *Le commerce maritime de la Bretagne;* Teneur, "Les commerçants dunkerquois"; J. T. Viaud and E J. Fleury, *Histoire de la ville et du port de Rochefort,* 2 vols. (Rochefort, 1845).

27. When his eldest brother died a bachelor in 1768, Daniel used Sara's dowry and his inheritance to start his own business. This death and earlier deaths in the family provided another brother, Jean, with the cash to purchase a plantation in Santo Domingo, where two other brothers had already established themselves as merchants en société. Another brother, Pierre, operated a business at Marans. Still another, Benjamin, died a ship's captain, leaving an estate of 47,000 lt. Daniel's four sisters were married, three to Rochelais merchants and one to a Montaudoin in Nantes. All of the children of Daniel Garesché père had been provided for through inheritances derived from his marriage to Henriette Delacroix and his own endeavors. In 1788 the son of Daniel fils, Isaac David, established himself in Santo Domingo with the financial assistance of his father. Robert, *Trafic coloniaux,* p. 185, and Etat des biens de Benjamin Garesché, 1773, and Isaac Garesché, 1769, 1774, Garesché Papers, ACM, Ms. 4J1610–14.

28. Elie Nicolas Rasteau continued to command vessels. He was captured by the English in 1757 and died in England; Requeste par Elie Nicolas Rasteau, 1737, AMLR, Ms. 1425; Le navire, *l'Union,* facture des marchandises, ACM, Ms. B229; Etat des comptes billets et sentence laissés à Mrs. Rasteau frères négt au cul-de-sac, 1751, ACM, Ms. B229; John G. Clark, *New Orleans, 1718–1812: An Economic History* (Baton Rouge, La., 1970), pp. 93–99, 102, 144–45.

29. Charles Bonfils à Théodore Delacroix, St. Marc, 8 août 1737, AMLR, Ms. 2645; Jacques Belin à Henri Belin, Léoganne, 15 juin 1722, Belin Papers, ACM, Ms. E292; Procuration par Jean Baptiste Belin du Verger, 2 février 1726, ACM, Ms. E293; E. Belin à Belin Desmarais à

Paris, La Rochelle, 14 février 1767, ACM, Ms. E298; Transport Boury, Pommier, Bonneau, 1 mars 1715, Rivière et Soulard, Notaries, ACM, Registers 1715–18; Extrait du Registre des sousmissions du greffe du Seige de l'Amirauté de La Rochelle, 22 mai 1750 pour M. Goguet, ACM, Ms. B5740; Facture et reconnaissance de Louis Charuyer l'aîné, La Rochelle, 8 mai 1766, AMLR, Ms. 1913.

30. Accounts concerning la Valeur, [untitled ms.], Belin Papers, ACM, Ms. E297; Claude Etienne Belin à Belin Desmarais à Paris, La Rochelle, 14 février 1767, ibid., Ms. E298.

31. Emile Garnault, *Le commerce rochelais au XVIIIe siècle d'après les documents composant les anciennes archives de la chambre de commerce de La Rochelle,* 4 vols., (La Rochelle, 1888–98) 1:49–66. See accounts based on Garnault in Robert, *Trafics coloniaux,* pp. 188–90, and Elinore G. Barber, *The Bourgeoisie in Eighteenth-Century France* (Princeton, N.J., 1955), pp. 64–65.

32. Chapter 8 explains the basis for shipper antagonism toward the venal officers connected with the brandy trade.

33. Garnault, *Le commerce rochelais,* 1:95–99, is accurate. His narrative of the debate was based upon CCLR, carton 13. See Paul Logié, *Les institutions du commerce à Amiens au XVIIIe siècle: Juridictions consulaire et chambre de commerce sous l'Ancien Régime et pendant la période révolutionnaire* (Amiens, 1951), pp. 96–98, for a similar controversy between négociants and manufacturers. Both debates reflected the multifaceted character of the moyenne bourgeoisie.

34. Registrations and declarations of proprietorship, [untitled documents], ACM, Ms. B4197 and B5589 (juridiction consulaire); Partage de la communauté du Sieur Jacques Brisson, 7 février 1766, AMLR, Ms. 1070; L. J. Nazelle, *Le Protestantisme en Saintonge sous le régime de la Révocation, 1685–1789* (Paris, 1907) pp. 260–61.

35. See Clark, *New Orleans,* pp. 141–48, for the efforts of Rasteau and others to exploit New Orleans's proximity to Spanish markets; Etat de navires du port du La Rochelle et du montant de leurs chargements, pris par les Anglais, 29 novembre 1745, CCLR, carton 7; Etat des Vaisseaux, ACM, Ms. B250–51.

36. Etat des vaisseaux, ACM, Ms. B259; Etat des navires de La Rochelle arrêtés par les Anglois soit en Europe ou en Amérique, avant la guerre déclarée, 18 septembre 1756, CCLR, carton 17.

37. Documents divers concernant les familles Rasteau et Charuyer, AMLR, Ms. 1918, contains the essential information of *l'affaire Rasteau;* Pierre Van Hoogwerf à P. G. Van Hoogwerf à St. Petersbourg, La Rochelle, 28 avril 1781, Van Hoogwerf Papers, ACM, Ms. 4J2847; Etat des vaisseaux, ACM, Ms. B259 and 259bis; Périer, *La prospérité rochelaise,* pp. 60–66.

Chapter Five

1. Jean Meyer, *L'armement nantais, dans la deuxième moitié du XVIIIe siècle* (Paris, 1969), pp. 77, 90–92; see also H. du Halgouet, *Nantes: Ses relations commerciales avec les îles d'Amérique au XVIIIe siècle* (Rennes, 1939), p. 47. All of the families listed on table 5.1 were among the ninety families.

2. Data about Bordeaux were adapted from Françoise Thésée, *Négociants bordelais et colons de Saint-Domingue: Liaisons d'habitations la maison Henry Romberg, Bapst et Cie., 1783–1793* (Paris, 1972), p. 82.

3. Meyer, *L'armement nantais,* pp. 90–92.

4. Floyd Hunter, *Community Power Structure* (Chapel Hill, 1953); Delbert Miller, "Industry and Community Power Structure: A Comparative Study of an American and an English City," *American Sociological Review* 23 (February 1958); Robert S. and Helen M. Lynd, *Middletown: A Study in Modern American Culture* (New York, 1929); Robert A. Dahl, *Who Governs? Democracy and Power in an American Community* (New Haven, 1961); Ritchie

P. Lowry, *Who's Running This Town?* (New York, 1962); Robert O. Schulze, "The Role of Economic Dominants in Community Power Structures," *American Sociological Review* 23 (February 1958).

5. Liste des négociants qui ont payés les fraix des batteries dressés sur le havre et murs de cette ville lors de séjour des Anglois dans nos rades, 1757, AMLR, Ms. EE16; Emile Garnault, *Le commerce rochelais au XVIIIe siècle d'après les documents composant les anciennes archives de la chambre de commerce de La Rochelle,* 4 vols. (La Rochelle, 1888–98), 2:198–200; Carlo Cipolla, *Before the Industrial Revolution: European Society and Economy, 1000–1700* (New York, 1976), p. 51–53, calls attention to that part of total wealth siphoned off by military requirements at both state and local levels. Unknown but probably quite large resources at La Rochelle, an exposed and relatively isolated port, were necessarily committed to defense during the war-ridden eighteenth century. These would include not only military hardware such as defensive batteries but maintenance of the walls, salaries to local militia, and expenses incurred by the quartering and boarding of royal troops. While the large convoys that gathered in La Rochelle's waters undoubtedly stimulated business, the convoys also carried troops to the colonies and, prior to embarkation on the transports, those troops were housed in La Rochelle at local expense. Too, as mentioned in Chapter 1, capital resources were diverted from port repair to the construction of an arsenal despite the objection of the Rochelais.

6. Paramount among the excluded families were the Noordingh de Witt, Claëssen, and Oüalle. Gustave Noordingh de Witt succeeded his father, Jean, in 1715 as commercial consul of Demark in the Atlantic ports of France, serving until his death in 1776. The Noordingh family made no armements after 1715, intermarried only with the Benoist family, and did not participate in other activities used to identify the most significant families. The members of the Claëssen family had been residents of La Rochelle since at least 1596. Nicolas Claëssen, a merchant-banker, served as a *syndic* in the La Rochelle Chamber of Commerce and as a director during the 1730s. He was also mayor of the city from 1725 to 1727, a deputy of commerce from La Rochelle, and had been consul and judge of the juridiction consulaire. Of all the families outside the ninety, the Claëssen was the only one which attained an importance comparable to those among the lower ranks on table 3.1. As were the Claëssens, the Oüalles were old Rochelais Protestants. David Oüalle served as the first director of the local chamber and had been a judge and consul at the admiralty. The Oüalles married into the Claëssen and de Richemond families, but nothing was known of their economic activities except that none served as armateurs. Pierre Bonnassieux, *Conseil de Commerce et Bureau du Commerce, 1700–1791: Inventaire analytique des procés-verbaux* (Paris, 1900), p. 1; Power of Attorney to Pierre Jean Van Hoogwerf, La Rochelle, 16 janvier, 3 mai 1776, Van Hoogwerf Papers, ACM, 4J2847. Van Hoogwerf succeeded Noordingh as Danish consul and took over Noordingh's commission business; Emile Garnault, *Livre d'or de la chambre de commerce de La Rochelle contenant la biographie de directeurs et présidents de cette chambre de 1719 à 1891* (La Rochelle, 1902), pp. 7–8, 15–16, provided further information for these sketches.

7. Garnault, *Le commerce rochelais,* I:134, and Arie Théodorus Van Deursen, *Professions et métiers interdits: Un aspect de l'histoire de la Révocation de l'Edit de Nantes* (Groningen, Neth., 1960), p. 337, both state erroneously that no Protestants were selected for the admiralty until 1789.

8. Compte générale de toutes les avances faitte par Paul Depont à La Rochelle pour Messieurs de la Compagnie des Indes, 14 février 1722, 15 avril 1722–29 décembre 1722, Depont des Granges Papers, ACM, Ms. E486.

9. Paul M. Bondois, "Les centres sucriers français au XVIIIe siècle," *RHES* 19 (1931): 45; G. Debien, "Le club des colons de La Rochelle (septembre 1789-octobre 1790)," *RHCF* 43 (1956): 347–48; Henri Robert, *Les trafics coloniaux du port de La Rochelle au XVIIIe siècle,* Mémoires de la Société des Antiquitaires de l'Ouest, 4th ser., vol. 4 (Poitiers, 1960), pp. 181–82.

10. Elinor G. Barber, *The Bourgeoisie in 18th Century France* (Princeton, 1955), pp. 94–95, 100–103; Pierre Goubert, *L'Ancien Régime,* vol. 1, *La Société* (Paris, 1969), pp. 207–8; Ernest

Labrousse et al., *Histoire économique et sociale de la France*, vol. 2, *Des derniers temps de l'âge seigneurial aux préludes de l'âge industriel (1660–1789)* (Paris: Presses Universitaires de France, 1970), pp. 632–33; Léon, *Economies et sociétés préindustrielles*, p. 365; George V. Taylor, "Noncapitalist Wealth and the Origins of the French Revolution," *American Historical Review* 72 (January 1967): 473–86.

11. Pierre Jean Van Hoogwerf à Odilé Van Hoogwerf à Edinbourg, La Rochelle, 16 juin 1773, Van Hoogwerf Papers, ACM, 4J2847.

12. Between 1770 and 1772, Van Hoogwerf regularly corresponded with agents in Cayenne about the purchase of a plantation. His correspondence did not reveal whether or not he actually purchased the land. Pierre Jean Van Hoogwerf à Gme. Scott à Cayenne, La Rochelle, 4 septembre 1770, 28 mars 1772; à Robert à Cayenne, La Rochelle, 11 février, 10 septembre 1772; Robert à Van Hoogwerf, Cayenne, 29 juin 1772. ibid.

13. Ventes et transport de different rentes par Paul Vivier, 6 juin, 12 novembre 1753, AMLR, Ms. 1938; Succession et partage du Jean Denis le jeune, 20 avril 1774, AMLR, Ms. 1597.

14. Marcel Delafosse and Claude Laveau, *Le commerce du sel de Brouage aux XVIIe et XVIIIe siècles* (Paris, 1960), pp. 28–29, 46; Meynardie jeune à Madame Veuve Delacroix, à Marrennes, 28 juillet 1773, AMLR, Ms. 2645; Déclaration des demoiselles Gastumeau, 12 février 1791, Gastumeau Papers, ACM, Ms. E393; Acquisition de Romphlac par M. Deverigny, 5 décembre 1741, ACM, Ms. E523–24; Goguet materials, AMLR, Ms. 1673; Etienne Van Hoogwerf à Pierre Van Hoogwerf, La Rochelle, 1 novembre 1795, AMLR, Ms. 1947; Notarial documents in ACM, Ms. 4J46; Arrentement d'une maison située au village de Rompay, ACM, Ms. 4J1062.

15. Goubert, *L'Ancien Régime*, pp. 131–32; Jean Périer, *La prospérité rochelaise au XVIIIe siècle et la bourgeoisie protestante* (Mesnil, n.d. [1899]), pp. 61–64, mistakenly wrote that the Rochelais did not invest capital in agricultural pursuits at home or in the colonies.

16. Meyer, *L'armement nantais*, pp. 244–45; Marcel Delafosse, "La Rochelle et les îles au XVIIe siècle," *RHCF* 36 (1949): 260–63; François-Georges Pariset, ed., *Bordeaux au XVIIIe siècle*, vol. 5, *Histoire de Bordeaux*, ed. Ch. Higounet (Bordeaux, 1968), pp. 217–19; Pierre Léon, *Marchands et speculateurs dauphinois dans le monde antillais du XVIIIe siècle: Les Dalle et les Raby* (Paris, 1963), p. 144.

17. E. Jourdan, "La cahier des plaintes, doléances et remontrance du Tiers-Etat de La Rochelle en 1789," *Revue de l'Aunis* (April 1864), pp. 340–50, 421. De Missy, Jean Baptiste Nairac, Pierre Henri Seignette, Joachim Debaussay, Jean Gilbert, Etienne Isaac Rasteau, Jean Perry, Jean Louis Gastumeau, and others summarized in one document all cahiers from the généralité of La Rochelle.

18. Debien, "Le Club des Colons," pp. 349–51; Inventaire et partage après la mort de M. Henri Belin, 27 août 1740, Belin Papers, ACM, Ms. E292; Liste des nègres se soustrouves sur l'habitation de M. Paul Belin desmarais à l'Artibonitte, 25 juin 1763–66, Belin Papers, ACM, Ms. E295; Claude Etienne Belin bill, 10 juillet 1775, [untitled document], AMLR, Ms. 1923; Statement of Jacques Bernon, 1774, [untitled document], ACM, Ms. B229; Collet l'aîné à Made, Veuve Labbé, St. Marc, 12 février 1748, ACM, Ms. B229; Transport-Boury, Pommier, Bonneau, 1 mars 1715, ACM, Ms. B229; Registre 1715–18, Rivere et Soulard, Notaries, ACM.

19. Procès Verbal d'ouverture des lettres saisier à la porte par les créanciers de Beltremieux, en failitte, 19 novembre 1745, ACM, Ms. B1729.

20. Henri Mariage, *Evolution historique de la législation commerciale de l'ordinance de Colbert à nos jours, 1673–1949* (Paris, 1951), pp. 40–47.

21. Lepage frères à M. [torn], La Rochelle, 1790, CCLR, carton 10; [minister of the Marine] à Chambre de Commerce de La Rochelle, 17 janvier 1777, ibid.

22. Copies of letters from the minister of the Marine and from the comptroller general to the La Rochelle Chamber of Commerce, March 7 and July 7, 1770, ibid.

23. Paillet à les directeurs et sindics de La Chambre de Commerce d'Aunis, à La Rochelle, 2 août 1784, and De par la roi lettres de réhabilitation pour les Sieurs Paillet et Meynardie, 11 février 1784, ibid.

24. Herbert Lüthy, *La banque protestante en France de la Révocation de l'Edit de Nantes à la Révolution,* 2 vols. (Paris, 1959–61), 1: 281; Gaston Martin, *Nantes au XVIIIe siècle: L'ère des négriers (1717–74), après les documents inédits* (Paris, 1931), pp. 184–85; Edouard Dupont, *Histoire de La Rochelle,* (La Rochelle, 1830), pp. 524–26.

25. Etat des failletés en la ville de La Rochelle et les environs dont les bilans et livres ont été déposés au greffe de la juridiction consulaire de la cette ville, depuis le premier janvier 1749 jusqu'au 9 juin 1753, CCLR, carton 10.

26. Copie de la lettre écrite par Monseigneur le comte de Maurepas, 10 février 1746, ibid.; Noordingh & Domus contre Pierre Hardy père et fils, 1741, AMLR, Ms. 1956; Extrait du concordat passé entre Mrs. Bessie de la Barthe et leurs créanciers, 5 décembre 1754, AMLR, Ms. 1956; Mémoir pour le Sr. Jean Elie Giraudeau l'aîné négociant, caissier, syndic & Directeur des créanciers du Sr. Pierre Blavout & des Srs. Marchand & veuve Blavout, demandeur, 1784, CCLR, carton 10; Etat des navires du port de La Rochelle et montant de leurs chargements pris pas les Angolis, 29 novembre 1745, CCLR, carton 7.

27. Bankruptcies in La Rochelle, 1769–72, [untitled ms.], CCLR, carton 7; Jugement sur la nomination des directeurs des créanciers Sr. Bourgine, 4 août 1765, ACM, Ms. 5757; De Par le Roi lettres de réhabilitation pour les Sieurs Paillet et Meynardie, 11 février 1784, CCLR, carton 10; E. Belin à Belin Desmarais à Paris, 2 janvier 1769, Belin Papers, ACM, Ms. E287; papers regarding Bedenc, de Richemond, and De Missy failures, [untitled ms.], CCLR, carton 10; Pierre Jean Van Hoogwerf à Odilé Van Hoogwerf à Edinbourg, La Rochelle, 20 février 1773, and à P. G. Van Hoogwerf à St. Petersbourg, La Rochelle, 25 avril 1779. Van Hoogwerf Papers, ACM, Ms. 4J2847; John G. Clark, *New Orleans, 1718–1812: An Economic History* (Baton Rouge, La., 1970), pp. 124–25, 158–61.

28. De Par le Roi lettres de réhabilitation pour les Sieurs Paillet et Meynardie, 11 février 1784, CCLR, carton 10; E. Belin à Belin Desmarais à Paris, 2 janvier 1769, Belin Papers, ACM, Ms. E278; Delaire l'aîné à E. Belin, La Rochelle, 25 mai 1774, AMLR, Ms. 1933. See also Pierre Dardel, "Importanteurs et exportateurs rouennais au XVIIIe siècle: Antoine Guymonneau et ses opérations commerciales (1715–1741)," *Etudes d'histoire économique* 4 (Dieppe, 1954), for the spread effects of failures elsewhere on an Rouennais merchant.

29. Récapitulation de toutes les marchandises sorties du royaume par les divers ports de mer de la direction de La Rochelle allant aux pays étrangers et les colonies, 1770–80, CCLR, carton 27; Pierre Jean Van Hoogwerf à Jenner à Marseille, La Rochelle, 2 mai 1779, Van Hoogwerf Papers, ACM, Ms. 4J2847.

30. [illegible] à M. Van Hoogwerf, 1777, AMLR, Ms. 1955; Copy of a letter from the minister of the Marine to the Chamber of Commerce of La Rochelle concerning the failure of Jouanne de St. Martin, January 17, 1777, CCLR, carton 10; Pierre Jean Van Hoogwerf à Jenner à Marseille, La Rochelle, 24 décembre 1778, à P. G. Van Hoogwerf à Utrecht, La Rochelle, 14 décembre 1782, Van Hoogwerf Papers, ACM, Ms. 4J2847; Augustin Bridault failure, [untitled manuscript], 13 octobre 1779, AMLR. Ms. 1956; Van Hoogwerf bilan, 1777–84, AMLR, Ms. 1946; George V. Taylor, "The Paris Bourse on the Eve of the Revolution, 1781–1789," *American Historical Review* 67 (July 1962): 956–57; André Remond, "Marchands normands dans la seconde moitié du XVIIIe siècle," *RHES* 30 (1952): 40–43.

31. Pierre Jean Van Hoogwerf à P. G. Van Hoogwerf à St. Petersbourg, La Rochelle, 27 mai 1783, 18 juillet 1784, ACM, Ms. 4J2847; Veuve Admyrauld à Van Hoogwerf, 4 juin 1783, AMLR, Ms. 1946; E. Seignette à M. Delaire, secretaire de La Chambre de Commerce, [n.d.], CCLR, carton 10; Augustin Leclerq à la Chambre de Commerce de La Rochelle, 28 novembre 1783, CCLR, carton 18; E. Jousselin à La Chambre de Commerce de La Rochelle, 29 mai 1784, CCLR, carton 18; Taylor, "Paris Bourse," p. 951.

32. Augustin Leclerq à la Chambre de Commerce de La Rochelle, 28 novembre 1783, CCLR, carton 18; Registre des sousmissions, ACM, Ms. B259–259bis; materials concerning de Richemond, and Garnault located in: Correspondance de J. J. Garnault à M. de Richemond, AMLR, Ms. 2247–48, 2295–96, and Ms. 1914, 1946, and 2275, and Meschinet de Richemond Letterbook, ACM, Ms. E450.

33. Pierre Jean Van Hoogwerf à Odilé Stuart à Edinbourg, La Rochelle, 31 juillet 1787, à P. G. Van Hoogwerf à St. Petersbourg, La Rochelle, 2 août 1787. Van Hoogwerf Papers, ACM, Ms. 4J2848; Fleuriau frères et Thouron à La Chambre de Commerce de La Rochelle, [n.d.], CCLR, carton 10; Jacques Carayon fils aîné à la Chambre de Commerce de La Rochelle, 2 septembre 1788, CCLR, carton 10; d'Ebez à Pierre Jean Van Hoogwerf, 26 décembre 1789, AMLR, Ms. 1955.

34. Registre des Sousmissions, ACM, Ms. B259bis.

35. See Chapter 7 for further discussion of colonial debts.

Chapter Six

1. Aside from a small glass plant, three starch manufacturers, and an earthenware factory, La Rochelle had no major industries except sugar refining. In 1716, one Etienne Riguaud requested permission to start a textile mill but apparently nothing came of it. In 1786, a manufacturer of indiennes did commence production in the city but nothing else is known of it. Clothes were manufactured at Saintes, Saint-Jean-d'Angely, and Niort, and the Rochelais did use those goods. Petition of Etienne Riguaud [untitled ms.], June 26, 1716, AMLR, Ms. 327; Priaud l'aîné à la Chambre de Commerce, 26 avril 1782, CCLR, carton 18; Résponse de la Chambre de Commerce, 1789. *ibid.;* Germain Martin, *La grande industrie en France sous le règne de Louis XV* (Paris, 1900), pp. 104, 122–29, 137.

2. This discussion is based upon Récapitulation de toutes les marchandises sorties du royaume par les divers ports de mer de la direction de La Rochelle allant aux pays étrangers et les colonies, 1718–80. CCLR, carton 27.

3. Simone Berbain, *Etudes sur la traite des noirs au golfe de Guinée: Le comptoir français de Judah (Ouidah) au XVIIIe siècle,* Mémoires de l'Institut francais d'Afrique noire no. 3 (Paris, 1942), pp. 82–83.

4. Gaston Martin, *Nantes au XVIIIe siècle: L'ère des Négriers (1717–74), après les documents inédits* (Paris, 1931), p. 47, estimated that "Indian goods" made up three-quarters of the barter cargo on a slaver, but this is high for La Rochelle where cloth of all types rarely surpassed 60 percent of the cargo and was normally under 50 percent.

5. L'Aimable Esther, cargaison pour Guinée, 15 décembre 1751, and le navire la Reine de Golconde, 2eme voiage, 1786, AMLR, Ms. 1132; Armement du Meulan, premier voyage de Guinée, 1776, AMLR, Ms. 1977.

6. M. J. Conan, "La dernière compagnie française des Indes," *RHES* 25 (1939): 300–301; Louis Dermigny, *La Chine et l'Occident Le commerce à Canton au XVIIIe siècle, 1719–1833,* 3 vols. (Paris, 1964), 2:707; [J. B. Nairac], Prospectus d'armement d'un navire d'environ 450 tonneaux pour un voyage aux Indes Orientales, [n.d.], AMLR, Ms. 1417.

7. Van Hoogwerf Livre de Ports de Lettres, 1777 à 1812, Van Hoogwerf Papers, ACM, Ms. 4J2851; Meschinet de Richemond Letterbook, ACM, Ms. E446.

8. Jean Cossart & Fils & Bouvier à Théodore Delacroix, Amsterdam, 28 mars, 10, 28 octobre, 4, 13, 28 novembre, 2 décembre 1737, Delacroix Papers, AMLR, Ms. 2645. Letters equally descriptive of the business dealings of Rochelais merchants have been preserved in great abundance in both AMLR and ACM, but it is generally impossible to sort out values or volume. Few merchants practiced double-entry bookkeeping and those who did adapted it to their own purposes, employing methods known only to themselves.

9. Henri Levy-Bruhl, *Histoire de la lettre de change en France aux XVIIe et XVIIIe siècles* (Paris, 1933), pp. 21–24, argues for the primacy of the remittance function; Jean Bouchary, *Le marché des changes de Paris à la fin du XVIIIe siècle (1778–1800) avec les graphiques et le relevé des cours* (Paris, 1937), p. 13, emphasized the credit function; Raymond de Roover, *L'évolution de la lettre de change, XIV–XVIIIe siècles* (Paris, 1953), George V. Taylor, "Types of Capitalism in Eighteenth-Century France," *EHR* 79 (July 1964): 485–86, point to the dual

nature of the instrument. A contemporary treatment, M. Dutot, *Réflexions politiques sur les finances et le commerce ou l'on examine quelles ont été sur les Revenus, les Denrées, le change étranger, le conséquemment sur nôtre commerce, les influences des Augmentations & des Diminutions des valeurs numéraires des Monnays,* 2 vols. (Paris, 1743), 2:2–13, recognized both functions.

10. Charles Carrière, *Négociants marseillais au XVIIIe siècle,* 2 vols. (Marseilles, 1973), 2:793–811; see also Jacques Teneur, "Les commerçants dunkerquois à la fin du XVIIIe siècle et les problèmes économiques de leur temps," *Revue du Nord* 48 (January-March 1966): 24–26.

11. Louis Charuyer à Lambert à Paris, La Rochelle, 22 mai 1756, AMLR, Ms. 1913; various accounts in Depont des Granges Livre no. 1, 1723–63, Depont des Granges Papers, ACM, Ms. 483; Etat de vente des marchandises de la cargaison du navire la Daphne commence à Léoganné le 16e juin jusqu'au 2 août 1741, Delacroix Papers, AMLR, Ms. 2645; Compte de vente et net produit pour le compte et risques des intéressés du batteau le Balon, 1784, de Richemond & Garnault Papers, AMLR, Ms. 2292–93.

12. Taylor, "Types of Capitalism," pp. 486–87.

13. Act de dépose de conséquence le Sr. Bordier et Surreau, 28 novembre 1729, ACM, Fleury Notaire, La Rochelle, Actes 1729; for de Richemond and Van Hoogwerf see n. 7; Paul Butel, "Contribution à l'étude de la circulation de l'argent en Aquitaine au XVIIIe siècle: Le commerce des rescriptions sur les recettes des finances," *RHES* 52 (1974): 82–109.

14. For excellent treatments of the evolution of commercial specialization, see Jean Cavignac, *Jean Pellet, commerçant de gros, 1694–1772: Contribution à l'etude du négoce bordelais au XVIIIe siècle* (Paris, 1967), pp. 88–89; Felix Olivier Martin, *L'organisation corporative de la France d'Ancien Régime* (Paris, 1938), pp. 273–76; and George V. Taylor, "Some Business Partnerships at Lyon, 1785–1793," *JEH* 23 (March 1963): 59–60. Virtually every collection of the papers of a Rochelais merchant cited to this point is filled with material reflecting the variety of functions performed by a single merchant. Special attention will be given to the brandy trade and insurance industry in subsequent chapters.

15. Rochelais ownership of vessels engaged in the coasting trade cannot be determined. The Registre des Sousmissions, ACM, Série B247–59bis, rarely contains registrations for other than voyages le long cours and fishing. Counts of the number of vessels entering the port do not list the ships by name. Rochelais serving as armateurs in le petit cabotage were available for one year only, 1784, in Visites des Vaisseaux, ACM, Ms. B5788. Pierre Jean Van Hoogwerf used *la Betsy* and *la Suzanne et Odélie* for le grand cabotage to Trieste, Van Hoogwerf Papers, ACM, Ms. 4J2847. How common this was during the century was not determined. The processes of armement and désarmement will be explained in following pages.

16. No vessels departed for Africa from 1745 to June 1748. The "Arrêt de conseil d'état du roi concernant le commerce de l'Inde," 13 août 1769, opened the trade in the seas beyond the Cape of Good Hope to individual merchants but stipulated that all returns be made at Lorient, AMLR, Ms. 431.

17. Between 1740 and 1749, Delacroix & Bonfils outfitted twenty ships; Rasteau, fourteen; Bonfils, twelve; Labbé, Belin, and Blavout, nine each; and Dubeignon and Bonneau, eight each. From 1780–89, Garesché ventured fourteen ships; Rasteau and Poupet, eight each; Goguet and Guibert, six each; and Carayon and de Richemond & Garnault, five each.

18. Pierre H. Boulle, "Slave Trade, Commercial Organization, and Industrial Growth in Eighteenth-Century Nantes," *Revue française d'histoire d'outre-mer* 59 (1972): 84; François-Georges Pariset, ed., *Bordeaux au XVIIIe siecle,* vol. 5, *Histoire de Bordeaux,* ed. Ch. Higounet (Bordeaux, 1968), pp. 238–39.

19. Boulle, "Slave Trade in Eighteenth-Century Nantes," p. 85.

20. Jean Meyer, "Le commerce négrier nantais (1774–1792)," *Annales ESC* 15 (January-February 1960): 123. See also Gaston Martin, *Nantes au XVIIIe siècle,* p. 238. At Honfleur, a minor slaving port, according to Jean Mettas, "Honfleur et la traite des noirs au XVIIIe siècle," *Revue française d'histoire d'outre mer* 60 (1973): 12, some five families accounted for the bulk of

slaving ventures. The findings of Boulle, Meyer, and Mettas have reference only to the number of armateurs sending out ventures to Africa. They did not identify the sources of investment capital for the trade. The proportionate role of Nantais capital and Nantais intéressés in the trade remains unclear.

21. Meyer, "Commerce négrier nantais," p. 123.

22. Boulle, "Slave Trade in Eighteenth-Century Nantes," p. 85.

23. De Richemond & Garnault à Texier à Paris, La Rochelle, 15 mars 1785, Meschinet de Richemond Letterbook, ACM, Ms. E450.

24. For 1727–31, eight armateurs directed 73 vessels of which 12 were for Africa; from 1740 to 1749, twenty-six armateurs directed 236 vessels of which 71 were for Africa; from 1780 to 1789, twenty-two armateurs managed 196 vessels of which 100 were for Africa.

25. Between 1740 and 1749, the six leading armateurs outfitted 59 percent of the armements and included (in order): Jean Labbé l'aîné, Allard Belin, Elie Giraudeau, Delacroix & Bonfils, Rasteau father and son, and Harouard Dubeignon; the six leaders in the period 1780–89 sent out 58 percent of the slavers and included: Daniel Garesché, Dumoustier de Fredilly, E & N Weis and Sons, Dumontier & Dejarnac, Jacques Guilbert, and Pierre Jean Van Hoogwerf; Registre des Soumissions, ACM, Série B250, 251, 259–59bis.

26. Gaston Martin, *Nantes au XVIIIe siècle,* pp. 286–87.

27. Jean Baptiste's older brother, Paul, was a major négociant in Bordeaux.

28. De Missy was sole proprietor of at least two vessels engaged in the East Indian trade, Déclaration de Samuel de Missy fils, 26 avril 1784, ACM, Ms. B5786; Déclaration de Missy fils, 4 décembre 1787, ACM, Ms. B5794.

29. During a portion of the 1780s, Fleuriau Brothers operated in partnership with Gabriel Thouron, Déclaration de Ms. Fleuriau frères et Thouron, 20 avril 1784, ACM, Ms. B5786; Déclaration de Ms. Fleuriau frères et Thouron, 20 juillet 1784, ACM, Ms. B5787; Acte de propriété du navire les Deux Maries allant à l'île de France, 15 septembre 1784, ACM, Ms. B5787.

30. Note that the costs of armement included the original cost of the vessel, a practice that will be discussed shortly.

31. Le navire l'Elisabeth expédié par L. Vivier au St. Domingue, 1780, de Richemond & Garnault Papers, AMLR, Ms. 2295–96; Compte d'achat, armement, mise hors, vivres, cargaisons & assurances du navire Het Kerperlick Zeepaert, expédié pour la côte d'Angole en Affrique, 30 janvier 1783, ibid.

32. Compte du Radoub, Doublage, armement & Mise Hors du navire le Mars expédié de La Rochelle de l'île de France, 1781, AMLR, Ms. 2248; Garnault à de Richemond, Paris, 20 novembre 1782, ibid.; Meyer, *L'armement nantais,* pp. 145–48, has noted the variety of components included in the mise hors at Nantes. Carrière, *Négociants marseillais,* 2:910–13, was more concerned with what to call the process of armement—*société anonyme, société général, etc.*— than with the functions it served and how it was accomplished. His discussion was disappointing.

33. These estimates assume a 2 percent commission and a mise hors that included all armement costs plus the value of the cargo. These armements represented only a part of the outfits made by these individuals or firms during the period. Data were obtained from many of the sources already cited and from the Registre des polices sur navires, commence le 7 avril 1784 à fini le 6 août 1787, CCLR. In Théodore Delacroix's Etat des commissions gagnée, 1722–24, he indicated that he earned 1955 lt. from armements and désarmements, Delacroix Papers, AMLR, Ms. 2645.

34. Compte d'achat, radoub, armement & Mise Hors de navire le Montgolfier, aller à Cayenne et Tabago, 1784, de Richemond & Garnault Papers, AMLR, Ms. 2292–93; see also n. 31.

35. Compte des retours pour compte des intéressés au navire le Saint Louis, 6 novembre 1738, 2e voyage, 1740–41, 3e voyage, 16 février 1743, Depont des Granges Papers, ACM, Ms. E486, and Depont des Granges, Livre no. 1, 1723–63, ibid. Ms. E483. Dale Miquelon, *Dugard of Rouen: French Trade to Canada and the West Indies, 1729–1770* (Montreal and London, 1978), pp. 199–201, links the arbitrariness in handling the value of the ship to the "absence of

systematic depreciation or amortization over time." Shipowners like Dugard or Jacques Rasteau, "lacking a concept of amortization," continued to charge the full value of the ship against total mise hors in each voyage after the first. As this raised the value against which commissions were charged, it was a method advantageous to the armateur.

36. In addition to the account of the voyage of *le Saint Louis* in n. 35, see the account of the voyage of *le Henoc* in AMLR, Ms. 1916, and material on the voyage of de Richemond & Garnault's *la Balon,* bound for Cayenne in 1784, in de Richemond & Garnault Papers, AMLR, Ms. 2272, 2292–93. Considerable data of this nature were scattered throughout the archives in La Rochelle.

37. Compte curant avec Isaac Garesché, 1727–29, Delacroix Papers, AMLR, Ms. 2646.

38. J. B. Nairac, Prospectus pour un voyage aux Indes Orientales, AMLR, Ms. 1417; Pierre Jean Van Hoogwerf à Deshommets à Paris, La Rochelle, 18 mai 1773. Van Hoogwerf Papers, ACM, Ms. 4J2487; Garnault à de Richemond, Brest, 1 octobre 1779, de Richemond & Garnault Papers, AMLR, Ms. 2247, and Convention entre Frederic Romberg de Bruxelles et de Richemond et Garnault de La Rochelle, pour le navire nommé l'Illustre Voyageur au Havre, 11 avril 1782, de Richemond & Garnault Papers, AMLR, Ms. 2295; Prospectus d'armement d'un navire de 250 à 300 tonnx pour la Louisianne, 1781, de Richemond & Garnault Papers, AMLR, Ms. 2286–88.

39. Postponed, too, will be a discussion of insurance, a matter of very large importance to armateurs and an important element in capital flow in La Rochelle. Insurance and the use of loans *à la grosse aventure,* or bottomry loans, will be treated in Chapter 9.

40. Two basic sources, previously cited, are Registre des Sousmissions, ACM, and Registre des policies, CCLR, Data from those sources have been necessarily supplemented by hundred of separate items located in other collections.

41. Figures were arrived at by calculating the average tonnage for each time period, based on samples of between 50 and 60 percent of all departures, and dividing that into the known total costs, thus producing an average value (lt.) per average ton. That result was then multiplied by total tonnage. For example, in 1724 La Rochelle recorded twenty departures. The average tonnage for fourteen was 138 tons and the inferred total tonnage, 20×138, was 2,760. Inferred total tonnage was multiplied by the average value per average ton, 2760×261 lt., yielding total inferred costs of 720,360 lt., or an average mise hors, 720,360 lt. $\div$ 20, of 36,018 lt. The credibility of this calculation is supported by the narrow difference in table 6.3 between the known mise hors for the sample vessels and the inferred mise hors for all departures.

42. Ernest Labrousse et al., *Histoire économique et sociale de la France,* vol. 2, *Des derniers temps de l'âge seigneurial aux préludes de l'âge industriel (1660–1789),* (Paris, 1970), pp. 386–87, 523; Léon, *Economies et sociétés préindustrielles,* vol. 2, 1650–1780, *Les origines d'une accélération de l'histoire* (Paris, 1970), p. 198.

43. CCLR, carton 27 contains annual unit prices for most years between 1720 and 1780 for these and other commodities such as indigo, coffee, and Dutch cheeses. No information is available that hints at the method of calculation. In the case of salt and brandy, price distinctions were made according to the source. Eau-de-vie from Île de Ré was less costly than from Cognac. Salt from Île de Ré normally cost more than salt from Île d'Oleron.

44. Lucien Peytraud, *L'esclavage aux Antilles françaises avant 1789* (Paris, 1897), pp. 59–62; Gilles Y. Bertin, "Les aspects comptables et financiers du commerce colonial de la Compagnie des Indes entre 1719 et 1730," *RHES* 40 (1962): 478; André Delcourt, *La France et les établissements français au Sénégal entre 1713 et 1763,* Mémoires de l'Institut français d'Afrique noire, no 17 (Ifan-Dakar, 1952) p. 62.

45. Gaston Martin, *Histoire de l'esclavage dans les colonies françaises* (Paris, 1948), p. 54, and idem., *Nantes au XVIIIe siècle,* p. 74; Pierre Dardel, *Navires et marchandises dans les port de Rouen et du Havre au XVIIIe siècle* (Paris, 1963), p. 135.

46. Remnants of a letter from Captain Palmie to Henri Brevet, 1750, AMLR, Ms. 1916. Slave revolts during the passage were not uncommon, usually taking place as the vessel made ready to

depart African waters. In 1738, a vessel of Jacques Rasteau was burned by rebelling captives; Partial copy of a letter written by the captain and officers of *la Galatée*, November 8, 1738, ACM, Série B226.

47. Gaston Martin, *Nantes au XVIIIe siècle*, pp. 113–16; Compte des retours pour compte des intéressés au navire le St. Louis, 6 novembre 1738, 2e voyage, 1740–1741, 3e voyage, 16 février 1743, Depont des Granges Papers, ACM, Ms. E486; Compte général du 2e voyage du navire la Victoire, 1740, Depont des Granges Papers, ACM, Ms. E486; Tableau général de la traitte des noirs du navire le Joly et de la corvette la Petite Suzanne de La Rochelle, 1 juillet 1785, AMLR, Ms. B57; Commencement d'operations, 11 janvier 1784 à 1785, la goelette la Creole, AMLR, Ms. EE277; Pierre Jean Van Hoogwerf à P. G. Van Hoogwerf à St. Petersbourg, La Rochelle, 6 décembre 1785, Van Hoogwerf Papers, ACM, Ms. 4J2848; St. Macary, Beaucamp & Poupier frères à Pierre Jean Van Hoogwerf, St. Marc, 18 novembre 1788, AMLR, Ms. 1949.

48. Meyer, "Commerce négrier nantais," p. 121; Henri Robert, *Les trafics coloniaux du port de La Rochelle au XVIIIe siècle*, Mémoires de la société des Antiquitaires de l'Ouest, 4th ser., vol. 4 (Poitiers, 1960), pp. 37–40.

49. Gaston Martin, *Nantes au XVIIIe siècle*, pp. 56–57, and idem., *L'esclavage dans les colonies françaises*, p. 47; Observations du commerce de La Rochelle sur ce mémoire, CCLR, carton 27.

50. Gaston Martin, *Nantes au XVIIIe siècle*, p. 56–57; Robert Stein, "The Profitability of the Nantes Slave Trade, 1783–1792," *JEH* 35 (December 1975): 790.

51. Meyer, *L'armement nantais*, pp. 162–65; Stein, "Nantes Slave Trade," p. 780.

52. Stein, "Nantes Slave Trade," p. 789.

53. Unfortunately, the data presented in table 6.5 are based upon an inferior sample. For most armements, either mise hors or tonnage is missing; only in rare cases are mise hors, cost of vessel, and tonnage known. It is thus impossible to distinguish between cost of vessel per ton and cost of cargo per ton. Average value per ton for all armements is inferentially derived for the years covered in table 6.5. For example, in 1784, the tonnage of forty of forty-four departures is known and the average tonnage is 284. The mise hors of forty-three departures are known, averaging 141,813 lt. Dividing the average mise hors by the average tonnage yields an average mise hors per ton of 499 lt. Such a large sample, however, is obtainable only for 1784. In all other years, far fewer mise hors are known than tonnages and only occasionally are both items known for the same vessel. Calculations based on the above method produce mise hors per ton values of 838 lt. (1783), 499 lt. (1784), 411 lt. (1785), 573 lt. (1786), and 458 lt. (1787).

54. Stein, "Nantes Slave Trade," table 2, pp. 786–87.

55. Cost estimates offered by other authors are difficult to compare with the Rochelais structure. Louis Dermigny, *Cargaisons indiennes: Solier et Cie. 1781–1793*, 2 vols. (Paris, 1959–60) 1: 79, presented the value of cargoes for nine Solier & Company ventures from Marseilles to America during the 1780s. Mise hors were not given. If Solier & Company used vessels equivalent in size to those used in La Rochelle, the firm's costs were roughly similar; Robert Richard, "Les financements des armements maritime du Havre du XVIIIe siècle: Position de problèmes," *Revue d'histoire économique et sociale* 47 (1969):5–31, offered mise hors per ton figures for four vessels destined for the Antilles in 1776—70 lt., 183 lt., 269 lt., and 598 lt.—which on the average are far below my estimates for La Rochelle; Stein, "Nantes Slave Trade," pp. 786–87, itemized "cost of expedition" figures for twenty-six slavers which were quite similar to La Rochelle's.

Chapter Seven

1. François-Georges Pariset, ed., *Bordeaux au XVIIIe siècle*, vol. 5, *Histoire de Bordeaux*, ed. Ch. Higounet (Bordeaux, 1968), pp. 217–19; Pierre Léon, *Marchands et speculateurs dauphinois dans le monde antillais du XVIIIe siècle: Les Dalle et les Raby* (Paris, 1963), pp.

27–32; Maurice Begouen-Demeaux, *Mémorial d'une famille du Havre: Stanislas Foäche, 1737–1806* (Paris, 1951), pp. 17–18.

2. Henri Robert, *Les trafics coloniaux de La Rochelle au XVIIIe siècle,* Mémoires de la Société des Antiquitaires de l'Ouest, 4th ser., vol. 4 (Poitiers, 1960), p. 7; Pariset, *Bordeaux,* pp. 217–19; Léon, *Dauphinois dans le monde antillais.* Dugard and Company of Rouen adopted the policy of bypassing colonial agents by authorizing its ships' captains to handle all transactions, thereby saving commissions. For the Rochelais, with many relatives on the islands, this policy made little sense. The reliability of kinship connections more than compensated for the cost of commissions that, in any event, flowed both ways; Dale Miquelon, *Dugard of Rouen: French Trade to Canada and the West Indies, 1729–1770* (Montreal and London, 1978), p. 95. Many manuscript collections contain correspondence between Rochelais armateurs and relatives in the colonies; see, for example, Delacroix Papers, AMLR, Ms. 2645, and Belin Papers, ACM, Ms. E292.

3. At some time during the mid-1770s, Garesché concluded a partnership agreement with Billoteau, and the firm transferred its center of operations to Port-au-Prince. Data on this firm are located in Garesché Papers, ACM, Ms. 4J1610–14.

4. Facture des marchandises à consignation M. Jean Mazin, chirugien major, 1748, ACM, Série B228; [Desgaults], Facture & Compte des marchandises, 29 octobre 1741, ibid., B227.

5. Invoice of goods shipped aboard *la Marquise Surgère* consigned to J. M. Vivier, officer, for Louisiana, 1749, [untitled ms.], ACM, Série B229; Déclaration des Noordingh & Domus, 1 mars 1748, ACM, Ms. B5738, relative to the purchase of parts of *pacotilles* from Jean Vivier; Facture des marchandises, 1748, ACM, Série B228, relative to Meynardie pacotilles.

6. See Chapter 5 for an earlier discussion of Rochelais plantation owners.

7. De la Vencendière fils à Belin de Marais à Paris, St. Marc, 25 octobre 1766–23 décembre 1768, Belin Papers, ACM, Ms. E298; Compte current des heritiers Belin de Marais avec Duvay, Maprit & St. Macary, St. Marc, 30 septembre 1778, AMLR, Ms. 1933. Letters from Claude Etienne Belin to Paul detail the disposition of various shipments and the purchases made from the proceeds.

8. Françoise Thésée, *Négociants bordelais et colons de Saint-Domingue: Liaisons d'habitations: La maison Henry Romberg, Bapst et Cie., 1783–1793* (Paris, 1972), pp. 84–85, 207–9; Saintard à Etienne Belin, Bordeaux, 8 août, 9 octobre 1753, AMLR, Ms. 1992; J. Corperin & Courtois à Etienne Belin, Nantes, 29 janvier 1772, AMLR, Ms. 1993.

9. Déclaration du Mathieu Benoist, 1 décembre 1730, ACM, Ms. B5725; Lettres-Patentes du Roi, portant Règlement pour le commerce des colonies Françaises, du mois d'avril 1717, in René Josué Valin, *Commentaire sur l'ordonnance de la marine du mois d'août 1681, avec des notes par V. Bécane,* 2d ed. (Paris, 1841), I: 417–21.

10. Déclaration du Jacques Rasteau, 7 décembre 1724, ACM, Ms. B5721; Déclaration du Allard Belin, 25 juillet 1729, ACM, Ms. B5725; Déclaration du Louis Vivier, 9 avril 1785, ACM, Ms. B5786; De Richemond & Garnault à Coirin à St. Pierre, Martinique, La Rochelle, 15 mars 1785, De Richemond Papers, ACM, Ms. E450.

11. Delauney Montaudoin à Théodore Delacroix, Nantes, 9 décembre 1737, Delacroix Papers, AMLR, Ms. 2645; Gazette de la Martinique, du jeudi, 21 août 1766, CCLR, carton 14; Récapitulation de toutes les marchandises entrées dans le royaume par les divers ports de mer de la direction de La Rochelle venant des pays étrangers pendant l'année, 1766–68, CCLR, carton 27; Boissinot de Ballessus à Belin Desmarais à Paris, St. Malo, 24 mars 1765, and De la Vincendière fils à Belin Desmarais à Paris, St. Marc, 24 janvier 1768, Belin Papers, ACM, Ms. E298.

12. J. Paillet à Théodore Delacroix et Trésahar Bonfils, au cap, 23 février and 2 mars 1752, Delacroix Papers, AMLR, Ms. 2645; Bretourrière & Quesdoes à Etienne Belin, St. Pierre, Martinique, 3 avril 1751, 25 mars, 6 juin 1753, AMLR, Ms. 1992.

13. Béville à M. Molinier, au çap, 24 octobre 1748–28 mai 1750, ACM, Série B229.

14. Registre des Sousmissions, ACM, Série B250–251; Facture des marchandises chargées

dans le navire le Robuste alant à la coste de Guinée et St. Domingue par Giraudeau l'aîné, Guinée, 25 mars 1750, cul de sac, 19 septembre 1750, Port au Prince, 31 janvier 1751, ACM, Série B229.

15. See Chapter 5. Even more bankruptcies shook La Rochelle during the late 1770s and 1780s.

16. Jean Meyer, *L'armement nantais dans la deuxième moitié du XVIIIe siècle* (Paris, 1969), p. 235; George V. Taylor, "The Paris Bourse on the Eve of the Revolution, 1781–1789," *American Historical Review* 67 (July 1962): 951–77; André Remond, "*Marchands normands dans la seconde moitié du XVIIIe siècle,*" *RHES* 30 (1952): 40–43; Paul Butel, "Contribution à l'étude de la circulation de l'argent en Acquitaine au XVIIIe siècle: Le commerce des rescriptions sur les recettes des finances," *RHES* 52 (1974): 108; Léon, *Dauphinois dans le monde antillais,* p. 144; Meynardie, Picard & Cie. à P. J. Van Hoogwerf, Port au prince, 5 février 1788, AMLR, Ms. 1949.

17. Benjamin Giraudeau à Garesché & Billoteau à Port au Prince, La Rochelle, 18 juillet 1780 and 19 avril 1781, Garesché Papers, ACM, Ms. 4J1610–12.

18. Emile Garnault, *Le commerce rochelais au XVIIIe siècle d'après les documents composant les anciennes archives de la chambre de commerce de la Rochelle,* 4 vols. (La Rochelle, 1888–98), 4:xiii–iv, 51–53; Jean Cavignac, *Jean Pellet, commerçant de gros, 1694–1772: Contribution à l'étude du négoce bordelais au XVIIIe siècle* (Paris, 1967), pp. 177–79; Thésée, *Négociants bordelais et colons de Saint-Domingue,* p. 85; Henri Sée, *Le commerce maritime de la Bretagne au XVIIIe siècle, d'après les papiers des Magon, Mémoires et documents pour servir a l'histoire du commerce et de l'industrie en France,* ed. Julien Hayem, 9th ser. (Paris, 1925), pp. 78–81; Pierre H. Boulle, "Slave Trade, Commercial Organization, and Industrial Growth in Eighteenth-Century Nantes," *Revue française d'histoire d'outre-mer* 59 (1972): 82–83; Meyer, *L'armement nantais,* pp. 206–7, 215–19.

19. Miquelon, *Dugard of Rouen,* p. 159, emphasized the speed of return on investments in commercial ventures as an advantage over slow returns on rentes. But speed was only the hope, not the reality. In fact, returns on a sizable number of investments dribbled in over a number of years.

20. Cavignac, *Pellet,* pp. 100–101; John G. Clark, *New Orleans, 1718–1812: An Economic History* (Baton Rouge, La., 1970), pp. 99, 111, 144–45; Louis-Philippe May, *Histoire économique de la Martinique (1635–1763)* (Paris, 1930) 189–97; Observations relatives au bien de l'agriculture et du commerce dans les îles françaises de l'Amerique, 15 novembre 1785 par la Chambre de Commerce à La Rochelle, CCLR, carton 15. Efforts in Canada, Louisiana, Martinique, and elsewhere to circulate special currencies—copper money, for example—were failures. This money depreciated rapidly, and merchants, local and metropolitan, refused to accept it in payment for goods. For the money introduced into Louisiana, see Clark, *New Orleans* pp. 107–25; for the importance of Spain, see Albert Girard, *Le commerce français à Seville et Cadix au temps des Hapsbourg: Contribution à l'étude du commerce étranger en Espagne au XVI et XVIIe siècle* (Paris, 1932); Gaston Rambert, "La France et la politique commerciale de l'Espagne au XVIIIe siècle," *RHMC* 18 (October–December 1959): 269–88.

21. Cavignac, *Pellet,* pp. 99–100, and Gaston Martin, *Histoire de l'esclavage dans les colonies françaises,* (Paris, 1948) pp. 78–79, emphasized barter.

22. Marcel Delafosse, "La Rochelle et les Îles au XVIIe siècle," *RHCF* 36 (1949): 259 noted the use in the seventeenth century of instruments of credit in the colonial trade; May, *Histoire économique de la Martinique,* p. 197; Acknowledgment of receipt of money by Elie Nicolas and Jean Benjamin Rasteau, Port au Prince, March 7, 1750, [untitled ms.], ACM, Série B228; Etienne Belin à Belin Desmarais à Paris, La Rochelle, 24 décembre 1768, Belin Papers, ACM, E298; Louis Charuyer à Jean Charuyer, St. Pierre, 7 décembre 1772, AMLR, Ms. 1994; Antoine Giraudeau à Garesché & Billoteau, au cap, 12 septembre 1781, Garesché Papers, ACM, Ms. 4J1610; Carrière, *Négociants marseillais,* 2:864–68, noted the general unimportance of letters in the traffic between Marseilles and the Antilles.

23. Louis Dermigny, *La Chine et l'Occident: Le commerce à Canton au XVIIIe siècle, 1719–1833,* 3 vols. (Paris, 1964), pp. 686, 707; Compte d'achat, armement, mise hors du bateau

l'Indien de quarante toneaux destiné pour les îles de France et de Bourbon, 10 janvier 1782, and Le navire le Prevost de Languistin, armement pour l'île de France et le Bengale, 1783, de Richemond & Garnault Papers, AMLR, Ms. 2295–97.

24. Table 7.1 and the discussion in the above three paragraphs were derived from Compte des retours pour compte des intéressés au navire le St. Louis, 6 novembre 1738, and Compte général du navire le St. Louis, 3e voyage, 16 février 1743, and Compte général du 2e voyage du navire la Victoire, 1740, Depont des Granges Papers, ACM, Ms. E486; Achat, armement, mise hors et cargaison du navire le Henoc, 27 décembre 1748, and Henri Brevet à O'Heguerty à Paris, La Rochelle, 11 juillet 1750, AMLR, Ms. 1916; Tableau général de la traitte des noirs du navire le Joly et de la corvett la Petite Suzanne de La Rochelle, 1 juillet 1775, AMLR, Ms. 857; Le navire le Meulan, compte du retour du dit navire, 1777, AMLR, Ms. 1977; Compte des désarmement à Nantes du navire la Belle Pauline, juillet 1784, AMLR, Ms. 2286–88; G. Desmarais Fleury à Pierre Jean Van Hoogwerf, au cap, 27 mars 1786, and St. Macary, Beaucamp, et Pouyer Brothers à Pierre Jean Van Hoogwerf, St. Marc, 19 février 1788, 5 décembre 1788, and Rasteau and Company à Pierre Jean Van Hoogwerf, Port au Prince, 31 mars 1790, AMLR, Ms. 1949; E. Belin à Belin Desmarais à Paris, La Rochelle, 24 décembre 1768, 28 février 1769, Belin Papers, ACM, Ms. E298.

25. Only for the last three voyages were distinctions made in accounts between cash and letters of exchange. The next to the last column of table 7.1 represents the total debt outstanding as of the date in the last column. The difference between the lt. value of total sales and the lt. value of receipts in cash or in notes does not represent the initial debt because payments were also made in goods.

26. In trying to explain the continued growth of the slave trade at Nantes, Robert Stein, "The Profitability of the Nantes Slave Trade, 1783–1792," *JEH* 35 (December 1975): 792, concluded that in this system, which depended upon credit, "promises of payment were, in practice, more important than hard currency. Indeed, it is very possible that the Nantais used colonial credits to finance further expeditions." The explanation offered in my study, emphasizing the significance of cash flow and its relatively large proportions, seems a much more reasonable explanation for La Rochelle than the Stein interpretation. Fixed charges, i.e., désarmement, final salary and wage payments, and divisions among intéressés, could not be satisfied with promises. Nor did credits suffice to organize the next venture.

27. Compte de désarmement à Nantes du navire la Belle Pauline, juillet 1784, AMLR, Ms. 2286–88; Pierre Jean Van Hoogwerf à P. G. Van Hoogwerf à St. Petersbourg, La Rochelle, 8 septembre 1789, Van Hoogwerf Papers, ACM, Ms. 4J2848; Poupet frères et Cie., au cap, 1, 15 février 1788; St. Macary, Beaucamp, et Pouyer frères à Pierre Jean Van Hoogwerf, St. Marc, 19 février, 12 mars 1788, AMLR, Ms. 1949; Récapitulation des nos interest dans les fonds à St. Domingue, 1772, par Van Hoogwerf père et fils AMLR, Ms. 1947.

28. Depont des Granges, Livre no. 1, 1722–63, Depont des Granges Papers, ACM, Ms. E483. Paul's father outfitted *le Post Gallere* and *la Paix;* Rasteau, *le Saint Paul* and *la Perle,;* Belin, the others. In each case, the senior Depont sold a fraction of his investment to his son. Paul's investment of 5,075 lt. in *le Saint Philippe* represented one-ninth of his father's investment of 45,677 lt., a five-sixteenth share in the total cost of the voyage.

29. The armements of Depont, Rasteau, and Belin were derived from a variety of sources including the citation in n. 28 and Chambre du Conseil des juges consuls, 1717–46, juridiction consulaire de La Rochelle, ACM, Série B339; Registre des Sousmissions, ACM, Série B247. The scale of returns on table 7.3 assumes a constant but declining rate of return beginning in the second year of an armement and complete amortization in the fifth year. Obviously, the pattern varied in reality. Profits, beginning in the sixth year, and income from other services would provide additional increments to working capital.

30. La navire la Fortune, premier armement, 12 avril 1733, Depont des Granges Papers, ACM, Ms. E486; Déclaration du Sr. Robert Beltremieux, 17 janvier 1749, ACM, Ms. B5739; Dulary, Majoret, & St. Macary à Madame Delacroix, St. Marc, 15 mai 1777, Delacroix Papers, AMLR, Ms. 2644; Benjamin Giraudeau à Garesché et Billotteau à Port au Prince, La Rochelle,

18 juillet 1780. Garesché Papers, ACM, Ms. 4J1610–11; Le navire les Trois Cousins compte d'armement pour le cap et le port au prince, 1782, de Richemond & Garnault Papers, AMLR, Ms. 2297.

31. See Chapter 3; Inventaire du meubles et effets du Sr. Allard Belin, 20 janvier 1748–10 septembre 1749, Belin Papers, ACM, Ms. E291.

32. St. Macary, Beaucamp & Poupet frères à Pierre Jean Van Hoogwerf, St. Marc, 10 décembre 1789, Rasteau et cie. à Pierre Jean Van Hoogwerf, Port au Prince, 19 mars 1790, AMLR, Ms. 1961; Récapitulation de nos Intérêts dans les fonds à St. Domingue, 1792, ibid. Etat des debiteurs aux divers Négriers de M. P. J. Van Hoogwerf de La Rochelle dont la vente à été faite au cap par Mrs. Poupet, Guymet & Gauvain au dit lieux, Philadelphie, 1803, ibid.; and Regarding creditors of the estate of Pierre Jean Van Hoogwerf, December 1828, [untitled ms.], ibid.

33. Stein, "Nantes Slave Trade," p. 790, suggested that colonists consciously refused to pay about 10 percent of their debts. Volition aside, subjectively it would seem that uncollected debts approached at least 15 percent and perhaps 20 percent.

34. Garnault, Le commerce rochelais, 3: 44; Jules Ballet, La Guadeloupe: Renseignements sur l'histoire, la flore, la faune, la géologie, la minéralogie, l'agriculture, le commerce, l'industrie, la législation, l'administration, 5 vols. (Basse terre, Guadeloupe, 1899), 2:113; Sée, Commerce de la Bretagne, 9:29–30; Begouen-Demeaux, Stanislas Foäche, pp. 25–26; Lettres patentes du Roy, en forme d'édit, concernant le commerce étranger aux Îsles & Colonies de l'Amerique, Données à Fontainebleau au mois d'octobre 1727, CCLR, carton 15; Fleury à la Chambre de Commerce à La Rochelle, 19 septembre 1727, CCLR, carton 14; Claessen à la Chambre de Commerce à La Rochelle 5 août 1730, CCLR, carton 4; Delaunay Montaudoin à Théodore Delacroix, Nantes, 31 janvier 1737, Delacroix Papers, AMLR, Ms. 2645.

35. Clark, New Orleans, pp. 42, 135; Garnault, Le commerce rochelais, 3:17–18, 4:75–118; H. du Halgouet, Nantes: Ses relations commerciales avec les îles d'Amérique au XVIIIe siècle (Rennes, 1939), pp. 32–33; Richard Pares, War and Trade in the West Indies, 1739–1763 (Oxford, 1936), pp. 326–27; Jacques Teneur, "Les commercants dunkerquois à la fin du XVIIIe siècle et les problèmes économiques de leur temps," Revue du Nord 48 (January-March, 1906): 23; A Messieurs les directeurs et sindics de la Chambre de Commerce de La Rochelle, 22 décembre 1744; Orry à la Chambre de Commerce de La Rochelle, 27 décembre 1744, 6 janvier 1745, CCLR, carton 14.

36. Charles Frostin, "Les colons de Saint-Domingue et la metropole," Revue historique 237 (April-June 1967): 397; Garnault, Le commerce rochelais, 4:238–47; Théophile Malvezin, Histoire du commerce de Bordeaux depuis les origines jusqu'à nos jours, 4 vols. (Bordeaux, 1892), 3:156; Pariset, Bordeaux, pp. 294–95; Henri Wallon, La Chambre du Commerce de la province de Normandie, (1703–1791) (Rouen, 1903) pp. 302–10. Louis Charuyer à Jean Clanchy à Nantes, La Rochelle, 15 août 1756, AMLR, Ms. 1913; Rasteau l'aîné et Gastumeau à la Chambre de Commerce de La Rochelle, Paris, 11, 25, 31 mai, 5, 8 juin 1756, and Joseph Pascaud à la Chambre de Commerce de la Rochelle, Paris, 14 juillet, 1761, 11 décembre 1762, CCLR, carton 4.

37. Pierre Isaac Rasteau à M. de Sartine [minister of the Marine], Paris, 3 juillet 1778, and Pierre Isaac Rasteau à la Chambre de Commerce de la Rochelle, 4, 5, juillet, 1 août 1778, CCLR, carton 4; Torterue Bonneau à la Chambre de Commerce de La Rochelle, Paris, 29 décembre 1781, 4 février 1783, ibid.

38. Frostin, "Saint-Domingue et la metropole," pp. 402–8; Halgouet, Nantes et les îles d'Amerique, pp. 116–17; Copie d'une lettre écritte le 20 juillet 1783 par M. le Mch de Castries aux administrateurs des îles du vent, CCLR, carton 4; Torterue Bonneau à la Chambre de Commerce de La Rochelle, 19 février 1785, 4 juillet 1789, CCLR, carton 4; Représentations de La Chambre de Commerce de La Rochelle, janvier 1785, CCLR, carton 15; Représentations de la Chambre de Commerce de Dunkerque sur l'arrêt du conseil du 30 août 1784, janvier 1785, CCLR, carton 15; Observations de la Chambre de Commerce de Marseille sur l'arrêt du 30 août 1784, 10 janvier 1785, CCLR, carton 15; Les six corps des marchands de Paris à la Chambre de Commerce de La Rochelle, 25 mars 1785, CCLR, carton 15; Mémoire de la Chambre de Com-

merce & des négocians de Bayonne au sujet de l'arrêt du conseil du 30 août 1784, 30 avril 1785, CCLR, carton 15; Observations relatives au bien de l'agriculture et du commerce dans les îles françaises de l'Amerique, 15 novembre 1785, par la Chambre de Commerce de La Rochelle, CCLR, carton 15; Rélevé des navires arrives à St. Domingue & partis de cette colonie dans le quatre premiers mois de 1788, CCLR, carton 21.

39. Paul Walden Bamford, *Forests and French Sea Power, 1660–1789* (Toronto, 1956), p. 162, and "French Shipping in Northern European Trade, 1660–1789," *Journal of Modern History* 26 (September 1954): 209–10; Garnault, *Le commerce rochelais,* 3:98; Halgouet, *Nantes et les îles d'Amerique,* pp. 57–60; A.M. de Boislisle and P. de Brotonne, ed eds., *Correspondence des contrôleurs-généraux des finances avec les intendants des provinces,* 3 vols. (Paris, 1897), 3:167; Mémoire à Messieurs les directeurs & sindics de la Chambre de Commerce de La Rochelle, 18 septembre 1744, Petitions to the Chamber of Commerce of La Rochelle, 1756–58, [an assortment of mémoires by the principal armateurs], CCLR, carton 17; Extrait du journal historique au sujet de tentative d'une Flotte Angloise sur les côtes du Pays d'Aunis, AMLR, Ms. EE16.

40. Valin, *Commentaire l'ordonnance d'août 1681,* 1:51; Violet Barbour, "Marine Risks and Insurance in the Seventeenth Century," *Journal of Economic and Business History* 1(August 1929): 563–68; Garnault, *Le commerce rochelais,* 3:158; Miscellaneous petitions from armateurs, 1744–48, to the Chamber of Commerce of La Rochelle, CCLR, Carton 14.

41. J. T. Viaud and E. J. Fleury, *Histoire de la ville et du port de Rochefort* 2 vols. (Rochefort, 1845), I:393–400; G. Lacour-Gayet, *La marine militaire de la France sous le règne Louis XV* (Paris, 1902), pp. 187–88; Garnault, *Le commerce rochelais,* 3:217–23; David Ogg, *Europe of the Ancien Regime, 1715–1783* (New York, 1965), p. 168; Ordonnance du Roy qui règ le payement des équipages des navires expédiez pour les iles de l'Amerique sous l'escorte des vaisseaux de Sa Majesté, pendant le tems qu'ils aouront été retenus dans les Rades pour attendre le depart des convois, 21 avril 1746, AMLR, Ms. EE16; Liste des navires partis de La Rochelle de 18 octobre 1747 sous le convois de M. de Letenduere, CCLR, carton 17; Déclaration du Louis Perdriau, 17 avril 1748, ACM, Ms. B5738; Récapitulation général de la marine de la France en 1756 et de la marine d'Angleterre en 1756, CCLR, carton 17, indicated that the English navy had twice the number of warships and guns as the French navy.

42. Garnault, *Le commerce rochelais,* 1:107; Miscellaneous petitions from armateurs, 1779–80, CCLR, Carton 17; Liste des navires marchands partis des Rades de La Rochelle, le 2 septembre 1782 sous le convoi commandé par le Comte de Soulanges, 1782, CCLR, carton 17; Daniel Garesché à Garesché et Billoteau, La Rochelle, 5, 28 juillet 1780, Garesché Papers, ACM, Ms. 4J1610–11; Pierre Jean Van Hoogwerf à P. Van Hoogwerf à La Brille, La Rochelle, 14 janvier 1781, Van Hoogwerf Papers, ACM, Ms. 4J2847; Pierre Hardy fils aîné à Garesché et Billoteaux à St. Marc, La Rochelle, 15 septembre 1781, Garesché Papers, ACM, Ms. 4J1612.

43. See table 2.2; Jean Delumeau, "Le commerce malouin à la fin de XVIIIe siècle," *Annales de Bretagne* 56 (September 1959): 281–86; Arthur M. Wilson, *French Foreign Policy during the Administration of Cardinal Fleury, 1726–1743: A Study in Diplomacy and Commercial Development* (Cambridge, Mass., 1936), pp. 86–87; Emile Garnault, *Le commerce rochelais,* 3:170–72, and *Livre d'or de la chambre de commerce de La Rochelle contenant la biographie de directeurs et présidents de cette chambre de 1719 à 1891* (La Rochelle, 1902), pp. 23, 65; Etat des navires du port de La Rochelle et du montant de leurs chargements, pris par les Anglais, 29 novembre 1745, CCLR, carton 7.

44. Garnault, *Le commerce rochelais,* 4:188–89, and *Livre d'or,* pp. 72–75; Gaston Martin, *Nantes au XVIIIe siècle: L'ère des négriers (1717–74), après les documents inédits* (Paris, 1931) pp. 266–68; Meyer, *L'armement nantais,* p. 81; Pariset, *Bordeaux,* pp. 290–93; Déclaration de Jacques Carayon, 10 mars 1756, and Bertraud à Admyrauld fils, Plymouth, 24 janvier 1757, ACM, Ms. B6086; Joseph Pascaud à la Chambre de Commerce de La Rochelle, 13 juin 1761, CCLR, carton 4; Boissinot de Bellessus à Belin desmarais à Paris, St. Malo, 19 octobre 1763, Belin Papers, ACM, Ms. E298; Mémoir pour le payemens aux négocians des affreteurs fair par le Roy, 15 décembre 1761, CCLR, carton 17; Etat des navires de La Rochelle arretés par les

Anglois soit en Europe ou en Amerique, avant la guerre déclarée, 18 septembre 1756, CCLR, carton 17.

45. For the above four paragraphs, see Begouen-Demeaux, *Stanislas Foäche,* p. 84; Pariset, *Bordeaux,* pp. 289–93; Paul Butel, "Le trafic européen de Bordeaux de la guerre d'Amérique à la Revolution," *Annales du Midi* 78 (1966): 37–82; Crossus à M. Crossus, capne du navire le Baron de Montmorency, La Rochelle, 11 août 1782, AMLR, Ms. EE277; Nicolas Suidre à Garesché et Billoteau, La Rochelle, 24 novembre 1779, and Jacques Guibert à Garesché et Billoteau, La Rochelle, 17 août 1779, 22 mai 1780, 21 juin 1781, Garesché Papers, ACM, Ms. 4J1610–11; De Richemond à Bernard Fontaine et Hilscher à Rouen, La Rochelle, 20 juin 1780, de Richemond à Herault à Chaillevette, La Rochelle, 2, 11, 16, 22, 29 mai, 29 juillet, 15 août 1780, Meschinet de Richemond Letterbook, ACM, Ms. E447; Pierre Jean Van Hoogwerf à P. G. Van Hoogwerf, La Rochelle, 25 avril 1779, 14 décembre 1782, Pierre Jean Van Hoogwerf à Jenner à Marseille, La Rochelle, 2 mai 1779, Van Hoogwerf Balance, September 1, 1777 to December 20, 1784 [untitled document], Van Hoogwerf Papers, ACM, Ms. 4J2847.

46. Boulle, "Slave Trade and Industrial Growth in Nantes," 103–8.

Chapter Eight

1. Skins were shipped to Niort's leather manufacturers and a portion of the codfish catch was consumed locally. Coal, grain (on occasion), and some wood products were the only items imported from northern Europe that were used on the spot.

2. Rochelais opposition to the extension of the privilege of colonial commerce to other ports (i.e., Saint-Valéry-sur-Somme in 1741) and negotiations relative to domaine d'occident tax rates are treated in Chapter 1.

3. At Bordeaux, coffee formed 30 percent of the value of colonial imports during 1775–77, 38 percent in 1784–86, and 49 percent in 1789. See Francois-Georges Pariset, ed., *Bordeaux au XVIIIe siècle,* vol. 5, *Histoire de Bordeaux,* ed. Ch. Higounet (Bordeaux, 1968), pp. 228–29.

4. Récapitulation entrées, and Récapitulation sorties, CCLR, carton 27; H. du Halgouet, *Nantes: Ses relations commerciales avec les îles d'Amérique au XVIIIe siècle* (Rennes, 1939), pp. 30, 130–34; Jean Meyer, *L'armement nantais dans la deuxième moitié du XVIIIe siècle* (Paris, 1969), p. 247; Michel Morineau, "La balance du commerce franco-néerlandais," p. 184; Paul Butel, "Bordeaux et la Hollande au XVIIIe siècle," *RHES* 46 (1967): 79. As Chapter 2 points out, La Rochelle's share of the French sugar trade with northern Europe declined from about 9 percent in 1750 to less than 2 percent in the 1770s.

5. Conflicting interests also developed within the local merchant community regarding the brandy trade and the production and importation of rum (*tafia* or *guildive*) for use in the slave trade. This will be treated in later pages.

6. The above four paragraphs are based on Charles Woolsey Cole, *Colbert and a Century of French Mercantilism,* 2 vols. (New York, 1939), 2:55; Halgouet, *Nantes et les îles d'Amérique,* pp. 29, 133–34; Emile Garnault, *Le commerce rochelais du XVIIIe siècle d'après les documents composant les anciennes archives de la chambre de commerce de La Rochelle,* 4 vols. (La Rochelle, 1888–98), 4:xvi, 39–41; Marcel Delafosse, "La Rochelle et les îles au XVIIIe siècle," *RHCF* 36 (1949): 256; Paul M. Bondois, "Les centres sucriers français au XVIIIe siècle," *RHES* 19 (1931): 28–45; Pariset, *Bordeaux,* pp. 277–78; Gaston Martin, *Capital et travail à Nantes au cours du XVIIIe siècle* (Paris, 1931), p. 15; G. Debien, "Le club des colons de La Rochelle (septembre 1789–octobre 1790)," *RHCF* 43 (1956): 347–48; Henri Robert, *Les trafics coloniaux du port de La Rochelle au XVIIIe siècle,* Mémoires de la société des antiquitaires de l'Ouest, 4th ser., vol. 4 (Poitiers, 1960), pp. 181–84; Raffineurs à La Rochelle, AMLR, Ms. 330.

7. The above five paragraphs are based on Emile Gabory, *La marine et le commerce de Nantes au XVIIe siècle et au commencement du XVIIIe siècle (1661–1715)* (Rennes, 1901), pp. 42–47; Delafosse, "La Rochelle et les îles," pp. 257, 277–79; Pierre Bonnassieux, *Conseil de Commerce et Bureau du Commerce, 1700–1791: Inventaire analytique des procès-verbaux*

(Paris, 1900), pp. 15, 18, 132, 215; Paul M. Bondois, "Centres sucriers français," p. 32, and "L'industrie sucrière française au XVIIIe siècle: La fabrication et les rivaltés entre les raffineries," *RHES* 19 (1931): 334–35; Warren C. Scoville, "The French Economy in 1700–1701: An Appraisal of the Deputies of Trade," *JEH* 22 (June 1962): 249; Germain Martin, *La grande industrie en France sous le règne de Louis XV* (Paris, 1901), pp. 144–45; Halgouet, *Nantes et les îles d'Amérique,* p. 134; Robert, *Trafics coloniaux,* pp. 182–83; Mémoire au conseil de commerce pour les négocians de La Rochelle, 1711–12, Juridiction Consulaire de La Rochelle, ACM, Ms. 4197; Veuve Faneuil & Cie. à M. Corneau, advocat au conseil prés St. Eustache à Paris, La Rochelle, 16 juillet, 18 août 1712, Juridiction Consulaire de La Rochelle, ACM Ms. 4197; Bonneau à Chambre de Commerce à La Rochelle, Paris, 24 juin 1786, CCLR, carton 4; Réponse de la Chambre de Commerce de La Rochelle [on manufacturing at La Rochelle], 1789, CCLR, carton 20.

8. For indigo: Récapitulation entrées, and Récapitulation sorties, CCLR, carton 27; Robert, *Trafics coloniaux,* p. 5; John G. Clark, *New Orleans, 1718–1812: An Economic History* (Baton Rouge, La., 1970), pp. 55–56, 187–88; Dauril Alden, "The Growth and Decline of Indigo Production in Colonial Brazil: A Study in Comparative Economic History," *JEH* 25 (March 1965): 35–60; Pariset, *Bordeaux,* pp. 228–29; Charet à Belin Desmarais à Paris, Nantes, 26 octobre 1763, Belin Papers, ACM, Ms. E298; Correspondence concerning indigo, [untitled documents], CCLR, carton 14.

9. For cotton: Récapitulation entrées, and Récapitulation sorties, CCLR, carton 27; Insurance policy on merchandise loaded aboard the *Comtesse de Pierreux* for Le Havre, La Rochelle, October 10, 1775, [untitled document], AMLR, Ms. 1916; A Messieurs les directeurs et sindics de la Chambre de Commerce de la ville de La Rochelle, 19 juin 1753, CCLR, carton 14; de Richemond à Guinebeau, Peteau à Orléans, and de Richemond à Delahaye & Père à Amiens, La Rochelle, 14 mars 1780, de Richemond Letterbook, ACM, Ms. E447; Paul Butel, "Le trafic européen de Bordeaux de la guerre d'Amérique à la Révolution," *Annales du Midi* 78 (1966): 79.

10. For coffee: Récapitulation entrées, and Récapitulation sorties, CCLR, carton 27; Mémoir sur les cafées, par la Chambre de Commerce de La Rochelle, 22 janvier 1755, CCLR, carton 14; Mémoire des directeurs de la Chambre de Commerce de Guienne sur les dispositions de l'arrêt du conseil du 29 mai 1736, CCLR, carton 14; Mémoire des places maritimes du Royaume sur l'entrepôt des caffé et les droits de consommation auxquels ils sont assujettes, 1774, CCLR, carton 14; A Messieurs les directeurs & Sindics de la Chambre de Commerce d'Aunis à La Rochelle, 10 novembre 1774, CCLR, carton 14; A Messieurs les directeurs et sindics de la Chambre de Commerce de La Rochelle, 2 janvier 1783, CCLR, carton 14; De Richemond à M. Duverge, Directeur des Fermes à Paris, La Rochelle, 30 mars 1780, de Richemond Letterbook, ACM, Ms. E447; Offres de la Chambre de Commerce de La Rochelle pour l'évaluation du prix des marchandises des îles sujettes aux droits du domaine d'occident pour 1774, CCLR, carton 20; Etat de'évaluation du prix des marchandises du crû des îles sur lesquelles droits des trois et demy pour cent du Domaine d'occident seront perçus dans tous les ports du Royaume pendant 1783, 1789, CCLR, carton 20; Coffee prices, import and export, 1736–1780, [untitled documents], CCLR, carton 27; Pariset, *Bordeaux,* pp. 228–29; Halgouet, *Nantes et les iles d'Amérique,* pp. 44–45; Louis Dermigny, *La chine et l'Occident: Le commerce à Canton au XVIIIe siècle, 1719–1833,* 3 vols. (Paris, 1964), 2:518–19; W. Adolphe Roberts, *The French in the West Indies* (Indianapolis, 1942), 141–42; Pierre Dardel, *Navires et marchandises dans les ports de Rouen et du Havre au XVIIIe siècle* (Paris, 1963), p. 147.

11. For tobacco: Clark, *New Orleans,* chaps. 4–7; Jacob M. Price, *France and the Chesapeake: A History of the French Tobacco Monopoly, 1674–1791, and Its Relationship to the British and American Tobacco Trades,* 2 vols. (Ann Arbor, Mich., 1973), vol. 1; Droits sur le tabac, Establissement et perception, 1629–1749, AMLR, Ms. CC20; Droits sur le tabac, Procédure et jugements divers, AMLR, Ms. CC26.

12. For furs and skins: Récapitulation entrées, and Récapitulation sorties, CCLR, carton 27; Mémoire des négocians assujet des droits atribués aux officiers de controlleurs prudhomme et vendeurs de cuirs au Roy et à nos Seigneurs de son conseil, 24 janvier 1733, CCLR, carton 21;

Réponse de Mr. Mercier, juin 1733, CCLR, carton 21; Relevé fait au Bureau des Fermes de La Rochelle des peaux de chavreuils venues de la Louisiane, 1773, CCLR, carton 21; Droits d'entrée sur les pelleterries, La Rochelle, 1778, CCLR, carton 21; Pierre-Isaac Rasteau à La Chambre de Commerce de La Rochelle, Paris, 21 février 1778, CCLR, carton 4; Représentations de la Chambre de Commerce de La Rochelle à l'effet d'obtenir que les pelleterries qui y seront importées cessent d'y être assujeties à de plus forts droits que ceux que cette marchandises aquite à l'entrée du Royaume par les Provinces réputées étrangères, 1784, CCLR, carton 21; Copie la supplique de la Chambre de Commerce de La Rochelle, du 15 juillet 1785 à Son Ex. Mgr. de Galvez du Conseil d'État et Ministre des Indes à Madrid, CCLR, carton 25; Galvez à la Chambre de Commerce a La Rochelle, 19 septembre 1785, CCLR, carton 25; Arrêt du conseil d'état du Roy, portant exemption des droits de traite à l'entrée des peaux d'Agneaux et de chevreaux en poil, et fixation des droits de sortie sur les peaux mégissées et sur les gants favriques, 13 avril 1786, CCLR, carton 21.

13. For fish: Récapitulation entrées, CCLR, carton 27; Etat des vaisseaux qui se sont expédier à La Rochelle pour le peche de la morue en 1700 et 1709, La Rochelle, 1709, ACM, Ms. B5633; Arrêt du Conseil d'Etat qui accorde des primes d'encouragement aux négocians françois qui transportent de morues sèches de pêche nationale dans les îles du Vent et sous le Vent, ainsi que dans le Ports de l'Europe tels que ceux d'Italie, d'Espagne, et de Portugal, 18 septembre 1785, ACM, Ms. B5633; Arrêt du Conseil d'Etat du Roy portant à cinq livres par quintal la taxe imposée sur la morue de peche étrangère qui Sera importée aux îles de l'Amerique du Vent et sous le Vent, 25 september 1785, ACM, Ms. B5633 Arrêt du Conseil d'Etat du Roi, qui porte à huite livres le droit de cinq livres par quintal établie par l'Arrêt du 25 septembre 1785, sur la morue sèche de pêche étrangère importée aux îles du Vent et sous le Vent, et à douze livres la Prime de dix livres accordée par l'Arrêt du 18 du même mois, par quintal de Morue sèche de pêche françoise, importée aux mêmes Îles, 11 février 1787, ACM, Ms. B5633; Comte d'Achat, Radoub et Armement et mise-hors du navire L'Alexandre expédié pour Miquelon le 7 juin dernier [1782], AMLR, Ms. 2286–88; Jean Delumeau, "Le commerce malouin à la fin de XVIIIe siècle," *Annales de Bretagne* 56 (September 1959): 274–78; Charles de la Morandiere, *Histoire de la pèche française de la morue dans l'Amérique septentrionale: Des origines à 1789,* 3 vols. (Paris, 1962), 2:523, 595, 597; Robert de Loture, *Histoire de la grande pèche de Terre-Neuve* (Montrouge, 1949), pp. 208–9; for a revealing account of noble investment during the 1750s in a fishing company operating out of Les Sables d'Olonne and selling cargoes in La Rochelle, Nantes, and Bordeaux, see J. Bosher, "A Fishing Company of Louisbourg, Les Sables d'Olonne, and Paris: La Société du Baron d'Huart, 1750–1775," *French Historical Studies* 9 (Fall 1975): 261–77.

14. For the external trade in grain: Arrêt pour les chargement des bleds, 1699–1700, ACM, Ms. 5646; A. M. de Boislisle and P. de Brotonne, eds., *Correspondence des contrôleurs-généraux des finances avec les intendants des provinces,* 3 vols. (1897), 3:13, 25, 41–42, 151–52, 186. For regulations dealing with the export of grains to foreign markets: AMLR, Ms. 432; Extrait des Registier des délibérations du Corps de ville de La Rochelle, 7 juin 1773, AMLR, Ms. 419; Extrait d'une lettre de M. le Contrôlleur Général du 1er décembre 1744, CCLR, carton 13; Commerce de graines, CCLR, carton 13; Simonde frères à Théodore Delacroix, London, 27 janvier, 15 février, 28 mars, 14 avril, 30 mai, 25 août 1737, Delacroix Papers, AMLR, Ms. 2645; J. C. Toutain, *Le produit de l'agriculture française de 1700 à 1958,* 2 vols. (Paris, 1961), 2:6–13; Gabory, *Marine et commerce de Nantes, 1661–1715,* pp. 37–38; Bonnassieux, *Conseil de Commerce,* p. 52; Dardel, *Les ports de Rouen et du Havre,* pp. 163–65.

15. Mémoire soumis à la Chambre de Commerce le 5e avril 1720, CCLR, carton 13; Arrêt du Conseil d'Etat du Roy, qui permet à toutes personnes de quelque état et condition qu'elles soient de faire sortir de la Province de Saintonge, telle quantité de grains de l'espece, dite Bled d'Espagne, Mahis, ou Bled de Turque, qu'ils jugeront à propos, pour être transporté à l'étrangère, pourvû que ce soit par les Ports de La Rochelle, Charente et Marennes, 18 février 1755, AMLR, Ms. 432; A Messieurs les directeurs et sindics de la Chambre de Commerce de la ville de La Rochelle, 1760, CCLR, carton 13; Notes of a meeting of the La Rochelle Chamber of Com-

merce, January 14, 1768, [untitled ms.], AMLR, Ms. 419; Mémoire ou lettre à un ami sur les avantages qu'il y auroit pour La Rochelle, et même en général, que l'exportation des graines qui se fait au Bourg de Marans en Aunis, se fit à l'avenir dans cette ville, 1769, CCLR, carton 13; De Richemond à Rucher & Wortmann à Hambourg, La Rochelle, 20 juin 1780, de Richemond Letterbook, ACM, Ms. E447.

16. For *ménage:* Concerning the defense of La Rochelle against the English in 1696, [untitled document], AMLR, Ms. EE16; Déclaration du Roy portant que les bleds, farines, & autres grains, ne pourront . . . [illegible] . . . être vendus, achetez, ni mesurez ailleurs que dans les Halles et Marchez, 19 avril 1723, AMLR, Ms. 419; Arrêt de réunion du Ménage à la Ville de La Rochelle, 23 février 1751, AMLR, Ms. 419; Compte Rendus par du Corps de ville de La Rochelle de la contestation qu'il est levée entre le fermier du ménage et le Sr. Carayon, le corps de ville ayant été appellé par le fermier et ayant prier son fait et cause, 2 août 1774, AMLR, Ms. 419; Mémoire concernant le droit du ménage de La Rochelle, 1750, AMLR, Ms. 419; Bassett, fermier du ménage, à Messieurs les maire, echevins et officiers du corps de ville de La Rochelle, 14 mai 1753, AMLR, Ms. 419; [Nineteen merchants] à Messieurs les Directeurs et Sindics de la Chambre de Commerce de la ville de La Rochelle, [1760s], CCLR, carton 13.

17. See Chapter 1 for a discussion of the armateur-rural landowner controversy over the levying of the *taille,* a tax impinging heavily on rural owners of brandy producing properties.

18. E. J[ourdan], "Sur les vignes et les vins d'Aunis," *Revue de l'Aunis et de la Saintonge* (April 1866), pp. 258–60, 272; Dion, *Histoire de la vigne,* 360–63, 442–48; Emile Garnault, "Les bourgeois rochelais des temps passés et les causes de la decadence du commerce rochelais," *Revue historque* 70 (1899): 57–58.

19. For *agréeurs* and *courtiers:* Extrait du registre de la Police de La Rochelle, 1712, AMLR, Ms. 326; Procés-verbal contre Jean Chabot, 21 et 24 mars 1722, AMLR, Ms. 326, Pétition des agréeurs à l'acceptation, 21 février 1754, AMLR, Ms. 326; Instance relative à une vente d'eau-de-vie, 27 août 1762, AMLR, Ms. 326; Requêtte Réception de Jean Chariaux, 12 janvier 1717, AMLR, Ms. 329; Pétition de Jean Chariaux, maitre tonnelier et étabonneur juré de cette ville, 1744, AMLR, Ms. 329; Results of inspection of brandy shipped by Noordingh & Domus, 1749, [untitled document], AMLR, Ms. 325; Déclarations des Mrs. Jean Chariaux, Gustave Noordingh, Abraham Domus, 1749, AMLR, Ms. 325; Réflexion de la Chambre de Commerce sur les abus qui se commettjant tant sur la fabrication des futailles à eau-de-vie que dans sa qualité, 1748, AMLR, Ms. 430; Blaire de Boisemont [intendant] à Mrs. les Maire et Echevins de la Rochelle, 15 juillet 1751, AMLR, Ms. 430; Arrêt du conseil d'état du roy concernant la Fabrication de l'Eau-de-vie dans la Province d'Aunis, 28 mai 1753, AMLR, Ms. 430; Ordonnance de M. le Lieutenant-Général de la Sénéchaussée de la ville et gouvernement de La Rochelle concernant des eaux-de-vie, 1786, AMLR, Ms. 857.

20. For taxation: Explanation of aydes, [untitled ms.], AMLR, Ms. CC7; [La Rochelle Chamber of Commerce] à Cardinal Fleury, [n.d.], AMLR, Ms. 311; Droits qui se levant dans La Rochelle, 1706 AMLR, Ms. 318; Mémoire des officiers du corps de ville en réponse de celluy de Messieurs des fermiers généraux, 1728, AMLR, Ms. 430; Copie de la lettre, Orry à Begnon, Intendant à La Rochelle, 8 décembre 1730, AMLR, Ms. 430; Claëssen à la Chambre de Commerce de La Rochelle, Paris, 14 avril 1730, CCLR, carton 4; Tarif et reglèmens concernant les droits de courtiers, jaugeurs, inspecteurs aux Boissons, et Inspecteurs aux Boucheries, 1722, AMLR, Ms. CC9; Mémoire contre Jacques Hué, 1749, AMLR, Ms. 311; Torterue Bonneau à la Chambre de Commerce de La Rochelle, Paris, 29 octobre 1785, 1 avril 1786, CCLR, carton 4; Ordonnance de M. le Lieutenant-Général de la Sénéchaussée de la ville et gouvernement de La Rochelle concernant des eaux-de-vie, La Rochelle, AMLR, Ms. 857.

21. Dardel, *Les ports de Rouen et du Havre,* pp. 68–69; Marcel Rouff, *Les mines de charbon au 18e siècle, 1774–1791* (Paris, 1922), pp. 32–35, 174–81; Copie de la lettre écritte par M. de Trudaine à M. de Blaire de Boisemont, Intendant de la Généralité de La Rochelle, 29 mars 1754, CCLR, carton 20; Réponse de la Chambre de Commerce de La Rochelle, 1789, CCLR, carton 20.

22. For the coalition against rum imports: Rastieau l'aîné à Mrs. les Maire et Echevins à La

Rochelle, Paris, 21 août, 14 septembre 1763, 26 mai 1764 AMLR, Ms. 433; Joseph Pascaud à la Chambre de Commerce de La Rochelle, Paris, 28 avril, 5, 12, 30 mai, 2 juin 1764, CCLR, carton 4; Mémoire sur les vins et sur les eaux-de-vie de l'Aunis, par Nairac, AMLR, Ms. 1417; Torterue Bonneau à la Chambre de Commerce de La Rochelle, 9 décembre 1783, 27 mars 1784, Paris, CCLR, carton 4; Chambre de Commerce de La Rochelle à M. le Marechal de Castries, La Rochelle, 3 décembre 1784, CCLR, carton 17; Dardel, *Les ports de Rouen et du Havre*, p. 171.

23. For salt: M. Beaupied Dumenils, *Mémoire sur les marais salans des provinces d'Aunis et de Saintonge* (La Rochelle, 1765), pp. 68–71, 80–81; Charles de La Morandière, "Le sel et la pêche, particulierement pour la pêche de la morue," in *Le rôle du sel dans l'histoire*, ed. Michel Mollat (Paris, 1968), pp. 97–101, 108–11; Gabory, *Marine et commerce de Nantes*, pp. 33–36; Dardel, *Les ports de Rouen et du Havre*, p. 176; Marcel Delafosse et Claude Laveau, *Le commerce du sel de Brouage aux XVIIe et XVIIIe siècles* (Paris, 1960), pp. 25–29; P. Giradot à Théodore Delacroix, Paris, 24 avril 1752, Delacroix Papers, AMLR, Ms. 2645; Meynardie jeune à Madame veuve Delacroix à Marenne, La Rochelle, 2 juin, 28 juillet 1773, AMLR, Ms. 2645; Miscellaneous receipts, 1750s and 1760s [untitled ms.], Depont Papers, ACM, Ms. 4J1226; Récapitulation sorties, CCLR, carton 27; Arrêts de conseil d'état du roy, 25 juin 1737, 20 janvier, 31 mars, 7 juillet 1739, AMLR, Ms. 369; Mémoire des négocians de La Rochelle contre la pretention de Pierre Carlieu, adjudicataire des cinq grosse fermes sur les sels, 27 janvier 1731, CCLR, carton 15; Arrêt du conseil d'état du roi portant révocation de la permission accordée aux armateurs, de tirer de l'Espagne et du Portugal les sels necessaires à la pêche de la Morue, 20 mai 1779, CCLR, carton 18; Torterue Bonneau à la Chambre de Commerce à la Rochelle, Paris, 17 juin, 5 septembre 1786, CCLR, carton 4; Statement of the proprietors of salt marshes at La Rochelle, 1775, [untitled document], AMLR, Ms. CC16.

24. Louis Dermigny, "De Montpellier à La Rochelle: Route du commerce, route de la medecine au XVIIIe siècle," *Annales du Midi* 67 (1955); Dardel, *Les ports de Rouen et du Havre*, pp. 71–75; Letter from the Admiralty at La Rochelle to an official in the ministry of the Marine, May 7, 1720, [untitled ms.], ACM, Ms. B5632; M. de St. Sauveur à la Chambre de Commerce de La Rochelle, Fiume, 9 janvier, 17 mars 1778, CCLR, carton 18; De Richemond & Garnault à Fred. Romberg à Bruxelles, La Rochelle, 25 août 1783, AMLR, Ms. 2275; Observations sur le commerce du nord relativement à la France, par de Baussay & Daniel Garesché, 1783, CCLR, carton 18; Pierre Jean Van Hoogwerf à Odilé Van Hoogwerf à Edinbourg, La Rochelle, 16 janvier, 1 mai 1776, Van Hoogwerf Papers, ACM, Ms. 4J2847.

Chapter Nine

1. Material from this chapter appeared in John G. Clark, "Marine Insurance in Eighteenth-century La Rochelle," *French Historical Studies* 10 (fall 1978): 572–98. Useful for a general understanding of the legal principles of insurance are Harold E. Raynes, *A History of British Insurance* (London, 1950); P. J. Richard, *Histoire des institutions d'assurance en France* (Paris, 1956); Barry Supple, *The Royal Exchange Assurance: A History of British Insurance, 1720–1970* (London, 1970); Charles Wright and E. Ernest Fayle, *A History of Lloyd's from the Founding of Lloyd's Coffee House to the Present Day* (London, 1928); The major study of French insurance, L. A. Boiteaux, *La fortune de mer: Le besoin de sécurité et les débuts de l'assurance maritime* (Paris, 1968), is of some value regarding insurance law. The most informative studies include Violet Barbour, "Marine Risks and Insurance in the Seventeenth Century," *Journal of Economic and Business History* 1 (August 1929); Jacques Heers, "Rivalité ou collaboration de la terre et de l'eau? Position générale des problèmes," in Mollat, ed., *Les grandes voies maritimes dans le monde;* A.H. John, "The London Assurance Company and the Marine Insurance Market of the Eighteenth Century," *Economica*, 25 (May 1958): 126–41; J. S. Kepler, "The Operating Potential of London Marine Insurance in the 1570s: Some Evidence from 'A Book of Orders of Assurances within the Royall Exchange'," *Business History* 17 (January

1975): 44–55; Richard Pares, *War and Trade in the West Indies, 1739–1763* (Oxford, 1936), pp. 303, 304; Florence Edler de Roover, "Early Examples of Marine Insurance," 5 (November 1945): 172–200; Henri Sée, "Notes sur les assurances maritimes en France et particuliérement à Nantes au XVIIIe siècle," *Revue historique du droit française et étranger,* 6th ser. 4 (1927): 287–311. For contemporary syntheses see Nicolas Magens, *An Essay on Insurances . . .,* 2 vols. (London, 1755), and J. Weskett, *A Complete Digest of the Theory, Laws, and Practice of Insurance* (London, 1781).

2. *Avaries simples* (simple averages) applied to expenses sustained by equipment, the body of a ship or cargo as a result of a storm, high winds, etc. *Avaries grosses* (gross averages) were extraordinary expenses compelled by the necessity of protecting the safety of the vessel such as ransom or jettisoning cargo during a storm. *Menues avaries* (petty averages) were claimable for damage suffered while entering or leaving a port under a pilot or under tow. See Magens, *Essay on Insurances;* Sée, "Les assurances maritimes," p. 300; Raynes, *British Insurance,* p. 173.

3. English policies during the mid-eighteenth century carried a deductible clause of 2 percent on the body of the vessel, 3 percent on corn and fish, 5 percent on sugar, tobacco, flax, hides, and hemp. Policies issued by an insurance company at La Rochelle during the 1780s carried deductible clauses of 3 percent on the body of the ship and on all dry goods, 6 percent on liquids, and 10 percent on all grains, flour, salt, fish, flax, and wool, CCLR, carton 7.

4. Jugement sur requête en faveur de la veuve Legriel et fils aîné pour des réassurances, 10 mai 1776, ACM, Ms. B5758.

5. Déclaration du Sr. Jean Ezeckiel Couillandeau, capt. de navire, 4 novembre 1749, ACM, Ms. 5739; Déclaration du J. Pascaud, 25 janvier 1757, ACM, Ms. 5747.

6. For the above three paragraphs, see P. J. Richard, *Assurance en France,* p. 14; Barbour, "Marine Risk and Insurance," pp. 576–78; Henry Levy-Bruhl, *Histoire juridique des sociétés de commerce au XVIIe et XVIIIe siècles* (Paris, 1930), pp. 39, 235, 245–46; Sée, "Les assurances maritimes," pp. 287–91; Supple, *Royal Exchange Assurance,* pp. 22–28; Raynes, *British Insurance,* pp. 100–109; Louis Dermigny, *La Chine et l'Occident: Le commerce à Caton au XVIIIe siècle, 1719–1833,* 3 vols. (Paris, 1964), 2:161.

7. Weskett, *Complete Digest of Insurance,* p. 92; Jean Meyer, *L'armement nantais dans la deuxième moitié du XVIIIe siècle* (Paris, 1969), pp. 34–38, 111–12, 116–17; Sée, "Les assurances maritimes," p. 294; Pierre Dardel, "Importateurs et exportateurs rouennais au XVIIIe siècle: Antoine Guymonneau et ses opérations commerciales (1715–1741)," *Etudes d'histoire économique* 4 (Dieppe, 1954): 112–13; Charles Carrière, *Négociants marseillaise au XVIIIe siècle,* 2 vols., (Marseilles, 1973), 2: 900.

8. Petition of a group of Rochelais, including Abraham Delacroix and Théodore Pages, regarding insurance, 1695, [untitled ms.], ACM, Ms. B5624; Société d'Assurance de La Rochelle, 23 octobre 1751, ACM, Ms. B229; Observations du commerce de La Rochelle, 1784, CCLR, Copie des mémoires de la Chambre de Commerce de La Rochelle.

9. Société d'Assurance de La Rochelle, 23 octobre 1751, ACM, Ms. B229; Acte de société de la compagnie d'assurance tant pour le cabotage que pour les voyages de long cours, à Nantes, 6 février 1783, CCLR, carton 7; Carrière, *Négociants marseillaise,* 2:900.

10. For the above three paragraphs; see the Rochelais documents cited in n. 9 above; Acte de Société de la Chambre d'Assurance et Grosse Aventure, à Paris, 1750 janvier, ACM, Ms. B228; Règlement général de l'association et la compagnie sous la tittre d'assurances généralles de Paris, enregistré au Chastelot de Paris le 6 mars 1754, ACM, Ms. B6086; Délibérations de Messieurs les Intéressés d'une la Compagnie d'Assurance establie à Paris le autres places maritimes et commerçante, 19 septembre 1754, ACM, Ms. B6086; Enregistrement de règlement général de la compagnie d'assurance à La Rochelle, 5 avril 1754, ACM, Ms. B5624; Enregistrement en faveur de Nicolas Weis & Louis Fort, négocians de La Rochelle, 13 septembre 1768, ACM, Ms. B5624; Mrs. Richemond & Garnault leur compte courant avec Dumoustier & Dejarnac, 17 janvier 1786, de Richemond & Garnault Papers, AMLR, Ms. 2273; Livre d'assurance de Nicolas Suidre, 1783–1789. AMLR, Ms. 1780.

11. Déclaration des Elie du Jardin, Allard Belin, Jean Labbé, Jacques Carayon, Jacques Rasteau, Michel Stuckey, Sebastian Auriel, Jean Faneuil, Pommier père et fils, Isaac Anger, Pierre Bonfils jeune, Jean Esprinard, et Guillaume Alexandre, 11 septembre 1720, ACM, Ms. B5717; Déclaration du Robert Butler, 17 septembre 1720, ACM, Ms. B5717; Achat du navire le Henoc et le construction du navire le Noé, pour Guinée, 27 décembre 1748, AMLR, Ms. 1916; Miscellaneous Insurance receipts of Théodore Delacroix, 1730–1770, [untitled ms.], AMLR, Ms. 2646.

12. Compte de la perte du vaisseau le Lion d'Or, capne Jacques Rasteau de Havane, 1708, Depont de Granges Papers ACM, Ms. E486; Effets et assurances rentrés du navire le St. Pierre, 1732, ACM, Ms. E486; Affirmation de M. Rodrigue pour l'assurance que à fait faire l'Aimable Catherine, 13 octobre 1757, ACM, Ms. B5747; Jean Cossart & fils et Bouvier à Théodore Delacroix, Amsterdam, 14 janvier, 23 septembre, 10 octobre, 29 octobre 1737, Delacroix Papers, AMLR, Ms. 2645.

13. The registered policies appeared to cover only the *corps* (body) of the vessel and not the cargo, Registre des policies sur navire Commencée le 7 avril 1784 à fini le 6 août 1787, CCLR.

14. Carrière, *Négociants marseillais,* 1: 98–100, stated that Marseilles had an insurance capacity in excess of its own needs and sold insurance for ventures launched elsewhere. This does not mean, however, that insurance made at Marseilles by local merchants necessarily exceeded in value the insurance made elsewhere by Marseillais.

15. Registre des policies, 1784–1787, CCLR; Livre d'assurance de Nicolas Suidre, 1783–89, AMLR, Ms. 1780; Van Hoogwerf insurance accounts, 1776–1791, [untitled ms.], Van Hoogwerf Papers, AMLR, Ms. 1962.

16. Livre d'assurance de Nicolas Suidre, 1783–89, AMLR, Ms. 1780; Compte d'assurance, de Richemond & Garnault, 1783, de Richemond & Garnault Papers, AMLR, Ms. 2286–88. These very tentative estimates assume total coverage of each armement, a condition that did not obtain during any part of the eighteenth century.

17. C. Ernest Fayle, "Shipowning and Marine Insurance," *The Trade Winds: A Study of British Overseas Trade during the French Wars, 1793–1815,* ed. C. Northcote Parkinson, (London, 1948), pp. 25–48; Gordon Jackson, *Hull in the Eighteenth Century: A Study in Economic and Social History* (London, 1972), apps. 27–29.

18. De Richemond & Garnault à Peltier, Carrière et cie, à Nantes, La Rochelle, 4, 12, 21 juin, 7 juillet 1785, de Richemond Letterbook, ACM, Ms. E450.

19. At La Rochelle, the admiralty courts heard disputes over claims. When a dispute ensued over a claim, the justice of which was investigable, the admiralty appointed experts to study the situation. Expert findings were then presented to admiralty appointed arbiters, who decided the issue. Occasionally, arbiters selected by the contending parties attempted a settlement. If unsuccessful, the official arbiters took over the case. If the damage occurred or a claim was filed in another jurisdiction, the procedures of that particular jurisdiction prevailed. Rochelais who made insurance elsewhere on their ventures presented claims before the admiralty of that place. Similarly, Rochelais customs were followed when a non-Rochelais presented a claim against Rochelais underwriters. Appeals to higher authorities such as the various *parlements,* the Council of Commerce, and the ministry of the Marine, while possible, seem to have been resorted to infrequently. A significant exception involved disputes over premiums paid when wartime rates were in effect.

20. Magens, *Essay on Insurance,* 1: 83; Henri Sée, *commerce maritime de la Bretagne,* p. 87; De Roover, "Early Marine Insurance," pp. 192–93.

21. Douglas C. North, "Ocean Freight Rates and Economic Development, 1750–1913," *JEH* 18 (December 1958): 537–55, considers the decline of piracy as a reason for reduced freight rates and, presumably, insurance rates; James F. Shepherd and Gary M. Walton, *Shipping, Maritime Trade, and the Economic Development of Colonial North America* (Cambridge, 1972), pp. 80–85, note a direct relationship between the decline of piracy and privateering and a reduction in armaments and crew size, all of which reduced capital costs of shipping and insurance costs as well.

22. According to the peacetime insurance rates offered in Shepherd and Walton, *Economic Development of Colonial North America*, pp. 77, 89, English and French rates for similar trips were about the same by the mid-eighteenth century. French insurance rates, however, had declined more radically than English rates, suggesting that French premiums during the late seventeenth century were generally higher than English.

23. Insurance receipts of Jean Charuyer, 1768–77. [untitled documents], AMLR, Ms. 1916, 1929; Etienne Belin à Belin Desmarais à Paris, La Rochelle, 24 décembre 1768, Belin Papers, ACM, Ms. E298; Désarmement du le Henoc, 18 novembre 1750, AMLR, Ms. 1916; Construction du navire le Noé pour Guinée, 1748, AMLR, Ms. 1916; Compte générale du navire le Saint Louis, 3e voyage, 16 février 1743, Depont Papers, ACM, Ms. E486; M. J. Conan, "La dernière compagnie française des Indes," *RHES* 25 (1939): 300–301.

24. England was without a system of ship inspection. Some influence was exerted by underwriters, especially after 1760, when the Society of Underwriters published the *Register Book on Shipping*, which classified vessels according to build and upkeep, Fayle, "Shipowning and Marine Insurance," p. 47.

25. Pierre Isaac Rasteau à la Chambre de Commerce à La Rochelle, Paris, 11, 25 juillet 1778, CCLR, carton 4; Déclaration du Roi, 17 août 1779, CCLR, carton 7. Interest in this issue abated as the War of the American Revolution heated up and as the old question of wartime rates came to the fore. Whether or not the new system was applied is not revealed in extant documents in La Rochelle.

26. Emphasizing the primacy of the capital loan function are Boiteux, *La fortune de mer*, p. 77; Richard, *Assurance en France*, p. 8; Georges Musset, *Les rochelais à Terre-Neuve, 1500–1789* (La Rochelle, 1899), pp. 53–55; Marcel Delafosse, "La Rochelle et les Îles au XVIIe siècle," *RHCF* 36 (1949): 245. Focus on the insurance component is found in Heers, "Rivalité ou collaboration," 37; Raynes, *British Insurance*, p. 5; De Roover, "Early Marine Insurance," p. 175. Meyer, *L'armement nantais*, pp. 151–53, recognized the dual nature of the loan.

27. Magens, *Essay on Insurances*, 2:168, 171; P. J. Richard, *Assurance en France*, p. 8; Heers, "Rivalité ou collaboration," p. 37; Assurance, Gitton aux Bonfils frères, 20 avril 1715, Rivère et Soulard Notaries, ACM, Registres, 1714–18; Déclaration du Sr. Alexandre, 25 juillet 1719, and Déclaration du Paul Depont, 18 novembre 1719, ACM, Ms. B5716; Statement of the creditors of the estate of Louis Allaire, [untitled ms.], August 19, 1720, ACM, Ms. B5717; Enregistrement par la Sr. Louis Auboyneau, 11 août 1749, ACM, Ms. B5739; Acknowledgment of a debt by Captain Jean Frémon, September 12, 1767, [untitled ms.], AMLR, Ms. 1960; Enregistrement d'un billet de grosse de 4,600 lt., le Sr. Et. Jolly, ngt., 10 janvier 1787, ACM, Ms. B5794.

28. R. Richard, "Armements maritimes du Havre," p. 22; Carrière, *Négociants marseillais*, 2:958; Labrousse et al., *Histoire économique et sociale de la France*, vol. 2, *Des derniers temps de l'âge seigneurial aux préludes de l'âge industriel (1660–1789)* (Paris, 1970), p. 210.

29. Labrousse et al., *Histoire économique et sociale de la France*, p. 309.

30. Ibid., p. 319; Contrat à la grosse aventure, J. Garesché et veuve Labbé, 5 octobre 1750, ACM, Ms. B228.

31. Delacroix-Dangiraud & Cie., compte, 1754–1755, Delacroix Papers, AMLR, Ms. 2646; M. Paul Depont de La Rochelle, son compte, 1707–09, Depont Papers, ACM, Ms. E486.

32. Pétition des Pierre Papineau, Michel Rodrigue, Jacques Goguet, négociants, directeurs, et syndics de la Chambre de Commerce à cette ville, 1760, ACM, Ms. 5624; Jean Baptiste Soumbrun à Messieurs les directeurs et sindics de la Chambre de Commerce à La Rochelle, 1757, CCLR, carton 17; Mémoire signifie pour le Sieur Jean Baptiste Soumbrun, Négociant et Armateur à La Rochelle contre la chambre et compagnie d'assurance à Paris, 1760, ACM, Ms. 4J2069; P. I. Rasteau, Thouron frères, Jacques Goguet, E. Belin, Paillet et Meynardie, Lebouef et cie., Couillandeau, Denis l'aîné, Chas. Ranson, [and others], à Messieurs les Directeurs et sindics de la Chambre de Commerce de La Rochelle, 14 avril 1763, CCLR, carton 17; La Première Chambre des Assurances de Paris, Intimée contre le Sieur Pierre Boudet, Négociant en la ville de La Rochelle, Appellant, août 1764, ACM, Ms. 4J2062; Précis pour le sieur Etienne Belin, Négociant à La Rochelle contre la Compagnie d'Assurances de Paris, 1767–73, AMLR,

Ms. 1960; Mémoir pour Denis Goguet, écuyer, Président Trésorier de France au Bureau des Finances de La Rochelle, appellant, contre la Chambre des Assurances de la même ville, intimée, 1769, ACM, Ms. 4J2036; Précis pour les Syndics, Directeurs et Intéressés en la première Chambre des Assurances de Paris contre la Demoisselle Giraudeau, veuve du Sieur Admyrauld, Négociant à La Rochelle et les Sieurs et Demoiselles leur enfans, 1784, ACM, Ms. 4J2088.

33. Pierre Isaac Rasteau à la Chambre de Commerce de La Rochelle, 14 mars, 10, 13, 25 avril 1779, CCLR, carton 4; Règlement des commissaires nommés par le commerce de La Rochelle pour fixer les augmentations d'Assurances, de fret et de profits aventureux, 9 avril 1779, CCLR, carton 7.

34. For Rochelais armateurs, intéressés, and other shippers, higher insurance costs were felt more intensely and for a longer period of time during the War of the American Revolution than during the Seven Years' War. Armements continued at about prewar levels during the American war, while they had fallen off drastically during the Seven Years' War.

35. Commencing on May 20, 1763, all policies made in La Rochelle were to be registered with the secretary of the Chamber of Commerce. He was to maintain one book for insurance on vessels and another for insurance on cargoes. Insurers paid scant attention to the requirement during the 1760s and 1770s. The few registered policies still extant from those decades suffered such water damage as to be illegible. Règlement fait par le commerce de La Rochelle, le 2 mai 1763, sur l'Enregistrement des Polices d'assurance, et nouveaux modeles de Police, and Thomas Delaire aîné à le Chambre de Commerce de La Rochelle, 1788, CCLR, carton 7.

36. Miscellaneous insurance receipts of Théodore Delacroix, 1730–54, [untitled ms.], Delacroix Papers, AMLR, Ms. 2646; Miscellaneous insurance receipts, La Rochelle, 1736–39, [untitled ms.], CCLR, carton 7; Construction du navire le Noé pour Guinée, 1748, and Achat du navire le Henoc, 27 decembre 1748, AMLR, Ms. 1916; Registre des polices sur navires, commencé le 7 avril 1784 à fini le 6 août 1787, CCLR. Most of the discussion that follows was derived from this basic source.

37. The "Registre," cited in note 36 above, commenced in April 1784. A nine-month average for 1784 is multiplied by twelve in order to obtain an annual figure. Only armements le long cours are considered.

38. For table 9.4: the derivation of the total value of outgoing ships and cargoes is explained in Chapter 6, note 41. The total insurance on sixty-three vessels and their cargoes for which the total value of vessels and cargoes is known yields an average coverage of 80 percent. That figure is used to derive the amount of insurance taken on all Rochelais armements le long cours.

39. The tonnage of each of the thirty missing ships is known. The tonnage is multiplied by the average value of vessels and cargoes. Eighty percent of that product produces an amount representative of the insurance coverage for each vessel. The resulting sum is divided by the ratio between locally made insurance and total insurance made and distributed proprotionately between Rochelais and non-Rochelais.

40. Deductions from the premium costs, including commissions charged against non-Rochelais who insured at La Rochelle through the agency of a Rochelais, would be more than balanced by adding the cost of similar commissions charged against Rochelais who used correspondents in other cities to make insurance on Rochelais vessels. Premium rates also varied from place to place. Such factors have been ignored in this discussion.

41. Navires en risque pour le compte de Monsieur Boivon de Paris, 23 mai 1764, ACM, Ms. B5758; De Richemond & Garnault à Peltier, Carrière & Cie. à Nantes, La Rochelle, 4 12, 21 juin, 7 juillet 1785, de Richemond Letterbook, ACM, Ms. E450; Louis Dermigny, *Cargaisons indiennes: Solier et Cie., 1781–1793,* 2 vols. (Paris, 1959–60), 2:360.

42. Livre d'assurance de Nicolas Suidre, 1783–89, AMLR, Ms. 1780; Van Hoogwerf insurance accounts, 1776–91, [untitled documents], Van Hoogwerf Papers, AMLR, Ms. 1962. Compte d'assurance, de Richemond & Garnault, février 1783, AMLR, Ms. 2286–88.

43. M. Paul Depont de La Rochelle, son compte, 1707–09, Depont Papers, ACM, Ms. E486; Delacroix-Dangiraud & Co., insurance accounts, 1754–57, [untitled documents], Delacroix Papers, AMLR, Ms. 2646.

44. Compte d'assurance, de Richemond & Garnault, février 1783, AMLR, Ms. 2286–88; Livre d'assurance de Nicolas Suidre, 1783–89, AMLR, Ms. 1780.

Chapter Ten

1. The method used to derive total value of outgoing ships and cargoes is explained in Chapter 6, note 41.

2. Only those years are included for which the actual value of investment in armements is fully known for at least 20 percent of departures le long cours. In 1722, sixteen departures were recorded. Total value of ships and cargoes was inferred according to the procedure explained above. But the value of investment and the residence of each intéressé are known for only five ventures. The proportion attributable to Rochelais for those five armements is used to derive total Rochelais investments for the sixteen recorded departures.

3. Jean Périer, *La prospérité rochelaise au XVIIIe siècle et la bourgeoisie protestante* (Mesnil, n.d. [c. 1899]), pp. 70 –75; Henri Robert, *Les trafics coloniaux du port de La Rochelle au XVIIIe siècle,* Mémoires de la société des antiquitaires de l'Ouest, 4th ser. vol. 4 (Poitiers, 1960), pp. 190–95.

4. Figure 4.1 suggests a normal non-Rochelais investment of about 20 percent while table 10.1 shows a non-Rochelais investment of 40 to 50 percent. An unknown number of intéressés, living elsewhere and therefore counted as non-Rochelais, were probably relatives. Relatives and nonkin also frequently deposited investment capital with an armateur, who invested it according to his best judgment. These sums are subsumed within the armateurs' share. Accurate knowledge about these practices would require some refinement of the figures, bringing them into closer harmony with table 10.1.

5. Jean Meyer, *L'armement nantais dans la deuxième moitié du XVIIIe siècle* (Paris, 1969), pp. 276–77; Francois-Georges Pariset, ed., *Bordeaux au XVIIIe siècle,* vol. 5, *Histoire de Bordeaux,* ed. Ch. Higounet (Bordeaux, 1968), p. 276; Robert Richard, "Le financement des armements maritime du Havre au XVIIIe siècle: Position de problèmes," *Revue d'histoire économique et sociale* 47 (1969): 28–29; Charles Carrière, *Négociants marseillais au XVIIIe siècle,* 2 vols. (Marseilles, 1973), 2:923–25, 944: For Solier & Co., see Louis Dermigny, *Cargaisons indiennes: Solier et Cie., 1781–1793,* 2 vols. (Paris, 1959–60), 1: 69–75, 169–75; Henri Sée, *Le commerce maritime de la Bretagne au XVIIIe siècle, d'après les papiers des Magon, Mémoires et documents pour servir à l'histoire du commerce et de l'industrie en France,* ed. Julien Hayem, 9th ser. (Paris, 1925), pp. 3–9, noted that Magon de la Balue of Saint-Malo drew investment capital from Nantes, Paris, Rennes, and Lyon for ventures to Spanish America.

6. Meyer, *L'armement nantais,* pp. 90–92.

7. See table 3.2 for the armements administered by the Carayon, Rasteau, and twenty-four other families.

8. For 1748–49, the estimated value of outgoing ships and cargoes reached 12,749,116 lt. Of that, Rochelais investors supplied an estimated 7,169,359 lt. Each share was given the value of 1,234 lt., or 1 percent of the average mise hors. No distinction was made between slaving voyages and direct voyages to the colonies. The families that appear in table 10.2 but not in table 10.3 did not participate either as armateurs or investors in 1748–49.

9. The total value of direct and slave armements for the period 1783–86 is calculated by multiplying the number of each type of voyage for each year by the average value of mise hors established in table 6.4, 152,241 lt. for direct voyages and 272,102 lt. for slavers. For the earlier period, the values adopted are 165,400 lt. for direct voyages and 191,500 lt. for slavers (see Chapter 6),

10. The rates of return (the percentage of total value of vessels and cargoes collected over time) adopted are as follows: direct voyages, 1748–51—year one, 45 percent, year two, 35 percent, year three, 20 percent; direct voyages, 1783–86—year one, 45 percent, year two, 25 percent, year three, 15 percent, year four, 5 percent; slave voyages, 1748–51—year one, zero, year two, 40

percent, year three, 30 percent, year four, 20 percent, year five, 10 percent; slave voyages, 1783–86—year one, zero, year two, 40 percent, year three, 25 percent, year four, 20 percent, year five, 10 percent, year six, 5 percent.

11. Delacroix & Bonfils and Co. and Etienne Belin received disheartening reports of glutted markets in the colonies from their colonial correspondents in 1750 and 1751.

12. Meyer, *L'armement nantais,* p. 168–88.

13. Ibid., pp. 181–88. Meyer estimated that four-hundred négociants were established at Nantes by 1789. The wealthiest of these, many of whom were noble, possessed far greater riches than the wealthiest in the 1720s. Some twelve to twenty possessed estates exceeding one million lt. These figures were educated guesses rather than precise calculations.

14. Meyer, *L'armement nantais,* p. 181–88.

15. Ibid.

16. Dermigny, *Cargaisons indiennes,* 1:183; a daughter of François Gabriel Admyrauld married the Nantes manager of the Bourcard firm, Benoist Bourcard; see also Herbert Lüthy, *La banque protestante en France de la Révocation de l'Edit de Nantes à la Révolution,* 2 vols. (Paris, 1959–61), vol. 2; identifying foreign intéressés is next to impossible since French law prohibited foreign participation in the ownership of French vessels. Most foreign investments appeared in the name of a French agent, most frequently an armateur.

17. Paul Depont son cte court avec Jean Regain aux Sables, 1720–22, Depont des Granges Papers, ACM, Ms. E486; Déclaration du Allard Belin pour Sr. Montaudoin de Nantes, 16 juin 1719, ACM, Ms. B5716; Déclaration du Sr. Busquet, 5 juin 1723, ACM, Ms. B5721; Déclaration du Monfort du Rouen, 17 janvier 1727, ACM, Ms. B5723; Etat des Intérest du Andre Chabot, 29 mai 1741, ACM, Série B229. Chabot's investments totaled 67,075 lt.; Déclaration du Weis et cie. à La Rochelle, 1756, ACM, Ms. B5747; Déclaration par les Sieurs Rigaud, Ternil en compagnie à Marseille par Trésahar Bonfils, 28 avril 1757, ACM, Ms. B5747; In addition to Bonfils, Théodore Delacroix, Jean Perry, and Couillandeau had shares in the Marseillais vessel *le Chenaguere.* Altogether, Rochelais held 42 percent of the shares; Déclaration du Sr. Gilbert, 8 août 1765, ACM, Ms. B5747; Garnault à de Richemond, Nantes, 15 août, 7 septembre, Brest, 1 octobre 1779, de Richemond & Garnault Papers, AMLR, Ms. 2247; Garnault et de Richemond compte avec Marion frères, St. Malo, 1784–85, AMLR, Ms. 2286–88; De Richemond à Martin fils et Landre à Marseille, La Rochelle, 22 février 1785, Meschinet de Richemond Letterbook, ACM, Ms. E450; Dermigny, *Cargaisons indiennes,* 1:91, 95.

18. Déclaration du Sr. Vincent Bureau, 10 janvier, 20 août 1721, ACM, Ms. B5718; Jean Cossart et fils et Bouvier à Théodore Delacroix, Rotterdam, 13 novembre 1737, Delacroix Papers, AMLR, Ms. 2645; Daniel Garesché à Garesché, et Billotteau, La Rochelle, 15 août 1780, Garesché Papers, ACM, Ms. 4J1610–11; St. Macary Beaucamp & Pouyer frères à Pierre Jean Van Hoogwerf, St. Marc, 15 août 1788, AMLR, Ms. 1949; Compte Lambert et De Richemond & Garnault, 26 janvier 1784, AMLR, Ms. 2275; De Richemond & Garnault à Mésnage au Havre, La Rochelle, 21 mai 1785, Meschinet de Richemond Letterbook, ACM, E450. The letters of this firm, describing their investments also identify co-intéressés in their own and others' armements.

19. Sée, *Commerce maritime de la Bretagne,* p. 3–9; Pierre Dardel, "Importateurs et exportateurs rouennais au XVIIIe siècle: Antoine Guymonneau et ses opérations commerciales (1715–1741)," *Etudes d'histoire économique* 4 (Dieppe, 1954): 90–92; Guy Richard, "La noblesse de France et les sociétés par actions à la fin de XVIIIe siècle," *RHES* 41 (1962): 492–93; Dermigny, *Cargaisons indiennes,* 1: 69–70, 75.

20. Dermigny, *Cargaisons indiennes,* 1: 69–70, 75; Meyer, *L'armement nantais,* p. 213; Van Hoogwerf accounts, 1784, [untitled ms.], AMLR, Ms. 1946; Déclaration de M. Dumoustier de Fredilly, 19 janvier 1787, ACM, Ms. B5794; Déclaration de propriété et des intéressés au navire la Jolly, 19 juillet 1787, ACM, Ms. B5796.

21. Van Hoogwerf accounts, 1784, [untitled ms.], AMLR, Ms. 1946; P. Giradot à Théodore Delacroix, Paris, 2 juin 1752, Delacroix Papers, AMLR, Ms. 2645; D. Dubrocq à Théodore

Delacroix, Bayonne, 27 juillet 1773, Delacroix Papers, AMLR, Ms. 2646; Dardel, "Antoine Guymonneau," pp. 90–92.

22. Investments in the coal mines of Languedoc and Bourgogne or Bourbonnais over a two- or three-year period required development capital of close to five million lt., one-fifth of the funding requirements of 1748–49, to support La Rochelle's fleet, Marcel Rouff, *Les mines de charbon au 18e siècle, 1774–1791* (Paris, 1922), pp. 254–77; Labrousse et al., *Histoire économique et sociale de la France*, vol. 2, *Des derniers temps de l'âge seigneurial aux préludes de l'âge industriel (1660–1789)* (Paris, 1970), 2: 253–57.

Chapter Eleven

1. William Williams, Jr. to Thomas W. Williams at New York, La Rochelle, 2 September 1807, Thomas Williams Papers, 1800–35, New York Public Library.

2. André Danière, "Feudal Incomes and Demand Elasticity for Bread in Late Eighteenth-century France," *JEH* 18 (September 1958): 326.

3. Henri Wallon, *La Chambre de commerce de la province de Normandie (1703–1791)* (Rouen, 1903), pp. 99–102.

4. Guy Chaussinard-Nogaret, *Les financiers de Languedoc au XVIIIe siècle* (Paris, 1970), pp. 161–89.

Index

Admyrauld, François, offices of, 212–13

Admyrauld, Pierre Gabriel: and insurance companies, 185–86, 196: offices of, 212

Admyrauld family: as insurance company agents, 98; and Protestant school, 50; significance of, 99; Swiss investors in *armements* of, 221

Admyrauld & Sons: *armements* of, 122

Agricultural lands, of Rochelais families, 99–102

Agriculture: in Aunis, 3; investment in, 101; of La Rochelle's hinterland, 169–71, 173

Amortization, of Rochelais ships, 124

Armateurs, French: at Bordeaux and Nantes, 89–91; use of kin by, 135; and trade risks, 110, 134; and wartime naval protection, 154

Armateurs, Rochelais: *armements* of, 89, 126, 229; banking by, 74, 115; bankruptcy of, 105–9; and brandy lands of, 19; and business agents, 113–14, 134–36; business routines of, 79–80, 123–25; and coffee trade, 165–66; colonial debts owed to, 140–50 passim; *droit de ménage* contested by, 172; commission income of, 123; and fishing, 169; foreign trade with colonies opposed by, 152–53; *grande cabotage* ignored by, 181; insurance company organized by, 185; insurance on *armements* of, 184, 186–89 passim, 203; as insurance underwriters, 198–205 passim; and investors, 124–25; leading families as, 47, 109, 211–14; and letters of exchange, 114, 141–43; liability for losses of, 137–38; and loans *à la grosse aventure,* 192; and *pacotilles,* 136; as ship captains, 81; ship inspection opposed by, 191; shipping ownership of, 34, 36, 74, 79; and sugar trade, 160–62; and tobacco trade, 166–67; trade specialization of, 115–22 passim, 230–31; wartime insurance rates for, 196; wartime shipping losses of, 154–55

Armements, Rochelais: costs of, 123–24; insurance policies on, 186–89, 201; investment in, 116, 203, 208–11, 221–23, 229; of leading families, 48; and slaving, 143–44, 214, 230; trading losses of, 138; during wartime, 155–56. See also *Mise hors;* Shipping, Rochelais

Arrêts du conseil: (1671), French sugar trade regulated by, 159–60; (1710–47, intermittently), grain exports regulated by, 170–71; (1743), brandy barrels proscribed by, 174; (1762), wartime insurance rates established by, 194; (1779), foreign salt in codfishing prohibited by, 180; (1783 and 1784), foreign trade with colonies allowed by, 8–9, 153; (1784), brandy export duties repealed by, 177–78; (1784), colonial sugar refining regulated by, 160

Atlantic economy, 22–24, 226, 232

Artisans, Rochelais: and competition from outsiders, 15; elite families as, 85

Auboyneau family: on *juridiction consulaire,* 96; plantations owned by, 102

Augmentation, of wartime insurance premiums, 193–97 passim, 231. See also Insurance, marine

Aunis: population characteristics of (1790s), 5; products of, 3; switch from wine to brandy in, 173

Aydes, 176

Bankruptcy, at La Rochelle, 103–9

Banque royale, at La Rochelle, 15, 97

Bayonne: fishing fleet of, 169; foreign trade with colonies opposed by, 153, merchant fleet of (1646–1787), 27

Belin, Allard: *armements* of, 145–46; estate of, 53, 61–65; offices of, 46; size of family of, 54

Belin, Claude Etienne: as co-inheritor of business, 46; and colonial crops, 82, 136–37; and colonial markets, 137–39; debtors of, 107; division of estate of, 62–65; helps Rasteau, 86–87; as insurance company agent, 186; and letters of exchange, 142; use of inheritance of, 62; and wartime insurance rates, 196

Belin, Elie Allard: as co-inheritor of business, 46; use of inheritance by, 62

Belin, Paul: sugar plantation of, 81–82, 136–37

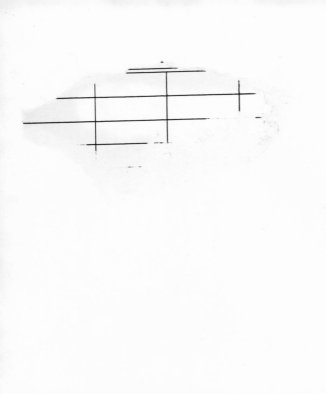